Kabbalistic Visions

In 1944 C. G. Jung experienced a series of visions which he later described as "the most tremendous things I have ever experienced." Central to these visions was the "mystic marriage as it appears in the Kabbalistic tradition," and Jung's experience of himself as "Rabbi Simon ben Jochai," the presumed author of the sacred Kabbalistic text, the *Zohar*. *Kabbalistic Visions* explores Jung's 1944 Kabbalistic visions, the impact of Jewish mysticism on Jungian psychology, Jung's archetypal interpretation of Kabbalistic symbolism, and his claim late in life that a Hasidic rabbi, the Maggid of Mezhirech, anticipated his entire psychology. This book places Jung's encounter with the Kabbalah in the context of the earlier visions and meditations of his *Red Book*, his abiding interests in Gnosticism and alchemy, and what many regard to be his Anti-Semitism and flirtation with National Socialism. In this second revised edition the author also provides a comprehensive discussion of Eric Neumann's recently published work on the relationship between Hasidism and Jungian/archetypal psychology. *Kabbalistic Visions* is the first full-length study of Jung and Jewish mysticism in any language and the first book to present a comprehensive Jungian/archetypal interpretation of Kabbalistic symbolism.

Sanford L. Drob, PhD, teaches at Fielding Graduate University in Santa Barbara, CA, and the C.G. Jung Institute in New York. His most recent book is *Archetype of the Absolute: The Unity of Opposites in Mysticism, Philosophy and Psychology*. He is a visual artist whose paintings on archetypal themes can be viewed at www.sanforddrobart.com.

Kabbalistic Visions

C. G. Jung and Jewish Mysticism

Second edition

Sanford L. Drob

 Routledge
Taylor & Francis Group

LONDON AND NEW YORK

Cover image: "The Tree of Light and Dark" (Frontispiece from V. Weigel's Stadium Universale.)

Second edition published 2010
by Routledge
4 Park Square, Milton Park, Abingdon, Oxon OX14 4RN

and by Routledge
605 Third Avenue, New York, NY 10158

Routledge is an imprint of the Taylor & Francis Group, an informa business

© 2023 Sanford L. Drob

X BR325.C8. Special Collections and University Archives, Rutgers University Libraries.

Second edition published 2023 by Routledge

British Library Cataloguing-in-Publication Data
A catalogue record for this book is available from the British Library

Library of Congress Cataloging-in-Publication Data
Names: Drob, Sanford L., author.
Title: Kabbalistic visions : C. G. Jung and Jewish mysticism / Sanford L Drob.
Description: [Second edition]. | Milton Park, Abingdon, Oxon ; New York, NY : Routledge, 2023. | "First published 2010 by Spring Journal Books"--Title page verso. | Includes bibliographical references and index. |
Identifiers: LCCN 2022015158
Subjects: LCSH: Jung, C. G. (Carl Gustav), 1875-1961. | Cabala. | Mysticism--Judaism.
Classification: LCC BF109.J8 D69 2022 | DDC 296.1/6--dc23/eng/20220407
LC record available at https://lccn.loc.gov/2022015158

ISBN: 978-0-36746-123-2 (hbk)
ISBN: 978-0-36746-124-9 (pbk)
ISBN: 978-1-00302-704-1 (ebk)

DOI: 10.4324/9781003027041

Typeset in Times New Roman
by Taylor & Francis Books

Contents

Illustrations

Preface

This has been a difficult book to research and write, one that involved a great deal of personal anguish and soul-searching, not only in relation to what would be said, but how and whether it should be said at all. On the one hand, I am of the belief that Jungian psychology provides us with a very significant piece of the puzzle regarding the human psyche. Moreover, I am convinced that Jung's perspective upon myth, mysticism, and religion is critical for any contemporary interpretation of the Kabbalah. On the other hand, in the course of researching this book, I have become acutely aware, more aware than I would have perhaps preferred, of Jung's problematic attitudes towards both Jews and Judaism, and the ethical and social dangers that certain aspects of Jung's thought pose with regard to both anti-Semitism and other forms of irrational prejudice. The questions that I have been forced to ask are further complicated by my discovery and belief that Jung is highly Kabbalistic in some of his doctrines, and that some of the ideas he shares with certain strands within Jewish mysticism are the very ideas that caused him to lose his bearings with respect to the threat of National Socialism prior to World War II.

My initial intention in writing this work was simply to expand upon the cross-fertilization between the Kabbalah and Jungian psychology that I had described in several prior publications;[1] to provide further evidence for my thesis that Jung, by extracting the spiritual core of alchemy, was in many ways rediscovering and reinterpreting the Kabbalah;[2] and to show that Jungian psychology is thus eminently suited to a contemporary under-standing of Kabbalistic myths, symbols, and ideas. However, as I proceeded with my work, it became increasingly clear that a simple rapprochement between Jung and the Kabbalah was impossible, and that neither could emerge unchanged from an encounter with the other. A second purpose eventually emerged, one that involved a critique, reinterpretation, and in some cases reformulation of certain key Jungian and Kabbalistic notions that have the potential for dire consequences. In writing this book, I have become far more appreciative of the age-old rabbinic dictum that among those who enter the "garden" (of mysticism) very few emerge spiritually, morally, and psychologically whole. In this work, I ponder the question of whether Carl Jung (and by extension, Jungian psychology) can be a valuable guide in our own spiritual/psychological quest. While in the end, and with certain provisos, I answer this question in the affirmative, I have come to recognize that the journey into the garden, as both Jung and the Kabbalists well understood, must inevitably take us through the shadow world of the "Other Side," and I found that it is to this shadowy realm of Jung's attitudes towards Judaism, race, Hitler, and the Nazi party that any full examination of Jung and the Kabbalah must eventually arrive.

Thus, while this book focuses upon an examination of Jungian psychology and Jewish mysticism, it also includes an assessment of Jung's relationship to Jews and Judaism. It considers both Jung's very harsh *and* very kind words and deeds with regard to the Jewish people and religion and continues with an extended meditation on the question of whether and how Jung *compensated* for some of his earlier prejudices. Although this is not a biographical study *per se*, I have felt compelled to discuss some of the personal, psychological, social, and theoretical factors that led Jung into certain prejudicial statements and sentiments while he was, at the same time, developing a psychology that in his own later estimation was wholly anticipated by the Jewish mystics.

I realize that by openly discussing the purportedly "anti-Semitic" material I run a grave risk of losing many readers, both Jewish and non- Jewish, who, unfamiliar with the full compass of Jung's writings and ideas, will see him in the most negative of terms and close their minds to the ideas I present and the arguments I make regarding the significance of Jung's thought for our under- standing of the Kabbalah. I also realize that many other readers will regard my consideration of Jung's personal attitudes largely or even wholly irrelevant to the question of Jung's theories and their applicability to a wide range of religious symbols and experience.[3] I can only say that I have labored long and hard with respect to whether and where the "biographical" material should be examined and included in a work of this kind. I ultimately concluded: (1) that if Jungian psychology is to be made relevant to the study of Kabbalah, then that psychology must be strong enough to pass the test of its weakest link; (2) that one cannot understand Jung's Kabbalistic visions and his entire relation- ship to both the Kabbalah and alchemy without considering his attitudes towards Freud, Judaism, and the rise of National Socialism; and (3) that the dangerous path that Jung flirted with may well be intrinsic to the very world- view that Jungian psychology shares with the traditional Kabbalah, and that thus any consideration of Jung's relationship to the Kabbalah without an examination of Jung's shadow or "other side" would be woefully incomplete. I hope that the reader will bear with me and stay the course through the moral and spiritual uncertainties of this examination in the hope of experiencing a bit of psychological and perhaps spiritual understanding. As the Zohar, profoundly if dangerously, says: "There is no light except that which issues from darkness…and no true good except it proceed from evil."[4]

I would like to thank Stanton Marlan, Michael Sokal, and Aryeh Maidenbaum for encouraging the completion of various chapters in this book, several of which have appeared in somewhat altered form in the journals or books for which each of them has served as editor, and Nancy Cater for her encouragement and assistance with the first edition of this work. I would also like to thank Alexis O'Brien, Susannah Frearson, Driss Fatih, and Reanna Young at Routledge for their assistance in bringing this second edition of *Kabbalistic Visions* to fruition.

I have, in this second edition of Kabbalistic Visions, added an appendix which considers the significance of the 2019 publication of Erich Neumann's long concealed *The Roots of Jewish Consciousness*. Neumann's work sheds important light on the parallels between Jungian and Hasidic thought and provides considerable insight into Jung's late life claim that the Hasidic Maggid of Meseritiz anticipated his entire psychology in the 18th century.

Introduction

The proposition that one of the twentieth century's giants in psychology, C. G. Jung, can be understood as a Jewish mystical thinker, whose theories not only reflect Kabbalistic sources but can actually breathe new life into them, is an idea that is likely to be looked upon skeptically by scholars of both Jung and the Kabbalah alike. While it is hard to avoid the obvious fact that Jung, especially in his later years, quoted fairly extensively from Jewish, especially Kabbalistic, sources, his references to Judaism are rather few in comparison to those he made to Christianity, Gnosticism, and alchemy. Further, Jung's interest in the Kabbalah is generally understood as merely one example of his more general interest in world religions (including Taoism, Buddhism, and Hinduism), each of which he regarded as the "data" for his hypothesis of the archetypes of the collective unconscious. Given Jung's predilection for Christian theology, and his early ambivalent and at times derogatory view of Judaism, it would seem to be a difficult task to argue, as I will in this book, that Jung's relationship to Jewish mysticism played an important role in the development of analytic psychology, a role that he himself initially may have sought to minimize, but which he ultimately embraced. It will be my task in this work to overcome each of these potential prejudices.

To understand Jung's intimate relationship with Jewish mysticism, one need look no further than Jung's own autobiographical account of a series of visions that he had after his heart attack in 1944, and which he described, in his *Memories, Dreams, Reflections,* as "the most tremendous things I have ever experienced."[1] These visions, which occurred at a point when, according to Jung's own report, he "hung on the edge of death,"[2] involve decidedly Jewish, moreover Kabbalistic, themes:

> Everything around me seemed enchanted. At this hour of the night the nurse brought me some food she had warmed. For a time it seemed to me that she was an old Jewish woman, much older than she actually was, and that she was preparing ritual kosher dishes for me. When I looked at her, she seemed to have a blue halo around her

DOI: 10.4324/9781003027041-1

head. I myself was, so it seemed, in the Pardes Rimmonim,[3] the garden of pomegranates, and the wedding of Tifereth with Malchuth was taking place. Or else I was Rabbi Simon ben Jochai,[4] whose wedding in the afterlife was being celebrated. It was the mystic marriage as it appears in the Cabbalistic tradition. I cannot tell you how wonderful it was. I could only think continually, "Now this is the garden of pome-granates! Now this is the marriage of Malchuth with Tifereth!" I do not know exactly what part I played in it. At bottom it was I myself: I was the marriage. And my beatitude was that of a blissful wedding.[5]

The vision continues with what Jung describes as "the Marriage of the Lamb" in Jerusalem, complete with angels and light. "I myself," he tells us, "was the Marriage of the Lamb." The vision concludes with Jung in a classical amphitheater situated in a verdant chain of hills: "Men and women dancers came on-stage, and upon a flower-decked couch All- father Zeus and Hera consummated the mystic marriage, as it is described in the *Iliad*."[6]

Jung relates that as a result of these experiences he developed the impression that this life is but a "segment of existence," and that time as it is ordinarily experienced is an illusion, since during the visions past, present, and future fused into one. There can be little doubt that Jung took these impressions seriously, as according to him, "the visions and experiences were utterly real; there was nothing subjective about them."[7]

This book is, in many ways, a sustained meditation on Jung's Kabbalistic vision. Interpreting this vision requires that we not only venture into the details of Kabbalistic theosophy and Jungian psychology, but also into the question of Jung's personal relationship to Judaism and what he termed "Jewish psychology."

Jung and Jungism

Although I originally believed that the controversy regarding Jung's personal and professional stance with regard to the Jews and the Nazis was beyond the scope of this book, I am now convinced that a full exploration of Jung's attitudes on these issues is a necessity for progress in Jungian studies of Jewish mysticism.[8] This is not only because Jung's purported early anti-Semitism has been an obstacle to such studies, but for the more basic and urgent reason that the very celebration of the nonrational and emotional aspects of the psyche and the openness to its dark side, which Jung shares with certain trends within the Kabbalah, may actually have contributed to Jung's negative attitudes towards normative Judaism and his early optimism regarding the spiritual potential of the Nazi party. Jung's relationship to Judaism will therefore be a major concern, especially in the second half of this book, where I will consider the literary and historical record, and argue that this record supports the view that Jung achieved a compensation and transformation in his views towards Jews and Judaism in the years during and after the Second World War.

After decades of avoiding the problem the Jungian community has, more recently, to its credit, taken careful stock of Jung's record on the "Jewish question" before, during, and after the Nazi era. The "Lingering Shadows" conference,[9] which was held in New York in the spring of 1989, has greatly broadened the dialog and "soul-searching" on these important questions. While there has now been much written on the subject of Jung's personal relationship to the Jews, what has been missing has been a deep and sustained reflection on Jung's theories and Judaism, in particular the relationship between Jungian psychology and Jewish mysticism. This work, which grows out of an appreciation for both Jewish mysticism and Jungian psychology, is meant to continue and expand upon the reflections on this theme that I began in my earlier articles and books.[10]

The Purpose of the Book

My goal in this book is threefold. First, through a careful analysis of both Jung's texts and his sources, I will explore the impact that Kabbalistic ideas had upon the development of Jungian psychology. I will show, for example, how, in extracting the psychological and spiritual "gold" that lay buried in the alchemists' texts and practices, Jung was, in many respects, reconstituting the Kabbalah, which had to a large extent been alchemy's spiritual foundations, and in the process provided himself with a framework through which he could make sense of the profound and transforming experiences he had years earlier, and which eventuated in his *Red Book* and related writings.[11] Second, through an archetypal analysis of the Kabbalistic symbols, I will explore the profound psychological insights afforded by a Jungian approach to Jewish mysticism. As such, it is my hope that this work will be a contribution both to Jungian and Kabbalistic studies. Finally, I will critically examine a view on the non-rational nature of the psyche, aspects of which are shared by Jung and the Kabbalists, and which may have attracted Jung to the Kabbalah in the first place. In doing so, I will raise certain questions regarding the values inherent in the Kabbalah as it is often understood and take some tentative steps towards a "New Kabbalah,"[12] one that is perhaps more balanced in its approach to the rational and nonrational aspects of both theology and the human psyche.

Jung brought the same interpretive posture to the Kabbalah as he had brought to Gnosticism and alchemy, the two spiritual disciplines that had received his most sustained attention. Throughout most of his career, Jung regarded Gnostic and alchemical symbols and practices to be projections of mostly unconscious psychological processes. Where the Gnostic saw the infinite divine "Pleroma," Jung saw the infinite expanse of the individual and collective unconscious. Where the alchemist saw a procedure for combining

base metals into gold, Jung saw the symbolic formation of a unified "self."
Jung's approach to the Kabbalah was similar, but less systematic, and his
views on Jewish mysticism must occasionally be pieced together from his
discussions of parallel Gnostic and alchemical themes. Further, as will
become evident in the late chapters of this work, Jung's ideas concerning the
significance of mystical symbols and experience changed later in his life, a
change that was arguably in large measure precipitated by his Kabbalistic
visions of 1944.[13]

In this book I will survey a number of Kabbalistic symbols and ideas
that were of significance to Jung, and several others that are significant
from a Jungian perspective. Among these symbols and notions are *Ein-Sof*
(the Infinite God), *Tzimtzum* (the Divine Contraction), *Adam Kadmon*
(Primordial Human), the *Sefirot* (divine archetypes), *Shevirat ha-Kelim*
(the Breaking of the Vessels), *Kellipot* (Shells or Husks), the separation/
unification of the King and Queen, *Tikkun ha-Olam* (the Restoration of
the World), and *Partzufim* (Divine "Faces" or "Visages"). While I will
endeavor herein to elucidate the significance of each of these Kabbalistic
symbols, both from traditional and Jungian perspectives, those interested
in a more detailed treatment are referred to my earlier books, *Symbols of
the Kabbalah* and *Kabbalistic Metaphors*.[14]

In his later writings and letters, Jung acknowledged a great affinity with the
Jewish mystical tradition. Yet as great as was Jung's acknowledged affinity to
the Kabbalah, his unacknowledged relationship was even greater. For every
reference to the Kabbalah in Jung's writings there are several to Gnosticism,
and perhaps dozens to alchemy—yet, as I will detail in this book, the interpretations that Jung places on Gnosticism and the very texts that Jung refers
to on alchemy were profoundly Kabbalistic, so much so that one could call
the Jung of the *Mysterium Coniunctionis* and other later works a Kabbalist in
contemporary guise. Jung has frequently been called a "Gnostic,"[15] but for
reasons that I will provide, Jung is far more Kabbalistic than he is Gnostic,
and he is "alchemical" largely to the extent that the alchemists borrowed
from and relied upon Kabbalistic ideas.

In this study, I will argue that Jung read Gnosticism in such a manner as to
transform a radical anti-cosmic, anti-individualistic doctrine into a world-
affirming basis for an individual psychology, one that is remarkably close to
the psychology of Kabbalah and, especially, Chasidism. Indeed, near the end
of his life, Jung himself came to the conclusion that "the Hasidic Rabbi Baer
from Mesiritz...anticipated [his] entire psychology in the eighteenth century."[16] Further, I will show that Jung interpreted alchemy so as to extract its
Kabbalistic spiritual and psychological core. Had Jung been sufficiently
familiar with the Kabbalists (and Chasidim), his task could have been far
easier, for their writings provide a richer and more psychologically oriented
imagery and symbolism than either the "otherworldly" theories of the
Gnostics or the radically material practice of the alchemists. Indeed, in some

instances, the Gnostics, the alchemists, and the Kabbalists share the same symbols and images (e.g., the "sparks," "Primordial Human"), but in each case the Kabbalistic approach to these symbols is the closest to Jung's own. In short, by providing a "this-worldly" interpretation of Gnosticism and a spiritual-psychological interpretation of alchemy, Jung arrived at a view that was essentially Kabbalistic in spirit. To use an alchemical metaphor, Jung, in his interpretation of alchemy, succeeded remarkably in extracting the Kabbalistic gold that lay buried in the alchemists' texts and methods.

The Plan of This Book

Chapter 1 provides a brief survey of Kabbalistic symbols and ideas, with specific attention to the Kabbalistic theosophy of Isaac Luria, which is of particular relevance to Jungian psychology. The relationship between the Lurianic Kabbalah and (Freudian) psychoanalysis is briefly considered. Jung's interpretation of Gnosticism is revealed as a model through which he was to later comprehend both alchemy and the Kabbalah. The relationship between Gnosticism and the Kabbalah is explored, and Jung's familiarity with Kabbalistic sources is surveyed.

Chapter 2 examines the relationship between the Kabbalah and alchemy. The impact of the Kabbalah on alchemy is explored in some detail as background for the assertion that Jung, in extracting the spiritual and psychological core of alchemy, was, in effect, reconstituting a Kabbalistic perspective on humanity.

Chapters 3 through 8 explore a variety of Kabbalistic symbols and ideas that had a significant impact on Jung's thinking. The Kabbalists' "wedding" and erotic symbolism (Chapter 3) and their conception of the complementarity of opposites (Chapter 4) are seen as an important foundation for Jung's understanding of the human psyche as a *coincidentia oppositorum* of masculine and feminine, good and evil, etc. Chapter 5 is a comparative study of the Kabbalistic symbol of the "Other Side" and the Jungian "Shadow." Chapter 6 discusses the Kabbalistic symbols of *Adam Kadmon* and the *Sefirot*, which Jung understood as important symbols of the self. Chapter 7 focuses upon the Lurianic symbols of the Breaking of the Vessels (*Shevirat ha-Kelim*) and their restoration (*Tikkun*). These symbols embody the dialectic of fragmentation and restoration, chaos and order, which, for Jung, is an essential dynamic of the human psyche. Chapter 8 considers the *"scintillae"* or "sparks," an image utilized by both the Kabbalists and Gnostics, and which Jung interprets to be symbols of the collective unconscious.

Chapter 9 requires a bit more explanation. Jung can in some ways be understood as a contemporary Kabbalist, yet one who provides the basis for a radical *psychological* interpretation of the Kabbalists' symbols and ideas. Such a psychological interpretation was not altogether foreign to the

Kabbalists themselves, who, on the principle of the microcosm mirroring the macrocosm, held that their own descriptions of cosmic events were also, and equally profoundly, descriptions of the dynamics within men's souls.[17] Indeed, such an interpretation of the Kabbalah provided the major impetus for the doctrines of the Chasidim. Still, Jung took this psychologization process further than either the Kabbalists or Chasidim, living in a pre-psychoanalytic age, could ever have hoped to do them- selves. In Chapter 9 I follow Jung's example and method in providing a psychological interpretation of certain Kabbalistic symbols and texts that Jung himself did not consider. Indeed, my goal in this chapter (and throughout this book) is to apply Jung's method to the basic metaphors of the Lurianic Kabbalah, a task that Jung did not even attempt to complete himself.

Chapter 10 considers in detail the vexing issue of Jung's relationship to Judaism and his controversial stance with regard to National Socialism. My intent in this chapter is not to provide an apology for Jung, but rather to review the historical record in order to provide the reader with an opportunity to evaluate Jung and Jung's personal relationship to Judaism and the Kabbalah. This chapter raises the question of whether Jung suppressed the Jewish mystical sources of his psychology and considers the possible motives he might have had for doing so. The chapter also considers several possible explanations for Jung's apparently contradictory words regarding Judaism, Hitler, and the Nazi party. While throughout this book I will present a perspective from which a Jungian approach to Jewish mysticism can be *welcomed* by those (such as myself) who continue to be deeply troubled by Jung's behavior before, and also to a more limited extent after, World War II, I acknowledge that others may come to different conclusions on this matter.

Regardless of what we conclude regarding Jung's personal behavior, it is clear that Jungian psychology is in many ways compatible with and in some instances indebted to Jewish mystical ideas and symbols. Even if one were to remain firmly (and I believe wrongly) convinced that Jung was anti-Semitic, one would ignore his psychology at the peril of ignoring insights that are compatible with, based upon, and, perhaps most significantly, illuminative of the Jewish mystical tradition.

Chapter 11 provides a detailed examination of Jung's 1944 "Kabbalistic vision." Jung's vision is explored from Jungian and Kabbalistic dream perspectives, providing both a comparison between Jung and the Kabbalah on the subject of dreams and a basis for the idea that Jung's dreams/visions served a compensatory and redemptive function in connection with his activities and writings prior to World War II.

Chapter 12 considers the question, raised by any characterization of Jung as "Gnostic" or "Kabbalistic," regarding the extent to which Jung shared in the metaphysical as well as the psychological assumptions of these spiritual movements. Throughout most of his career, Jung himself denied any metaphysical aspirations, asserting that his discussions of "God" or "Primordial Human," to take two examples, were merely meant to illuminate aspects of the empirical psychology of the self, and that any inquiry into the external "truth" of these archetypal images was beyond the scope of his own investigation.[18] In spite of these disavowals, Jung has been adopted (and criticized) by the theologians, and his work can be taken to have important theological, axiological, and metaphysical implications. Further, toward the end of his life, Jung seemed to open the door to theology, stating, amongst other things, that for him the existence of God was a matter of knowledge as opposed to belief, an assertion that, with the publication of *The Red Book*, we now see had been made by Jung much earlier in his life.[19]

Philosophically, Jung can be understood as part of a tradition that can be traced back to the Kabbalah and early Christian mystics (and which achieved supreme *rational* expression in Hegel), which sees the Absolute and man as progressing through a series of contradictions or oppositions in a quest for unity and, as Jung put it, "individuation." One of the goals of Chapter 12 is to situate Jung within this tradition, comparing his views with those of the Kabbalists as well as with the views of such thinkers as Kant, Hegel, and Derrida, all in the hope of illuminating not only Jung's work, but the contemporary situation of the Kabbalah as well. Such issues as the metaphysical status of psychological and philosophical antinomies and oppositions, the role of reason and myth in resolving such antinomies, and the nature of mythical symbols (each of which are raised by Jung's work) must be addressed if the age-old tradition of the Kabbalah is to gain new life in our own time, rather than remain the province of historians and philologists.

Chapter 1

Kabbalah and Depth Psychology

Late in his life, when Carl Jung was asked to comment on "the significance of Freud's Jewish descent for the origin, content and acceptance of psycho-analysis," Jung responded that in order to adequately answer this question "one would have to take a deep plunge into the history of the Jewish mind... into the subterranean workings of Hasidism...and then into the intricacies of the Kabbalah, which still remains unexplored psychologically."[1] Freud himself is said to have exclaimed, "This is gold!" after having read a German transla-tion of the Kabbalistic work *Sefer Etz Chayyim*,[2] and Jung, in an interview on his eightieth birthday in 1955, declared, "the Hasidic Rabbi Baer from Mesiritz anticipated my entire psychology in the eighteenth century."[3]

It would seem, at least according to Jung's evaluation, that the Jewish mystical tradition, as expressed in Kabbalah and Chasidism, is of more than passing significance for the origins of depth psychology. This chapter examines this proposition in some detail, beginning with an overview of the relevant Kabbalistic symbols and ideas, and then exploring the significance of these ideas for both Freudian and Jungian thought.

The Kabbalah

The Kabbalah, the major tradition of Jewish mystical theosophy, theology, and practice, is a vast spiritual and intellectual arena that in our time has come to both ignite the public's imagination and command its own field of university study. Rooted in early Jewish mysticism and, according to many, a Jewish form of Gnosticism,[4] the Kabbalah achieved its own unique expression toward the end of the twelfth century in the anonymous *Sefer ha-Bahir*, generally regarded to be the earliest extant text in this mystical genre.[5] It is in *Sefer ha-Bahir* that the theory of the ten *Sefirot*, the value archetypes (e.g., Will, Wisdom, Under-standing, Kindness, Judgment, Beauty, etc.), which the Kabbalists held to be the elements of creation, first takes distinctive form. The *locus classicus*, how-ever, for our understanding of the *Sefirot* and other Kabbalistic symbols is *Sefer haZohar* (The Book of Splendor), which, according to Jewish tradition, was authored by the second-century rabbinic sage Simon ben Yochai.

DOI: 10.4324/9781003027041-2

Contemporary scholars, however, believe that the Zohar originated in Spain sometime in the thirteenth century, and was for the most part written by Rabbi Moses de Leon (c. 1250–1305), who claimed to have "rediscovered" this "ancient" text, and who first brought it to the attention of the world.[6] The Zohar, much of which is written as a loose and far-reaching commentary on the Torah (the Five Books of Moses), is the source of much of the "wedding symbolism" (unifications of the various *Sefirot*) that preoccupied the alchemists studied by Jung. The Zohar's homilies on the nature of the unknowable infinite, the soul, the masculine and the feminine, the *Sefirot* (archetypes of God, mind, and world), the relationship between good and evil, dreams, death, and many other subjects provide much of interest to analytic and archetypal psychologists. As we shall see, Jung himself quoted a number of Zoharic passages, and appears to have been acquainted not only with a Latin, but also a German and an English translation of portions of this book.

It is, however, the radical reformulation of the Kabbalah, initiated by Isaac Luria (1534–72) and his disciples, notably Chayyim Vital (1542–1620), in the final decades of the sixteenth century, that will be the focus of much of our interest in this work.[7] Vital, who outlived Luria by fifty years, had acted as Luria's "Boswell" during the latter's most produc tive period in Safed, taking down his words as if they were the words of a prophet. It was through Vital and Luria's other disciples that the Lurianic Kabbalah was transmitted from Palestine to Europe and later became the foundation for the Sabbatean heresy[8] in the seventeenth century and the Chasidism in the eighteenth century. Luria's ideas were little known outside orthodox Jewish circles, however, until Gershom Scholem brought them to the attention of the intellectual world in the 1930s.[9] Even today, only a fraction of the Lurianic corpus has been translated into English. Luria himself wrote comparatively little, and the main source for our knowledge of Luria's theosophy, Chayyim Vital's *Sefer Etz Chayyim*, is an extremely complex and baroque work. While it is rich in archetypal material, its study requires familiarity with the specialized Kabbalistic terminology used by its author.[10] A more lucid volume by Moses Luzatto has been translated as *General Principles of the Kabbalah*. Written one hundred years after Vital's death, it summarizes many of the basic symbols and principles of the Lurianic system.[11]

One can also find many ancient Gnostic themes reappearing suddenly in the Lurianists, and the study of both Christian and Jewish Gnostic sources is invaluable as a background for comprehending the ideas of the Kabbalah.[12] Lurianic ideas are prominent in the seventeenth-century messianic movement surrounding Sabbatai Sevi in Poland.[13] They are also to be found among the Chasidim, whose psychological interpretation of the Kabbalah is invaluable for our own understanding of this tradition.[14]

There is also a Christian Kabbalah, which translated into Latin and at times creatively expanded upon some of the Jewish sources. For example, Knorr von Rosenroth's *Kabbala Denudata*, a Latin compendium of Zoharic and other Kabbalistic texts, was relied upon by Jung in his interpretation of alchemy.[15] We should also note that the Kabbalah has important affinities to many of the themes in Plato and Neoplatonism, Christian mysticism, German Idealism (Schelling and Hegel), and, interestingly, both Hindu and Buddhist thought.[16] A comprehensive contemporary interpretation of the Kabbalah would indeed take into consideration these and many other mystical, theological, and philosophical movements, a number of which I have examined in my previous works, *Symbols of the Kabbalah, Kabbalistic Metaphors*, and *Kabbalah and Postmodernism*.

The Lurianic Kabbalah

With this background in mind, I will now briefly summarize the main Lurianic symbols and ideas. As the Lurianic Kabbalah incorporated much of the previous Kabbalah, this summary will provide the necessary background to comprehend not only Jung's use of the Kabbalistic symbols, but also a contemporary psychological reading of the Kabbalah as a whole.

The Lurianic Kabbalah is of interest in part because of its systematic treatment of many of the symbols and conceptions of the earlier Kabbalah. Indeed, many of the ideas in the Lurianic Kabbalah are dynamic developments of concepts and symbols that appear in the Zohar. Luria adopted the earlier Kabbalistic term *Ein-sof* to designate the primal, allencompassing "Infinite All." This "All," according to the Kabbalists, is both the totality of being and the abyss of complete "nothingness."[17] As such, it is the union of all things and their opposites.[18] For the Kabbalists, *Ein-sof* is completely ineffable and unknowable prior to its manifestation in creation. Regarding *Ein-sof*, the Zohar declares, "High above all heights and hidden beyond all concealments, no thought can grasp you at all…You have no known Name for You fill all Names and You are the perfection of them all."[19] Vital holds that the term *Ein-sof* "indicates that there is absolutely no way to comprehend Him, either by thought or by contemplation, because He is completely inconceivable and far removed from any kind of thought."[20] Nearly all Kabbalists agree that *Ein-sof* is at least one step removed from the personal, biblical God.

Luria departed from the majority of the earlier Kabbalists, who had put forth a Neoplatonic, "emanationist" view of creation. According to Luria, *Ein-sof* created the world through a negative act of divine concealment, contraction, and withdrawal. This act, known in the Lurianic corpus as the *Tzimtzum*, was necessary to "make room" in the divine plenum for the emanation of the worlds. In the act of *Tzimtzum*, the Infinite God withdraws himself from himself, leaving a void. According to Vital:

> When it arose in His simple will to create the world and emanate the emanations, and to bring to light the perfection of His acts and names, then He contracted Himself into the central point that was in the middle of His light. He contracted Himself into this point and then retreated to the sides encircling this point. Then there remained an empty space or ether, an empty hollow (or void).[21]

This void, known as the *tehiru* or *chalal*, is a metaphysically empty circle or sphere (or on some accounts a square), which *Ein-sof* surrounds equally on all sides. Once established, this void becomes the metaphysical "space" in which an infinite number of worlds will take form through a positive, emanative phase in the creative process. But even without a positive emanation the stage has already been set for a finite world; like a photographic slide, which selectively conceals various portions and aspects of a projector's homogenous light, the *Tzimtzum* creates a differentiated matrix of finite things by selectively *concealing* aspects of the full divine presence.

According to Luria, with the advent of the *Tzimtzum*, a thin line (*kav*) of divine light (the *Or Ein-sof*) penetrates the void but does not completely transverse it. From this line, as well as from a residue (*reshimu*) of the divine light that had remained in the metaphysical void after the divine contraction, the first created being, Primordial Human (*Adam Kadmon*), is formed. (The *Or Ein-Sof*, the divine light, is subsequently revealed to be a sexual or erotic energy which informs the conjugal relations between the masculine and feminine aspects of God and the world.)

Vital holds that it is the Primordial Human who is responsible for emanating the archetypal structures of the created world, the *Sefirot*. Lights flashing from the ears, nose, mouth, and eyes of this Primordial Human create the *Sefirot*, which are understood by the Kabbalists to be the ten essential elements or value-dimensions of creation. Each light from the Primordial Human beams down into the void and then returns, leaving a residue of divine energy from which the "vessel" for each *Sefirah* is formed. A second light is projected from the eyes of *Adam Kadmon* and then returns, leaving behind a second residue, which fills the vessels, thereby completing the formation of each of the ten *Sefirot*. The ten *Sefirot*, in order of their emanation (and with their alternate appellations), are as follows: *Keter* (Crown) or *Ratzon* (Will), *Chochmah* (Wisdom), *Binah* (Understanding), *Chesed* (Loving-kindness) or *Gedullah* (Greatness), *Gevurah* (Strength) or *Din* (Judgment), *Tiferet* (Beauty) or *Rachamim* (Compassion), *Netzach* (Glory), *Hod* (Splendor), *Yesod* (Foundation), and *Malchut* (Kingship) or Shekhinah (the feminine aspect of God).

The *Sefirot* are themselves organized into the "body" of Primordial Human, with *Keter, Chochmah*, and *Binah* forming the "crown" and "brains"; *Chesed* and *Gevurah*, the arms; *Tiferet*, the torso; *Netzach* and *Hod*, the legs; and *Malchut*, the mouth, or in some accounts the feminine counterpart to *Adam Kadmon*. The *Sefirot* are also organized into a series of five worlds (the worlds of Primordial Human, "Nearness," "Creation," "Formation," and "Making"—the lowest of which, *Assiyah* [Making], provides the substance of our earth). The cosmos, as it was originally emanated via ten discrete *Sefirot*, is known as the "World of Points."

In addition to the emanation of the *Sefirot, Adam Kadmon* is said to emanate the *Otiyot Yesod*, the twenty-two "Foundational Letters" that form the linguistic-conceptual structure of the world. According to the Kabbalists, the worlds and everything within them are comprised of both *Sefirot* and letters. Together the ten *Sefirot* and twenty-two *Otiyot* (letters) comprise the "thirty-two paths of wisdom" through which the world was created.

Luria is completely original in his description of the fate of the *Sefirot*, letters, and worlds after their original emanation from *Adam Kadmon*. The *Sefirot* "closest" to *Adam Kadmon*, the so-called "psychical" *Sefirot*, are comprised of the most powerful vessels, and they alone can withstand the impact of the second series of lights emanating from the eyes of the Primordial Human. As we have seen, these lights were intended to fill the sefirotic vessels with divine life and energy. According to Vital:

> The light that shines into the vessels of the ten *Sefirot* and keeps them alive, is enclothed within the vessel in the same way that the soul enters into the body, enclothed within human limbs, giving them life and illuminating them from the inside. This is called the inner light.[22]

However, the vessels were unable to effectively contain their lights. The first three vessels were merely displaced by the lights' impact, but the next six, from *Chesed* to *Yesod*, shattered, causing displacement, exile, and discord to hold sway throughout the cosmos. This event is known in the Lurianic Kabbalah as the "Breaking of the Vessels" (*Shevirat ha-Kelim*). The shattering of the *Sefirot* is paralleled by an equivalent catastrophe in the linguistic realm:

> All the stages of extended Light are also represented by combinations of letters. These are the functioning lights from which everything comes into being. Since they were unable to endure the abundance of Light, the combination of letters became disarranged and were severed from each other. They were thus rendered powerless to act and to govern. This is what is meant by their "shattering."[23]

As a result of the cosmic catastrophe, shards from the broken vessels tumble down through the void, entrapping sparks of divine light in "evil husks" (the *Kellipot*) that form the lower worlds and, ultimately, the "other side," a realm of evil, darkness, and death that is alienated from the source of divine light in God. Chaos reaches the upper worlds as well, where the masculine and feminine aspects of the deity, the celestial "Mother" and "Father," represented by the *Sefirot Chochmah* and *Binah*, are prompted to turn their backs on one another, thus disrupting the flow of divine erotic energy to all the worlds.

The broken vessels must be reassembled and restored. This is possible because not all of the divine light that fell out of the broken vessels is entrapped in the *Kellipot*. Some of this light returns spontaneously to its source, commencing a repair and reconstruction of the cosmos. This process, spoken of as *Tikkun ha-Olam*, the restoration of the world, involves the reorganization of the broken vessels into a series of *Partzufim*, "visages" or personality-structures of God, each of which is dominated by one or more of the original *Sefirot*.

However, the *Partzufim* organize within themselves all of the *Sefirot* and are hence stronger than any of the original *Sefirot* were in and of themselves. According to Scholem, these visages represent the development of the Primordial Human (*Adam Kadmon*) as it evolves towards a restored and redeemed world.[24] The Lurianists held that the stages of *Tikkun* are actually brought about by means of lights streaming from the forehead of *Adam Kadmon*.

The Kabbalists understood the *Partzufim* to be aspects or partial personalities of the deity. The five major divine personas are constellated as follows:

Attika Kaddisha (The Holy Ancient One) or Arikh Anpin
(The Long-suffering One),
Abba (The Father),
Imma (The Mother),
Zeir Anpin (The Impatient One) or *Ben* (The Son),
Nukvah (The Female) or *Bot* (The Daughter).

The *Partzufim* engage in certain regular relationships or unifications. *Abba* and *Imma* are unified in an enduring relationship of mutual friendship and support, and *Zeir Anpin* and *Nukvah* are unified in a passionate romance, which brings them alternately together and apart. The lower *Partzufim* (and *Sefirot*) are "born" in the womb of *Imma*, the Mother.

According to Luria the erotic relations (and ruptures) of the various *Partzufim* determine the fate of God, man, and the world. It is mankind's spiritual task to help raise the sparks of divine light entrapped in the evil husks of the other side. Man must, in effect, have dealings with the evil realm in order to realize the world's and his own redemption. As put by the Zohar:

There is no true worship except it issue forth from darkness, and no true good except it proceed from evil.[25]

Schneur Zalman, the first Lubavitcher rebbe, tells us:

The ultimate purpose [of creation] is this lowest world, for such was His blessed will that He shall have satisfaction when the *Sitra Achra* is subdued and the darkness is turned to light, so that the divine light of the blessed *Ein-sof* shall shine forth in the place of the darkness and *Sitra Achra* throughout the world, all the more strongly and intensely with the excellence of light emerging from darkness than its effulgence in the higher worlds.[26]

According to the Chasidic rebbe Dov Baer of Mesiritz, the "Maggid," who, as we have seen, Jung later praised for having anticipated his "entire psychology":[27]

It was...necessary that there should be a *shevirah* (Breaking of the Vessels), for by this means forgetfulness occurs in the Root, and each one can lift up his hand to perform an act…and they thereby elevate the sparks of the World of Action.[28]

According to the Lurianists, the "raising of the sparks" liberates divine energy for the service of erotic unions among the various *Partzufim*, not only between the "Mother" and "Father," but also between the Son and the Daughter and even between the "Old Holy Man" (*Attika Kaddisha*) and his consort. In raising these sparks, mankind is said to provide the "feminine waters" for the renewed divine activity. The result of these erotic recouplings, and the overall effect of the "World of Tikkun," is that cosmic alienation and exile is overcome and the flow of divine erotic energy is restored. The restored cosmos is far superior to the original "World of Points," which was comprised of the *Sefirot* as they were emanated prior to the Breaking of the Vessels. By assisting in the process of *Tikkun ha-Olam*, humanity, as Jung himself later declared, truly becomes a partner in the creation of the world. The Kabbalists themselves went so far as to hold that humanity's *Tikkun* (Restoration) is actually the completion, if not the creation, of *Ein-sof*, the Infinite God. As put by the Zohar:

> He who "keeps" the precepts of the Law and "walks" in God's ways, if one may say so, "makes" Him who is above.[29]

With the "raising of the sparks" the process of divine manifestation is complete. In Jungian terms, it might be said that *Ein-sof* and the world have become fully individuated, i.e., have achieved their respective identities. However, for the Kabbalists, the deity is not an external, transcendent being who creates a separate and distinct world. Rather, the world is itself an integral part of *Ein-sof's* identity. Divinity, for the Kabbalists, is the entire theosophical process. This process is summarized in Box 1.1, which can be understood as a "verbal picture" which begins with, develops, and ends with *Ein-sof*, the infinite God:

Box 1.1 The Lurianic System

Ein-sof (The infinite godhead),
of which nothing can be said…
is the union of being and nothingness, of "everything and its opposite."
Ein-sof performs a *Tzimtzum* (Divine Concealment, Contraction,
Withdrawal) which leads to a…
Metaphysical Void (*tehiru*), a circle surrounded by *Ein-sof* on all sides…
containing a residue (*reshimu*) of divine light, and into which
is emanated…
the light of the infinite (*Or Ein-sof*), a thin line (*kav*) through which…
Adam Kadmon (Primordial Human) spontaneously emerges.
Lights flashing and recoiling from *Adam Kadmon*'s eyes, nose, mouth,
and ears form Vessels (*Kelim*) for containing further lights,

thus forming the "World of Points" comprised of…

the *Sefirot* (Archetypes of Value and Being,

which are the constituents of the body of *Adam Kadmon):*

Keter (Crown, Will, Delight, the highest *Sefirah)*

Chochmah (Intellect, Wisdom, Paternal) *Binah* (Understanding, Maternal)

Chesed (Loving-kindness) *Tiferet/Rachamim* (Beauty, Compassion)

Din/Gevurah (Judgment, Strength)

Netzach (Glory) *Hod* (Splendor)

Yesod (Foundation)

Malchut /Shekhinah (Kingship / Feminine principle)

The ten Sefirot are complemented by the twenty-two *Otiyot Yesod*

(Foundational Letters), together forming the "thirty paths of wisdom"

which are organized into…

Worlds (*ha-Olamot*)

Adam Kadmon (A'K, identified with *Ein-sof* and *Keter)*

Atziluth (Nearness)

Beriah (Creation)

Yetzirah (Formation), and

Assiyah (Making, the lowest world, which includes our material earth).

The weakness and disunity of the *Sefirot* leads to their

shattering and displacement, known as…

The Breaking of the Vessels (*Shevirat ha-Kelim*), which

produces… a disruption in values and language and a

rupture in the conjugal flow

between Masculine and Feminine aspects of God.

Netzotzim (Sparks) from the shattered vessels fall and

become entrapped in…

Kellipot (Husks), which comprise the…

Sitra Achra (the Other Side, a realm of darkness and evil).

Lights from the forehead of *Adam Kadmon* reconstitute the

vessels as:

Partzufim (Faces or Personalities of God):

Attika Kaddisha (The Holy Ancient One) /

Keter Abba (The Father) / *Chochmah*

Imma (The Mother) / *Binah*

Zeir Anpin (The Impatient One) *Chesed - Yesod*

Nukvah (The Female) *Malchut/Shekhinah*. … This

begins…

Tikkun ha-Olam (The Impatient One), completed by

man, via the "raising of the sparks" which brings about the

reunification of the *Partzufim*, the masculine and

feminine principles of God,

and an end to division, alienation, and exile within the cosmos,

and the realization of *Ein-sof*, the infinite Godhead.

In subsequent chapters we will see that Jung himself makes reference to several of these symbols and that, moreover, the entire system is readily comprehensible in Jungian terms.

The Lurianic Kabbalah and Psychoanalysis

Before we explore the details of the relationship between Jung and the Kabbalah it will be worthwhile to orient ourselves by considering the basic connection between Lurianic and (Freudian) psychoanalytic thought. There have, of course, been numerous works that treat of the presumed Jewish pedigree to psychoanalysis.[30] However, with the exception of David Bakan's *Sigmund Freud and the Jewish Mystical Tradition*, none of them deal specifically with Jewish mysticism and most understand Freud's Judaism as only a kind of general impetus to his work in psychoanalysis. Bakan argued that Freud was greatly influenced by Kabbalistic ideas and was in fact a "crypto-Sabbatean," a follower of the seventeenth-century false messiah, Sabbatai Sevi.[31] Unfortunately, Bakan provided insufficient data to substantiate these claims, and his book also suffered from a failure to consider any of the symbols and ideas specific to the Lurianic Kabbalah; this despite the fact that in the book's second edition Bakan records a story, related to him by the late Lithuanian Rabbi Chayyim Bloch, that Freud had taken a keen interest in a German translation of a manuscript by Chayyim Vital, Luria's most prominent disciple.[32] In his book, first published in the 1950s, Bakan had argued that Freud had either consciously or unconsciously made use of Jewish mystical ideas in formulating psychoanalysis. After the book's publication, Bakan received a letter from a Rabbi Chayyim Bloch, who reported that he had been an acquaintance of Freud some years back. Bloch had read Bakan's book and informed Bakan that he had some information that might be of interest to him.

According to Chayyim Bloch, many years earlier he had been asked by his own mentor, the eminent Rabbi Joseph Bloch, to do a German translation of a work by Chayyim Vital, the most important student of Isaac Luria, the great master of the theosophical Kabbalah. Chayyim Bloch told Bakan that he'd begun work on the translation, but soon lost interest and ceased work altogether when Joseph Bloch died in 1923. Some time later, however, Chayyim Bloch had a dream in which Joseph Bloch came to him and asked him why he had not finished the project.

Chayyim Bloch then completed the translation, but felt he needed someone to write a foreword to the book and to help assume responsibility for its publication. Apparently Bloch had some understanding of the psychological significance of Chayyim Vital's work, because he decided to approach his acquaintance, Sigmund Freud. Freud agreed to read the manuscript, and upon doing so exclaimed to Bloch, "This is gold!" and wondered aloud why Chayyim Vital's work had never previously been brought to his attention. Freud agreed to write the foreword to the book and also agreed to assist in securing its publication.

At this point, Freud informed Bloch that he too had written a book that was relevant to Judaism, and hurriedly presented Bloch with the manuscript of what was to become *Moses and Monotheism*. Freud and Bloch were meeting in Freud's library, and Bloch quickly perused Freud's manuscript. The work, however, incensed Bloch, who saw that Freud had not only denied that Moses was Jewish but had placed responsibility for Moses' death on the Jewish people. Bloch exclaimed that the Christian world had always blamed the Jews for the death of their Christ, and now Freud would blame the Jews for the death of their own liberator, Moses.

Freud was himself deeply angered by Bloch's reaction to *Moses and Monotheism* and left the room, leaving Bloch alone in Freud's library for a period of time. During that time Bloch reports he had nothing to do but to browse through the books on Freud's shelf, among which was a French translation of the classic Kabbalistic text, the Zohar, as well as several German-language books on Jewish mysticism.

What, we might ask, was the "gold" that Freud had seen in the pages of Bloch's translation of Chayyim Vital's work? Interestingly, and somewhat surprisingly, David Bakan, in his own book on Freud and Jewish mysticism, barely even mentions Vital or Luria. This is the case even though it is plain that the Lurianic Kabbalah is a system of thought that cries out for interpretation in psychoanalytic terms.

As we have seen, Jung himself held that Jewish mysticism as expressed in the Kabbalah and Chasidism was an important key to understanding the origins of psychoanalysis.[33] Let us, then, examine the relationship between Freudian psychoanalysis and Kabbalistic, specifically Lurianic, theosophy, a relationship that is summarized in Table 1.1 below.

According to Freudian theory, the development of the individual involves the channelling and vicissitudes of libidinal energy, much as, for the Lurianists, the development of the cosmos involves the channeling and vicissitudes of the sexual/procreative energy of the Infinite God. Like the energy of the Kabbalists' *Ein-sof*, which is concealed and contracted to form a world, the libidinal energy spoken of by Freud is *concealed* and *contracted* (via repression), and modified into *structures*, the ego and superego, that form components of a psychic self. The function of these structures is to channel and modulate further "emanations" of the individual's *libido*, much as, according to the Kabbalists, the *Sefirot* were designed as vessels for channelling God's light, energy, and will. For psychoanalysis, the structures of the ego and superego are essential for the formation of *human character* in much the same way as, in the Kabbalah, the *Sefirot* are essential for the formation of *Adam Kadmon*, the Primordial Human.

For reasons that are inherent in the nature of the conflict between instinct and culture, the Freudian structures (ego and superego) are not

Table 1.1 The Basic Metaphor in Luria and Freud

Metaphor	Luria	Freud
Primary procreative and sexual energy	*Or Ein-sof* (Light of the Infinite God)	The Libido
Negation or concealment of energy	*Tzimtzum* (Contraction/ concealment of the infinite light)	Primary repression
Formation of value structures	The *Sefirot* (Value Archetypes)	Value structures of ego and superego
Creation of personality or man	*Adam Kadmon* (Primordial Human)	Individual character
Deconstruction	*Shevirah* (Breaking of the Vessels)	Shattering and splitting of ego structures
	"Sparks" entrapped in	Libido repressed in
Alienation in "underworld"	the *Sitra Achra* (the "Other Side")	Unconscious
Disruption in the erotic	Division of masculine and feminine principles in Godhead	Sexual dysfunction and pathology
Restoration	*Tikkun ha-Olam*: Restored flow of divine sexual energy	Psychoanalysis: libido restored

consistently able to maintain and modulate the libidinous energy in ways that are most adaptive to the individual. As with the Kabbalists' *Sefirot*, there is a partial shattering of each of these structures, resulting in a splitting off or alienation of ideas and emotions from the main fabric of the individual's personality. In the Lurianic system, this is analogous to the way in which divine sparks are separated or exiled from their main source in God. For Freud, the psychological splitting off occurs, for example, when the individual becomes aware of an impulse, thought, or desire that his conscious self finds unacceptable. The impulse or idea, and its associated affect, is repressed and subsequently exists in a nether psychological realm known as the unconscious, which is quite analogous to Luria's *Sitra Achra* or "Other Side." Once in the unconscious, these complexes of thought and affect, which are akin to the Kabbalist's *kellipot* ("husks"), are inaccessible to the individual. They are, in effect, exiled psychosexual energy, which becomes the source of an imbalance that the individual experiences as depression or other neurotic symptoms, in much the same way as the *kellipot* entrap and exile divine sexuality, thereby becoming the source of cosmic negativity and evil. Further, in Freudian theory, the splitting of the ego resulting from repression creates a disruption in the individual's erotic life, just as for Luria the Breaking of the

Vessels causes a blockage in the flow of divine sexual energy and a rupture in the *coniunctio* between the masculine and feminine aspects of God.

The task of psychoanalysis, at least as it was originally conceived, is to make the unconscious thoughts and emotions conscious and, more importantly, to free the libidinal energy attached to them so that it can again be made available to the individual for his erotic and life goals; just as in Kabbalah the energy trapped in the *Sitra Achra* must be freed and made available for divine service and a renewed relationship between the masculine and feminine aspects of God. From a Kabbalistic perspective, psychoanalytic therapy is itself a form of *tikkun* or restoration, which brings an end to a *galut* or exile of aspects of the individual's personality and ushers in a *geulah* or psychological redemption.

The relationship between Freudian psychoanalysis and the Kabbalah is certainly a fascinating topic in its own right, one that is made even more interesting by Freud's father's background and other circumstances in Freud's life.[34] We will see, however, that as strong as is the link between the Lurianic Kabbalah and Freudian psychoanalysis, it is the non-Jewish disciple of Freud, Carl Jung, who creates a psychology that is most profoundly Kabbalistic in nature. As we have seen, it is Jung who has Kabbalistic visions, which he describes as the "most tremendous things I have ever experienced," and it is Jung who (via Gnosticism, alchemy, and the Kabbalah itself) turns to the symbols of Jewish mysticism in constructing his theory of the human psyche and, in effect, extracts the psychological "gold" buried in the Jewish mystical tradition.

Jung's Familiarity with the Kabbalah

Jung makes very few references to the Jewish mystical tradition in his pre-alchemy writings and does not appear, even in his later writings, to have had in-depth knowledge of original Kabbalistic texts. While *Mysterium Coniunctionis* includes citations to the Sperling and Simon English translation of the Zohar (first published in 1931–34) as well as to a German translation of the Zohar by Ernst Mueller (1932),[35] nearly all of Jung's specific citations to Kabbalistic symbols and ideas are to the writings of Knorr von Rosenroth, whose *Kabbalah Denudata* (1684) is a Latin translation of passages from the Zohar, other Kabbalistic writings, and essays on the meaning of the Kabbalah.[36] Knorr von Rosenroth's work, however, was a formidable one, and Jung's close disciple James Kirsch asserts that Jung had read all three thousand pages in its entirety.[37] While Jung's "visions" were inspired by the symbolism of the Kabbalist Moses Cordovero's *Pardes Rimmonim* (Garden of Pomegranates), and this work is cited in the bibliography of *Mysterium Coniunctionis*, the only specific reference is in a single footnote, and this is cited through Knorr von Rosenroth.[38] While Jung was undoubtedly aware of the writings of Gershom Scholem (whose *Major Trends in Jewish Mysticism* first appeared in the mid-1930s), if we take him at his word, he appears unlikely to have read them closely prior to 1954. Otherwise he would have undoubtedly been familiar with certain doctrines of the Lurianic Kabbalah such as the Breaking of the Vessels and *Tikkun* prior to the date he acknowledges in his letter to Reverend Erastus Evans in February of that year.[39] Jung carried on a correspondence with a number of students who had first-hand knowledge of Kabbalistic texts, and even acknowledges to R. J. Zwi Werblowsky that he received a copy of the Kabbalist R. Gikatila's text on dreams.[40] In addition, with the publication of Erich Neumann's *The Roots of Jewish Consciousness* in 2019 (see Appendix) it is tempting to speculate that the rich psychological understanding of Hasidism present in that work was imparted to Jung by one of his closest disciples, but at this point the evidence is that Jung derived his working knowledge of the Kabbalah from Knorr von Rosenroth, references to the Kabbalah in the writings of such alchemists as Dorn, and an occasional perusal of the European literature on the Kabbalah (French, German, English) that was extant before the field was thoroughly transformed by Scholem.

I will argue in Chapter 10 that, for reasons to be adduced there, Jung may have originally suppressed his more direct dependence upon Kabbalistic sources. Regardless, in his later work Jung commented quite profoundly on certain Kabbalistic symbols and ideas. The major Kabbalistic symbols and ideas that concerned Jung were those that had clear parallels in Gnosticism and alchemy: the notion of a spark of divine light contained within man, the concept of Primordial Human who contains within himself in *coincidentia oppositorum* the various conflicting tendencies within the human spirit, the theory of the *Sefirot* and their unifications, particularly the unifications of good and evil and masculine and feminine, etc. Despite an occasional reference to Luria, absent from any detailed consideration in Jung's major works are the symbols of *tzimtzum* (divine contraction), *shevirah* (the "breaking of the vessels"), *tikkun ha-olam* (the "restoration of the world"), etc., which are unique to the Lurianic Kabbalah. It is true, however, that just as these concepts were implicit in the Kabbalah that preceded Luria (e.g., the Zohar), they are, as we will see, also implicit in the alchemical writings that borrowed so heavily from the earlier Kabbalah. Had Jung been aware of these symbols prior to 1954, they would have been of invaluable service to him, not only in his attempt to grasp the spiritual and psychological nature of alchemy, but also in the expression of his own psychology of the self.[41]

Jung and Gnosticism: The Seven Sermons to the Dead

Jung's interpretation of Gnosticism is critical to his understanding of the Kabbalah. This is because many major Kabbalistic themes are anticipated in the Gnostic sources with which Jung was familiar.[42] Jung's comments on Gnosticism are scattered throughout his writings;[43] his major statement on the subject coming in his essay "Gnostic Symbols of the self."[44] However, long before he had systematically considered Gnosticism from the point of view of his own analytical psychology, Jung had been familiar with Gnostic theology and even constructed, in 1916, his own "Gnostic myth," which he had circulated privately among friends but which, at his own request, was excluded from his collected works. This myth, as we now know, was originally embedded within a much larger set of writings, which eventuated in *The Red Book*, and was reported by Jung to have been communicated to him by Philemon, one of the psychic figures that emerged during his early visions and experimentations with active imagination. In the "*Septem Sermones ad Mortuos*" (Seven Sermons to the Dead), as well as in other passages in *The Red Book*, Jung registers a number of "Gnostic" themes to which he was to return to many times in his later writings.

Among these themes, perhaps the most significant and pervasive is a concern with the coincidence of opposites and the unification of antinomies. "Harken," Jung writes, "I begin with nothingness. Nothingness is the same as fullness. In infinity full is no better than empty. Nothingness is both empty and full."[45] The "Pleroma" (or fullness of being, which for the Gnostics is the equivalent of the Kabbalists' *Ein-sof*, the Infinite) is characterized, Jung tells us, by "pairs of opposites," such as "living and dead," "good and evil," "beauty and ugliness," "the one and the many." These opposites are equal and hence void in the Pleroma but are "distinct and separate" in man. "Thus," Jung writes, "we are victims of the pairs of opposites. The Pleroma is rent in us."[46] "Abraxas," the "forgotten god," who stands above the God who is worshipped and who would be the first manifestation of the Pleroma if the Pleroma indeed had "being," speaks "that hallowed and accursed word which is life and death...truth and lying, good and evil, light and darkness, in the same word and in the same act."[47] In *The Red Book*, we learn "the melting together of sense and nonsense... produces the supreme meaning,"[48] "immense fullness and immense emptiness are one and the same,"[49] and "madness and reason want to be married.... The opposites embrace each other, see eye to eye, and intermingle."[50] The doctrine of *coincidentia oppositorum*, also played a prominent role in *Psychological Types*, which Jung wrote and published during the period of his Gnostic visions.

A variety of other typically Gnostic themes make their appearance in "The Seven Sermons." Among these is the doctrine that "because we are parts of the Pleroma, the Pleroma is also in us." We are also, according to Jung, "the whole Pleroma"[51] on the principle that each smallest point in the microcosm is a perfect mirror of the cosmos.[52] Man, as a finite creature, is characterized by "distinctiveness," and the natural striving of man is towards distinctiveness and individuation. However, this battle against sameness and consequent death is ultimately futile, because as we are immersed in the Pleroma our pursuit of various distinctions inevitably leads us to seize each of their opposites. In pursuing good and beauty we necessarily lay hold of evil and ugliness as well. Hence, man should not strive after that which is illusory, but rather after his own being, which leads him to an existential (rather than an epistemological) awareness of the pleromatic "star" that is his ultimate essence and goal.[53]

Jung's prescription for man in "The Seven Sermons" is significant because it appears to be so typically Gnostic. This world of distinctiveness and individuation offers man nothing. Man must turn his back on the world of "creatura" and follow his inner star beyond this cosmos, for, according to Jung:

> Weakness and nothingness here, there eternally creative power. Here nothing but darkness and chilling moisture. There wholly sun.[54]

Years later, when Jung comes to take a second look at Gnosticism through the eyes of a more fully developed archetypal psychology, he interprets it in a manner that is far more Kabbalistic than Gnostic, that is, far more friendly to the world and the individual's struggle within it. Interestingly, there are passages in *The Red Book* that anticipate this "world-embracing" turn. For example, in *Liber Primus*, Jung writes, "this life is the way, the long sought after way to the unfathomable, which we call divine. There is no other way. All other ways are false paths."[55]

Several other ideas that were to become significant for Jung's later psychology make their appearance in *The Red Book* and the "Seven Sermons." These include the themes of accepting the evil or shadow side of God and human nature, welcoming "chaos" as a path to the discovery of one's soul, valuing the unknown, and giving "(re)birth" to both God and self. We will later see how each of these themes is developed by Jung in conjunction with alchemical, and particularly, Kabbalistic, symbols and ideas.

One more point regarding "The Seven Sermons" bears mention: its view of sexuality. Jung adopts the Gnostic theme of sexuality pervading the cosmos. For Jung, as for the Gnostics, sexuality is a numinous phenomenon and not simply a natural function of mankind:

> The world of the gods is made manifest in spirituality and in sexuality. Spirituality and sexuality are not your qualities, not things which you possess and contain but they possess and contain you; for they are powerful demons, manifestations of the gods, and are therefore things which reach beyond you, existing in themselves. No man hath a spirituality unto himself, or a sexuality unto himself. But he standeth under the law of spirituality and of sexuality.[56]

This passage is of particular interest with respect to Jung's own polemic against Freud. Years later, Jung would relate how Freud appeared to take an almost religious, worshipful view of the sexual instincts in man, but was not able to acknowledge the true spirituality of Eros.[57] Jung, of course, would later locate spirituality and sexuality among the archetypes of the collective unconscious, and in this sense they would remain for him a law that exists beyond any human individual. Here in this Gnostic flight of fancy he sees them, however, as manifestations of the gods, "Platonic forms" that have an existence independent of the human mind. We will see how the Kabbalists came to epitomize the divine nature of sexuality in their theosophical writings.

The themes expressed in "The Seven Sermons," and many of the themes in *The Red Book* in general, are well represented in the Gnostic sources[58] and, as we shall see, in the Kabbalah. We will now turn to Jung's unique contribution in this area, the psychologistic interpretation of Gnosticism that crystallized in his essay "Gnostic Symbols of the self."

Jung's Interpretative Method

Jung's interpretation of Gnosticism, indeed his interpretation of religious phenomena in general, rests upon his theory of the history of the psyche in man,[59] a theory that builds upon Freud's understanding of the origins of the mythological and religious worldview. In *The Psychopathology of Everyday Life* (1904), Freud had written:

> I believe that a large part of the mythological view of the world, which extends a long way into most modern religions, is nothing but psychology projected into the external world. The obscure recognition... of psychical factors and relations in the unconscious is mirrored...in the construction of a supernatural reality, which is destined to be changed back once more by science into the *psychology of the unconscious*. One could venture to explain in this way the myths of paradise and the fall of man, of God, of good and evil, of immortality, and so on, and to transform *metaphysics* into *metapsychology*.[60]

However, according to Jung, modern man has moved from a state in which he projects the contents of his unconscious onto the world and heavens to one in which, as a result of his total identification with the rational powers of the ego, he has withdrawn his projections from the world. In this state, he fails completely to recognize the formerly projected contents (what Jung terms the "archetypes") of his unconscious mind. The world's great religions, Christianity and Gnosticism among them, developed at a time when men projected their collective unconscious onto the world and then worshipped these contents as gods. In essence, the ancients understood these unconscious contents as events independent of their own psyches. According to Jung, as a result of the development of a fully independent rational and conscious ego, modern man has withdrawn his unconscious projections from the world and heavens. This has resulted in a loss of faith in the gods and a loss of interest in mythological language and symbols. Today, Jung writes, "we lack all knowledge of the unconscious psyche and pursue the cult of consciousness to the exclusion of all else."[61] The unconscious, however, cannot be ignored or eliminated, and it forces itself on modern man in the form of ennui, superstitious fears and beliefs (e.g., "flying saucers,"[62] or, in our time, "new age ideas"), and, most significantly, in neurosis and aggression. According to Jung:

> The gods have become diseases; Zeus no longer rules Olympus but rather the solar plexus, and produces curious specimens for the doctor's consulting room, or disorders the brains of politicians and journalists who unwittingly let loose psychic epidemics on the world.[63]

Jung's prescription for contemporary man is a new non-projective awareness and experience of the collective unconscious to replace the dead projective metaphors of religion. Psychology, specifically Jungian psychology, is in a position to provide man with a direct awareness of the archetypes within his own psyche. This, Jung believes, can be accomplished through an interpretation of the spontaneous symbolic projections of the unconscious in fantasy, art, and dreams, guided by a new *psychological understanding* of the basic archetypal images, which have presented themselves in the history of myth and religion. Jung turns to this history for a catalogue or map of the contents of the collective unconscious, and he interprets his patients' (archetypal) dreams and images accordingly. His interest in the "dead" religion of Gnosticism, as well as in the forgotten science of alchemy, lies in the fact that their symbolisms presumably contain a more or less pristine crystallization of the collective unconscious, undisturbed by the ego-oriented reinterpretations of reason and dogma. Indeed, the long incognizance of the Kabbalah in official Judaism suggests that it too preserves elements of the collective unconscious in a relatively pure form.

Jung's Interpretation of Gnosticism

Jung interpreted the Gnostic myths—including the origin of the cosmos in the Pleroma, the emergence of an ignorant God or demiurge, the creation of a Primordial Human, and the placing of a spark of divinity within individual humans—in psychological terms.[64] The Gnostic myths do not, according to Jung, refer to cosmic or even external human events, but rather reflect the basic archetypal developments of the human psyche. The Pleroma, within which is contained the undifferentiated unity of all opposites and contradictions, is, according to Jung, nothing but the primal unconscious from which the human personality will emerge.[65] The "demiurge," which the Gnostics disparaged as being ignorant of its pleromatic origins, represents the conscious, rational ego, which in its arrogance believes that it is both the creator and master of the human personality. The spark, or *scintilla*, which is placed in the soul of man, represents the possibility of the psyche's reunification with the unconscious, and the primal anthropos (*Adam Kadmon* or Christ), which is related to this spark, is symbolic of the "self," the achieved unification of a conscious, individuated personality with the full range of oppositions and archetypes in the unconscious mind. "Our aim," Jung tells us, "is to create a wider personality whose centre of gravity does not necessarily coincide with the ego,"[66] but rather "in the hypothetical point between conscious and unconscious."[67] Jung sees in the Gnostic (and Kabbalistic) image of Primordial Human a symbol of the goal of his own analytical psychology.

Jung's Interpretation of Alchemy

Jung provides a similar, if more daring and far-reaching, interpretation of alchemy. According to Jung, what the alchemist sees in matter and understands in his formulas for the transmutation of metals and the derivation of the *prima materia* "is chiefly the data of his own unconscious which he is projecting into it."[68] For example, the alchemist's efforts to bring about a union of opposites in his laboratory and to perform what he speaks of as a "chymical wedding" are understood by Jung as attempts to forge a unity, e.g., between the masculine and feminine, or the good and evil aspects of his own psyche.[69] "The alchemical opus," Jung tells us, "deals in the main not just with chemical experiments as such, but with something resembling psychic processes expressed in pseudochemical language."[70] It is for this reason that the alchemists have occasion to equate their chemical procedures with a vast array of symbolical processes and figures, for example, equating the *prima materia* not only with the philosopher's stone (*lapis philosophorum*), but also with the Spirit Mercurius, a "panacea," and a divine hermaphroditic original man.[71] Indeed, according to Jung, alchemy is of special interest to the psychologist because the alchemists, in projecting their unconscious onto their work, laid bare their psyche without ever realizing that they were doing so.[72] As such, alchemy provides a pure crystallization of the collective unconscious, unaltered by conscious censorship or obfuscation.

In his *Mysterium Coniunctionis*, Jung provides a catalog of alchemical symbols, interpreted in the context of the alchemists' principle of *solve et coagula* (separation and bringing together). According to Jung, "the alchemist saw the essence of his art in separation and analysis on the one hand and synthesis and coagulation on the other."[73] The process, ending in what the alchemists spoke of as the *coniunctio*, is personified as a "marriage" or union between sun and moon, Rex and Regina (King and Queen), or Adam and Eve. This union, according to Jung, reflects "the moral task of alchemy," which is "to bring the feminine, maternal background of the masculine psyche, seething with passions, into harmony with the principle of the spirit."[74] In Jungian terms, this amounts to the unification of *animus* and *anima* or of the ego with the unconscious.

The *solve et coagula* (separation and unification) of the alchemist is, according to Jung, perfectly paralleled in the contemporary process of psychotherapy. Therapy, according to Jung, approaches a personality in conflict, separates out—i.e., analyzes—the conflict, and ultimately aims at uniting the dissociated or repressed elements with the ego. The alchemist, in striving for a permanent, incorruptible, androgynous, divine "unification," was himself unconsciously striving after a process of individuation, the forging of a unified self.[75] As we shall see, the alchemists consciously borrowed such Kabbalistic symbols as the "spiritual wedding," "the raising of the sparks," and *Adam Kadmon* (Primordial Human) to further articulate this unification process.

It is interesting to note, if just in passing, that Jung, without much elaboration, interprets astrology in a similar, psychological manner. Indeed, he applauds alchemy and astrology for their ceaseless preservation of man's bridge to nature (i.e., the unconscious) at a time when the church's "increasing differentiation of ritual and dogma alienated consciousness from its natural roots."[76] In regard to astrology, Jung writes:

> As we all know, science began with the stars, and mankind discovered in them the dominants of the unconscious, the "gods," as well as the curious psychological qualities of the zodiac: a complete projected theory of human character.[77]

As we proceed to examine Jung's relationship to Jewish mysticism, we will do well to remember that such Kabbalists as Chayyim Vital were often also practitioners of both alchemy and astrology.[78]

Kabbalah, Gnosis, and Jungian Psychology

Regardless of the direction of influence, it is clear that nearly all of the basic symbols and ideas of Gnosticism are to be found in one form or another in the Kabbalah, and vice versa. The notion of an unknowable Infinite Godhead that contains within itself a coincidence of metaphysical opposites, the gradual manifestation of the Infinite through an emanation of *logoi* or *Sefirot*, the notion of a cosmic accident giving birth to the manifest world, the distinction between the God of the Bible and the true Infinite, the estrangement of man from his true essence, and the entrapment of a divine spark within man's material nature are all themes that found their way into both

Gnosticism and the Kabbalah. The question of origins is complicated by the fact that although, according to contemporary scholars, the Kabbalah arrives on the scene centuries after the first manifestations of Gnosticism, many of these same scholars hold that Gnosticism itself grew out of an even earlier Jewish mystical tradition that (centuries later) also gave rise to the Kabbalah.[79] There is also speculation to the effect that apparent Gnostic themes arose *de novo* among the Lurianic Kabbalists in the sixteenth century in Safed.[80]

Yet for all the similarities between Gnostic and Kabbalistic doctrine, certain essential differences emerge that are of ultimate significance for Jungian psychology. The major difference is that Gnosticism has no equivalent concept or symbol for the Kabbalistic notion of *Tikkun ha-Olam*, the Restoration of the World. For the Gnostics, the goal of religious life is not a restoration, but an *escape* from what they regard to be this worthless, evil world. The Gnostic identifies with the divine spark within himself in order that he might transcend his physical self and the material world. The Kabbalist, on the other hand, holds, in the main, a radically different view. Although there are also escapist or "gnostic" trends within the Kabbalah, the majority of Kabbalists held that the realization of the divine spark both in man and the material world brings about an elevation, restoration, and spiritualization of both humanity and its environment.[81] In Gnosticism the world is escaped; in the Kabbalah it is elevated and restored. The latter view is one that is much more congenial to Jungian psychology, not only on the obvious principle that for Jung life in this world, and the world itself, is worthwhile, but also with respect to the (less obvious) psychological interpretation that Jung places on the Gnostic myths. As Robert Segal has pointed out, the Gnostic ethic, as interpreted by Jung, would strictly speaking lead to a complete identification of the ego with the unconscious mind.[82] This is because the Gnostic attempts to escape from the world (which Jung equates with the ego) into a complete identification with the infinite Pleroma—which, as we have seen, Jung identifies with the unconscious.

By way of contrast, for the Kabbalists and Jung (and the alchemists as interpreted by Jung) the Godhead creates the world in order to fully realize itself within it. By analogy, the unconscious mind manifests itself in a reflective ego in order to complete and know itself as a conscious "self." "The difference," Jung writes, "between the 'natural' individuation process, which runs its course unconsciously, and the one which is consciously realized, is tremendous. In the first case consciousness nowhere intervenes; the end remains as dark as the beginning."[83]

As Idel points out (and as will be detailed in the Appendix to this volume) Jung's early Jewish disciple, Erich Neumann, well understood the "this-wordly" nature of Jewish mysticism, as well as its implications for a psychology of the self. As Neumann put it, "Normally the ego, transformed by the experience of the numinous, returns to the sphere of human life, and its transformation includes a broadening of consciousness....Whenever the ego returns to the sphere of human life, transformed by the mystical experience, we may speak of an immanent world-transforming mysticism."[84] Jung himself was well aware of the worldly orientation of Judaism. For example, in his seminar on Nietzsche's *Zarathustra* he averred that "the Semitic temperament... believes in the glorification of the world," and "The Jew has the temperament of a reformer who really wants to produce something in this world."[85]

For Jung, as for the Kabbalists and alchemists, the world, and its psychological equivalent, the self, far from being the superfluous, harmful, and lamentable conditions envisioned by the Gnostics, are actually necessary, beneficial, and laudable.[86] For Jung the process of individuation, of raising the spark within one's psyche, reveals the archetypal richness of the collective unconscious, and has the effect of bringing one into the world (Judaism), rather than escaping from it (Gnosticism). According to Jung, with the revelation of the collective unconscious:

> there arises a consciousness which is no longer imprisoned in the petty, oversensitive, personal world of the ego, but participates freely in the wider world of objective interests. This widened consciousness is no longer that touchy, egotistical bundle of personal wishes, fears, hopes, and ambitions which always has to be compensated or corrected by unconscious counter-tendencies; instead, it is a function of relationship to the world of objects, bringing the individual into absolute, binding, and indissoluble communion with the world at large.[87]

For Jung, both God and man must pass through the world and redeem it in order to realize their full essence. This is precisely the view of the Kabbalists, as expressed in their symbol of *Tikkun ha-Olam*. As Segal has pointed out, Gnosticism actually advocates the precise opposite of Jungian psychology.

Interestingly, the alchemists are far more compatible with Jung (and the Kabbalah) on this crucial point than are the Gnostics. The *raison d'être* of alchemy is the transformation of worldly matter,[88] not the escape from it. For Gnosticism, the dissolution of the world is an end in itself. For the alchemists, it is a precondition for a new creation, just as in the Kabbalah the *Shevirat ha-Kelim*, the breaking of the vessels and destruction of earlier worlds, sets the stage for the world's redemption in *Tikkun ha-Olam*. It is thus understandable that Jung would write at the close of *The Red Book* that it was only an encounter with alchemy beginning in 1930 that enabled him to arrange the experiences that produced *The Red Book* into a coherent whole. As we will see in Chapter 2, European alchemy was itself indebted to the Kabbalah for its spiritual core.

Jung is more Kabbalistic than Gnostic on a number of other crucial points as well. For example, according to the Gnostics, the demiurge or creator God (the God archetype in Jung) is thoroughly evil, whereas for Jung (and the Kabbalah) it represents both good and evil, persona and shadow, a coincidence of opposites.[89] Indeed, Gnosticism holds a radical dualism of good immateriality and evil matter; while for Jung, as for the Kabbalah, good and evil originate (and end) in the same source, are mutually dependent upon one another, and are not simply to be identified with spirit and matter. This, again, is a theme that permeates Jung's thoughts and experiences in *The Red Book*, a theme that is essentially Jewish in origin.[90] Had Jung been more familiar with the Kabbalah, particularly in its Lurianic form, he would have found a system of mythical thought that was far more compatible with his own psychology than Gnosticism. In 1954, shortly after his discovery of the Lurianic Kabbalah and after essentially completing *Mysterium Coniunctionis*, Jung all but acknowledged this point of view. In a letter to James Kirsch (16 February 1954), he writes:

> The Jew has the advantage of having long since anticipated the development of consciousness in his own spiritual history. By this I mean the Lurianic stage of the Kabbalah, the breaking of the vessels and man's help in restoring them. Here the thought emerges for the first time that man must help God to repair the damage wrought by creation. For the first time man's cosmic responsibility is acknowledged.[91]

For Jung, in contrast to the Gnostics, humanity is not enjoined to escape the world, but is rather responsible for its repair and restoration. It is this notion of "world-restoration," what the Kabbalists referred to as *Tikkun ha-Olam*, that most connects Jung to the Jewish mystical tradition.

Jung's Gnosticism

Before turning to our next major theme, the relationship between the Kabbalah and alchemy, I will comment briefly on a question that has been a subject of controversy for many years, the question of Jung's so-called "Gnosticism." The question takes on a certain moment in the present context for the fact that Jung's main "accuser" in this regard was the Jewish philosopher Martin Buber, himself an expositor of Chasidism and sometime interpreter of the Kabbalah. Buber castigates Jung for reducing God to an aspect of the self, and for failing to recognize that the primary experience of the deity is via a relationship to one who is wholly "other," as in the experience that Buber himself had articulated in *I and Thou*.[92] Jung's theology, according to Buber, is Gnostic in the disparaging sense that Jung reduces God to humanity.

Jung bitterly rejected the Gnostic epithet, not because he rejected any particular Gnostic symbol or theory, but because he viewed himself as an empirical scientist who was, in his work, completely *agnostic* with respect to any metaphysical or theological claims.[93] For Jung, God, the Pleroma, the divine spark, etc., are real psychologically, but Jung insists that he can make no judgment regarding their metaphysical status. As for Buber's criticisms, Jung held that a genuine encounter with the self was a necessary prerequisite for a genuine and sustained "I-Thou" encounter with God.[94]

Still, others have not been willing to let Jung off the hook with such a general disclaimer. Maurice Friedman, a disciple and expositor of Buber, calls Jung a Gnostic because Jung offers the psychological equivalent of salvation, a salvation of turning inward into one's own psyche or soul.[95] Thomas J. J. Altizer, a theologian who himself proclaimed the "death of God" and the deity's subsequent dispersal throughout humanity, writes:

> Despite his frequently repeated and even compulsive scientific claims, Jung has found his spiritual home in what he himself identifies as the Gnostic tradition.[96]

One cannot readily demur to Altizer's characterization, a characterization that is particularly apt given Jung's late-life confession that the fantasies and dreams that culminated in his Gnostic "Seven Sermons" prefigured and guided all of his later work. In *Memories, Dreams, Reflections*, he writes:

> All my works, all my creative activity, has come from these initial fantasies and dreams which began in 1912, almost 50 years ago. Everything that I accomplished in later life was already contained in them, although at first in the form of emotions and images.[97]

Indeed, in *The Red Book* Jung speaks forcefully about the discovery of God within his self and, despite occasional references to the singular significance of love,[98] he holds that there are enormous difficulties in achieving relational mutuality:

> two things have yet to be discovered. The first is the infinite gulf that separates us from one another. The second is the bridge that could connect us.[99]

Yet even with this confession, and even if we discount Jung's own professed agnosticism, Jung, as we have seen, makes a radical break from the Gnostics in his affirmation of both the individual human being and, more importantly, the world. In addition, with his discovery of the psychological significance of alchemy, Jung became deeply involved with its wedding/ *coniunctio* symbols, symbols that were in many cases imported from the Kabbalah, and which, in their Kabbalistic form, became the central theme in Jung's 1944 visions. These *coniunctio* symbols, which would provide Jung with a notation for unifying the masculine and feminine aspects of the self, as well as representing the union of man and woman, and humanity and God, are absent from *The Red Book* and Jung's other early writings. It is for these reasons that I have described Jung as more Kabbalistic than Gnostic, and they are, in part, the reasons why Jung turned from Gnosticism to the more "worldly" (and Kabbalistic) alchemy in his historical exploration of the symbols of the unconscious.

Chapter 2

Kabbalah and Alchemy

In October 1935, over a year after Erich Neumann had emigrated from Germany to Palestine, Neumann wrote Jung about his fear that his absorption in Jungian psychology would place him in "danger of betrayal to [his] own Jewish foundations." Neumann further wrote of his realization that analytical psychology "stands on its own ground... Switzerland, Germany, the West, Christianity," and that Jewish individuation must be based "on our own archetypal collective foundations which are different because we are Jews."[1] Jung, in his response, wrote that analytical psychology "has its roots deep in Europe, in the Christian Middle Ages, and ultimately in Greek philosophy," adding, "the connecting-link I was missing for so long has now been found, and it is alchemy."[2] Neither Neumann nor Jung would allow that analytical psychology as it then stood was rooted in anything Jewish, a fact that was troubling to Neumann, who had thought of Jung as his spiritual teacher but who chided Jung for his "general ignorance of things Jewish."[3]

Although, later in his life, Jung was more than happy to acknowledge Jewish, specifically Jewish mystical, precursors to his own work,[4] during the 1930s, at a time when he sought to distinguish analytical psychology from the "Jewish" psychologies of Freud and Adler, Jung was unlikely to acknowledge any Jewish sources of his own thinking. There is a certain irony here, because what Jung failed to realize, or mention, at the time of his letter to Neumann (though he would later openly acknowledge it) was that alchemy, the "connecting link" to analytical psychology, was itself imbued with Jewish mystical symbols and ideas.

In this chapter, I discuss the historical connection between alchemy and the Kabbalah. I will provide evidence supportive of the hypothesis that the spiritual/psychological aspects of alchemy were in no small measure derived from the Kabbalah, thus providing grounds for regarding Jung as further immersed in Kabbalistic ideas than his more limited quotation of Kabbalistic texts might suggest. Indeed, I will argue here and in later chapters that there is good reason to believe that in extracting the "psychological gold" that lay buried in the alchemists' texts and procedures Jung was, in effect,

DOI: 10.4324/9781003027041-3

reconstituting Kabbalistic ideas that had been absorbed by the alchemists themselves.

Jung's Understanding of the Impact of Kabbalah on Alchemy

It is well known that Jung's interest in alchemy consumed him for the last thirty years of his life. Most of his writings in the 1940s and 1950s are concerned, in one way or another, with alchemical themes, and it is fair to say that the most mature developments in his thinking regarding such topics as the self, the coincidence of opposites, and the archetypes of the collective unconscious came about as a result of meditations upon alchemical texts and ideas. Jung held that the pseudo-chemical language and goals of the alchemists concealed and were symbolic of spiritual and, moreover, depth-psychological principles and themes.[5] In his investigations of alchemical texts, Jung sought to uncover what he understood to be the psychological principles that the alchemists projected into their chemical and metallurgical formulas.

By the time Jung wrote *Mysterium Coniunctionis*,[6] he was well aware of the strong relationship that had developed between the Kabbalah and later alchemy, and he often spoke of specific Kabbalistic influences upon the alchemists. "Directly or indirectly," Jung writes, "the Cabala [Jung's spelling] was assimilated into alchemy. Relationships must have existed between them at a very early date, though it is difficult to trace them in the sources."[7] Further, in a discussion of the symbol of the "Primordial Human," Jung tells us that "traces of cabalistic tradition are frequently noticeable in the alchemical treatises from the sixteenth century on."[8] Jung informs us that by that time the alchemists began making direct quotations from the classic Kabbalistic text, the Zohar. For example, Jung quotes the alchemist Blasius Vigenerus (1523–96), who had borrowed the Zohar's comparison of the feminine *Sefirah Malchut* with the moon turning its face from the intelligible things of heaven.[9] Jung notes that the alchemists Vigenerus and Knorr von Rosenroth had related the alchemical notion of the *lapis* or philosopher's stone to certain passages in the Zohar that had interpreted verses in the books of Genesis (28:22), Job (38:6), and Isaiah (28:16) as referring to a stone with essential, divine, and transformative powers.[10]

Jung takes an interest in the Kabbalistic symbol of *Adam Kadmon* (Primordial Human), and references a number of alchemists, who made extensive use of this symbol.[11] Jung points out that in these texts "the alchemists... equate Mercurius and the Philosopher's Stone with the Primordial Man of the Kabbalah."[12] It is significant that in exploring the Primal Anthropos, which he calls "the essential core of the great religions," Jung works his way through its material representation in alchemy as the "stone," to the quasi-physical spiritual entity "Mercurius," to its purely spiritual and, moreover, psychological representation in the Kabbalah as *Adam Kadmon*. This is an example of what I mean by Jung extracting the spiritual/Kabbalistic "gold" out of the material practice of alchemy. In this context, we should note that Jung references Isaac Luria's view that every psychic quality is attributable to Adam,[13] quoting Knorr von Rosenroth's Latin translation of Luria's text and stating that he is indebted to Gershom Scholem for an "interpretive translation," presumably from the Hebrew.[14]

Jung notes that Paracelsus had introduced the sapphire as an "arcanum" into alchemy from the Kabbalah.[15] Jung took a lively interest in two alchemists, Knorr von Rosenroth and Heinrich Khunrath, who composed entire treatises on the Kabbalah, as well as other alchemists, e.g., Dorn and Lully, who were heavily influenced by Kabbalistic ideas.[16] The symbol of the "sparks" (or "*scintillae*"), which was to become a key element in the Lurianic Kabbalah, is present in their work, where it is provided a this-worldly Kabbalistic (as opposed to otherworldly or Gnostic) interpretation. Jung points out, for example, that Dorn held that wisdom is an awareness of the "spark of (God's) light," which is an "invisible sun,"[17] the equivalent to the image of God within man. Khunrath, who wrote at a time when the Lurianic Kabbalah was rapidly spreading across Europe, held that "there are...fiery sparks of the World-Soul...dispersed or scattered at God's command in and through the fabric of the great world into all fruits of the elements everywhere,"[18] a quintessentially Kabbalistic idea that Jung interpreted as a "projection of the multiple luminosity of the unconscious."[19]

Kabbalah as the Spiritual Foundation of Alchemy

While Jung was clearly aware of the impact of Kabbalah upon alchemy, more recent scholarship has provided further support for the idea that the spiritual aspects of alchemy, those which interested Jung, were to a large extent Jewish in origin.[20]

In this regard, Raphael Patai has provided an invaluable service in collating and presenting many of the Jewish alchemical sources and in tracing the influence of Kabbalah and Jewish alchemy on the Christian alchemists.[21]

Interestingly, Jung's own view that alchemy is essentially a spiritual/ psychological, rather than a purely material, discipline appears to have originated in Jewish sources. The Egyptian Hellenistic Jewess, Maria the Prophetess, who is regarded by Zosimos (third century) to be the founder of alchemy (and by modern scholarship to be among its earliest practitioners), viewed the alchemical work as fundamentally a process through which the adept attains spiritual perfection.[22] According to Maria, the various metals in the alchemical work are symbols of aspects of humanity. Her famous maxim "Join the male and the female and you will find what is sought"[23] anticipates Jung's interpretation that alchemy provides the feminine background of the masculine psyche. Later we will see that this very "Jungian" view of the human psyche is deeply Kabbalistic.

Centuries later, Heinrich Khunrath (1560–1601), an alchemist who is cited in many of Jung's works, was influenced deeply by the Kabbalah in his view that the alchemical opus reflects a mystical transformation within the adept's soul.[24] Khunrath, whose highly influential compendium, *Amphiteatrum sapientiae* (1602), is illustrated with Kabbalistic symbols, including an elaborate depiction of the ten *Sefirot*, held that the alchemical "philosopher's stone" is equivalent to the spirit of God, *haRuach Elohim*, which hovered over the waters at the time of creation.[25] According to Patai, "Under the impact of the Kabbalah and its gematria the medieval alchemical tradition underwent a noticeable change, and became during the Renaissance a more mystically and religiously oriented discipline."[26]

We are only now becoming aware of the extensive influence of Jewish mystical sources on the history and direction of alchemy. Indeed, alchemy was already linked to the Kabbalah in the Middle Ages, and Jewish mystical ideas are evident in an alchemical manuscript dating from the eleventh century, *Solomon's Labyrinth*.[27] Patai marshals evidence that the alchemical works attributed to the theologian and missionary Raymund Lully (ca. 1234–1315), who is often quoted by Jung, were actually composed by a Marrano Jew, Raymond De Tarregga, probably several decades after Lully's death.[28] Tarregga, like other Jewish alchemists, maintained a special interest in the medical applications of his art, and applied alchemical principles to the cure of melancholy and possession, taking a rather psychological view of these afflictions. In his work on demonology, Tarregga held that demons come to possess men because they are attracted to their ill humour, melancholy, and their "horrible images in fantasy." According to Tarregga, by treating the possessed's melancholy with the alchemical *quinta essentia* (the fifth essence) and other medicines the patient will be freed from the demons because he no longer provides a psychological environment hospitable to them.[29] Interestingly, Tarregga was accused by the ecclesiastical authorities of holding the heretical belief that the sinner conforms to the will of God, on the grounds that "good and evil please God equally."[30]

By the close of the fifteenth century, a number of Christian scholars had written works in Latin that made the doctrines of the Kabbalah readily accessible to the Christian alchemists.[31] Among these scholars were Johann Reuchlin[32] ([1455]–1522), Pietro Galatinus (1460–1540), and Pico della Mirandola (1463–1522).[33] Cardinal Egidio da Viterbo (ca. 1465–1532) translated significant portions of the Zohar and other Kabbalistic works into Latin and even composed his own work on the *Sefirot*. While Jung had noted that Reuchlin and Mirandola had made the Kabbalah accessible in Latin translation, Phillip Beitchman[34] has documented the wide impact and prevalence of the Kabbalah on thought during the Renaissance and later and has collated numerous works in Latin and several European languages through which the alchemists and others not versed in Hebrew and Aramaic were able to absorb Kabbalistic ideas. The

Kabbalistic writings of the sixteenth-century monk Giordano Bruno were particularly noteworthy in this regard.[35]

Paracelsus (1493–1541), an alchemist whom Jung held in high regard, and to whom he devoted an entire work ("Paracelsus as a Spiritual Phenomenon"[36]), was of the opinion that expert knowledge of the Kabbalah was a prerequisite for the study of alchemy.[37] His teacher Solomon Trismosin (six of whose alchemical illustrations adorn Jung's *Psychology and Alchemy*[38]) claimed that he drew his teachings from Kabbalistic sources that had been translated into Arabic, which he acquired during his travels to the south and east.[39]

In the sixteenth century, Johann Reuchlin (*De Arte Cabbalistica*), and later Cornelius Agrippa, placed the Kabbalah at the center of theosophical and occult studies, respectively, and from Agrippa's equivalence of the Kabbalah with "experimental magic" many alchemists concluded that alchemy was itself a Kabbalistic discipline. According to Scholem, this blending of alchemy and Kabbalah reached an apex in the work of Heinrich Khunrath of Leipzig, who under the influence of Johann Nidanus Pistorius's *Artis Cabalisticae* (Basel, 1587) brought together Kabbalistic notions of divine creation and the alchemical *opus*.

By the end of the sixteenth century, European alchemists were, in effect, claiming an identity between Kabbalah and alchemy. This was a view advocated by Khunrath and his contemporary Pierre Arnaud de la Chevallerie, who held that advanced knowledge of traditional Kabbalah was necessary for an understanding of alchemy. Similar ideas were echoed by Paracelsus's disciple Franz Kieser, and later by the Welsh philosopher and alchemist Thomas Vaughan (1621–66), who held that the *summa arcani* (the highest secrets) were only open to those who are versed in magic and Kabbalah.[40]

Beginning around 1614, the Rosicrucians, in particular Johann Valentin Andreae (1586–1654), took up the mystical conception of alchemy, and the English theosophist Robert Fludd (1574–1637) popularized the equivalence of Kabbalistic and alchemical symbols, arguing that the alchemical production of gold was a material symbol for the transformation of humankind. Scholem points out that, under the influence of Reuchlin, Fludd adopted the thirteenth-century Kabbalistic notion (articulated by the Spanish Kabbalist Jacob ha-Cohen) that there are two forms of the Hebrew letter *alef*: the first, a material dark form, and the second, represented by white spaces (between the letters of the Torah), a light, "mystical" form. Fludd adopted this Kabbalistic imagery in his account of the transmutation of the dark *prima materia* into the bright philosopher's stone of wisdom. Authors like Fludd and Vaughan later found in Knorr von Rosenroth's *Kabbalah Denudata* a strong confirmation of their belief in the equivalence of Kabbalah and alchemy.[41] Scholem references two German theosophists, Georg von Welling (1652–1727) and Friedrich

Christoph Oetinger (1702–82), who attempted a union of Kabbalistic theosophy and alchemy. Welling makes clear that he is not interested in "physical alchemy," but rather the teaching of how God and nature can be recognized in one another. Welling popularized the symbol of the Shield of David as an alchemical representation of perfection. While Scholem credits Welling with having made use of some authentic Jewish Kabbalistic ideas, such as divine action through the vehicle of the *Sefirot*,[42] Welling actually rejected Jewish Kabbalah in favor of a Christian Kabbalistic discipline, and Scholem holds that on the whole Welling's Kabbalah "relates to the Jewish tradition in name only."

Scholem is more generous to Oetinger, who he sees as having made an "authentic connection" between Jewish Kabbalah and Christian alchemical-mystical symbolism. Oetinger was influenced by the German mystic and philosopher Jacob Boehme (1575–1624), who developed Kabbalistic symbolism in his theosophical writings, and whose work was introduced to Oetinger by Koppel Hecht (d. 1729), a Frankfurt Kabbalist.

For the alchemists, the Kabbalistic doctrine of the *Sefirot* provided a theosophical justification for their belief in the infinite malleability and underlying unity of all things. In the Kabbalah, the *Sefirot*, the ten divine traits, which serve as the archetypes for creation, are in constant flux, breaking apart, being emended and restored, all for the purpose of reestablishing divine unity. In the Kabbalistic doctrines of the *Sefirot* and gematria (the view that words and thus things are transformable and equivalent by virtue of the arithmetical properties of their letters) the alchemists saw a vehicle for explaining and rationalizing such transformations.[43]

The notion that Hebrew letters and words concealed within themselves an indefinite variety of secrets, meanings, and associations intrigued the alchemists, who saw in this aspect of the Kabbalah an underlying rationale for their own worldview. As a result, the Christian alchemists became intrigued with the Hebrew alphabet and, according to Patai, "from about the fifteenth century on, there was scarcely an alchemical book or treatise written by Christian alchemists that did not display conspicuously some Hebrew power-words on the title page or inside the text."[44] Patai points to Heinrich Khunrath as a striking example of this tendency. Khunrath, in his *Amphitheatrum sapientiae*, one of the most widely read alchemical compendiums, not only equates the alchemical philosopher's stone with the *Ruach Elohim* but illustrates his volume with an impressive "world of the spheres" that encompasses not only the ten *Sefirot* and twenty-two Hebrew letters (which according to the Kabbalists are the primary elements of creation) but also a wide variety of other Hebrew inscriptions of Jewish religious significance.[45]

We thus find that a "Kabbalistic alchemy" developed not mainly among Jewish alchemists but among their non-Jewish counterparts.[46] The Christian alchemist-Kabbalists endeavored to learn Hebrew, and they sought out Jewish spiritual mentors from whom they could learn the mysteries of Kabbalah and gematria as a means of attaining the highest alchemical art and knowledge.[47]

The Kabbalah provided the alchemists with a spiritual and metaphysical foundation for their view that there was just one basic substance in the universe, the so-called *prima materia*, which took on a multitude of manifestations and forms. The alchemists were intrigued by such Kabbalistic doctrines as the notion that *Ein-sof* inheres and sustains all things and that all the multifarious objects in the universe are comprised of the ten *Sefirot*, which are themselves comprised of one another. By joining itself to the Kabbalah, alchemy not only developed a rationale for its material enterprise but also developed itself as a spiritual discipline.

A review of Jung's works on alchemy reveals that many of the alchemists he discusses were Jews, Christians posing as Jews in order to give their works "authenticity," or Christians who openly acknowledged their debt to Kabbalistic sources. For example, Gerhard Dorn, whom Jung cites dozens of times throughout his later works, wrote an alchemical commentary on the opening verses of the Book of Genesis,[48] spoke of Adam as the "invisibilus homo maximus"[49]—an allusion to the Kabbalistic doctrine of *Adam Kadmon*—and held that the legendary patriarch of alchemy, Hermes Trismegistus, though Egyptian, was taught by the "Genesis of the Hebrews."[50]

Like many of the alchemists, Jung was aware of the correspondence between the alchemists' *chymical marriage*—of sun and moon, gold and silver, spirit and body, king and queen—and the conjugal unifications of the various *Sefirot* and *Partzufim* that are central themes in the Kabbalah. Jung himself had Kabbalistic visions[51] that illustrated these themes, and which he interpreted as exemplifying the coincidence of opposites, e.g., *animus* and *anima,* and held to be requisite for the unification and individuation of the self. Whether or not the alchemists actually derived their "wedding symbolism" from the Kabbalists, it is clear that, in its encounter with the Kabbalah, alchemy attained a new spiritual interpretation of these symbols. Alchemical metaphors with only latent spiritual and psychological overtones became rooted in an established spiritual/psychological discipline once alchemy had incorporated the Kabbalah. According to Patai:

> the Kabbalah supplied the alchemists with a quasi sanctification of their views by opening up to them the doctrine of the cosmological structure of the sefirot, which taught them that not only the hidden essence of *materia* but even the divine unity itself was expressed in multiple mystical manifestations.[52]

Patai points out that among Jewish alchemists alchemy occupied a middle position between philosophy and medicine,[53] and the Jewish search for the philosopher's stone was often more closely associated with healing the sick than in obtaining earthly wealth.[54] In this sense, the Jewish alchemists approximated Jung's therapeutic use of alchemical symbols and ideas.

The Jewish Alchemists: Abraham Eleazar and *Esh M'saref* (The Refiner's Fire)

Patai describes the work of the Jewish alchemist Abraham Eleazar, whose *Uraltes Chymisches Werck* (Age-Old Chymical Work) is referred to several times by Jung in *Mysterium Coniunctionis*,[55] and which Jung regarded as the work of a Christian posing as a Jew.[56] However, according to Patai, Eleazar's is the most "Jewish" alchemical treatise in existence.[57] The author is unknown except for this work, which was first printed in 1735. According to Patai, the content of the work likely goes back to an earlier Jewish thirteenth-century alchemist. Patai describes *Uraltes Chymisches Werck* as "mysticism clothed in alchemical garb."[58] It is a work that essentially concerns itself with the healing and consolation of the Jewish people, and a fervent religious, nationalistic, and "Zionistic" spirit pervades the work. Eleazar focuses at length on the "supernal serpent," which signifies the *mundi universalem*, the universal world spirit, and which he describes as "the most lovely and also the most terrible, who makes everything live, and who also kills everything, and takes on all shapes of nature." Eleazar continues: "In sum: he is everything, and also nothing."[59] This last description, which is remarkably similar to both Gnostic descriptions of the Pleroma and Kabbalistic descriptions of the infinite Godhead, *Ein-sof*, is an exceptional example of the *coincidentia oppositorum*, which, according to Jung, is the essential characteristic of the human psyche. It is also an example of how Kabbalistic/mystical ideas came to permeate alchemical treatises.

Jung drew extensively from Eleazar's writings; twice in *Mysterium Coniunctionis*, quoting a lengthy passage from the *Uraltes Chymisches* that makes reference to the Kabbalistic doctrines of the sparks[60] and *Adam Kadmon*.[61] Jung interprets Eleazar's account of the Talmudic story in which God prevents the mating of the Leviathan serpents (lest their union destroy the world) as symbolic of a premature, unconscious, and hence dangerous integration of the masculine and feminine aspects of the self,[62] and he refers to Eleazar's description of the "King and Queen perishing in the same bath" as an example of spirit and soul (*anima*) dissolving in the unity of the self.[63]

Cornelius Agrippa (1486–1535) discussed the relationship between alchemy, astrology, and the Kabbalah in a work entitled *De Occulta Philosophia* (printed in 1533 but written ca. 1510). In this work, Agrippa drew a connection first between the planets and the Kabbalistic *Sefirot*, and then between the planets and the alchemists' metals.[64] Shortly thereafter there appeared a work by an unknown Jewish alchemist that provided a direct one-to-one correspondence between the metals and the *Sefirot*. This work, entitled *Esh M'saref* (The

Refiner's Fire), is known to us only through a Latin translation of major sections that Knorr von Rosenroth included in the first volume of his *Kabbalah Denudata* (*The Kabbalah Unveiled*, 1677–84), a book with which, as we have seen, Jung was quite familiar.[65]

Like other Jewish alchemists, the author of *Esh M'saref* viewed alchemy on the analogy of medicine, as a process of healing degenerate or impure metallic substances. Further, the author held that the secrets of alchemy "do not differ from the supernal mysteries of the Kabbalah."[66] The various metals, because they are essentially impure, correspond to the heavenly *Sefirot* as they are manifest in the lowest and hence most degenerate world of the Kabbalah, that of *Assiyah*, the world of "Action." For example, *Keter*, the highest *Sefirah*, is regarded as the "Metallic Root," the origin of all other metals; lead is equivalent to the *Sefirah Chochmah* (Wisdom); tin to *Binah* (Intelligence); silver to *Chesed* (Kindness); gold to *Gevurah* (Strength); iron to *Tiferet* (Beauty); and quicksilver, which is said to be equivalent to the ninth *Sefirah, Yesod* (Foundation). The final *Sefirah, Malchut* (Kingdom) is "the true medicine of metals...(and) it represents the rest of the natures under the metamorphosis of both gold and silver, right and left, judgment and mercy."[67] The transformation of metals is conceived in this work on the analogy of the Kabbalistic elevation of the *Sefirot*, and as such *Esh M'saref* provides a theoretical blending of Kabbalistic and alchemical theory.[68]

By the time Knorr von Rosenroth published selections from *Esh M'saref* in his Latin compendium of Kabbalistic texts in Sulzberg in 1677, alchemy had taken a pronounced mystical turn. For many alchemists of the seventeenth century and later, alchemy had actually become synonymous with the Kabbalah.[69] Gershom Scholem, who, as we will see, was rather skeptical regarding the connections between an *authentic Jewish* Kabbalah and alchemy, acknowledged that "for more than four hundred years, the terms alchemy and Kabbalah have been synonymous among the Christian theosophists and alchemists of Europe."[70] While Scholem criticizes Eliphas Levi's view that "alchemy is but a 'daughter of the Qabalah,'" Scholem holds that with alchemy "we are without doubt dealing essentially with a mystical movement whose scientific tendencies are byproducts of their symbolism and symbolic practices," and that "it is precisely in these circles that the identification of the Kabbalah with alchemy has asserted itself, most emphatically."[71]

Many alchemists adopted the Kabbalistic theories of the *Sefirot*, gematria (numerology), and letter combinations, and inscribed Hebrew characters in their vessels in the belief that such letters would facilitate the combining of metals.[72] In certain alchemical writings, the transformative alchemist's stone (the *lapis*) is represented by a *Magen David* enclosed in a circle. For the alchemists, the two triangles comprising the *Magen David* represented the primal elements of fire and water (in Hebrew, *Esh* and *Mayim*), which when combined form the Hebrew word for heaven (*SheMayim*), and the circle

alluded to *Ein-sof* (the Infinite God).[73] The alchemists believed that by combining fire and water they could extract "Mercurius" and thereby obtain the
mysterious spiritual substance that they believed to be equivalent to the
prima materia, Adam, and Christ, and which, for Jung, is the *principium
individuationis* of the self.[74]

Alchemical References in Kabbalistic Texts

Although the main direction of influence was from the Kabbalah to
alchemy, certain Kabbalists took a lively interest in and were influenced by
alchemy, and the Zohar and other Kabbalistic writings occasionally make
reference to alchemical ideas in order to illustrate mystical, religious
themes.[75] For example, in the Zohar (2:23b-24a) we read:

> The first four elements have a deep significance for the faithful: they
> are the progenitors of all the worlds, and symbolize the mystery of the
> Supernal Chariot of Holiness. Also [from] the four elements of fire,
> air, earth and water...come gold, silver, copper, and iron, and beneath
> these other metals of a like kind....North brings forth gold, which is
> produced by the side of fire-power....When water is united with earth,
> the cold and moist brings forth silver.[76]

In reference to another Zoharic passage on the mystical significance of
gold, Scholem writes that "not even Christian and Gnostic mystics and
alchemists could have described the 'gold' within the human soul more
clearly than this characteristic piece of kabbalistic theosophy." According
to the Zohar:

> And such is [this gold] that, when it appears in the worlds, whoever
> obtains it hides it inside himself, and from there [i.e., from this mys-
> tical gold] all other types of gold emanate. And when is gold [rightly]
> called gold? When it shines and ascends to the glory [of the mys-
> tical region] of the "fear of God," and then it is in [the state of]
> the "mystical bliss."[77]

The presence of alchemical terminology in works of the Kabbalah, and
the specific prescriptions for making gold in works of "practical Kabbalah" gave both Jewish and Christian alchemists a certain Jewish mystical
warrant for alchemical beliefs and practices.

Scholem points out that, in the fourteenth century, the Toledo rabbi
Judah ben Asher drew parallels between the alchemical refining of metals
and the Kabbalistic understanding of Gilgul, which involves the transmigration and purification of souls.[78] Late in the fifteenth century, even
before the Christian humanists and alchemists identified Kabbalah as the

spiritual source of alchemy, Joseph Taitazak, who Scholem identifies as both a Kabbalist and humanist, identified alchemy with Kabbalistic theology. Scholem quotes from a handwritten manuscript in the British Museum:

> And this is the science of alchemy, which is the science of the God-head, as you will understand when you reach it [in these revelations]. And who does not know the science of the upper world [Kabbalah] beforehand, cannot practice it [alchemy].[79]

According to Taitazak the secret of Jacob's ladder in the Bible is the secret of the "science of the Godhead," which is also "the secret of the upper [mystical] gold and silver."

The Kabbalists' efforts to create a *Golem* (an artificial man)[80] can be understood as a parallel to the alchemists' efforts to derive Mercurius, and in so doing to create a Primordial Adam. Interestingly, Paracelsus was himself concerned with the alchemical creation of a homunculus, which certain scholars equate with the Kabbalists' Golem[81] (Idel, however, holds that the two notions are not historically or integrally connected[82]). The creation of an artificial man, perhaps even more so than the alchemists' efforts to create gold, can be understood, in Jungian terms, as an attempt to forge a self, and is therefore deserving of close attention by Jungian psychologists. The fact that the Kabbalists conceived of the Golem as being created through the permutations and combinations of Hebrew letters reinforces the parallels between the Golem and the self. This is because the self, too, is on many levels a construction of language. Idel, in his work on the Golem, may go too far when he says "it was the linguistic alchemy which interested the Jews, not the metallurgic or organic ones,"[83] but it is no exaggeration to hold that the letter combinations of the Kabbalah, no less than the chemical operations of alchemy, mirror important psychological dynamics.

Idel's view that Jews were not interested in "metallurgic" alchemy is belied by the fact that Chayyim Vital (1542–1620), the foremost disciple of the Kabbalist Isaac Luria and the man to whom much of our knowledge of Luria's Kabbalistic system is due, was steeped in the study of alchemy and wrote a manuscript with practical recipes involving the creation and improvement of gold.[84] Vital was dissuaded from engaging in alchemy during the two years he had contact with Luria, but returned to it after Luria's death.[85] Scholem points out that Vital confessed that he "neglected the study of the Torah for two-and-a-half years while being occupied with the science of alchemy." However, even after his involvement with Isaac Luria he continued to use alchemical imagery, for example, drawing an equivalence between the metals silver, gold, copper, tin, lead, mercury, and iron and the seven lower *Sefirot*, from Chesed to Malchut, as well as to the seven planets of astrology.[86]

Vital's interest in alchemy, however, was largely technical, and he wrote about alchemy without generally making reference to his mystical writings and ideas. It would seem that Vital managed to remain unconscious of or ignore the parallels between the earthly combinations and transformations of alchemy and the cosmic unifications and transformations among the *Sefirot* and worlds he was describing in his Kabbalistic texts. It is as if in his alchemical work Vital had an opportunity to unconsciously act out the very transformative forms of thought that occupied him in his study of the Kabbalah.

In 1570 Simeon Labi of Tripoli drew parallels between Kabbalah and alchemy when he wrote at length about the equivalence of gold and silver, explaining this with the dictum that "nothing from the natural sciences was concealed from the sages of the Zohar. Because they also knew that nothing exists in the natural world without having roots in the upper [world]."[87] During the first half of the seventeenth century, the physician and Kabbalist Joseph Solomon Delmedigo wrote a treatise on the philosopher's stone, a small portion of which remains in manuscript form in the library of the Jewish Theological Seminary.[88] Finally, as late as 1924 Scholem himself made the acquaintance of an old Kabbalist/alchemist in Jerusalem who reported that years before he had been the "court alchemist of the Sharif of Morocco."[89]

Scholem on Kabbalah and Alchemy

While Kabbalistic texts occasionally incorporated alchemical ideas, and certain Kabbalists engaged directly in alchemy, the main direction of influence was from the Kabbalah to alchemy, and this influence helped propel alchemy from being a protoscience to a spiritual (and psychological) discipline.[90] The intimate relationship between Kabbalah and alchemy has only slowly been acknowledged by the scholarly community. As Raphael Patai has pointed out, until recently the study of this relationship was received with the same skepticism with which the study of Kabbalah in general had been received during the nineteenth century.[91] Even Gershom Scholem, who almost single-handedly overcame the neglect and disrepute of the Kabbalah in academic circles, was quite skeptical regarding the possibility of a significant relationship between Kabbalah and alchemy, a skepticism that rested in part upon his claim that in the main those alchemists who identified alchemy with the Kabbalah were ill informed, and provided confusing accounts of Kabbalistic symbols. One example of this cited by Scholem is the confusion between gold and silver, the hierarchy of which is reversed in the Kabbalah—this reversal was unrecognized by many of the "Kabbalistic alchemists."[92] To take another example: in discussing von Welling's amalgam of Kabbalah and alchemy, Scholem points out the centrality of a myth about the "revolt of Lucifer" that, although it derives from the Jewish apocalyptic *Book of Enoch*, is "foreign to kabbalist tradition."[93]

I believe that Scholem was in danger of losing the forest for the trees. What the Kabbalah provided the alchemists was not so much a set of specific doctrines or symbols, but rather a general warrant for reconceptualizing their efforts to manipulate the natural world as a spiritual/ psychological practice, the goal of which is the redemption of both the individual practitioner and, ultimately, the entirety of humankind. As I have argued elsewhere, in spite of Scholem's central position in bringing the Kabbalah into step with intellectual life in the twentieth century, his own philosophical and theological understanding of Kabbalistic symbols was at times quite narrow. For example, Scholem held that the symbols of the Kabbalah were largely incomprehensible in rational/philosophical terms,[94] and he argued that mystical symbols in general have no cognitive or even semantic content.[95] Scholem's lack of vision is illustrated in his account of the Kabbalistic symbol of *Shevirat ha-Kelim*, the Breaking of the Vessels. Scholem writes that as a consequence of the *Shevirah*:

> Nothing remains in its proper place. Everything is somewhere else. But a being that is not in its proper place is in exile. Thus, since that primordial act, all being has been in exile, in need of being led back and redeemed.[96]

Scholem holds that "before the judgment seat of rationalist theology such an idea may not have much to say for itself,"[97] and he proceeds to provide a historical explanation of this symbol in terms of the Jewish response to the expulsion from Spain. While Scholem suggests another possibility when he writes that "the mighty symbols" of Jewish life can be taken as "an extreme case of human life pure and simple," he ultimately holds that "we can no longer fully perceive, I might say, 'live,' the symbols of the Kabbalah without a considerable effort if at all."[98] What Scholem failed to recognize was that it is precisely the implications of the *Shevirah* doctrine as *alienation and exile* that make it so relevant and comprehensible to twentieth- (and twenty-first)-century philosophy. The Kabbalists' understanding of the *Shevirah* as an alienation of God from himself and of humanity from God, and their view that all of reality is somehow broken, flawed, and incomplete, enables this symbol to encompass the contemporary experience of the exile of human beings from one another (existentialism), of the individual from himself (Freud), and of humanity from the products of its creative labor (Marx), as well as to gather under a single heading the apparently unbridgeable chasms between nature and spirit, freedom and necessity, appearance and reality, good and evil, universal and particular, theology and science—each of which might be said to be illustrative of the basic "fault" in the cosmos.[99] It also provides a powerful symbolic expression of the insight, deeply embedded both in the

Kabbalah and alchemy (and later adopted by Jung), that a return to chaos and disorder is a prerequisite for spiritual and psychological renewal.

The alchemists, in their efforts to bridge the gap between spirit and nature, and to reintegrate and redeem the world by converting (and thereby spiritually transforming) base metals into gold, turned to *and adapted* the Kabbalah as a spiritual foundation for their discipline. More specifically, as will be recounted in more detail in later chapters, various alchemists availed themselves of the Kabbalistic symbol of *Adam Kadmon* (the Primordial Human) as a spiritual equivalent of Mercurius and the philosopher's stone; utilized the Kabbalistic image of the divine "sparks" scattered throughout the world and humanity as symbolic for the search for wisdom, and made reference to the Kabbalists' union of male and female *Sefirot* as a symbol of *coincidentia oppositorum*, the union of all opposites and contradictions. In addition, for the alchemists, Kabbalah provided a foundation for the view that the *chymical opus* is a vehicle for transforming the adept's soul, and the Kabbalists' doctrine of the *Sefirot* provided a rationale for the alchemists' views regarding the malleability, transformability, and ultimate identity of all things. The Kabbalistic doctrine of *Otiyot Yesod* (letter combinations) supported their view that language could transform both material and spiritual worlds. Finally, the Lurianic notions of *Shevirah* (rupture) and *Tikkun* (repair) provided a spiritual analog to the alchemical notion of *solve et coagula*, the idea that things must first fall apart before they can be reintegrated on a higher level, a notion that, as will see, became of interest to Jung later in his career. In sum, the alchemists absorbed from the Kabbalah the notion that the natural world was infused with divine energy that could be harnessed in the service of individual and world redemption, and which could be transformed in a manner that would overcome man's alienation from both his true self and God. It was these ideas that Jung found in alchemy, and which he sought to reconstitute in his archetypal psychology.

Jung's interest in alchemy was, of course, in its mystical and psychological aspects, and he thus focused upon those of its elements that were most compatible and assimilable to Kabbalistic ideas: the alchemical unification of opposites, the divine wedding, Primordial Human (*Adam Kadmon*), the *scintillae* (or sparks), and *solve et coagula* (fragmentation and restoration). All of these ideas appear in the alchemical texts Jung studied, and all were either rooted in or assimilated to Kabbalistic equivalents. Jung, as we have noted, also had access to, and read, various Kabbalah texts: Knorr von Rosenroth's Latin compendium, French and German translations of the Zohar, and even Scholem's earlier writings, and he undoubtedly read the Kabbalistic passages in alchemical writings through the lens of these works. As we examine Jung's treatment of these (and other) themes, we will see how close indeed he was to developing a Kabbalistic view of the cosmos and man.

Chapter 3

The Wedding and Eros Symbolism

Jung's 1944 Kabbalistic visions involved the divine wedding between *Tiferet* and *Malchut* (which, in the Kabbalah, are the masculine and feminine divine principles), and the wedding of Rabbi Simon ben Yochai (traditionally held to be the author of the Zohar) in the afterlife. Jung tells us that "at bottom" he himself was the marriage, his beatitude being that of a "blissful wedding." Jung's initial vision is followed by "the Marriage of the Lamb" in Jerusalem, with angels and light. Again, Jung tells us, "I myself was the 'Marriage of the Lamb.'" In a final image, Jung finds himself in a classical amphitheater situated in a landscape of a verdant chain of hills. "Men and woman dancers came on-stage, and upon a flower-decked couch All-father Zeus consummated the mystic marriage, as it is described in the Iliad."[1] The central theme of all three visions— Jewish, Christian, and Greek—is a "sacred wedding" of divine principles and, at least in the first two, the union is consummated within a single soul, Jung himself.

The Wedding Symbolism of the Kabbalah

Subsequent to his visions, in the works of his later years, Jung turned to alchemical and, to a lesser but still significant extent, Kabbalistic symbols of the "wedding" or sexual intercourse to express the union of opposites that is necessary for the realization of both God and man. Before turning to Jung's use of such Kabbalistic symbols, it will be worth our while to briefly explore the Kabbalistic notion of divine *coniunctio*.

The Kabbalists made prolific use of wedding symbolism to express both the original unification in the Godhead, which was rent apart by human sin, and also the reunification that can be brought about through humanity's adherence to the divine commandments. Such unifications are expressed in the Zohar and later writings as the union of the *Sefirot Chochmah* (Wisdom) and *Binah* (Understanding), which are personified as the *partzufim Abba* (father) and *Imma* (mother). The cosmic unification of male and female principles is also expressed in the image of the incestuous passion between the *Sefirot Tiferet* (beauty) and *Malchut* (royalty), which

DOI: 10.4324/9781003027041-4

are personified as the *partzufim Zeir Anpin* (the short-faced one) and *Nukvah* (the daughter). This latter relationship is frequently expressed as the "unification of the Holy One Blessed Be He and His feminine presence (or consort, the *shekhinah*)," such union being conceptualized as the vehicle through which the fault and disorder in the cosmos will be set aright. Other cosmic sexual unions are expressed in the Kabbalah as the sexual influx from the *sefirah Yesod* (identified with the phallus) into *Malchut*, often identified with the *Shekhinah* (the divine feminine), earth, and the created world.

The separation of the male from the female is, according to the Zohar, a source of evil and imperfection:

> Now when Adam sinned by eating of the forbidden tree, he caused that tree to become a source of death to all the world. He also caused imperfection by separating the Wife from her Husband. The imperfection was exhibited in the moon, until the time when Israel stood before Mount Sinai, when the moon was freed from its defect, and it was in a position to shine continually. When Israel sinned by making the calf, the moon reverted to its former imperfection.[2]

Both the world and humanity, according to the Kabbalists, can be made whole only through a harmonious integration of the masculine and feminine. According to the thirteenth-century Spanish Kabbalist Joseph Gikatila, "When a male is created, his feminine partner is necessarily created at the same time, because from above half a form (*hatzi tsurah*) is never made but only an entire form (*tzurah shlemah*) is made."[3] Man without woman, according to the Zohar, is defective, a mere "half body."[4] As Arturo Schwartz points out, similar ideas were (later) also expressed by the alchemists. For example, Gerhard Dorn wrote that "Adam bears an invisible Eve hidden in his body,"[5] and according to the early seventeenth century alchemist Dominicus Gnosius, "our Adamic hermaphrodite, though he appears in masculine form, nevertheless always carries about with him Eve or his feminine part hidden in his body."[6] Whether a result of influence or convergent thinking, the Kabbalists and alchemists were in remarkable accord regarding the androgynous nature of the primordial human. According to Schwartz, the implication of this androgyny is that "everything can be itself and something else at the same time [as they] contain their opposites without their identity being altered in any way."[7]

Among the Kabbalists, at times the female that completes "man" was understood as an actual woman, but at other times it is conceived of, as Jung later conceived the *anima* archetype, as a female "image" that arises within a man's soul and is viewed as his spiritual counterpart or completion. The Zohar speaks of such a counterpart accompanying a man and making him "male and female," when, for example, he is on a journey away from his wife and home.[8] The Chasidic rebbe Elimelekh of Lizhensk expands upon and psychologizes this theme when he writes:

> A man has two wives. One is the woman whom God commanded him to marry to *be fruitful and multiply* (Gen 1:28). The second is his holy soul—the intellective soul—which God placed in man....Because of her, man can attain the level of unending greatness.[9]

Early on, Jung held that both man and woman were completed by the opposite-gendered aspect of their own psyches:

> Do you know how much femininity man lacks for completeness? Do you know how much masculinity woman lacks for completeness?... You, man, should not seek the feminine in women, but seek and recognize it in yourself, as you possess it from the beginning.[10]

Jung's Use of the Kabbalah's *Coniunctio* Symbols

Jung was aware of the *coniunctio* symbolism in the Kabbalah, but initially discounted it, preferring to trace the history of the divine creative wedding to Christian and pagan sources. In "Psychology of the Transference" (1946) Jung writes:

> The *coniunctio* is an *a priori* image that occupies a prominent place in the history of man's mental development. If we trace this idea back we find it has two sources in alchemy, one Christian, the other pagan. The Christian source is unmistakably the doctrine of Christ and the Church, *sponsus* and *sponsa*, where Christ takes the role of Sol and the Church that of Luna. The pagan source is on the one hand the hierosgamos, on the other hand the marital union of the mystic with God.[11]

No mention is made of the profound impact of the Kabbalah, in particular its doctrines of the divine wedding and the dialectical coincidence of opposites, on alchemy. This is interesting in light of the fact that in Jung's visions, which he experienced after his near fatal heart attack in 1944, the Kabbalah *coniunctio* material is given priority, as Jung envisioned himself as the divine wedding between *Tiferet* and *Malchut*.[12] One might well ask whether his Kabbalistic vision served as a feeling-toned compensation for his own intellectual blind spot regarding the role of the Jewish material in the development of the *coniunctio* symbolism in alchemy.[13]

Later, Jung openly acknowledged the sexual and gender symbolism in the Kabbalah,[14] and he occasionally cited examples in which the Zoharic symbols were quoted or adapted by the alchemists Knorr von Rosenroth[15] and Vigenerus.[16] By the time he completed *Mysterium Coniunctionis*, Jung recognized the significance of the Kabbalah wedding symbolism, both in its own right and in relation to alchemy. In that work he discusses at length a text by the Jewish alchemist Abraham Eleazar in which such symbols are elucidated,[17] and refers to the *coniunctio* symbolism in the Mueller (German) translation of the Zohar,[18] in Knorr von Rosenroth's *Kabbalah Denudata*,[19] and even in the writings of Gershom Scholem.[20] In discussing the *sefirah Malchut*, which as the widow *Shekhinah* was abandoned by the *sefirah Tiferet*, Jung writes:

> In this wicked world ruled by evil Tifereth is not united with Malchuth. But the coming Messiah will reunite the King with the Queen, and this mating will restore to God his original unity.[21]

Jung continues with further commentary and quotation from a German translation of the Zohar:

> The Cabala develops an elaborate hierosgamos fantasy which expatiates on the union of the soul with the Sefiroth of the worlds of light and darkness, "for the desire of the upper world for the God-fearing man is as the loving desire of a man for his wife while he woos her."[22]

Jung recognizes the impact of the Kabbalistic wedding symbols on the alchemists. He cites Knorr: "The Cabala also speaks of the thalamus (bride chamber) or nuptial canopy beneath which *sponsus* and *sponsa* are consecrated, *Yesod* acting as paranymphus (best man)." It is here that Jung makes a comment, which I have already cited in the previous chapter, and which suggests that the alchemists' use of the *coniunctio* image was at least in part derived from the Kabbalah: "Directly or indirectly the Cabala was assimilated into alchemy. Relationships must have existed between them at a very early date, though it is difficult to trace them in the sources."[23]

The Zohar does not limit its erotic interest to marriage. For the Zohar and later Kabbalists, those sexual acts, such as incest, which are forbidden to man on earth, are permitted, even necessary on the divine level in order to restore the cosmic order. In *Tikkunei ha-Zohar* we learn, for example, that among the *Sefirot* incest is not forbidden:

> In the world above there is no "nakedness," division, separation or disunion. Therefore in the world above there is union of brother and sister, son and daughter.[24]

The same idea makes its appearance in alchemy. Jung notes that in contrast to Christianity, which allegorized or demonized sexuality, the alchemists exalted the most heinous transgression of the law, namely incest, into a symbol of the union of opposites, hoping in this way to bring back the golden age.[25]

According to Jung, incest has always been the prerogative of gods and kings, and is an important archetype that for modern man has been forced out of consciousness into criminology and psychopathology. For Jung, the alchemical union of King and Queen, and Sun and Moon, are archetypal symbols that express the incestuous union of opposites.

The Zoharic notion that man must be completed by his feminine half is also, as Jung understood, echoed in alchemy. As we have seen, Jung held that it is the "moral task of alchemy" to harmonize the rational spirit of the masculine psyche with the seething passions of its feminine background.[26] This, Jung intimates, is another, perhaps deeper, psychological meaning of the alchemical symbols uniting King and Queen, Adam and Eve, and brother and sister; a meaning that is clearly present in the Zohar's description of a man's "intellective soul" as his inner feminine counterpart, which enables him to attain "unending greatness."[27]

Wedding symbolism is also prominent in the Kabbalah of Isaac Luria. For example, disruption and reunification of male and female plays a decisive role in the Lurianic symbols of the "Breaking of the Vessels" and *Tikkun*, the restoration of the world. If these Lurianic symbols did not impact upon Jung's own thought, they clearly call out for explication within a Jungian framework. The "vessels," as described by Luria's most important disciple, Chayyim Vital, are located in, and constitute, the womb of the Celestial Mother. As a result of the Breaking of the Vessels, the Celestial Mother and Father (i.e., the *partzufim Abba* and *Imma*), who had hitherto been in a "face to face" sexual conjunction, turn their backs upon one another and become completely disjoined.[28] The "chaos" brought about by the Breaking of the Vessels is one of sexual and erotic alienation, a condition that can only be remedied through a rejoining of opposites via a renewed *coniunctio* of the sexes. At the same time, like the water that breaks signaling the birth of a new human life, the Breaking of the Vessels heralds a new birth, that of a new personal and world order to be completed by man via the process of *Tikkun* (restoration). Vital's description of this process illustrates the Jungian notion that the sexual can itself be symbolic of spiritual ideas.[29]

In this context we should note that Jung presents an interesting and important discursus on the ultimate significance of the sexual symbolism in the Kabbalah (and, by extension, alchemy). In discussing the sexual symbolism of the *sefirah Yesod* in the Zohar, Jung writes:

Insofar as the Freudian School translates psychic contents into sexual terminology there is nothing left for it to do here, since the author of the Zohar has done it already. This school (Freud's) merely shows us all the things that a penis can be, but it never discovered what the phallus can symbolize. It was assumed that in such a case the censor had failed to do its work. As Scholem himself shows and emphasizes particularly, the sexuality of the Zohar, despite its crudity, should be understood as a symbol of the "foundation of the world."[30]

Jung's (and Scholem's) position raises the question of the full significance of sexual imagery and symbols. Does this view mean that sexuality is simply a vessel or allegory for cosmic creative events, or does it suggest what the Zohar and the later Kabbalah itself implies, that the universe and humanity are somehow erotic in their own essences?

Gender Transformation and Gender Bias in the Kabbalistic Symbols

Recently, Elliot Wolfson has explored the use of erotic and gender symbolism in the Kabbalah and has commented in detail on several themes that are of relevance to Jungian thought. According to Wolfson, while the use of sexual symbolism is natural in mysticism to portray the ecstatic union between man and God,[31] Jewish mysticism is unique in the explicit use of erotic and gender-related language in its characterization of the divine itself.[32] For the Kabbalists, the esoteric is essentially tied to the erotic, and even divine thought is characterized in erotic terms. As Idel points out, in contrast to Greek, Gnostic, and Christian religion, the Jewish tradition occasionally sexualized reality, and this sexualization was emphasized in the Kabbalah.[33]

Wolfson points out that, in the view of certain Kabbalists, both God's self-creation and the creation of the world originate in *autoerotic* play, and that hence in the Kabbalah "the basic act of God is portrayed as precisely that activity that in the human sphere is viewed as the cardinal sin for which the unfolding of history is the gradual rectification."[34] Whereas Jung had pointed out that for the alchemists, the sin of incest is a divine prerogative that becomes a symbol of the union of opposites,[35] Wolfson argues that another sexual transgression, *onanism*, symbolizes a complex dialectic between creation, sin, and redemption.

Wolfson further shows that the theosophical Kabbalah utilizes the trope of *gender transformation* as a fundamental metaphor for the divine. Both the creation and redemption of the world involve a dynamic in which female is transformed into male and male is transformed into female. Wolfson holds that for the phallocentric Kabbalists the original divine essence is an androgynous male, a "singular male form that comprises both masculine and feminine."[36] However, while Wolfson argues that redemption, for the Kabbalists, "consists of the restoration of the female to the male...rather than a unification of two autonomous entities," this is not always fully borne out in the texts.[37] The Zohar, for example, states:

> All the souls in the world, which are the fruit of the handiwork of the Almighty, are mystically one, but when they descend to this world they are separated into male and female, though these are still conjoined. When they first issue forth, they issue as male and female together. Subsequently, when they descend (to this world) they separate, one to one side and the other to the other, and God afterwards mates them—God and no other, He alone knowing the mate proper to each.[38]

The Zohar does exhibit a certain gender bias when it continues:

> Happy is the man who is upright in his works and walks in the way of truth, so that his soul may find its original mate, for then he becomes indeed perfect, and through his perfection the whole world is blessed.

However:

> The desire of the female produces a vital spirit and is embraced in the vehemence of the male, so that soul is joined with soul and that they are made one, each embraced in the other.[39]

The Zohar further specifies that all souls are "mystically one," and that when they descend into this world they are separated into male and female. Each person, in order to perfect himself, must find his original heavenly mate,[40] and since "man is fashioned as a microcosm of the world...every day God creates a world by bringing the proper couples together."[41] Further: "Just as a palm tree does not grow unless the male is accompanied by the female, so the righteous cannot flourish save when they are male and female together, like Abram and Sarai."[42]

However, in other places the Zohar follows the biblical tradition in holding that the female originated in and is derivative of the male. For example, the Zohar explains that the letter Zade (Tsaday):

> consisted of the letter nun surmounted by the letter yod (representing together the male and female principles). And this is the mystery of the creation of the first man, who was created with faces (male and female combined)....The Holy One Blessed be He, said to her (the letter Zade) further, I will in time divide thee in two, so as to appear face to face.[43]

While for the Zohar, there is an explicit "superiority of the male over the female,"[44] and the female is associated with impurity, loathsomeness,[45] and death,[46] "the male is incomplete unless he is reunited with the female":

> "Man" implies the union of male and female, without which the name "man" (*Adam*) is not applied.[47]
>
> (Man) walks erect (and) mystically combines male and female.[48]
>
> Every figure which does not comprise male and female elements is not a true and proper figure....The male is not even called male until he is united with the female.[49]

Indeed, the continued separation of the female principle from the male results in discord and evil:

> When the moon was in connection with the sun, she was luminous, but as soon as she separated from the sun and was assigned the charge of her own hosts, she reduced her status and her light, and shells upon shells were created for covering the brain, and all for the benefit of the brain.[50]
>
> ...a woman enjoys no honour save in conjunction with her husband.[51]

For the Zohar, "it is incumbent on a man to be ever 'male and female,' in order that his faith may be firm, and that the Shekhinah may never depart from him."[52] As we have seen, the Zohar informs us that those who go on a journey or "students of the Torah who separate from their wives during the six days of the week in order to devote themselves to study are accompanied by a heavenly partner in order that they may continue to be 'male and female.'" This heavenly partner has been procured for the man by his wife and therefore it is his duty, when he returns to his wife, "to give his wife some pleasure."[53]

The Kabbalist not only held that *male* and *female* must be united, but also that *good* and *evil* must be joined, on the road to redemption. Interestingly, the Zohar suggests that the good and evil inclination are united in harmony within the female:

> The good inclination and the evil inclination are in harmony only because they share the female, who is attached to both, in this way: first the evil inclination sues for her and they unite with one another, and when they are united the good inclination, which is joy, rouses itself and draws her to itself, and so she is shared by both and reconciles them. Hence it is written, "and the Lord God formed man," the double name being made responsible for the good and evil inclination. *The man*: as we have explained, male and female together, and not separated, so as to turn face to face.[54]

While, as we have seen, there are passages in the Zohar that are suggestive of gender equality, in general, the Zohar's view of the *coniunctio* is biased on the side of the male and in this way corresponds perfectly to Jung's interpretation of the alchemical opus: "to bring the feminine background of the masculine psyche, seething with passions, into harmony with the principle of the rational (masculine) spirit."[55] The Kabbalists are at times exceptionally graphic in their symbolization of this union, depicting it, in a number of texts that Wolfson cites, as "the restitution of the female crown to the male organ."[56] Whatever our contemporary reaction to the assimilation of the female to the male, a *coniunctio* in which the female is reincorporated in the male is present in both Kabbalah and alchemy, and seems to have found a place in both Jung's visionary experience ("I myself was the marriage") and thought.

The *Coniunctio* and Language

The Kabbalists not only assimilated divine creativity to eros, but also assimilated language and especially writing to the sexual act. Wolfson points out that certain Kabbalists regarded the very act of divine and human *writing*, so important in the Jewish tradition, as an act of masculine engravure on a blank, passive feminine surface. According to Wolfson, for the Kabbalists, writing, as opposed to speech, is essentially an act of *phallic* eroticism. In the Zohar, for example, we read:

> I have seen in the mysteries of creation that says as follows: that concealed holy one engraved engravings in the womb of a luster in which the point is inserted.[57]

Since this act of engraving in a womb of luster presumably occurs at a point prior to any differentiation within the Godhead, Wolfson regards the primary creative act of the Kabbalists' deity as an autoerotic one within an androgynous god.[58] However, there are also passages in the Zohar that depict creation as a union of masculine and feminine aspects of writing:

> when the world was created it was the supernal letters that brought into being all the works of the lower world, literally after their own pattern....All these letters consist of male and female merging together into one union, symbolical of the upper waters and the lower waters, which also form one union. This is the type of perfect unity. Hence, whoever has a knowledge of them and is observant of them, happy is his portion in this world and the world to come; as therein is contained the root principle of true and perfect unity.[59]

Further:

There are letters of the female principle and letters of the male principle, the two classes of which come together to form a unity symbolical of the mystery of the complete divine Name.[60]

There is thus a dialectical movement in the Kabbalah between acts of
eroticism and *coniunctio* on the one hand, and language, and particularly
writing, on the other hand, which leads to the creation of all things. There
is also a further dialectic in which masculine and feminine principles are
transformed into one another in the creative process. For example, while
the Kabbalists regarded the instrument of engraving to be the divine
phallus, the act of engraving, which is also an act of self-arousal, is for
them also an expression of judgment and limitation, which the Kabbalists
regarded as the essence of the feminine.[61]

For the Kabbalists, both eros and writing are forms of *imitatio dei*.
According to Wolfson, writing is said to involve the unification of the
masculine with the feminine aspects of the divine through an act of phallic
engraving upon a passive feminine surface. This is especially true of mystical writing, for the writing of esoteric secrets is "a decidedly phallic
activity that ensues from an ecstatic state wherein the mystic is united with
the feminine divine presence."[62]

Thus we might say that, Kabbalistically speaking, Jung, in writing the
Mysterium Coniunctionis, himself performs the very union of the masculine and the feminine that his text describes. This, as we have seen, is also a
perspective that Jung himself took, upon his Kabbalistic vision: i.e., that
he himself was the holy union of God and his bride.

The work of a scribe is considered exceptionally holy in Jewish tradition,
and Wolfson refers to a manuscript that instructs a scribe how to ritually
prepare for writing a text concerning the ten holy *Sefirot*. The scribe is
instructed to wrap himself in a prayer shawl (*tallit*) and place the crown of the
Torah on his head. According to Kabbalistic tradition, this "crown" refers to
the feminine aspect of God, and the scribe, in placing it on his head, unites
himself with the divine feminine principle.[63]

Eros and Redemption

The Kabbalists related the divine wedding not only to the world's creation,
but to its redemption as well. For the Kabbalists, idolatry and evil stemmed from a reification of the feminine as a distinct entity.[64] Wolfson cites
a Kabbalistic text:

If, God forbid, she is separated from the (phallic) All, then "the Lord
has a sword; it is sated with blood" (Isaiah 34:6). She is aroused to
judge the world by harsh punishments and severe judgments.[65]

A similar thought is expressed in the Zohar regarding the male and female cherubs, which in Ezekiel's vision guard the throne of God:

> When their faces were turned one to another, it was well with the world—"how good and how pleasant," but when the male turned his face from the female, it was ill with the world.[66]

For the Kabbalists, the redemption from evil requires a *hierosgamos* that overcomes the distinction between male and female within the cosmos. According to Wolfson, the female is reabsorbed into the male and her powers of passivity, judgment, and restraint, the so-called powers of the left, are absorbed by the masculine powers of the right: activity and over-flowing mercy.[67]

Whereas Scholem had held that the Kabbalists, in contrast to the Gnostics, desired to conjoin male and female as opposed to making the female male, Wolfson points to a number of Kabbalistic texts that display the latter, typically Gnostic, point of view. There is, on this view, a clear phallocentrism in the Kabbalah, as there is in the entire Jewish tradition. For example, the Zohar records:

> And when is a man called "one"? When he is male with female and is sanctified with a high holiness and is bent upon sanctification: then alone he is called one without blemish. Therefore a man should rejoice with his wife at that hour to bind her in affection to him, and they should both have the same intent. When they are thus united, they form one soul and one body: one soul through their affection, and one body, as we have learnt, that if a man is not married he is, as it were, divided in halves, and only when male and female are joined do they become one body. Then God rests upon "one" and lodges a holy spirit in it: and such are called "the sons of God," as has been said.[68]

More radical is the view of the later Kabbalist Moses Zacuto, who held that "the essence of the creator is (the ninth *Sefirah, Yesod*/foundation), for the (tenth *Sefirah, Nukvah*, the female) is only a receptacle that receives semen that *Yesod* gives her, and she is the speculum that does not shine."[69] Some Kabbalists even went so far as to declare that when a woman gives birth she assumes a masculine role.[70] Isaac Luria held that when the males entered the Holy Temple in Jerusalem their very presence there transformed the feminine *Shekhinah* into male, thereby making her into the biblical God, *Adonay, Elohim*.[71]

Clearly, these texts are written from a masculine point of view. A similar phallocentrism is present in alchemy, and also (though less markedly) in Jung, who deals at length with integrating the *anima* (which he calls the soul) into the masculine psyche, but hardly at all with integrating the *animus* into the feminine. Nevertheless, there are Kabbalistic texts that speak of a transformation of the masculine into the feminine. In this transformation the male is required to become female in order to receive penetration and impregnation (*ibbur*) from the masculine God.

For example, as Wolfson points out the Lurianists held that the mystical significance of prayer, a significance that is enacted by the gesture of the worshipper closing his eyes, involves an effeminization of the male.[72] The male worshipper must divest himself of his masculinity, and assume the posture of the female, in order to draw down the masculine forces of the Godhead to earth. This begins a process in which the *Shekhinah* is impregnated and a male is born, which in turn brings about *Tikkun*, the rectification of a rupture within God. Both the homoerotic and the potentially christological aspects of this scenario are obvious. However, Kabbalistically we have another instance of gender transformation, this time from male to female, which is necessary for the world's redemption.

The Lurianists further held that the four-letter name of God, YHVH, the tetragrammaton, represents the deity, who perfectly encompasses both male and female characteristics. Vital refers to this in discussing the ritual of the palm branch and citron on the festival of Sukkoth. He states: "One must unite them together for the palm branch is the phallus and the corona is conjoined to it without separation."[73] According to Wolfson, Vital's image here is part of a long Kabbalistic tradition that history itself is a progressive restoration of the feminine to the masculine, in order that the Godhead can be restored to its purely homogenous condition prior to the separation of the feminine in the creation of worlds. The purpose of prayer and ritual is to catalyze the transformation of the feminine into the masculine, but in order for this to occur there are points at which the male worshipper must first be transformed into female.

Dangers of the Wedding Symbolism

In the next chapter we will develop the theme of *coincidentia oppositorum* (the coincidence of opposites), which, for both Jung and the Kabbalah, is an important theme underlying the wedding and erotic symbols. In holding that the self or God is a coincidence of the opposites of male and female, universal and particular, God and man, good and evil, etc., both Jung and the Kabbalah participate in a worldview that recognizes the vital importance of each pole of the classic oppositions, presumably without absorbing their differences in the process of their unification. However, the nullification of differences is an ever-present danger in such thought, particularly when, as is sometimes the case both with Jung and the Kabbalah, one pole of an opposition (e.g., the "masculine") is covertly privileged over the other (the "feminine"). As we will see, such covert "privileging" is only one of the dangers attendant to a worldview that takes seriously both poles of the oppositions that characterize human life and ideas. An equal danger exists when, in an effort to compensate for the "ruling discourse's" privileging of a single pole, a fetish is made of its opposite, often with disastrous results. In later chapters we shall see that this danger was encountered both by Kabbalah and Jung, when in an effort to compensate for an overemphasis upon the rational and regulatory aspects of the psyche a celebration of the nonrational and transgressive ensued.[74] This danger continues to pose a challenge to both the Jewish mystical and Jungian worldviews.

Another question raised by the wedding symbolism arises from its assumption of a clear-cut male/female dichotomy and with this the tendency to reify traits, attitudes and behavior that are presumably characteristic of each gender. This assumption, which had begun to be questioned in Jung's era, has become increasingly problematic in our own as traits traditionally attributed to "male" and "female" have to for many come to be viewed as social constructions and the very dichotomy male/female has itself been radically questioned. On the other hand, it can be argued that by emphasizing the coincidence of opposites between male and female and incorporating the "opposite gender" into the depths of the individual's psyche Jung (and even the Kabbalists) paved the way for a radical deconstruction of gender polarity.

Chapter 4

The Coincidence of Opposites in the Kabbalah and Jungian Psychology

For Jung, the key to understanding the "wedding" and erotic symbolism in the Kabbalah and alchemy is the psychological principle of *coincidentia oppositorum*. In fact, it would not be an exaggeration to say that for Jung the "coincidence of opposites" is not only the key to his interpretation of alchemy, but the cornerstone of his entire psychology. Indeed, long before he became acquainted with alchemy and the wedding symbolism, Jung had intuited that a *coincidentia oppositorum* stood at the foundation of both God and the human soul, and this idea is a major theme in both *The Red Book*[1] and *Psychological Types*.[2] In *Psychological Types* and other writings,[3] Jung developed the notion that the psyche unifies opposites via a process he termed the "transcendent function,"[4] which produces symbols that unite disparate and opposing aspects of the self, and which enables the individuals to transcend their conflicts. Indeed, Jung went beyond the basic Freudian insight that there are no contradictions in the unconscious, and that personality develops as a result of psychological conflict, to articulate a notion of the "self," which is a union of opposites and apparent contradictions. Among the opposites to be united are male and female, conscious and unconscious, personal and impersonal, and good and evil. "The self," Jung tells us, "is made manifest in the opposites and the conflicts between them; it is a *coincidentia oppositorum*."[5] For Jung, the measure of both the individual and culture is the ability to recognize polarity and paradox and to balance and unify oppositions.[6] "The union of opposites on a higher level of consciousness is not," according to Jung, "a rational thing, nor is it a matter of will; it is a process of psychic development that expresses itself in symbols,"[7] the most important of which is the union between male and female, *anima* and *animus*. It is, I believe, fair to say that Jung attempts in the realm of the symbolic, mythological, and psychic what Hegel had attempted in the sphere of reason: a dialectic of oppositions and antinomies leading to the full development of psyche or "mind."

The philosophical and psychological implications of the *coniunctio* symbolism were not lost on the Kabbalists and alchemists, who understood the cosmic union of male and female principles as symbolic of a *coincidentia oppositorum* on both cosmic and psychic levels. Arturo Schwartz has observed,

DOI: 10.4324/9781003027041-5

"For the kabbalist as well as for the alchemist, the two poles of a polarity are in a complementary rather than conflictual relationship. The male-female polarity is the fundamental model for all other polarities."[8] The universe is seen as having been created through a division of male and female divine principles, with the female principle identified with the material earth. The union of these gendered principles is necessary for redemption and return to wholeness on both a cosmic and individual level.[9] In short, a *coniunctio oppositorum* leads to a wider *coincidentia oppositorum*. This, according to Schwartz, became the foundation for Jung's concept of individuation, the etymological origins of which in *in-dividuus*, means "un-divided."[10] Such individuation corresponds to the *Rebis* (a double-headed male and female figure) and the *philosopher's stone* in alchemy and the primordial man, *Adam Kadmon*, in the Kabbalah.

Coincidentia Oppositorum in Jung's Interpretation of Alchemy

Jung utilizes a number of terms in describing the coincidence of opposites, including *unio mystica, unus mundus, complexio oppositorum*, and *mysterium coniunctionis*. Jung bases his discussion of the "coniunctio" in alchemy on the indisputable datum that the alchemists themselves viewed their activity as bringing about both a symbolic and material union of opposite tendencies and contradictory ideas. The alchemists not only conceived of their melting pots as vessels for the separation and unification of various metals, but also as vessels for the reunification of spiritual wholes that had been rent apart in the material world. The alchemist Barnaud, for example, speaks of "soul, spirit, and body, man and woman, active and passive, in one and the same subject, when placed in the vessel heated with their own fire and sustained by the outward majesty of the art."[11]

Among the symbols of unification used by the alchemists are the *coniunctio* of *sol* and *luna*,[12] the marriage (and identity) of water and fire,[13] the fertilization of earth by heaven,[14] the incestuous marriage of brother and sister,[15] the "chymical" wedding of King and Queen,[16] and the conjunction of *Nous* (Mind) and *Physis* (Matter).[17] Jung's *Psychology and Alchemy* presents a wonderful collection of (mostly fourteenth through sixteenth century) illustrations of these ideas, which can have the impact of producing in the viewer an intuitive sense of the harmony of soul brought about when a unified peace obtains between these oppositions.

The alchemists also expressed the fundamental *coincidentia* idea through the articulation of a number of paradoxes, which have a jarring and ultimately unifying effect on the listener:

> In lead is the dead life.
> Burn in water and wash in fire.
> Seek the coldness of the moon and ye shall find the heat of the sun.[18]

According to Jung, this alchemical juxtaposition and mixture of opposites corrects a basic tendency in the human spirit to rend itself apart into opposites, between conscious and unconscious, male and female, or persona and shadow:

> The essence of the conscious mind is discrimination; it must, if it is to be aware of things, separate the opposites.[19]

And:

> Since conscious thinking strives for clarity and demands unequivocal decisions, it has constantly to free itself from counterarguments and contrary tendencies, with the result that especially incompatible contents either remain totally unconscious or are habitually and assiduously overlooked. The more this is so, the more the unconscious will build up its counterposition.[20]

According to Jung, "unconscious processes...stand in compensatory relation to the conscious mind"[21] and, in effect, form a "shadow" that expresses itself in dreams, symptoms, etc., in an effort to balance the individual's "persona."

Jung points out that for the alchemists the tendency to separate opposites within the human psyche reflects an even deeper principle that "every form of life, however elementary, contains its own inner antithesis."[22] According to Jung, this idea itself is but one example of a perennial worldwide philosophy that takes as its basic axiom the universal idea of "the antithetical nature of the *ens primum*." He points out that in China, for example, this axiom is expressed in the notion of yin/yang, heaven and earth, odd and even numbers.[23] This idea can be extended to include all the basic oppositions within language and thought that in various cultures have served as expressions of the world-creative process. The biblical creation story with its distinctions between the firmaments, light and darkness, night and day, being and void, is only the most familiar example.

Because humanity's essence as a finite being is, as Jung affirmed in his *Seven Sermons to the Dead*, "distinctiveness," its psychological propensity is to identify with one pole of any given psychological dichotomy and neglect the other. As such, the oppositions between male and female, good and evil, reason and emotion, etc., are expressed within the individual's own being.[24] This is a necessary, but ultimately unhappy state, which the alchemical "conjunctions" are meant to correct.

According to Jung, the alchemical concept of *solve et coagula* provides a metaphor for a dialectic in which an original unity in God, being, or the unconscious is separated into component oppositions, and then reunited in an act that brings about a superior wholeness. This is precisely the dialectic expressed by the Lurianic Kabbalists in their concepts of *Sefirot* (archetypes), *Shevirah* (breakage), and *Tikkun* (restoration). With *Tikkun ha-Olam* (the restoration of the world), the unity provided by man is superior to the unity that existed in the Godhead prior to creation.

According to Jung, the "self" that is the goal of individual development can only be achieved through a confrontation with the "abysmal contradictions of human nature."[25] This is a theme that had already occupied Jung in *The Red Book*, where partly as a result of Nietzsche's influence, he was highly critical of conventional morality[26] and concluded that the human soul must include evil as well as the good.[27] Without such experience there can, on Jung's view, be no experience of either wholeness or the sacred. Religious orthodoxy, with its efforts to maintain firm distinctions between good and evil, rational and irrational, masculine and feminine, is actually a tool of the ego and an impediment to spiritual and psychological progress. According to Jung, alchemy became an undercurrent to Christianity, and thereby maintained a dim consciousness of the "even numbers" of earth, female, chaos, the underworld, the feminine, and evil, over against the "odd numbers" of Christian dogma. It is just a such an excursion into the rejected aspects of the human psyche that brings about a combination of the universal and the particular, the eternal and the temporal, the male and the female, etc., and which leads to an experience of the archetype of the self or God. This archetype is expressed in alchemy in the figure of Mercurius, the "world creating spirit":

> the hermaphrodite that was in the beginning, that splits into the classical brother-sister duality and is reunited in the *coniunctio* to appear once again at the end in the radiant form of the *lumen novum*, the stone. He is metallic yet liquid, matter yet spirit, cold yet fiery, poison and yet healing draught—a symbol uniting all opposites.[28]

Coincidentia Oppositorum in the Kabbalah

It will be instructive to examine the notion of *coincidentia oppositorum* as it appears in the Kabbalah, since Kabbalistic ideas, mostly mediated through alchemy, played a significant role in Jung's own understanding of this doctrine.

The Kabbalah is hardly the exclusive provenance of the coincidence of opposites. The notion that oppositions are dissolved in the plenum of the Infinite or Absolute is common to Indian thought, Gnosticism, and mystical thought in general. Nicholas of Cusa defined God as a *coincidentia oppositorum*.[29] A similar idea is also present in the philosophies of Eckhart, Boehme, and the German Romanticists, reaching its full rational articulation in the philosophy of Hegel. Still, the Kabbalah, with its dialectical scheme of the unifications of various opposing Sefirot; its views that man himself is incomplete unless he is both male and female; that God himself as the absolute being is also nothingness; that God creates man and yet man creates God; that the cosmos is, in effect, completed by the negative, evil world of the "other side"; that humanity, in order to reach its own salvation, must pay its dues to the realm of evil; that creation is negation (and vice versa); that destruction (the Breaking of the Vessels) is the condition of progress; and that the dialectical tensions of the cosmos are mirrored in the psychology of the individual, provided what was perhaps the Western world's richest symbolical scheme for expressing the *"coincidentia"* idea. This scheme was transmitted to the Christian world via the Christian Kabbalah and alchemy. As will be seen in more detail in Chapter 9, the Kabbalistic *coincidentia* material is particularly suited to a psychological, particularly Jungian, interpretation.

The identification of the deity with "Nothingness" is among the strangest of the Kabbalistic doctrines of God and can serve as an introduction to the Kabbalistic doctrine of *coincidentia oppositorum*. According to David B. Abraham ha-Lavan (end of the thirteenth century), the *Ayin* or nothingness that is to be identified with the highest aspect of God has:

> more being than any other being in the world, but since it is simple, and all other simple things are complex when compared with its simplicity, so in comparison it is called "nothing."[30]

There is in the Kabbalah a dialectical interdependence between being and nothingness: they are, as it were, welded together as a circle is to its own boundary. This interdependence is spoken of directly in the following passage from Azriel's work on the *Sefirot*:

> He who brings forth Being from Naught is thereby lacking nothing, for the Being is in the Naught after the manner of the Naught, and the Naught is in the Being after the manner [according to the modality] of the Being. And the author of the Book of *Yetzirah* said: He made his Naught into his Being, and did not say: He made the Being from the Naught. This teaches us that the Naught is the Being and Being is the Naught.[31]

For Azriel, the deeper we penetrate into the mystery of being the more we arrive at nothingness and vice versa; and like everything else in the world (e.g., night/day, beginning/end, male/female), being and nothingness have their opposites woven into their very essences. Indeed, from a certain perspective, the Infinite God, *Ein-sof*, can be understood as the negation that originates oppositions, antinomies, and dialectics in general—the very dialectics, as Isaiah Tishby points out, through which the world is created, transformed, and sustained.[32] According to the Kabbalist Ibn Ezra, the very "good" of creation (Genesis 1:31) is the communion of all things with "*Ayin*" (nothingness). The world, according to the Kabbalists, is constantly renewed through its contact with God's goodness, which is reinterpreted mystically as the Naught. Nothingness, for the Kabbalists, is "good" because it is the very principle that brings finitude, differentiation, and multiplicity into the world,[33] and, as such, it is the principle of the world's creation. From a psychological point of view, a full realization of the human psyche can only be achieved through a confrontation with nothingness and death. Nothingness, death, and finitude are, paradoxically, the source of all that is valuable and distinctive in human life.

The Kabbalist Azriel of Gerona, in discussing the nature of *Ein-sof*, says, "it is the principle in which everything hidden and visible meet, and as such it is the common root of both faith *and unbelief*" (my italics).[34] It is indeed very typical of Azriel, and of the Kabbalists in general, to make a thesis about *Ein-sof* and then to immediately hold that the opposite of this thesis is true as well, on the principle that *Ein-sof*, in its infinity, is the union of all opposites and contradictions. Indeed, according to Azriel, even the nature of the *Sefirot*, the archetypal values through which God created the universe, involve the union of "everything and its opposite."[35]

The "contradictoriness" of *Ein-sof* is expressed in the Zohar with such terms as "the head that is not a head."[36] More formally, the notion that *Ein-sof* is ontologically an indistinct unity of opposites is given (by Azriel and others) the Hebrew term *ha-achdut ha-shawah* (the "indistinguishable unity of opposites"), which denotes the equal presence of the divine throughout the universe, including in those aspects of the cosmos that oppose or contradict one another.[37]

The Kabbalistic notion of the coincidence of opposites is evident in their view that although God created man, man is also the creator of God. For example the Zohar adapts the wording of a rabbinic text (Midrash Leviticus Rabbah, 35:6) in affirming:

> Whoever performs the commandments of the Torah and walks in its ways is regarded as if he made the one above.[38]

This idea was quite widespread among the Kabbalists.[39] For example, we read in the Kabbalistic text *Sefer ha Yichud*:

> Each and every one [of the people of Israel] ought to write a scroll of Torah for himself, and the occult secret [of this matter] is that he made God Himself.[40]

A similar notion is expressed in an ancient Gnostic text where we read:

> God created men, and men created God. So is it also in the world, since men created gods and worship them as their creations. It would be fitting that gods should worship men.[41]

From a theological point of view, the Kabbalists and Gnostics, in their rather bold declarations, underscore the notion that there is a *reciprocal relationship between God and man*, an idea that Jung had become convinced of by the time he wrote *Psychological Types*.[42] God is indeed man's creator, but since man is the one being who through his actions can actualize the values that are only "ideas" in the mind of God, man can be said to complete, actualize, and even "create" God. This "reciprocity" is surprisingly premonitory of Jung, who held that the "gods" (in Jungian terms the archetypes, which traditional piety ascribes to the heavens) can be psychologically understood as a product of man's own collective unconscious.

A *coincidentia oppositorum* is present in the Lurianic theory of the creation of the world. Luria held that the central creative act was a negation— a contraction, concealment, and withdrawal of divine light and energy—which "provided room" for the existence of a finite world. According to Luria's disciple, Chayyim Vital:

> When it arose in His simple will to create the world and emanate the emanations, and to bring to light the perfection of His acts and names, then He contracted Himself into the central point that was in the middle of His light. He contracted Himself into this point and then retreated to the sides encircling this point.[43]

A similar paradox is present in the Lurianic notion of redemption, for *Tikkun ha-Olam*, the restoration of the world, is made possible only by its deconstruction, the *Shevirat ha-Kelim* or "breaking of the vessels." As we shall see, the very process of *Tikkun*, of both personal and world redemption, involves a blending of opposites, e.g., male and female, reason and emotion, kindness and judgment—the very blending of opposites that for Jung is the origin of the "self."

The Jewish mystical conception of coincidence of opposites is given further expression in the writings of the Chabad Chasidim. As R. Aaron Ha-Levi puts it:

> All created things in the world are hidden within His essence, be He blessed, in one potential, in *coincidentia oppositorum*...[44]

In their state of *Hashawah* within *Ein-sof,* opposites become united in a single subject and their differences are, in effect, nullified. Again, according to R. Aaron:

> He is the perfection of all, for the essence of perfection is that even those opposites which are opposed to one another be made one.[45]

Indeed, for R. Aaron, in *Ein-sof* there is such an interpenetration of opposing principles that "the revelation of everything is through its opposite,"[46] a notion that anticipates Jung's dictum that the full meaning of any conscious psychic trend is only revealed when we comprehend that which is opposed to it in the unconscious.

The Coincidence of Opposites in Psychotherapy

For Jung, the blending of the opposites becomes not just a principle of psychological reality, but also a prescription for psychotherapeutic change. Although Jung ultimately developed a conception of the unconscious that was radically different from that of Freud, he never abandoned the basic Freudian notion that psychotherapy involves the bringing into conscious awareness of psychological conflicts that had hitherto been repressed or, in Jung's preferred terminology, "dissociated" from consciousness.[47] Jung held that conflict was both inherent to, and necessary for the development of, the human spirit. For Jung, "a life without inner contradiction is either only half a life or else a life in the Beyond, which is destined only for angels."[48] Echoing the midrashic theme that a human life of freedom achieves a height above that of the angels, and the mishnaic (*Pirke Avot*) theme that one day in this world is superior to an eternity in the "world to come," Jung himself adds, "But God loves human beings more than the angels."[49]

Like the Chasidim, Jung held that conflict and contradiction are constitutive of both God and the human self: "The self is made manifest in the opposites and in the conflict between them; it is a *coincidentia oppositorum*. Hence the way to the self begins with conflict."[50] Among the Chasidim it was the first Lubavitcher rebbe, Schneur Zalman, who most fully developed the talmudic idea that man experiences conflict throughout his life between his *yetzer hara* (the evil inclination) and his *yetzer hatov* (the good inclination) or, as Schneur Zalman generally puts it, between his animal and Godly souls.[51] For the Chabad Chasidim, the human body is like a neutral battleground upon which these two souls compete like armies, each one seeking to subdue and conquer a "small city."[52] As such, human beings continually experience an inner tension or conflict, which can only be relieved in moments of inner harmony, such as those achieved during sincere ecstatic prayer.[53] At other times this conflict can lead to depression[54] or disturbing, intrusive thoughts.[55] However, conflict is also the vehicle through which mankind can elevate his basic instincts in the service of spiritual and ethical values.

Again, like the Chasidim, Jung held that it was possible to elevate the light that energizes human conflict:

> The stirring up of conflict is a Luciferian virtue in the true sense of the word. Conflict engenders fire, the fire of affects and emotions, and like

every other fire it has two aspects, that of combustion and that of creating light.[56]

Jung held that most serious conflicts involved an incongruity between feeling and thinking: typically one or the other has been dissociated from consciousness and must be reintroduced into one's intrapsychic dialog. While the psychotherapy patient, seeing that there is no external resolution to his or her conflict, is likely to believe that the conflict is insoluble, "a real solution comes only from within, and then only because the patient has been brought to a different attitude."[57]

Jung's views here closely correspond to those of the Kabbalists and Chasidim who held that inner conflict involves an inevitable clash between intrapsychic *Sefirotic* traits, most often between *Chesed* (love) and *Din* (Judgment), which must be dialectically blended or resolved in a third *Sefirah* or trait, *Rachamim* (Compassion). Jung held that such a resolution was possible only if the tension that exists between one's opposing ideas and affects can be held in awareness, at which point a spontaneous intrapsychic resolution, one that is neither predictable nor completely rational, will emerge. Jung called the "third" position that resolves the conflict between the initial opposites the *tertium non datur*, or the "transcendent function."[58] For the Kabbalists this function is epitomized in the *Sefirah Rachamim* (Compassion), which mediates between *Chesed* (Kindness) and *Din* (Judgment). By holding one's conflict in awareness, one's own compassionate stance towards oneself (a stance facilitated by either a rebbe or analyst) will bring about a spontaneous resolution. Interestingly, the *Sefirah Rachamim* is also known as *Tiferet* (Beauty), suggesting that the solution to intrapsychic conflict is a creative, aesthetic, imaginative one, as opposed to intellectual or physical achievement. Such a transcendent solution mirrors what some contemporary psychologists have come to understand as a critical aspect of wisdom, i.e., the bringing together and reconciliation of what initially appear to be opposing or incompatible ideas.[59] According to both Jung and the Kabbalists, the reconciliation of the opposites releases energy that is previously inhibited, inaccessible, or paralyzed by one's indecision. As Jung puts it: "During the progression of libido the pairs of opposites are united in the coordinated flow of psychic processes."[60] For Jung, the poles of the various conflicts and contradictions that are dissociated within the human psyche must be articulated, suffered, and ultimately reconciled in psychotherapy. While the goal of individuation may initially involve a process through which the conflict between conscious and unconscious is brought into awareness,[61] simply making the unconscious conscious is by itself insufficient to bring it about.[62] For Jung, the therapeutic process must invoke the production and interpretation of archetypal symbols—through which a creative synthesis of opposites, and thus the individuation of the self, can be attained.[63] It is for this reason that Jung turns to alchemy, mythology, and religious symbolism, which, on his view, both represent and actually promote the individuation process.[64] The wedding, erotic, and other alchemical symbols discussed by Jung are particularly important, for they symbolize the union and harmony of the contradictory poles of human life.

The psychotherapeutic process involves a creative act that occurs partly if not largely outside of conscious awareness. One of its main tasks is to reveal the unconscious as a collective phenomenon, the presence of which is indicated by the appearance of symbolic archetypes and mythologems in the patient's dreams and fantasies (e.g., creative work).[65] The emergence of these archetypes in psychotherapy can, on Jung's view, facilitate the integration and individuation of the personality.

Jung considers the ego and consciousness in general to be mere epiphenomena of the authentic psyche, which he identifies with the mostly unconscious self.[66] As such, psychotherapy involves an expansion of the subject beyond the conscious and rational ego towards a "center" that is closer to the unconscious, particularly the collective unconscious. This is achieved through the dialectical process between patient and therapist,[67] and is fully embodied in the "transference," which Jung understands as analogous to the "mystic marriage" in alchemy.[68] Jung describes an aspect of the therapeutic transference in which the contradictions of the psyche are unleashed on the therapist. The reconciliation of these opposites actually requires the development of a philosophy of life, one that can be derived from the symbolic systems of the great religions, or which must be individually crafted by the patient in treatment.[69] Jung considered the world's religions great therapeutic systems and held that the modern man's aversion to religion actually fosters the dissociation between ego and unconscious that gives rise to the neuroses.[70]

In this context it is worth noting that the basic function of the "Kabbalistic tree" is to harmonize opposing or discordant tendencies within the cosmos and human psyche. The third *Sefirah, Binah* or Understanding, is said to perform a reconciliation between the "will," "desire," and emotion of the first *Sefirah, Keter-Ratzon,* and the intellect of the second, *Chochmah.* It is interesting that the Kabbalists regard "understanding" as harmonizing the discord between intellect and emotion,[71] the role that Jung gives to intuition.[72]

The sixth *Sefirah, Tiferet/Rachamim* (Beauty/Compassion), also brings about an important reconciliation of opposites, that between *Chesed,* loving-kindness, and *Din,* stern judgment. The *Sefirah Rachamim* represents the capacity to tolerate, and indeed harmonize, conflict and contradiction. That *rachamim* or compassion is essential for psychological healing is clear, for it is only through compassion that one can live with the contradictions within oneself and others, and ultimately—as the alternative name of this *Sefirah,* Beauty, implies—realize the harmonizing beauty of the human soul.

Had Jung focused his attention more fully on the *Sefirot* and other Kabbalistic symbols—e.g., *Ein-sof* (the Infinite Godhead), *Tzimtzum* (Contraction/Concealment), *Shevirah* (Breaking of the Vessels), and *Tikkun* (Restoration, Emendation)—he would have discovered a wealth of symbolic material that resonates deeply with his own vision of psychotherapy. The identification of the self with an unknown (*Ein-sof*), the therapist's withdrawal as a means for permitting the patient's unconscious to emerge (*Tzimtzum*),[73] the shattering of both patient's and therapist's expectations and psychic structures during the course of therapy (*Shevirah*), and the patient's reconciliation, reorganization, and reinterpretation of his or her shattered life (*Tikkun*) are all themes that are present in both Jung[74] and the symbols of the Kabbalah, and which were, in fact, articulated in Chasidism. It is of small wonder that Jung came to believe that his entire psychology was anticipated by a Chasidic rabbi.

Chapter 5

The "Shadow" and the "Other Side"

Jung's views on the dark side of human nature, that aspect of the human personality that embodies the negative, discarded, and evil aspects of the self, distinguishes him not only as an original psychologist, but as a thinker of theological moment as well. As we have seen, Jung's critique of Christianity, indeed his critique of the entire Western tradition, points to its failure both to recognize and, in effect, welcome the archetype of the Shadow. European man, even up through the period between the two World Wars, had congratulated itself on the progress that had presumably been made in taming and controlling humanity's baser instincts. The prevailing philosophies of progress, science, and reason were but one expression of this optimism, an optimism that was to be shattered by the horrors of the Second World War.

Both Freud and Jung were, each in their own way, extremely distrustful of the view that humanity had or could eliminate its instincts for aggression, death, and evil, and Jung went so far as to hold that until the individual recognizes his or her "shadow," the hidden dark aspects of one's personality, there can be neither psychological healing nor wholeness. According to Jung, for individuation of the personality to occur, "consciousness must confront the unconscious and a balance between the opposites must be found."[1] This is a difficult moral challenge that "involves recognizing the dark aspects of the personality as present and real."[2] According to Jung, "this is not possible through logic," and "one is dependent on symbols to make an irrational union of opposites possible."[3] According to Jung, until we recognize the negativity within ourselves, the world, and even within God, there can be no adequate solution to the problem of evil.

In spite of Jung's interest in the Kabbalah and his reference to certain Kabbalistic themes in his major work on the problem of evil,[4] he draws no explicit connection between the Shadow archetype and its Kabbalistic equivalent, the *Sitra Achra*, or "Other Side." For the Kabbalists, the Other Side is a shadowy realm that both mirrors and complements the holy realm of the *Sefirot*. Within the Other Side, all of the negative tendencies inherent in the *Sefirot* are realized: the "kindness" of the *Sefirah Chesed*

DOI: 10.4324/9781003027041-6

becomes smothering and overwhelming, the "judgment" of the *Sefirah Din* becomes harsh and punitive, etc. Yet, like Jung hundreds of years later, the Kabbalists recognized that the Other Side plays a critical role both in the world and within the human psyche, and must be acknowledged and given its due. According to the Kabbalists, the world, including the soul of man, is partly immersed in the Other Side, and it is for this reason that the *Yetzer Hara*, the "Evil Impulse," cannot be banished from this world, but must instead be harnessed for good.

Such ideas were already present in Judaism before the advent of the Kabbalah, and played a critical role in the early Kabbalists' view of both God and humanity. According to ancient midrash, "If not for the evil impulse no one would build a house, marry, have children, nor engage in trade."

A similar idea is expressed by Jung in *The Red Book*:

> The evil one can only fail to make sacrifice. You should not harm him. Above all not his eye, since the most beautiful would not exist if the evil one did not see it and long for it. The evil one is holy.[5]

In the earliest Kabbalistic work, *Sefer ha Bahir*, we read: "The Holy One praise be He has a trait (*middah*) which is called Evil."[6] Since it is part of the deity, evil, according to the Kabbalists, is absolutely necessary for good. In discussing this very problem, the Zohar recites:

> For this reason it says "And behold it was very good" (Genesis 1:31). This is the angel of death. He should not be banished from this world. The world needs him....It is all necessary, good and evil.[7]

We have just seen that one reason provided by Jewish tradition for the necessity of evil is that the energy of the "evil impulse" is necessary for the very activities that mankind cherishes as the good. The Kabbalist also held that since evil brings into the world the possibility for choosing between sin and virtue it is also the very origin of (the possibility of) the good. Without the possibility of evil there could indeed be no value to this world. It is in this sense that evil is good, for it is the condition for good's realization. As the Zohar states:

> There is no light except that which issues from darkness, for when that "other side" (*Sitra Achra*) is subdued, the Holy One is exalted, and is glorified in His glory. In fact, there can be no true worship except it issue forth from darkness, and no true good except it proceed from evil. And when a man enters upon an evil way and then forsakes it, the Holy One is exalted in glory.[8]

The Kabbalists provide us with an image in which each layer of creation is a husk or shell to that which is above it and kernel to that which is below it. Elaborating upon the analogy of a fruit or nut, the Kabbalists conceived each husk or shell to be relatively lifeless, but containing (and protecting) a living, edible kernel. The Zohar draws upon this metaphor in its description of evil, in portraying the Other Side as a shell that "surrounds and protects the fruit inside."[9] The same idea is expressed more classically using the biblical image of the snake: "The Holy One, Blessed be He, has curled a serpent around the (realm of) holiness."[10] According to the Zohar there is no path to holiness except by way of the serpent, by way of the husk of darkness, which is the Other Side. Jung expresses a similar idea when he writes:

> If I had not become like the serpent, the devil, the quintessence of everything serpentlike, would have held this bit of power over me. This would have given the devil a grip and he would have forced me to make a pact with him just as he also cunningly deceived Faust. But I forestalled him by uniting myself with the serpent, just as a man unites with a woman.[11]

In the Kabbalah, the Other Side itself is sometimes understood as constituting a realm of "impurity," one that is completely parallel and intrinsically bound up with the ten *Sefirot* of holiness. Thus we read in the Zohar:

> The Holy One, blessed is He, emits ten crowns, supernal holy crowns. With these He crowns Himself and in these He vests Himself. He is they and they are He, just as a flame is bound up in the coal, and there is no division there. Corresponding to these are ten crowns beneath, which are not holy, and which cling to the uncleanness of the nails of a certain Crown called Wisdom, wherefore they are called "wisdoms."[12]

In the Zohar we also find the doctrine that just as one must have faith and grant sacrifices to the side of holiness, one must do the same for evil in order to "appease" the Other Side. Several of the *mitzvoth* (Torah commandments) are described in the Zohar as an appeasement or bribe, including among them the goat dispatched to "Azazel" (a ritual that the Cohanim performed on *Yom Kippur* when the Temple still stood in Jerusalem), and the inclusion of animal hair in the *tephillin* (phylacteries), which are donned by Jewish men during morning prayer.[13] The Other Side, which is here understood as our animal instincts or impulses, cannot simply be defeated or overcome; it must, in effect, be "granted its portion."

Here we have a powerful metaphor for the psychological truth, later recognized by Jung, that one's destructive urges cannot simply be willed away. The Kabbalah has a healthy respect for man's baser instincts, and it recognizes the real power of destructiveness in the human heart. Indeed, the Zohar criticizes the biblical Job for believing himself to be so righteous and pure that he failed to "give a portion" to the *Sitra Achra*.[14] By failing to take the evil impulse into consideration, he actually increased the powers of uncleanness and destruction:

> ...and when Job made sacrifices, he did not give Satan any part whatsoever....Had he done so, the Accuser would not have been able to prevail against him...had he given Satan his due, the "unholy side" would have separated itself from the holy, and so allowed the latter to ascend undisturbed into the highest spheres; but since he did not do so, the Holy One let justice be executed on him. Mark this! As Job kept evil separate from good and failed to fuse them, he was judged accordingly; first he experienced good, then what was evil, then again good. For man should be cognizant of both good and evil, and turn evil itself into good. This is a deep tenet to faith.[15]

The Kabbalistic notion that humanity must include its so-called baser instincts in its image of holiness is an idea that Jung, via alchemy, analyses in his consideration of "The Spirit Mercurius,"[16] and which is at the core of Jung's major work on evil, *Answer to Job*.[17] According to the alchemists, Mercurius is both good and evil, father and mother, young and old, strong and weak, death and resurrection, visible and invisible, dark and light, known and yet completely nonexistent.[18] The alchemists equated Mercurius with the Kabbalists' Primordial Human (*Adam Kadmon*). Jung points out that Mercurius:

> truly consists of the most extreme opposites; on the one hand he is undoubtedly akin to the godhead, on the other hand he is found in sewers.[19]

In *Answer to Job*, Jung proffers a similar dichotomous view of the Jewish God, which he says is reflected in the psychology of humanity:

> Yahweh...is an antinomy—a totality of inner opposites—and this is the indispensable condition for his tremendous dynamism, his omniscience and his omnipotence.[20]
>
> By this I do not mean to say that Yahweh is imperfect or evil, like a gnostic demiurge. He is everything in its totality; therefore, among other things, he is total justice, and also its total opposite.[21]
>
> The paradoxical nature of God has a like effect on man: it tears him asunder into opposites and delivers him over to seemingly insoluble conflict.[22]

This coincidence of good and evil, the holy and profane, is, as we have seen, very close to the Kabbalists' own conception of God.

While the Kabbalists clearly held that there is an asymmetry between good and evil that must tilt in the direction of good, this was not possible without a full recognition of and respect for evil. The Zohar interpreted the entire sacrificial system of pre-rabbinic Judaism, at least in part, as a method for appeasing the Other Side.[23] By channeling man's aggressive/thanatic urges, the animal sacrifices presumably provided the necessary appeasement to evil. Indeed, the strength of man's aggressive urges and the necessity for their sublimation and appeasement is made clear in the biblical story of the *Akedah*, where Abraham, the great patriarch of the Jewish people, nearly sacrifices his own son Isaac in the name of faith and holiness. This act serves as the somewhat unnerving paradigm for the faith of the Jewish people and illustrates the Zoharic axiom that evil (here in the guise of a filicidal impulse) must be included in the worship of God.

Just as there must be *a descent for the purpose of ascent* on the cosmic level, just as the potential for evil is a necessary condition for the good, each individual man and woman must, according to the Kabbalah, be prepared to descend into the realm of evil if he or she is to effect a personal *Tikkun*. The Zohar interprets Abraham's, and later Israel's, descent into Egypt as an earthly representation of the theosophical "descent for ascent" principle. According to the Zohar, Adam and Noah each descended into and became entangled in the "realm of the husks," but the patriarchs entered and emerged in peace. The Jews' four hundred years in *Mitzrayim* (Egypt) and their *aliyah*, or ascent with Moses to the Promised Land, is the paradigmatic example of the "descent for ascent" principle operating in history. Though it is a dangerous undertaking from which one may not return, the individual, it is said, achieves perfection by entering the domain of evil and refining himself there as in a crucible.

Evil, for the Kabbalists, is intrinsically connected to holiness. It is for this reason, the Zohar tells us, that we must learn to accept the evil or thanatic urges within our own nature:

> Hence we learn that even though this side (*Sitra Achra*) is nothing but the side of uncleanness, there is a brightness around it, and man does not have to drive it away. Why is this? Because there is a brightness around it; the side of holiness of faith exists there; and there is no need to treat it with disdain. Therefore one must give it a portion on the side of the holiness of faith.[24]

Jung expresses a similar thought in a contemporary, psychological idiom when he writes:

> A safe foundation is found only when the instinctive premises of the unconscious win the same respect as the views of the conscious mind.[25]

According to the Kabbalists, humanity itself is comprised of both good and evil. The Zohar recites that when the world was created, the letter

Teth (T), which is placed at the head of the word *Tov* (Good), did not wish to take its place anywhere near the letter *Resh* (R) which is at the head of the word *Ra* (Evil). God said to the letter *Teth*:

> Go to thy place, as thou hast need of the *Resh*. For man, whom I am about to create, will be composed of you both, but thou wilt be on his right side whilst the other will be on the left.[26]

According to the Zohar, God:

> made a Right and a Left for the ruling of the world. The one is called "good," the other "evil," and He made man to be a combination of the two.[27]

In a fascinating passage replete with mythological imagery, the Zohar describes how one of the seven nether earths:

> consists of two sections, one enveloped in light, the other in darkness, and there are two chiefs, one ruling over the light, the other over the darkness. These two chiefs were at perpetual war with each other, until the time of Cain's arrival (to this nether world), when they joined together and made peace; and therefore they are now one body with two heads. These two chiefs were named '*Afrira* and *Kastimon*. They, moreover, bear the likeness of holy angels, having six wings. One of them had the face of an ox and the other that of an eagle. But when they became united they assumed the image of a man. In time of darkness they change into the form of a two-headed serpent, and crawl like a serpent, and swoop into the abyss, and bathe in the great sea.[28]

It is, according to the Zohar, only after evil is fully recognized and takes its first actual form (Cain's slaying of his brother Abel) that the powers of good and evil can make peace. These powers become united in "the image of man." However, "in times of darkness," when man is ignorant of his origins in the powers of both darkness and light, this "image of man" is transformed into a "two-headed serpent," one that swoops into the abyss and bathes in the "great sea." In psychological terms, we might surmise that this "abyss" and "great sea" is the unconscious mind, within which the two-headed serpent "bathes" and thereby wreaks havoc upon the psyche and the world.

Chapter 6

Adam Kadmon and the Sefirot

Jung took a particular interest in the Kabbalistic symbol of Adam Kadmon (Primordial Human), which he understood to be both the archetype of all psychological being and an expression of the archetype of the self, which is man's goal. *Adam Kadmon* is spoken of directly by the alchemists and is taken by them to be an equivalent of the *prima materia*,[1] Mercurius,[2] and the philosopher's stone. In *Aion*, Jung sees the symbol of Christ as an expression of the Primordial Human or self archetype.[3]

The symbol of Primordial Human, the first being to emerge with the creation of the cosmos, is common to a number of religious and philosophical traditions. The Upanishads describe a primal man composed of the very elements—fire, wind, earth, sun, and moon—that were to become the world.[4] According to the Upanishads, this "gigantic divine being" is both infinitely far and deposited near the innermost recesses of the human heart.[5] Indeed, in the Hindu tradition, the Primordial Human is identified both with the entire universe and the soul or essence of all things.

The Primordial Human is also an important symbol in Gnosticism. The Gnostics inferred from the verse in Genesis, "Let us make man in our own image," that the first earthly man was created on the model of a cosmic Adam on high.[6] In the Nag Hammadi Gnostic text the *Apocryphon of John*, we learn that this Anthropos is the first creation of "knowledge and Perfect Intellect" and the first luminary of the heavens.[7] This Anthropos becomes the heavenly model through which the demiurge forges an earthly Adam. Other Gnostic sources relate how the "archons" (conceived of as female demigods corresponding to each of the seven planets) formed an earthly Adam to fulfill their sexual desire for the heavenly Anthropos who was beyond their spiritual reach. Among the Mandaeans (a Gnostic sect that today survives in Iraq), the primordial Adam is coextensive with the cosmos; his body is the body of the world, and his soul the soul of all souls.[8] In an image that would later reappear in the Kabbalah, the Gnostics held that individual human beings are descended from the cosmic Anthropos as a result of its fragmentation.

In the Lurianic Kabbalah, *Adam Kadmon* becomes a pivotal notion linking God, man, and the world. *Adam Kadmon*, as the first being to emerge

DOI: 10.4324/9781003027041-7

from the infinite Godhead, is essentially indistinguishable from the deity, yet at the same time the Primordial Human's body is said to both emanate and constitute the world. Man, having been created in God's image, is according to the Kabbalists made of the very same cosmic elements, the *Sefirot*, that comprise the "body" of *Adam Kadmon*. Finally, *Adam Kadmon* is said to play a critical role not only in the creation of the world but in its redemption as well, as lights from the Primordial Human's forehead act upon the broken vessels and restore them as *Partzufim* or primal personalities/visages of humanity and God. The symbol of *Adam Kadmon* can be said to express the idea that the cosmos itself has both a soul and body very much like that of man, and that the world too is garbed in the interest, value, and eros that is normally thought to be the exclusive province of humankind.

For Jung, *Adam Kadmon* is the invisible center in man, the hidden unified self that gives full personal expression to the *coincidentia oppositorum*. Jung quotes the purportedly Jewish alchemical text by Abraham Eleazar:[9]

> Noah must wash me...in the deepest sea, that my blackness may depart....I must be fixed to this black cross, and must be cleansed therefrom with wretchedness and vinegar, and made white, that...my heart may shine like a carbuncle, and the old Adam come forth from me again. O! Adam Kadmon, how beautiful art thou.[10]

Adam, Jung relates, is equated with the alchemist's transformative substance because he was made from clay, a piece of the original "chaos," yet infinitely formable and moldable.[11] Jung makes reference to the midrash *Pirke De Rabbi Eleazar*, which held that Adam was made from the dirt of the four corners of the earth.[12] In a rare reference to Isaac Luria, Jung says: "We can therefore understand why Isaac Luria attributed every psychic quality to Adam: he is psyche par excellence." Jung quotes a passage from Knorr von Rosenroth to the effect that *Adam Kadmon* contains all ideas from the lowest, most practical levels of the soul to the highest levels (the *yechidah* of *Atziluth*).[13] *Adam Kadmon*, we are told, is the equivalent of Plato's sphere-shaped "original man,"[14] and like Plato's man and Mercurius he is an apt symbol of the self because he is androgynous.

Adam Kadmon, Jung informs us, is the universal soul, the soul of all humankind. Jung reviews the Midrashic and Kabbalistic notions that suggest that all the righteous come from the different parts of Adam's body: his hair, forehead, eyes, nose, mouth, ears, and jawbone.[15] A midrash, Jung relates, describes the first Adam as extending from one end of the world to the other until God took away pieces from his limbs, instructing him to scatter these pieces to the ends of the earth, so that they could become the souls and bodies of all future men.[16] *Adam Kadmon* is the equivalent of Mercurius in alchemy, because the metallic element mercury has been disseminated throughout the physical world.[17]

Jung considers the concept of the "Old Adam"—which appears in the writings of Abraham Eleazar, and which Jung relates to the sinful, unredeemed man in Romans, but which he says can also readily be juxtaposed to the worthless man, Samael—a counterimage of *Adam Kadmon*, in the Kabbalah.[18] According to Jung, this "Old Adam" corresponds to the primitive man at the opposite extreme from *Adam Kadmon* but who is also sometimes equated with him.[19] It suggests a primitive identification of God and the self with an animal consciousness and, according to Jung, corresponds to the "shadow" archetype. There is a compensatory relationship between the highest spiritual image and the lowest instinct, and when their interdependence is lost, religion, on Jung's view, becomes petrified in formalism and compensation is converted to neurotic conflict.[20]

It is significant for Jung that "in the cabalistic view *Adam Kadmon* is not merely the universal soul or, psychologically, the 'self,' but is himself the progress of transformation."[21] Jung quotes Knorr von Rosenroth's Latin translation of a passage from the Kabbalist Abraham Ha Cohen Herrera:

> *Adam Kadmon* proceeded from the simple and the one, and to that extent he is Unity, but he also descended and fell into his own nature, and to that extent he is Two. And again he will return to the One, which he has in him, and to the Highest; and to that extent he is Three and Four.[22]

This passage is particularly noteworthy for its dynamic or dialectical view of a deity (or in Jung's terms, the self) that must become estranged from itself (in distinction and consciousness) in order to become itself (as man or ego), only to return to itself (in a unity between man and God, or consciousness and the unconscious). For Jung, as for the Kabbalah, the God archetype completes itself only in this dynamic process, a view that each shares with Hegel.[23] Because *Adam Kadmon* is essentially dynamic or transformative, "the alchemists could equate Mercurius and the Philosopher's Stone with the Primordial Human of the Kabbalah."[24] Jung points out that the conception of Primordial Human is common to other religious traditions, and makes particular reference to the Taoist P'an Ku, a primal man who is said to have transformed himself into the earth and all its creatures.[25]

In this light it is worth noting that, for Jung, "the archetype of Man, the Anthropos, is constellated and forms the essential core of the great religions." Jung writes: "There is in the unconscious an already existing wholeness, the 'homo totus' of the Western and the Chen-yen (true man) of Chinese alchemy, the round primordial being who represents the greater man within, the Anthropos, who is akin to God."[26] Jung, however, also believed that "every civilized human being, however high his conscious development, is still an archaic man at the deeper levels of his psyche."[27] Unlike civilized man, the archaic or primitive man projects his psyche onto the world at large and perceives the world as imbibed with soul and spirit. Jung relates, "In the idea of the *homo maximus* the Above and Below of creation are united."[28]

In the Kabbalah, while *Adam Kadmon* is often understood as a linear representation, it is also frequently seen as emerging from the same circular pattern of emanation that gives rise to the *Sefirot*. Jung makes reference to a similar idea in a seventeeth-century alchemical text, which also makes use of an astrological metaphor:

> The synthesis of the [four] elements is effected by means of the circular movement in time (*circulatio, rota*) of the sun through the houses of the Zodiac. the aim of the *circulatio* is the production (or rather, reproduction) of the Original Man, who was a sphere.[29]

It may be that both the Kabbalistic and alchemical concepts of an original man encased within, or manifest as, a sphere are attributable to Platonic influence.[30]

The Kabbalistic dual concepts of *Iggulim* and *Yosher* (circles and lines)[31] in the formation of the *Sefirot* and *Adam Kadmon* is reflected in a passage in Knorr von Rosenroth, also quoted by Jung:

> From *En Soph*, from the most general one, was produced the universe, which is *Adam Kadmon*, who is One and Many, and of whom and in whom are all things. The differences of genera are denoted by concentric circles. specific differences are denoted by a straight line.[32]

Jung, consistent with his psychological interpretation of the Kabbalah, notes that the concentric circles (the *Sefirot*) either proceed from *Adam Kadmon* or are contained within him,[33] but that at any rate he is a schema of *psychic structure*.

According to Jung, the figure of the circle is seized upon in various mystical traditions as a symbol of psychological containment. "It is intended to prevent the 'outflowing' and to protect the unity of consciousness from being burst asunder by the unconscious."[34] Such a view is completely consonant with the Kabbalists' own understanding of the *Sefirot* as vessels designed to contain the light and power of the Infinite God. Jung further suggests that "the circular movement has the moral significance of activating the light and dark forces of human nature, and together with them all psychological opposites of whatever kind they may be."[35] A similar view was also put forth by the Kabbalists, who held that each of the *Sefirot* represents a psychological or moral trait, and that it is incumbent upon man, at least with respect to the seven lower, "emotional"

Sefirot, to improve his character through the development of all forty-nine possible *Sefirotic* combinations, and to acknowledge the presence within his soul of their dark or negative opposites. It will be instructive to examine the doctrine of the *Sefirot* and its psychological ramifications in some further detail.

The *Sefirot*

Sefirah and its plural form *Sefirot* have no clear linguistic derivation. The term has been variously interpreted as meaning luminary, brilliance or sapphire, number, scribe, and book (the Hebrew word for which is *sefer*), and each of these proposed derivations can provide us with some insight into the nature of the *sefirah* symbol. Jung himself discusses the derivation in *Mysterium Coniunctionis*, where he points out that while some authorities relate *Sefirah* to the Greek word for sphere, more recent scholars (e. g., Gershom Scholem) have suggested that the word derives from the Hebrew root 'SFR,' primordial number.[36] The Kabbalists themselves describe the *Sefirot* as luminaries, dimensions, numbers, or archetypes through which God has created or *written* the world. The *Sefirot* are ten in number, and even their names (e.g., Wisdom, Understanding, Kindness) suggest that they represent values, archetypes, or dimensions of the human soul, and according to the Kabbalists they are also the foundational elements of the world. It is a fundamental tenet of Kabbalistic thought that the microcosm mirrors the macrocosm, that the elements of the soul of man mirror the ultimate constituents of God and the universe.

According to the Kabbalists, the ten *Sefirot* embody the dimensions of will, wisdom, understanding, love, power and judgment, beauty and compassion, endurance, majesty, foundation, and kingship. It might be said that the Kabbalists recognize additional "dimensions" beyond the four of space and time traditionally acknowledged by physics, and that these additional dimensions[37] characterize an object's spiritual, conceptual and psychological properties. The Kabbalist Moses Cordovero (1522–70), an older contemporary of Isaac Luria's in Safed, who understood the *Sefirot* as the constituent elements or "molecules" of the world, held that each thing obtains its specific character through the relative admixture and dominance of the *Sefirot* of which it is comprised.

The Kabbalists held that the *Sefirot* are distributed within, and actually comprise the body of, *Adam Kadmon*, the Primordial Human, with the final *Sefirah, Malchut*, comprising his feminine counterpart. Jung himself briefly alludes to this arrangement:

> Yesod signifies the genital region of the Original Man, whose head is Kether. Malchuth, conforming to the archetypal pattern, is the underlying feminine principle.[38]

The Kabbalists also organized the *Sefirot* into a "tree," which they regarded as essentially equivalent to *Adam Kadmon*, and which in some sources is described as having its roots in the air, a fact that Jung takes to be a symbol of the equivalence of heaven (the air) with the unconscious (wherein the human psyche is rooted).[39] Jung wrote a major essay on "The Philosophical Tree," where he acknowledged that the *arbor inversa* (the inverted tree) "found its way into alchemy via the Cabala."[40] He references both the Zohar and the Kabbalist Joseph Gikatila in his discussions of the sefirotic tree,[41] and he cites Knorr von Rosenroth, in relating how *Binah*, one of the upper *Sefirot* (and the cosmic Mother), is named the "root of the tree" and is the source of life brought down from the heavens.[42]

The Kabbalists also held that the *Sefirot* are organized into worlds (*olamot*), some of which (being spiritual) are dominated by the highest *Sefirot, Keter* (Will) and *Chochmah* (Wisdom), while others (being more material) are dominated by less exalted sefirotic archetypes. Estelle Frankel has pointed out that, according to the eighteenth-century Lurianist Moses Chaim Luzatto, the four main worlds of the Kabbalah—*Atziluth* (Emanation), *Beriah* (Creation), *Yetzirah* (Formation), and *Assiyah* (Action)—provide the root or foundation for four distinct types of soul (the higher *neshamah*, the *neshamah*, the *ruach*, and the *nefesh*). According to Frankel, these four types of soul correspond to the four personality types described by Jung: the higher *neshamah* corresponding to the intuitive personality type, the *neshamah* to the thinking type, the *ruach* to the feeling type, and the *nefesh* to the sensate type.[43]

In addition to being organized into worlds, the *Sefirot* are transformed into five major *Partzufim*, or "personalities": the Holy Ancient One, the Father, the Mother, the Impulsive One, and the Female, which, as we will detail in Chapter 9, correspond in a remarkable manner to the basic Jungian archetypes of the Senex, the Father, the Mother, the Puer, and the Anima. From a Jungian perspective, another important aspect of the *Sefirot* doctrine is the existence of the so-called ten negative crowns or "counter-*Sefirot*," which as we have seen are said to exist in an infernal realm, the "Other Side," and which provide an evil or negative counterpart to the *Sefirot*. As we have also seen, according to the Kabbalists man must pay his due to the world of the counter-*Sefirot* as well as to the upper realms. If he fails to recognize the negative forms of will, wisdom, strength, and kindness within himself, he runs the risk of being dominated by these same forces emerging from the Other Side. This is the same notion later expressed by Jung in his discussion of the individual's need to integrate his Shadow.

The symbols of the *Sefirot* are exceedingly rich from a psychological point of view. Not only does each embody a specific character trait or psychological value (e.g., will, wisdom, kindness, compassion, etc.), they each can be said to embody a particular principle of psychotherapeutics.[44]

For example, it can be said that the highest of the *Sefirot, Keter,* which the Kabbalists identified with the abyss of nothingness as well as with the supreme will, delight, and desire, embodies the principle that in order to achieve psychic wholeness one must seek one's true desire, a desire that is embedded within the abyss of the unconscious. *Chesed,* which the Kabbalists identified with loving-kindness, can be said to embody the psychological principle that there is no true psychic change except that which proceeds from the care and regard of an other. *Din,* the Kabbalistic archetype of judgment, embodies the principle that the overflowing kindness of *Chesed* must be tempered with self-criticism and judgment in the creation of the self. Indeed, the self is, according to the Kabbalists, only achieved when *Chesed* and *Din,* Kindness and Judgment, are united and harmonized in the *Sefirah Rachamim* (Beauty, Compassion).

We will have occasion to explore the *Sefirot* in more detail in Chapter 9. There we will see that the *Sefirot* doctrine, as it is articulated in the Lurianic Kabbalah, provides the foundation for an entire depth and archetypal psychology.

Chapter 7

Fragmentation and Restoration

For the Lurianic Kabbalah, the universe as we know it is in a fragmented, partially displaced, and chaotic state resulting from the Breaking of the Vessels (*Shevirat ha-Kelim*). According to the Kabbalists, this *shevirah* or "rupture" is the force behind human history and conditions the experience of each individual. The Breaking of the Vessels is an archetypal event that reflects the notion that the original unity of all things must be broken and a portion of the "original chaos" reintroduced into the cosmos in order for humanity to achieve its purpose in perfecting both itself and the world.

The Kabbalists provide a variety of metaphorical descriptions of the Breaking of the Vessels. On the most basic level, they hold that the ten original *Sefirot* were created as vessels to contain the divine light emanated by the Infinite God but were unable to do so and shattered from the light's impact. The shards from these broken vessels tumbled through the metaphysical void, entrapped sparks of divine light, and became the elements of both the "Other Side" and our world. On a second interpretation, the Kabbalists held that the Breaking of the Vessels caused a rupture in the bond between the Celestial Father and Mother (the *Partzufim Abba* and *Imma*), causing them to turn their backs upon one another, thus disrupting the flow of masculine and feminine "waters," which maintain the harmony of the worlds.[1] According to the Kabbalists, humanity's task is *Tikkun ha-Olam*, the "restoration" of the broken vessels, which will result in a renewed "face to face" (*panim a panim*) conjunction between the masculine and feminine aspects of God. The significance of the Kabbalist's doctrine of the Breaking of the Vessels is that a rupture in the status quo and re-introduction of chaos and negativity is paradoxically necessary for the soul's and world's perfection and wholeness.

Jung himself asserts in his correspondence that he was unaware of these Lurianic ideas until 1954 (probably after the completion of *Mysterium Coniunctionis*), and he expresses excitement over having found in them a confirmation of his own thoughts.[2] Prior to this time, however, he had considered analogues of the "breakage" (*Shevirah*) and restoration (*Tikkun*) concepts in

DOI: 10.4324/9781003027041-8

alchemy and elsewhere. As early as in *The Red Book*, Jung had spoken of the value of reintroducing chaos into the human psyche:

> There in the world of chaos dwells eternal wonder. Your world begins to become wonderful. Man belongs not only to an ordered world, he also belongs to the wonder-world of his soul. Consequently you must make your ordered world horrible....[3]

This is an idea that Jung adopted from Nietzsche who had written in *Zarathustra* (Prologue, Part V) that One must have a chaos inside oneself to give birth to a dancing star. In *The Red Book* Jung describes chaos as breaking down the walls of ones structured, equanimous soul.[4] However, it is only with his study of alchemy that Jung understood the full implications of chaos for the development of the human psyche. The alchemical formula of *solve et coagula* (dissolve and synthesize) calls attention to the fact that for alchemy a premature unity must first be separated and broken apart before the alchemical synthesis can achieve its desired effect, just as the premature order of the *Sefirot* must be ruptured in order to assure that a new synthesis can lead the redemption of the soul and world.

Jung informs us that the initial state in which opposite forces are in conflict is known in alchemy as *chaos*, and is considered the equivalent of the *prima materia*.[5] It is identical to the "chaotic waters" at the beginning of creation,[6] before the separation of opposites as symbolized by the "firmament." The alchemists *solve* (like the Breaking of the Vessels involves a breakthrough of the primordial chaos, According to Jung:

> The alchemists understood the return to chaos as an essential part of the opus. It was the stage of *nigredo* [blackness] and *mortificatio*, which was then followed by the "purgatorial fire" and the *albedo* [whiteness].[7]

Jung informs us that an element of chaos, negativity, or evil (often symbolized in alchemy by the element "lead") must enter into the alchemical work as the impetus to the stage of *solve*. Such chaos, incidentally, has the potential to drive the adept mad.[8]

"Chaos," for the alchemists, is symbolized by the sea,[9] the serpent,[10] and the anima, or feminine aspect of the world.[11] Paradoxically, however, all material transformation and psychic healing come about through chaos. A similar idea is expressed in the Kabbalah of Joseph Ben Shalom of Barcelona (ca. 1300), who held that there is no creation, alteration, or change in which the abyss of nothingness does not, at least for "a fleeting moment," become visible.[12]

An idea that in many respects parallels the Kabbalistic symbol of the *Shevirah* is reflected in the alchemists' view of healing as resulting from the "destruction of the bodies." Jung points out that according to the alchemist

Dorn, bodily and spiritual healing results when Mercurius (as quicksilver) destroys copper to the point of transforming it into powder. A battle between the elements is set up that brings about an alchemical *separatio, divisio, putrefactio, mortificatio,* and *solutio,* each representing an element of chaos, resulting in physical change in the substances and, more importantly, spiritual healing for the alchemist.[13]

Making reference to the "hermetic vessel," which is said to contain a portion of the original chaos from before the world's creation,[14] the alchemist Dorn writes:

> Man is placed by God in the furnace of tribulation, and like the Hermetic compound he is troubled at length with all kinds of straits, divers calamities and anxieties, until he die to the old Adam and the flesh, and rise again as in truth a new man.[15]

Similarly, the British alchemist and cleric Ripley (1415–90) held in his *Cantilena*[16] that in order to enter the Kingdom of Heaven the "king" must transform himself into the *prima materia* in the body of his mother and return to a state of primal chaos.[17]

According to Jung, the psychological equivalent of these transformations by chaos is a confrontation with one's own unconscious.[18] He writes:

> The meeting between the narrowly delimited, but intensely clear, individual consciousness and the vast expanse of the collective unconscious is dangerous, because the unconscious has a decidedly disintegrating effect on consciousness.[19]

Although perilous, the process of confronting the chaos of one's unconscious is a necessary prerequisite to psychological growth. Jung tells us:

> We must not underestimate the devastating effect of getting lost in the chaos, even if we know it is the *sine qua non* of any regeneration of the spirit and personality.[20]

Earlier, in *The Red Book*, Jung had written exuberantly, "If one opens up chaos, magic also arises,"[21] yet he already knew quite well from personal experience the dangers of a confrontation with the chaotic forces, images, and figures of the unconscious:

> Everything inside me is in utter disarray. Matters are becoming serious, and chaos is approaching. Is this the ultimate bottom? Is chaos also a foundation? If only there weren't these terrible waves. Everything breaks asunder like black billows.[22]

Jung's ideas closely correspond to the Lurianic/Chasidic notion that a personal "shevirah" or psychic rupture is a necessary prerequisite for a personal *Tikkun*, or restoration or regeneration of one's soul. This process of regeneration of the spirit is, according to Jung, symbolized by an egg, which stands for the primal chaos containing the divine seeds of life,[23] but which at the same time holds the world-soul captive.[24] Out of this egg will arise the phoenix, which symbolizes a restored Anthropos who had been "imprisoned in the embrace of *Physis.*"[25] This egg and captive world-soul parallel the Kabbalists' conception of the state of affairs existing after the Breaking of the Vessels, in which sparks of the divine light that had been emanated from *Adam Kadmon* are captured and contained by the *Kellipot*, or husks. The birth of the phoenix is a parallel image to the Kabbalistic symbol of *Tikkun.* According to Jung, the typical Gnostic and alchemical theory of "composition and mixture" involves a "ray of light from above," which mingles with the dark chaotic waters "in the form of a minute spark." Jung points out that "at the death of the individual, and also at his figurative death in mystical experience, the two substances unmix themselves."[26] "Like iron to a magnet," the Sethians held, the spark is drawn to its proper place. This procedure, according to Jung, is perfectly analogous to the process of *divisio* and *separatio* through which the alchemists sought to extract the *anima* or world-soul from the *prima materia* or chaos.[27] It is also essentially equivalent to the Lurianic process of *Birur* (extraction), in which sparks of divine light are separated from their evil, dark containers. Jung's ideas regarding the disintegrating but regenerating impact of the unconscious upon the conscious self are given an interesting symbolic expression in a gloss on the *Shevirah* provided by one of Isaac Luria's disciples, Israel Sarug. As recounted by Scholem, Sarug held that the world as originally emanated "was like a sown field where seeds could not bear fruit until they had first split open and rotted."[28] Looked at psychologically, this metaphor suggests that the Breaking of the Vessels, in its very destructiveness and negativity, is a necessary condition for the birth of the psyche or self. In Jungian terms, it suggests that an imperfect, "split open," even "rotted" psychic system is the prerequisite for individuation.[29]

Jung held that various processes of healing, separation, and extraction after an experience of chaos, represent efforts on the part of the individual to restore his own soul, or, as we will see momentarily, in theological language that is very close to that of the Lurianic Kabbalah, efforts to complete and perfect God. This process, according to the Kabbalists, is one in which humanity provides the "feminine waters" in service of reuniting a divided God. It is also one in which man must embrace his satanic side in order to create a whole self. In a letter to Erich Neumann in January of 1952, Jung wrote:

God is a contradiction in terms, therefore he needs man in order to be made One. Sophia is always ahead, the demiurge always behind. God is an ailment man has to cure. For this purpose God penetrates into man. Why should he do that when he has everything already? In order to reach man, God has to show himself in his true form, or man would be everlastingly praising his goodness and justice and so deny him admission. This can be effected only by Satan, a fact which should not be taken as a justification for Satanic actions, otherwise God would not be recognized for what he really is.

The "advocate" seems to me to be Sophia or omniscience. Ouranus and Tethys no longer sleep together. Kether [Jung's spelling] and Malkhuth are separated, the Shekhinah is in exile; that is the reason for God's suffering. The *mysterium coniunctionis* is the business of man. He is the nymphagogos of the heavenly marriage.[30]

In this passage, Jung makes reference to the Kabbalistic doctrine that man provides the "masculine waters" for the unification of the masculine and feminine aspects of God, which had been separated as a result of the Breaking of the Vessels. The theodicy presented here, like the one outlined in Jung's *Answer to Job*, is based on the idea that in order for humanity (and hence God) to become complete, the individual must come face to face with evil both within the deity and within his or her own soul.

Only then can humankind perform those acts that unify the opposites, acts that are necessary to complete the world and God. When the Holy One is reunited with his *Shekhinah*, then *Tikkun ha-Olam* is achieved, and the cosmic balance is restored.

Tikkun ha-Olam in the Kabbalah

Jung, late in his life, took a keen interest in the Kabbalistic concept of *Tikkun*. In 1954 he wrote to the Reverend Erastus Evans: "In a tract of the Lurianic Kabbalah, the remarkable idea is developed that man is destined to become God's helper in the attempt to restore the vessels which were broken when God thought to create a world."[31] It will be worth our while to explore the Kabbalists' *Tikkun* metaphor in some depth, as it affords another important bridge between the Kabbalah and Jungian psychology.

The concept of *Tikkun ha-Olam* is implicit throughout the history of Jewish mysticism. Its origins are, in part, to be found in the biblical conviction that the paradise that was lost to humankind because of Adam's sin would be restored in a future age, and in part in the late biblical belief that an exiled Jewish people would be returned to the land of Israel. While the repair or restoration of the world is a theme that is recurrent throughout Jewish history, the concept of *Tikkun ha-Olam* reaches its fullest development in sixteenth-century Safed in the Lurianic Kabbalah. Isaac Luria (1534–72)[32] and his disciples, most notably Chayyim Vital

(1542–1620),[33] dwelt upon *Tikkun* at great length, reinterpreting older Kabbalistic ideas, e.g., regarding the "death of the kings," and providing a grand symbolic scheme within which the "repair of the universe" plays the most prominent role. The Kabbalists of Safed understood every event in the created universe, indeed the very act of creation itself, as a mere introduction to, or preparation for, *Tikkun ha-Olam.*

The Kabbalists created a wide variety of symbols to express the *Tikkun* idea. We have already encountered one of these symbols in our discussion of the unification of the masculine and feminine aspects of God and the soul. We will have occasion to discuss another of these symbols, "the raising of the sparks," in Chapter 8.

Among the other similes through which the Kabbalists described the process of *Tikkun* are the "discovery of the roots of one's own soul," "development in the womb of the celestial mother," "the descent into the infernal world of the *Kellipot*," and "the reunification of the trees of life and knowledge." Each of the Kabbalistic metaphors is of interest from the point of view of contemporary analytic psychology.

Discovering the roots of one's soul: According to the Kabbalists, the Breaking of the Vessels resulted in the imprisonment of sparks not only from the Godhead but from human souls as well. Indeed, it was their view that the souls of all men and women are comprised of sparks from Adam's soul, most of which have been imprisoned in the *Kellipot* as a result of Adam's sin. It is the task of each individual to discover these sparks or roots within himself and, through a process known as *Birur* (extraction or disencumbrance), perform his own personal *Tikkun* or restoration. This task is described as follows by Chayyim Vital: "When man is born his soul needs to extricate those sparks that are his share which had fallen into the *Kellipot*... because of the sin of Adam."[34] According to the Kabbalist Moses Zacuto: "It behooves every man to inquire diligently and to know the roots of his soul so as to be able to perfect it and restore it to its origin which is the essence of his being."[35] Here, as Jung notes with respect to the Gnostics, the process of self-perfection is essentially one of self-discovery.

It is important to distinguish the self-discovery of the Kabbalists from self-discovery as it is understood today in the context of popular psychology. Discovering the roots of one's soul, performing the act of *Birur*, and achieving one's personal *Tikkun* do not lead to the enhancement of one's ego and the fulfillment of one's personal desires *per se*. Rather, it is a process through which one discovers one's unique spiritual task in life. The discovery of the roots of one's own soul leads to the realization of one's "Godly self,"[36] and to the transformation of the individual into a conduit for God's values and God's will, which in Jungian terms involves a re-centering of the self closer to the collective unconscious.

Development in the Womb of the Celestial Mother: Among the most difficult and seemingly opaque aspects of the Lurianic Kabbalah is its treatment of *Partzufim* (Visages). Like the *Sefirot*, the *Partzufim* are idea-tional or spiritual structures that are regarded as aspects of the deity and intermediaries between God and creation. However, unlike the *Sefirot*, which are generally regarded as impersonal structures or values, the *Part-zufim* are personal aspects of visages of the Primordial Adam that take on the form of various stages of individual human development. In general, the Lurianists held that the *Partzufim* emerged spontaneously as a result of the Breaking of the Vessels.[37] In Vital's account, lights from the fore-head of the Primordial Human shine on the broken vessels and sparks, revivify them, causing them to reorganize themselves into configurations that correspond to stages in the development of the individual.

The creation of the *Partzufim* is the initial phase of *Tikkun ha-Olam*. Each *Partzuf* represents a specific stage in the process of divine recon-struction, acts as a medium for the reception and transmission of divine influx from the upper worlds, and serves as an archetype for the union of the masculine and feminine aspects of God, symbolized in their "looking face to face" (*panim be fanim*).[38]

However, man must complete the *Partzufim*, and *Tikkun ha-Olam* itself. One *Partzuf, Zeir Anpin* (the "short-faced" or "impatient" one), is, according to the Kabbalists of Safed, integrally connected with the phase of *Tikkun* that involves the efforts of mankind. *Zeir Anpin* is said to organize within itself qualities of six of the ten *Sefirot*, precisely those that were completely shattered in the Breaking of the Vessels, including the "moral" *Sefirot* of *Chesed* (Kindness), *Din* (justice), and *Rachamim* (mercy). The Zoharic metaphor of "the unification of The Holy One Blessed Be He with His *Shekhinah*" is paralleled in the Lurianic writings by the metaphor of the union between "Zeir Anpin" and "Rachel." As symbols of *Tikkun*, these unions refer to the union of Godly values with each other and their instantiation on earth in humankind.

Of greater relevance here, however, is the fact that *Zeir Anpin* is itself described as developing within the womb of another *Partzuf, Imma*, the Celestial Mother, creating, according to Scholem, what appears to be a myth of "God giving birth to Himself."[39] In its development, *Zeir Anpin* is said to progress through five distinct stages: *ibur* (conception), *lidah* (pregnancy), *yenikah* (birth), *katanot* (childhood), and *gadolot* (maturity). The final stage, *gadolot*, is reflective of mankind's own intellectual and moral maturity. Significantly, the *Partzuf Imma*, within which this devel-opment takes place, is identified with the *Sefirah Binah*, which connotes intellectual understanding.[40] Before the six moral or emotional *sefirot* (the six that are embodied in *Zeir Anpin*) can fully participate in *Tikkun haOlam*, they must undergo a developmental process through which they come to be integrated with intellect and understanding. It is just such a process that one undergoes in the process of individuation, and that is facilitated in a Jungian analysis. We will have more to say about the

Partzufim in Chapter 10, when we consider the entire Lurianic system as a metaphor for the development and maturation of the self.

The Trees of Life and Knowledge: The Kabbalists used the metaphor of the "exile of the *Shekhinah*" (the estrangement of God's feminine, earthly aspect) to symbolize the alienated, exiled state of affairs on earth. The "exile" is given a moral interpretation in *Midrash HaNeelam* in the Zohar, where it is explained as follows: The *Sefirot* (the ten dimensions or aspects of Godliness) were revealed to Adam in the form of the twin trees of Life and Knowledge. By failing to maintain their primal unity, Adam placed a division between life and knowledge that has had far-reaching implications.[41] According to the Zohar, this division resulted in a fissure in both God and the world and prompted Adam to worship the tenth *Sefirah* (the *Shekhinah*, God's manifestation on earth) without recognizing its unity with higher, more spiritual forms. By worshipping the *Shekhinah* and failing to understand her unity with the other *Sefirot*, Adam became attached to the temporal, material world, as opposed to the values which that world instantiates or represents.

In the Zohar we thus have a concept of the world's redemption in which neither intellect nor experience, matter nor spirit is an adequate center for the world or the self. In effect, according to the Zohar (*Midrash HaNeelam*), humanity must turn from a purely intellectual perspective (symbolized by the tree of knowledge) and embrace the values of "life," which has escaped consciousness since the time of Adam. This union between knowledge and life is another example of *coincidentia oppositorum*, which for both the Kabbalah and Jung is essential for spiritual and psychological development.

The Descent into the Infernal World of the Kellipot: One of the most startling passages in all religious literature is to be found in the second book of the Zohar. "In fact," the Zohar tells us, "there can be no true worship of God except it issue forth from darkness, and no true good except it proceed from evil."[42] How, we must ask, can evil, which by definition is diametrically opposed to good, be at the same time the latter's source and foundation? The answer to this question goes to the very heart of *Tikkun ha-Olam*.

Recall that, according to the Kabbalists of Safed, if *Tikkun* is to be achieved, the sparks of divine light (*netzotzim*), which had been alienated from their source in God by the Breaking of the Vessels, must be liberated from the Husks (*Kellipot*) that entrap them in the dark world of the "Other Side." The extraction of the divine light, referred to in the Kabbalah as the act of "*birur*," is, metaphysically speaking, the very process of *Tikkun ha-Olam*, and the very essence of "the good" as it can be achieved by humankind. It should, however, be apparent that because the *Kellipot* (which are sustained by the sparks of divine light they contain) are the source and substance of both matter and evil, the process of extraction (and thus the very process of *Tikkun*) requires a sojourn into the realm of evil, the realm of the *Sitra Achra*, the "Other Side." *Tikkun*, the "raising of the sparks," proceeds, as it were, out of the *Sitra Achra* and as such there is no goodness, i.e., no liberated light, except that which issues forth out of the evil realm. "The perfection of all things," the Zohar tells us, "is attained when good and evil are first of all commingled and then become all good, for there is no good so perfect as that which issues out of evil."[43] This conception of *Tikkun* parallels Jung's thoughts on the Shadow, and brings an additional dimension to our discussion of Jung's conception of the unconscious and evil, which we began in Chapter 5.

The Differentiation and Blossoming of All Things: The Kabbalists held that the differentiation of the world into each of its particulars is necessary for *Tikkun ha-Olam*. According to Luria's chief disciple, Chayyim Vital:

> Everything was created for the purpose of the Highest One, but all do not suckle in the same way, nor are all the improvements (*tikkunim*) the same. Galbanum (an ingredient in incense, which by itself has a foul odor), for example, improves the incense in ways that even frankincense cannot. That is why it is necessary for there to be good, bad, and in-between in all these worlds and why there are endless variations in all of them.[44]

Rabbi Aaron ha-Levi, a disciple of the first Lubavitcher rebbe wrote that it was the divine intention that all realities and particulars be differentiated and revealed, and ultimately joined in their value.[45] We find in the Kabbalah and Hasidism, an enormous respect for difference, a respect that was clearly echoed by Jung, who in *The Red Book* made this startlingly postmodern pronouncement:

> Differentiation is creation. It is differentiated. Differentiation is its essence, and therefore it differentiates. Therefore man differentiates since his essence is differentiation.[46]

In this same work, Jung speak of a white bird that sits on his shoulder and says, "Let it rain, let the wind blow, let the waters flow and the fire burn. Let each thing have its development, let becoming have its day."[47]

"Complex" and *Kellipot*

For Jung, a "complex" is the image of a certain psychic situation that is strongly accentuated emotionally and is, moreover, incompatible with the habitual attitude of consciousness.[48] For Jung, "the *via regia* to the unconscious...is not the dream, as [Freud] thought, but the complex, which is the architect of dreams and of symptoms."[49] According to Jung, the complexes typically form around certain archetypes of "feeling-toned ideas," such as "Mother" or "Father,"[50] and "interfere with the intentions of the will and disturb the conscious performance; they produce disturbances in memory and blockages in the flow of associations."[51] Complexes act in a nearly autonomous fashion. Jung calls them "splinter psyches" and he traces their origin to "trauma, an emotional shock or some such thing, that splits off a bit of the psyche." One of the most common causes is a "moral conflict, which ultimately derives from the apparent impossibility of affirming the whole of one's nature."[52] Psychotherapy ideally produces a reintegration of the complex into the main fabric of the personality and a consequent restoration of the associative chain and the flow of psychic energy.

In the Lurianic Kabbalah, a "*Kellipah*" results from a spark of divine energy that as a result of a cosmic trauma has been split off from the divine core and entrapped in a husk or shell. However, the *Kellipot* are also active on the level of the individual psyche. Like Jung, the Kabbalists—and, in particular, the Chasidim—speak of the *Kellipot* as sources of negativity, which bind an individual's soul and lead him or her into wickedness and pathology. According to Chasidic psychology, one can fall into the grip of a *Kellipah*. Similarly, Jung tells us that while people may speak of "having a complex" it is perhaps better to speak of the complex "having us."[53] In the process of *Tikkun*, the energy from the *Kellipah* is released so that it can serve the ends of man and God, just as in psychotherapeutic treatment the affect that is bound to a complex is freed to serve the patient's individuation.

While the Kabbalists held that the *Kellipot* are the molecular components of the (fallen) world, Jung held that their psychic analogues, the complexes, are the building blocks of the human psyche, and the source of all emotional and other psychic activity. For Jung:

> Complexes are focal or nodal points of psychic life which we would not wish to do without; indeed, they should not be missing, for otherwise psychic activity would come to a fatal standstill.[54]

The Kabbalists held the *Kellipot* to be the constituents of the "Other Side," but nonetheless believed that they (like the *yetzer hara*, the evil impulse) were absolutely necessary for the progress and redemption of the world. According to Chayyim Vital, our world is partly immersed in the *Kellipot*, and as such it is a world that is mostly evil with only a bit of good mixed in. As the contemporary Kabbalist and sage Adin Steinsaltz has argued, because of this we live in the worst of all possible worlds in which there is yet hope—yet, paradoxically, such a world is "the best of all possible worlds."[55] This is because it is only in a world that is on the brink of total disaster that humanity is forced to put forth the ethical, spiritual, and intellectual efforts necessary to realize the values inherent in the *Sefirot* and thereby mend and restore the world. Jung makes a similar point when he says that having a complex "means that something dis-cordant, unassimilated, and antagonistic exists, perhaps as an obstacle, but also as an incentive to greater effort, and so, perhaps, to new possibilities of achievement."[56] Jung's view here echoes both the Kabbalistic and German Idealist idea that the world's trials and tribulations ultimately serve the development of both man and God.

According to Jung, complexes are not pathological in and of them-selves, but only become pathological when we believe that we do not have them.[57] For Jung, the aim of analysis is not to rid oneself of all complexes, but rather to minimize their negative effects by withdrawing our identifi-cations from them, and, paradoxically, by fully acknowledging and living them. For Jung:

> a complex can be really overcome only if it is lived out to the full. In other words, if we are to develop further we have to draw to us and drink down to the very dregs what, because of our complexes, we have held at a distance.[58]

Similarly, the Baal Shem Tov, the founder of the Chasidic movement, held that it was not useful to attempt to suppress one's baser motives and instincts, but rather to enter into and spiritualize them. The Baal Shem Tov is said to have taught that "a man should desire a woman to so great an extent that he refines away his material existence in virtue of the strength of his desire."[59] In the process of spiritualizing one's instincts one "raises a spark" of divine light and contributes to *Tikkun ha-Olam*, the restoration of the world. As descri-bed by the Chasidic rebbe Elimelekh of Lizhensk:

> He extracts something precious from something cheap, and even the evil urge becomes good. He now serves God with *both* impulses, the good and the evil. The animal soul that induces his physical desires now supports him also, for he hallows himself even in that which is permitted—eating, drinking, and other acts. Thus, he elevates every-thing to supreme holiness.[60]

Chapter 8

The Raising of the Sparks

Of all the Kabbalistic metaphors for world restoration, the one that has had the greatest and most lasting significance for the subsequent history of Judaism is the symbol of "the raising of the sparks." The notion of a spark of divine light trapped in a world of matter is a quintessentially Gnostic idea.[1] It is an idea that remains largely unarticulated in the Kabbalah until it erupts with great force in the system of Isaac Luria in the seventeenth century. Later it becomes a foundational concept in Chasidism.

Jung's interest in the symbol of the "sparks" is largely centered about its appearance in Gnosticism, alchemy, and Christian theology, but his interpretation of its meaning is essentially Kabbalistic, as he sees the raising of the sparks as a metaphor for psychological redemption in (as opposed to a Gnostic escape from) the world of individual human existence.

Jung makes brief mention of the theory of the sparks in *Psychology and Alchemy*, where, in speaking about the early (third century) alchemist Zosimos, he considers the idea of "the pneuma as the Son of God, who descends into matter and then frees himself from it in order to bring healing and salvation to all souls."[2] Jung, in a footnote, says that "the cabalistic idea of God pervading the world in the form of soul sparks (*scintillae*) and the Gnostic idea of the Spinther (spark) are similar."[3] Jung writes that these ideas suggest a parallel to the unconscious—and indeed, as we have seen, the notion of a buried psychic or spiritual energy that must be freed and returned to its source is a basic psychoanalytic idea. Jung had early on recognized the image of the spark to be a symbol of the unconscious. In his commentary on "The Secret of the Golden Flower," a Chinese alchemical text, Jung had interpreted the sparks and fire within the refining furnace as the unconscious impetus to the emergence of the "golden flower" from the "germinal vesicle."[4]

Jung discusses the doctrine of the sparks or *scintillae* in depth in *Mysterium Coniunctionis*, relating this symbol to his theories of the archetypes, the collective unconscious, and the self. Early in this work he quotes a passage from the presumably Gnostic *Gospel of Philip*, which states the theme of a God/self dispersed throughout mankind and the world:

DOI: 10.4324/9781003027041-9

I am thou and thou art I, and wherever thou art, there I am, and I am scattered in all things, and from wherever thou wilt thou canst gather me, but in gathering me thou gatherest together thyself.[5]

This passage, Jung tells us, reflects man's nature as a microcosm, and Jung interprets it through the words of the early Christian theologian Origen:

Understand that the fowls of the air are also within thee. Marvel not if we say that these are within thee, but understand that thou thyself art another world in little, and hast within thee the sun and the moon, and also the stars.[6]

Jung understands the image of the *scintillae* in alchemy against this background of man as microcosm, containing within himself both the world and the celestial luminaries. The *"scintillae"* are, in Jung's view, a symbolic expression of the archetypes of the collective unconscious.

Jung reviews the history of the spark doctrine as it is manifest in the teachings of the Gnostics, Sethians, Simon Magus, and later thinkers such as Meister Eckhart. He notes that, for at least the Gnostics, man carries within himself a spark from the "world of light," which enables him to ascend and dwell with "the unknown father and the heavenly mother."[7] Jung takes particular interest in the Sethian notion, as reported by Hippolytus, that darkness "'held the brightness and the spark of light in thrall,' and that this 'smallest of sparks' was finely mingled in the dark waters."[8] This idea, which is echoed in alchemy, is also premonitory of the notion of the *Kellipot* (sparks entrapped in dark "shells") in the later Kabbalah.

Jung quotes Abraham Eleazar to the effect that the sparks are to be identified with *Adam Kadmon*[9] and describes how for the alchemists the *scintillae* are often "golden and silver" or are called "fishes' eyes," which appear in clouds, water, and earth, and symbolize the omnipresence of the philosopher's stone, which according to the alchemists is equivalent to the heavenly sparks.[10] Eyes, sparks, light, and sun are, according to Jung, symbols of consciousness. The Gnostics, in their efforts to reintegrate sparks to reach "the father," and the alchemists who put *scintillae* together to form gold, are projectively attempting to reintegrate consciousness itself.

The alchemist Dorn provides a spiritual interpretation of the *scintillae* that is quite similar to that of the Kabbalists. Wisdom, according to Dorn, is an awareness of these sparks, for such sparks are equivalent to the image of God within man. In man, according to Dorn, there is an "invisible sun."[11] This "sun," however, also contains a dark side, for, according to Dorn, "there is nothing in nature that does not contain as much good as evil."[12] Jung considers the following passage in Dorn, which suggests to Jung that the *scintillae* contain as much potential for evil as for good:

> Man is the bait, wherein the sparks struck by the flint, i.e. Mercurius, and by the steel, i.e. heaven, seize upon the tinder and show their power.[13]

From the "nuptial" impact between the feminine Mercurius and the masculine heaven (steel), Jung informs us that a "fire point" is created in man that has potential as both danger and panacea. This, we might suppose, is the burning passion that resides in the heart of humankind.

Jung considers the work of Heinrich Khunrath (1560–1605), who, as we saw earlier, was both an alchemist and Christian Kabbalist. Khunrath, a contemporary of Luria and Vital, studied medicine in Basel and died in Leipzig.[14] It is in regard to Khunrath that Jung notes that Gnostic ideas reemerged after many centuries,[15] the same comment that Scholem made with regard to Luria.[16] According to Khunrath:

> There are…fiery sparks of the World-Soul, that is of the light of nature, dispersed or scattered at God's command in and through the fabric of the great world into all fruits of the elements everywhere.

Khunrath associates the theory of the sparks with both the divine spirit (*ruach Elohim*) and the Cosmic Anthropos or Primordial Human:

> The Son of the Great World…is filled, animated and impregnated… with a fiery spark of Ruach Elohim.[17]

Further, for Khunrath, the "fiery sparks of the World-Soul were already in the chaos, the *prima materia*, at the beginning of the world."[18]

Thus, in Khunrath we find a theory of the sparks that is remarkably close to that of Luria, who also held that sparks of the Primordial Human or World-Soul have been scattered throughout every corner of the universe. Jung, of course, provides a psychological interpretation of Khunrath's symbolism, noting that "the filling of the world with scintillae is probably a projection of the multiple luminosity of the unconscious."[19]

Elsewhere Jung is more explicit, equating the sparks with the archetypes of the collective unconscious:

> In the unconscious are hidden those "sparks of light" (*scintillae*), the archetypes, from which a higher meaning can be "extracted."[20]

Jung equates the sparks with the alchemists' Mercurius and with the *anima mundi* or world-soul of the Neoplatonists, referring to the hermetic doctrine that this soul is "that part of God which, when he 'imagined' the world, was as it were left behind in his creation,"[21] a wonderful metaphor that is reminiscent of the Kabbalistic notion of the *Reshimu* or trace of divinity that remains in the cosmic void after the *Tzimtzum* (withdrawal), the first creative act of *Ein-sof*.[22] Such metaphors have a deep resonance with human experience, for who has not felt that a part of a writer or artist is left behind, even long after his death, in his work.

Jung's idea of "extracting" significance from the sparks of light recalls the Lurianic notion of *Birur*, the extraction of the sparks themselves from the *Kellipot* ("husks") that contain them. This idea has its alchemical parallel in the concept of extracting the *caelum*, which, as Jung explains, is "the celestial substance hidden in man, the secret 'truth,' the 'sum of virtue,' the 'treasure which is not eaten into by moths nor dug out by thieves.'" According to the alchemist Dorn, for the world this *caelum* is the cheapest thing, but for the wise it is more precious than gold: the part of man's soul that survives his death.[23] It is precisely this *caelum*, this piece of "heaven," that is symbolically extracted by the alchemists in their procedures. Jung tells us that as a result of this extraction what remains is a *terra damnata*, "a dross that had to be aban doned to its fate."[24] The parallel to the Lurianic notions of *Kellipot* (the "husks") and *Birur* ("extraction") should be readily apparent.

Jung makes reference to a passage in St. Augustine's "Reply to Faustus the Manichean" in which a very early version of this theory of extraction is described in fantastic terms. According to Augustine's report, the divine spirit is, for the Manicheans, imprisoned in the bodies of the "princes of darkness," who are seduced by angelic male and female beings from the sun and the moon. By exciting their desire, these angels cause the wicked to break out into a sweat that releases the divine spirit and falls upon the earth to fertilize its plants.[25] This description is noteworthy, for in contrast to the Gnostic theory of divine sparks escaping from a useless and damned world, this Manichean image has the divine spirit returning to restore the earth, an idea that is premonitory of the Kabbalistic doctrine of *Tikkun*, and hence far more compatible with Luria (and Jung) than it is with the general tenor of Gnostic thought.

The alchemists, of course, believed that through their metallurgic procedures they could extract Mercurius or the *lapis*, the philosopher's stone, which were each conceived as the material representations of the Primordial Human[26] and the heavenly sparks or *scintillae*.[27] This *lapis* combines, in *coincidentia oppositorum*, elements that are "base, cheap, immature, and volatile" with those that are "precious, perfect, and solid,"[28] in such a manner as to create both a "figurative death" and a "panacea" for the disharmonies of both the physical world and the human spirit.[29] Jung sees this panacea as a unification of the ego with the shadowy and repressed contents of the unconscious mind, but the alchemists understood their procedure in metaphysical terms, as the extraction or distillation of the "foundation stone" of the world.[30]

The Chasidic Theory of the Sparks

It will be worth our while to examine in some detail the doctrine of the sparks as it appears in the later Kabbalah and in Chasidism, where it is provided a this-worldly and psychological interpretation that Jung, had he been aware of it, would have welcomed. (We will have the opportunity to further meditate on the relationship between Jung and Hasidism when we consider Neumann's *Roots of Jewish Consciousness* in the Appendix).

The doctrine of the "raising of the sparks" brought an *immediacy* to the concept of *Tikkun ha-Olam* (the Restoration of the World) that had not hitherto been present in the Kabbalah. The Kabbalists of Safed, and, particularly, the Chasidim, believed that sparks of divine light are contained in all things, and they held that each individual has the opportunity to engage in world redemption in each and every one of his or her activities, from the most mundane to the most spiritual. There is, according to the Lurianic point of view, something of value, something Godly, in all things, and it is incumbent upon humankind to discover, highlight and, as it were, bring out this value in the material world, thus transforming that world into a spiritual realm. As described by the Chasidic rebbe Levi Yitzhak of Berdichev:

> All your material, mundane actions should be intended primarily for the glory of heaven, elevating the holy sparks to their Source. For every material object contains love, fear, and beauty (the *Sefirot Chesed, Gevurah, Tiferet*); when you desire to eat, drink, or engage in some other mundane activity, and you intend it for the love of God, you elevate the material desire to a spiritual one, releasing the holy sparks in these objects.[31]

Tikkun ha-Olam, the Restoration of the World, will be complete when all of the sparks have been raised and the entire world has been informed with spiritual meaning and value. This conception of *Tikkun* is one that manages to fuse the spiritualism of mysticism with the "worldliness" of Judaism.

The Kabbalists held that each individual's soul contains sparks that derive from the soul of *Adam Kadmon*, the Primordial Human, who, as a result of the Breaking of the Vessels, was divided into a number of soul sparks. The notion that all souls ultimately derive from *Adam Kadmon* gave rise to the concept of soul-roots and soul-families. Scholem points out that R. Solomon Alkabez (ca. 1550) and R. Moses Cordovero developed the idea that the souls of certain individuals have a familial connection, which is completely independent of those individuals' biological familial status.[32] Parents and children, for example, are rarely from the same soul-root, but individuals from the same soul-root may meet and sense an immediate and profound spiritual connection. These Kabbalists held that the Cosmic Adam originally fragmented into 613 major soulroots, corresponding to the 613 divine commandments and the 613 organs that according to Jewish tradition comprise the human body. These soul-roots further divided into a multitude of "minor roots," each of which is referred to as a "Great Soul." The Great Soul further subdivides into individual souls and sparks.[33]

According to Solomon Alkabez, all of the sparks derived from a Great Soul are controlled by a law of sympathy,[34] suffering with one another and benefiting from each other's good deeds. A *tzaddik* or saintly individual, for example, is capable of restoring sparks within (but only within) his own soul-family.

Amongst the Chasidim, the doctrine of the holy sparks became the key to personal as well as world redemption. The Chasidim understand life as a providential journey in which the people, places, and events that a person encounters contain precisely those sparks which only that individual can redeem. As such, every moment in a person's life provides the opportunity for raising the sparks of personal and divine redemption, or, conversely, for plummeting both the self and the world even further into the grip of the Other Side.

Chayyim Vital had earlier held that each individual, in the course of a lifetime, encounters sparks that are his or her lot to redeem.

> When a person is born his soul must purify (*Birur*) the sparks which reach his portion, that fell through the sin of the first man (*Adam ha Rishon*)....This is the reason for a person being born in this world. Understand this well. Through the *mitzvot* (divine commandments) one extracts the good from those portions that were damaged and fell.[35]

We should not lose sight of the significance of this idea for the subsequent development of Judaism. Not only the Kabbalists, but generations of later Chasidim have lived their lives according to this theory: that the divinely appointed mission of each individual is to raise those sparks that reside within his own soul and that come his or her way in the course of a lifetime. It is in this manner that the individual is able to turn darkness into light, the bitter into the sweet, and take part in *Tikkun ha-Olam*, the restoration of the world.[36]

The Chasidim developed the beautiful doctrine that the people and objects one encounters in the course of a lifetime are presented precisely in order that one can liberate the spiritual energy within them and, in so doing, also liberate the sparks within one's own soul. There is thus a spiritually intimate, redemptive relationship between individuals, their possessions and all things they encounter. For this reason, one should take care to respect the events and experiences in one's life as divinely selected and ordained for one's own destiny and *Tikkun.* When an object changes hands it means that there are no longer any sparks within it that are sympathetic to its original owner.[37] When a person is inexplicably moved to travel to a distant corner of the world, it is because there are soul sparks in that place that only that individual can redeem.[38] Even today the Chasidim hold that their "rebbe" is capable of peering into the soul of each of his followers in order to advise them to undertake a marriage, job, or journey that is uniquely suited to the individual Chasid's mission in life, and which places the Chasid in contact with those aspects of the world that are sympathetic to his own soul-root.

The Kabbalistic symbol of the Raising of the Sparks is thus one that is of considerable interest to a psychology that seeks to uncover the relationship between the human psyche and the natural world. Jung's notion of "synchronicity," for example, according to which worldly events correspond to events in an individual's psyche, is very close to the Kabbalist's theories of the sparks and soul-roots. The psyche, for both the Chasidim and Jung, does not stand outside of, or opposed to, the natural world, but is rather intimately connected with it. As we have seen, Jung applauded the Kabbalistic view that psychological redemption involves a simultaneous turning inward and outward and prompts the individual to become a partner in the world's completion and perfection.[39]

Archetypes, *Adam Kadmon*, Mercurius, and the Sparks

As we have seen, throughout both *Psychology and Alchemy* and *Mysterium Coniunctionis* Jung variously equates *Adam Kadmon*, the *scintillae*, Mercurius, and the philosopher's stone with the archetypes of the collective unconscious. At other times, Jung equates various of these archetypes with the sefirotic "tree,"[40] and equates the individual *Sefirot* with specific archetypes e.g., *Yesod* with sexuality, and *Malchut* with the anima or underlying feminine principle.

A detailed discussion and evaluation of Jung's notion of the archetypes is beyond the scope of this study. Nevertheless, certain essentials must be addressed if we are to make full sense of Jung's interest in and interpretation of the Kabbalah.

The concept of "archetype" is never clearly and unequivocally defined in Jung. As "the contents of the collective unconscious," archetypes cannot, by definition, ever be completely known and circumscribed. According to Jung, an archetype is itself an "irrepresentable model" that can, at times, however, be represented in consciousness by "archetypal ideas."[41] These ideas are indeterminate in number, yet certain basic archetypes play a recurrent and profound role in both the history of humankind and in individual human development. Amongst these are the archetypes of the *anima* (feminine principle) and *animus* (masculine principle), the *persona* (the presentation of one's personality to self and others), the shadow (the unconscious converse of the persona, which balances or compensates for it), the *self* (the center of the psyche which encompasses both ego and shadow, and the psychic equivalent of God), the *Senex* (the old man), *Puer* (the young man), the Mother, the Father, the Hero, the Trickster, etc. Jungian psychology is in part an elaboration of the various archetypes as they are expressed in folklore and myth and as they appear in dreams and other fantasy productions of analytic patients. According to Jung, there are important archetypal ideas corresponding to the phenomena of human society (King, Queen, Fool, etc.), and also of nature. He relates:

> The mythological processes of nature, such as summer and winter, the phases of the moon, the rainy seasons, and so forth, are in no sense allegories of these objective occurrences, rather they are symbolic expressions of the inner, unconscious drama which becomes accessible to man's consciousness by means of projection—that is, mirrored in the events of nature.[42]

While there is an archetype corresponding to every significant event in the natural order, such archetypes are not merely the ideas (denotations) of such events, but rather contain the full panoply of (largely unconscious) associations and meanings (what Jung calls "projections") that humanity as a whole experiences in relation to them. Such generic associations or projections are what make the archetypes the content of the *collective* unconscious; *personal* associations, on the other hand, are what Jung calls the Freudian or *personal* unconscious. Because an archetypal idea is always experienced and expressed by individuals, "it takes its colour from the individual consciousness in which it happens to appear."[43]

Archetypes are, according to Jung, related closely to the Platonic ideas. In one place, he calls the archetypes "an explanatory paraphrase of the Platonic *eidos*."[44] In *Mysterium Coniunctionis*, he states that:

> within the limits of psychic experience, the collective unconscious takes the place of the Platonic realm of eternal ideas. Instead of these models giving form to created things, the collective unconscious, through its archetypes, provides the *a priori* condition for the assignment of meaning.[45]

The Jungian concept of "archetypes" shifts the whole discussion of ideas from the realm of *being* (as it was in Plato) to the realm of *meaning* and *significance* (which is more amenable to psychology). Archetypes are, in effect, the "human significances" of the things in the world. But because these significances are largely transpersonal and unconscious, they are frequently understood by humanity as elements of a "higher world." According to Jung:

This higher world has an impersonal character and consists on the one hand of all those traditional, intellectual, and moral values which educate and cultivate the individual, and, on the other, of the products of the unconscious, which present themselves to consciousness as archetypal ideas.[46]

Interestingly, Jung holds that Freud correctly recognized the "traditional values," calling them the superego, but because "the belief in reason and the positivism of the nineteenth century never relaxed their hold [on him]" he remained unaware of the archetypal ideas.[47]

Jung claims that the existence of archetypes is an empirical discovery rather than a metaphysical speculation or invention, and that they are "symptoms of the uniformity of *Homo Sapiens*."[48] They proceed from the structure and function of the human brain, which, in Jung's view, will in principle produce the same forms of thought in humans the world over. He views the production of certain myths and ideas (for example, Primordial Man, the theory of the sparks) in various times and cultures as evidence for the spontaneous production of ideas from an archetypal foundation.[49] Another piece of evidence for the uniformity of the collective unconscious is the appearance of universal archetypal symbols in insanity and in dreams.[50]

This is not the place to enter into the debate on the existence or nature of the collective unconscious as conceived by Jung. My own view of the archetypes is more phenomenological than biological. I do not believe, for instance, that the archetypes and collective unconscious must be hardwired into the brain as a result of heredity. An equally plausible view is that they are symbolic forms that arise spontaneously, simply as a result of our psychic interaction with the world, and have a universal existence because such interaction has certain invariants dictated by the human condition. No one need point to a special psychic apparatus or brain process to account for the fact that human beings spontaneously experience common meanings and significances (the archetypes) throughout the world and across time.

The question that concerns us here, however, is not the origin of the archetypes themselves but rather their purported equivalence to such Kabbalistic notions as *Adam Kadmon*, the *Sefirot*, and the sparks. Having considered the nature of Jung's archetypes in general, we are now in a position to explore the meaning of these alleged equivalencies.

The Kabbalistic symbols of the infinite divine light (*Or Ein-sof*) and the *Sefirot*, which are themselves comprised of this light, can perhaps best be understood as representing consciousness, significance, and value. Indeed, many of the names of the *Sefirot*—*Ratzon* (Will), *Chochmah* (Wisdom), *Chesed* (Loving-kindness), and *Din* (Judgment)—suggest basic meanings or *values* in human experience. These values, however, are organized into a system of "higher worlds" and set in the context of a dynamic in which, as we have seen, most of them are broken apart and encapsulated, falling into a nether realm, the *Sitra Achra*, which is analogous to the unconscious. As such, the *Sefirot* come very close to the Jungian concept of the archetypes as unconscious sources of value and meaning. Further, the *Sefirot* are then restored, partially as a result of the efforts of mankind, into five basic *Partzufim*: *Attika Kaddisha* (the Holy Ancient One), *Abba* (father), *Imma* (mother), *Zeir Anpin* (the short-faced one), and *Nukvah* (the female). As we have seen, the *Partzufim* correspond almost precisely to the Jungian archetypes of the *Senex*, Father, Mother, *Puer*, and *anima*, the *Sitra Achra* itself corresponding to the Jungian Shadow.

The Kabbalistic idea that *Adam Kadmon* (Primordial Human) spontaneously emanates and fully contains the light of the ten *Sefirot, Partzufim*, and worlds, provides a parallel to the idea of that the arche types arise spontaneously within are contained within humanity as symbols of the human condition. Indeed, as I will detail in Chapter 9, various phases in the Lurianic dynamic, e.g., the original divine contraction (*Tzimtzum*) and the Breaking of the Vessels (*Shevirat ha-Kelim*), correspond to archetypal patterns in human relationships and experience.[51] In short, Jung has sufficient warrant to regard the archetypes as very similar to and in some ways illuminative of the Kabbalistic symbols of *Adam Kadmon*, the *Sefirot*, higher worlds, Partzufim, etc. He also, I believe, has warrant for regarding the sparks (*netzotzim*) as buried unconscious meanings or archetypes that can erupt into consciousness with powerful effect; for, as we have seen, according to the Kabbalists these sparks are complexes of divine light that are entrapped in the nether realm of the "Other Side" and that must be released in order to repair the personality of both God and humanity.

I will not dwell any longer on Jung's own consideration of specific Kabbalistic (and related) symbols.[52] Our discussion has, I believe, been sufficient to demonstrate not only that Jung engaged in a vital dialogue with the ideas of the Kabbalah, but also that his interpretation of the metaphors of alchemy was conducted on a model that was very close to that of the Kabbalists, particularly the author(s) of the Zohar and Isaac Luria. Jung's psychological interpretation of Kabbalistic and alchemical ideas was anticipated by the Kabbalists themselves, who adhered to the principle that the microcosm (humanity) mirrored the macrocosm (God and the world). I think it is fair to say that a Jungian approach to the corpus of Kabbalistic symbols can yield further insights that are not only psychological, but that might well be deemed "Kabbalistic." Jung himself never undertook such a systematic exploration of the Kabbalah, in part because he did not have a wide enough range of Kabbalistic writings and ideas available to him, and in part because he understood himself as utilizing the Kabbalah largely as a tool to gain insight into alchemy, and rarely focused upon the Kabbalah *per se*. It is incumbent upon others, more familiar with the Kabbalistic corpus, to provide a contemporary psychological interpretation of a system of thought that purports to not only unlock the secrets of the Godhead, but to provide considerable insight into the nature of humanity as well. A preliminary step in this direction will be our task in the next chapter.

Chapter 9

Kabbalah and the Development of the Psyche

Jung held that the religious symbols of God, the heavens, cosmic happenings, and higher worlds could be empirically understood as projections of the archetypes of the collective unconscious—as reflections of the deepest, most universal structures of the human mind.[1] This is the simple basis of Jung's interpretation of Gnosticism and alchemy, and it is a major thesis of this book that this same approach can provide useful insights into Jewish mystical symbols and ideas. For reasons that I will detail in the final chapter of this study, I do not subscribe to the view that a psychological interpretation is the only reasonable and valuable interpretation of religious, particularly Kabbalistic, symbols. However, in this chapter, I will examine the Lurianic Kabbalah from a purely psychological perspective.

Psychological Hermeneutics in the Kabbalah and Chasidism[2]

My plan in this chapter is to view the Lurianic system as a whole as a metaphor for the development of the human psyche. Surprisingly, a similar psychological perspective is to be found among the Kabbalists and Chasidim themselves, who, far from being antagonistic to any "psychologization" of the divinity, held that the human mind is a mirror and, in some respects, the very origin of the theosophical realm.[3] While the validity of Jungian hermeneutics certainly does not rest upon the presence of Jungian principles of interpretation in the very texts to which this hermeneutic is to be applied, it will nevertheless be instructive to briefly examine the Kabbalistic and Chasidic sources which appear to provide an imprimatur for Jung's project.

One of the earliest of the *theosophical* Kabbalists, Azriel of Gerona (early thirteenth century), held that the energy of the human soul derives from the heavenly *Sefirot*, the archetypes through which God expresses himself in creation, and he equated each *Sefirah* with a psychological power or physical organ in man.[4] Moshe Idel has shown how the *ecstatic* Kabbalah, with its focus on the *experience* of the initiate, regarded the *Sefirot* themselves as human spiritual and psychic processes.[5] For example, Abraham Abulafia (1240–91) understood the names of the ten *Sefirot* (Thought, Wisdom,

DOI: 10.4324/9781003027041-10

Understanding, Mercy, Fear, Beauty, Victory, Splendor, etc.) as referring to processes taking place in the mind and body of human beings, and thought it possible for individuals to cleave to these attributes through proper meditation.[6] An even more radical viewpoint was advocated by R. Meir ibn Gabbay (1480–1540), who interpreted an ancient midrash to mean that God's anthropomorphic structure was itself copied from a human original![7]

According to Idel, the psychological understanding of the Kabbalah was eclipsed with the advent of Lurianism, with its emphasis upon the theosophical structure of the Godhead and divine worlds. However, even in the writings of the most thoroughgoing Lurianic Kabbalist, Chayyim Vital (1542–1620), we find the doctrine that the *Sefirot* are mirrored in the human body and soul.[8]

The notion that the divine macrocosm is mirrored in the human mind and body is provided new life in the Chasidic movement, whose founders, as we have seen, humanized and "psychologized" the Lurianic Kabbalah for their disciples. Rabbi Jacob Joseph of Polonnoye (1704–94) stated in the name of the Baal Shem Tov (1700–60), the founder of Chasidism, that the ten *Sefirot* appear in humanity as a result of a divine contraction, whereby the deity progressively instantiates himself in a series of personal structures until, upon reaching humanity, he (and humanity itself) is called Microcosmos (*Olam Katan*).[9] Rabbi Levi Yitzchak of Berdichov (1740–1809) held that "Man is a counterpart of the Attributes on high," and he provided a one-to-one correspondence between these attributes and the parts of the human body.[10] Similarly, Rabbi Yehoshua Heschel, the "Apter Rebbe" (1745–1825), held that "Man is a microcosm, a miniature universe, and his body therefore constitutes a complete structure."[11]

According to the Apter Rebbe, all universes, both spiritual and physical, have a similar configuration. Entire universes parallel the various parts of the human body. Some universes correspond to the head, others to the brain, nose, eyes, ears, hands, feet, and various other parts of the human anatomy. Further, each of these universes contains thousands upon thousands of worlds.[12]

Rabbi Dov Baer, the Maggid of Mesiritz (1704–72), who succeeded the Baal Shem Tov as the leader of the early Chasidic movement, taught that "everything written in [Vital's] *Sefer Etz Chayyim* [the major exposition of the Lurianic Kabbalah] also exists in the world and in man."[13] The Maggid went so far as to hold that the very significance of divine thought is contingent upon this thought making its appearance in the mind of man, a viewpoint that is surprisingly premonitory of Jung, who himself was later to state that his entire psychology was anticipated by this Chasidic sage.[14] According to the Maggid, the *Tzimtzum*, the act of contraction/concealment through which God created the world, condenses divine thought into the human intellect, and it is through this process that God's thought becomes actual and real. The Godhead itself is the foundation and source of thought, but actual thinking can only occur within the framework of the human mind.[15]

Thus, for the Maggid, the psychologization process is one that is necessary for the completion and fulfillment of God himself. For the Jewish mystics, there is a reciprocal relationship between the psyches of God and man. God is the ultimate source of the human attributes of thought and emotion, but the human psyche is the realization of what is only potentiality within God. Like Jung, who was to expound this view two centuries later with respect to the collective and personal unconscious, the Maggid held that the Godhead has a hidden life within the human mind.[16]

Archetypal Interpretation of the Lurianic Kabbalah

The very openness of the Kabbalists and Chasidim to a psychological interpretation of their own symbols facilitates a contemporary psychological interpretation of the theosophical Kabbalah. My discussion in this chapter is meant to be suggestive rather than complete and draws upon ideas that are not necessarily limited to Jungian thought. My purpose is simply to show that a psychological interpretation of the theosophical Kabbalah is possible and worthwhile,[17] not that the Kabbalistic symbols are reducible to psychology or that a theological interpretation of their symbols is to be discarded in favor of a "psychological" one.

At this point it may be helpful for the reader to recall the description of the Lurianic system that was presented in Chapter 1. Table 9.1, below, provides an outline of this system and the psychological (archetypal) interpretation, which will then be described in more detail in the pages to follow. In each phase, a theosophical event is understood as a psychological occurrence in the development of the human psyche. The table can either be read horizontally (as a series of interpretive statements) or vertically (as two parallel narrative structures).

I will now discuss the archetypal interpretation of the Lurianic Kabbalah in greater detail.

(1) *Ein-sof* (the infinite), of which nothing can be known or said, represents the primal unconscious, which is neither known nor can be known to consciousness.

The Kabbalists referred to *Ein-sof* as "the concealment of secrecy," "the concealed light," "that which thought cannot contain," etc.,[18] each of these appellations implying that *Ein-sof* is somehow beyond human knowledge and comprehension. However, there are other terms, e.g., "Root of all roots," "Indifferent Unity," "Great Reality,"[19] which imply that the Kabbalist's Infinite God is the foundation of all experience and being. Yet in spite of the positive connotations, even these terms are interpreted so as to refer to a God who is completely unknowable and concealed. According to Azriel of Gerona, *Ein-sof* is that which cannot be made a part of linguistic discourse:

Table 9.1 The Lurianic System and its Archetypal Interpretation

The Lurianic System	Archetypal Interpretation
(1) Ein-sof (The infinite Godhead), which is unknowable in and of itself,	(1) The Primal Unconscious, which is neither known nor can be known to consciousness,
(2) is the union of being and nothingness, of "everything and its opposite," male and female, good and evil, etc.	(2) is the union of everything and its opposite, of male and female, good and evil, etc.
(3) Ein-sof performs a divine conceal- ment, contraction (Tzimtzum), lead- ing to a...	(3) The primal unconscious is con- cealed from awareness through a primal repression, yielding...
(4) Metaphysical Void (tehiru), a circle surrounded by Ein-sof on all sides.	(4) the boundless, chaotic unknown that lies at the heart of the human psyche.
(5) This void contains a residue (reshimu) of divine light, and into it is emanated the Light of the Infinite (Or Ein-sof), a thin line (kav) through which...	(5) Here there is the smallest element of awareness of the unconscious and through this awareness
(6) Adam Kadmon (Primordial Human) spontaneously emerges.	(6) a primal self emerges.
(7) Lights (orot) flashing and recoiling from Adam Kadmon's eyes, nose, mouth, and ears form vessels (Kelim) for containing further lights, thus creating the "World of Points."	(7) This primal self directs its libido onto the world, and from the interaction between the libido and the world, the original, unmodified structures of the ego emerge.
(8) These vessels comprise the Sefirot (Archetypes of Value and Being), which form the body of Adam Kadmon. The Sefirot are:	(8) These structures are the archetypal values and tendencies of humanity that are embodied within the self. These include:
(9) Keter (Crown, Will, Delight, the highest Sefirah) Chochmah (Intellect, Wisdom, Paternal), Binah (Understanding, Maternal), Chesed (Loving-Kindness), Din/Gevurah (Judgment, Power), Tiferet/Rachamim (Beauty, Compassion) Netzach (Glory), Hod (Splendor), Yesod (Foundation, the Phallus/ Masculine Principle), and Malchut/ Shekhinah (Kingship/Feminine principle).	(9) Will or Desire, the fundamental motivating force, Cognition, the fundamental struc- turing attribute, Understanding, an amalgam of will and intellect, Love, the fundamental expression of will and desire, Judgment, the fundamental cognitive distinction, and the will to power (the origin of aggression), Beauty/Compassion, the dialectical blending of love and judgment, and all the glorious and splendorous accomplishments of mankind. All of these attributes are funda- mentally expressed in the erotic union of male and female.

The Lurianic System	*Archetypal Interpretation*
(10) The Sefirot are themselves comprised of primordial letters. Indeed, the molecular components of the world are at once both value archetypes (the Sefirot) and linguistic elements (Otiyot Yesod, foundational letters).	(10) The psyche is itself structured like a language and indeed structured by language. Language is the very substance of the psyche and without language there would be no "mind," values, or ideas.
(11) The Sefirot are organized into Worlds (ha-Olamot): Adam Kadmon (A'K, identified with Ein-sof and Keter), Atziluth (Nearness, Emanation), Beriah (Creation), Yetzirah (Formation), and Assiyah (Making, the lowest world; includes our material earth).	(11) These structures and values are further organized into the various "realms of experience" that constitute each individual; some are nearly identical to the inner psyche, others remain close to the heart, and still others are increasingly removed from the inner self but constitute a public persona and the individual's relationship to a public, objective world.
(12) The weakness and disunity of the Sefirot leads to their shattering and displacement, known as...	(12) The values and psychic structures as they are originally constituted early in life become disunified and do not serve the individual's overall "self," leading to conflict and ultimately to...
(13) The Breaking of the Vessels (Shevirat ha-Kelim), which produces	(13) a crisis or shattering of the psyche, frequently occurring in mid-life, which produces
(14) a rupture in the conjugal flow between Masculine and Feminine aspects of God.	(14) a rupture both in the individual's erotic life and between the masculine and feminine aspects of the psyche.
(15) Shards from the broken vessels and Netzotzim (sparks of the divine light) fall and become entrapped in the "shells" or "husks" (Kellipot), which comprise "the Other Side" (Sitra Achra), a realm of darkness and evil.	(15) Aspects of the shattered psyche (personal and collective thoughts, values, feelings, impulses) coalesce as "complexes" that are repressed in a Shadow and personal unconscious, and are experienced as a source of psychological conflict.
(16) Not all of the divine light is entrapped in the husks. Some of it returns spontaneously to its source where it initiates a new start to creation.	(16) After the crisis, some libido becomes attached to the archetypes of the collective unconscious and helps serve to restore the shattered ego.
(17) The entire cosmos must now be restructured and restored. This involves Tikkun ha-Olam, the restoration of the world.	(17) A new self must emerge by restoring and restructuring the elements of the old ego, which has been shattered by crisis. This is the process of individuation.

The Lurianic System	Archetypal Interpretation
(18) Lights from the forehead of Adam Kadmon reconstitute the broken Sefirot/vessels as...	(18) The libidinal energy from the primal self, the "collective unconscious," serves to restore the shattered psyche by means of...
(19) Partzufim (Faces or Personalities of God). Among these "personalities" are:	(19) human images and archetypes around which a mature self can become individuated. Among these archetypes are
(20) Attika Kaddisha (The Holy Ancient One) Abba (The Father) Imma (The Mother) Zeir Anpin (The Impatient One) Nukvah (The Female).	(20) The Senex (Wise Old Man) The Father The Mother The Puer (Youth), The Hero The Female (Anima).
(21) The Partzufim engage in erotic unifications that must now be facilitated by the activities of humankind...	(21) Opposing aspects of the psyche, in particular animus and anima, the male and female archetypes, must be reunited in the newly formed self...
(22) which, via the "raising of the sparks," brings about	(22) which, by raising the personal and collective complexes into consciousness (making the unconscious conscious), brings about a
(23) a reunification of the masculine and feminine principles and other oppositions within God.	(23) reunification of masculine and feminine principles, and other oppositions within the psyche.
(24) In performing Tikkun, humanity actually influences and restores the upper worlds as well as earth.	(24) In analytic work, the individual can restore the deeper layers of his/her soul and even impact creatively upon the world's collective psyche as well.
(25) However, humanity cannot by its own efforts reclaim all the sparks that had been dispersed as a result of the Breaking of the Vessels.	(25) However, the unconscious is not completely accessible to man.

Ein-sof cannot be an object of thought, let alone of speech, even though there is an indication of it in everything, for there is nothing beyond it. Consequently, there is no letter, no name, no writing, and no word that can comprise it.[20]

The infinite is unknowable, according to Azriel, precisely because it is a plenum "without end," and hence there is no *meta* point of view from which it can be circumscribed and made into an object. Indeed, *Ein-sof* is even in this difficult epistemological position with regard to itself, and it is for this reason that the Zohar can imply that *Ein-sof* (except through the medium of creation) has no knowledge of itself.[21] The Zohar speaks of the "Supernal Will," the "Secret of All Secrets," and the "Primal Nothing," but denies that even these exalted ascriptions apply to *Ein-Sof* itself, instead attributing them to the highest *Sefirah* or emanation.[22]

The Zohar describes *Ein-sof* as:

> ...the limit of inquiry. For Wisdom was completed from *ayin* (nothing), which is no subject of inquiry, since it is too deeply hidden and recondite to be comprehended. From the point at which its light begins to extend it is the subject of inquiry, although it is still more recondite than anything beneath, and it is called the interrogative pronoun, "Who?" Hence "Who (*Mi*) created these," and also, "From the womb of Whom (*Mi*) came forth the ice"; as much as to say, that about which we can inquire but find no answer.[23]

According to Erich Neumann, the "original question about the origin of the world is at the same time the question about the origin of man, the origin of consciousness and of the ego."[24] As such, from a psychological point of view, *Ein-sof* can be regarded as the infinite plenum of the unconscious, the foundation and origin of a subject or self, which, by definition, is beyond the reach of human awareness. Jung suggests an equivalence between the infinite God and the human unconscious when he states, "We cannot tell whether God and the unconscious are two different entities. Both are border-line concepts for transcendental contents."[25] According to Jung, the "archetype of the self" cannot be empirically distinguished from the God-image. Jung holds the same negative view regarding knowledge of the self that the Kabbalists hold with respect to *Ein-sof*:

> There is little hope of our being able to reach even an approximate consciousness of the self, since however much we make conscious there will always exist an indeterminate and undeterminable amount of unconscious material which belongs to the totality of the self.[26]

In a letter to Hans Schmidt, 6 November 1915, Jung writes: "the core of the individual is a mystery of life, which dies when it is grasped...."[27] There is thus an aspect of the self that remains forever unknown and unknowable. What this is can neither be specified nor circumscribed. According to Jung, the infinite plenum of the unconscious is represented in Gnosticism by the Pleroma. In the Kabbalah it is symbolized by *Einsof*. The Zohar perhaps hints at a completely unknown *inner self* when it speaks of *Ein-sof* as:

...the mysterious Ancient One whose essence can be sought but not found....He is ever to be sought, though mysterious and unrevealable, since further we cannot enquire. That extremity of heaven is called *Mi* (Who?), but there is another lower extremity which is called *Mah* (What?). The difference between the two is this. The first is the real subject of enquiry, but after a man by means of enquiry and reflection has reached the utmost limit of knowledge, he stops at *Mah* (What?), as if to say, what knowest thou? What have thy searchings achieved? Everything is as baffling as at the beginning.[28]

The Zohar's description here, it would seem, is quite applicable to the human psyche.

(2) **The Coincidence of Opposites:** According to the Kabbalists, *Ein-sof* is the union of both *Yesh* (being) and *Ayin* (nothingness),[29] male and female, good and evil, as well as all other oppositions. As we have seen, for the thirteenth-century Kabbalist Azriel of Gerona, the Godhead not only unites being and "the nought"[30] but also the visible and invisible as well as faith and unbelief,[31] and its emanations are the "union of everything and its opposite."[32] The Lurianists, and the Chasidim who followed in their wake, referred to *Ein-sof* as *ha-achdut ha-shawah*, a unity or coincidence (coinciding) of opposites,[33] a notion to which Jung turned to in describing the nature of both God[34] and the human psyche. Both the Kabbalists and Jung held that the psyche (*anima mundi* or "world-soul") begins and ends as an indistinguishable unity of opposites, but must first traverse a middle phase in which it is differentiated into an array of innumerable and conflicting details. According to Kabbalistic and Chasidic teaching, it is the fundamental divine purpose that the world should be differentiated and revealed in each of its finite particulars and yet ultimately united in a single infinite source.[35] Moses de Leon, the presumed author of the Zohar, wrote, "Everything is a unique secret and a unique Light, which admits no separation of any kind,"[36] and as the Chabad Chasidic Rabbi Aaron ha-Levi puts it:

...the entire essence of the [divine] intention is to reveal His blessed equalization, in actuality, that is, that all of reality in all of its details, should be revealed and that nevertheless they will be united and joined together in their equivalence, that is, they will be revealed as separate entities and nevertheless they shall be united.[37]

The fullest expression of divinity requires the Godhead to enter into a circular dynamic in which it becomes finite and differentiated, only to have this finitude and particularity transcended in a unity that embodies all particulars. Psychologically speaking, an original unitary psyche must differentiate itself into all of the details, conflicts, and particularities of an individual life, only to seek and ultimately discover an essential unity that informs and reconciles all these details and contradictions in the service of a fully developed self. Kabbalistically, this is the process of *Tikkun ha-Olam*; psychologically, it is the process that Jung referred to as *individuation*, a process that, as we have seen, involves an openness to and reconciliation of the opposing principles (male/female, good/evil, shadow/persona) in the individual and collective psyche. According to the contemporary scholar Joseph Dan, in the Kabbalah this reconciliation goes so far as to include a coincidence of opposites between sense and nonsense, meaning and absurdity,[38] the very *coincidentia oppositorum* that Jung, in *The Red Book*, had declared constitutive of the supreme meaning.[39]

In (3) *Tzimtzum* (contraction/concealment), *Ein-sof* withdraws itself from itself, and it is this process of withdrawal that allows a cosmos and humanity to emerge.

The notion of *Tzimtzum*, the divine concealment/contraction at the heart of creation, is a unique contribution of the Lurianic Kabbalah. Jung does not comment upon *Tzimtzum* directly. However, he does comment upon words of St. Ambrose that are in some ways premonitory of this Lurianic idea:

> Luna is diminished that she may fill the elements....He emptied her that he might fill her, as he also emptied himself that he might fill all things.[40]

St. Ambrose intended this passage as a homily on Christ. However, the notion of the deity's movement from the level of the divine to the level of creation via an "emptying" is close to Luria's idea of creation as a contraction and withdrawal of the infinite God.

The doctrine of *Tzimtzum* (concealment, contraction) was invoked by the Lurianic Kabbalists to explain the transition from an infinite, all-encompassing God to the existence of a pluralistic world. If *Ein-sof* is indeed the *Infinite All*, it must, Luria reasoned, limit itself, to "make room" for something other than itself. In order to create a world with a measure of independence, *Ein-sof* must contract itself and, moreover, conceal an aspect of itself from itself. That which is concealed, that which for the moment *Ein-sof* does not know, becomes the created, finite world, sustained in its being by a "primal repression" in which God's infinite plenitude has, at least temporarily, been limited. In this view, the world is akin to a cinematic projection in which the detailed rendering of the objects and persons projected on the screen is possible only by virtue of a selective diminution of the full light of the projector, as that light is dimmed by and filtered through the celluloid film. For the Kabbalists, the finite world, in all of its infinite variation and complexity, is, in effect, an illusion created by ignorance, ignorance of the absolute unity and infinitude of the "light" that is the essence of all things, the infinite God.[41] Yet, paradoxically, it is this illusion of finitude, separation, and complexity that allows God to complete himself as the Infinite All; for it is only when God is differentiated into a boundless expanse of finite entities, which are then understood as participating in his unified essence, that God's full infinity is achieved. A presumed infinite deity that has evolved through "difference," and includes within itself all possible finite things, is more complete in its infinity than one that has not.

For the Kabbalists, the divine concealment results in a world that is simultaneously real and illusory. Indeed, the Kabbalah (like the Hindu *Vedanta*) regards the whole of creation as akin to a dream in the infinite mind of the Absolute.[42] In withdrawing itself from itself and (what amounts to the same thing) by concealing itself from its own reality, the infinite God creates an illusion of finitude and multiplicity that is our world, an illusion that is in many ways akin to a human dream. Paradoxically, this illusion is, for the Kabbalists, the very perfection and completion of the deity himself, for without humanity in a finite world, God would have no capacity to see or comprehend himself or to instantiate the values that are implicit in his infinite goodness.

In *The Red Book* Jung advanced the notion that the imagination of man is the "cure" and completion of God. Indeed, Jung convinces the God "Izdubar" that the one way he can be healed of his mortal illness is to accept that he is a fantasy in the mind of man. Paradoxically, as in the Lurianic Kabbalah, it is this fantasy/illusion that maintains God himself. Jung tells Izdubar, "I do not mean to say that you are not real at all, of course, but only as real as a fantasy."[43] Jung proceeds to say The tangible and apparent world is one reality, but fantasy is the other reality.[44] Thus, Jungs conception of fantasy, image and the objective *psyche* comports closely with the Lurianic understanding of the symbol/doctrine of *Tzimtzum*.

From a psychological perspective, *Tzimtzum* is the act of concealment or repression that is fundamental to the very nature of the human psyche. Indeed, it is only through concealment and its variants—i.e., denial, repression, symbolization, displacement, condensation, etc.— that a division is set up between the conscious and the unconscious mind and our personalities are born. It is an important tenet of Jungian theory that it is the unconscious mind that adds depth and flavor to life and that is essential to the formation of an individual's character. Just as God, according to the Kabbalists, creates a world through an act of concealment (if you will, a cosmic repression), humans reates their own characters and culture, through an earthly concealment: the personal and collective repressions of the psyche.

Psychologically, the boundless expanse of the unconscious mind must itself be differentiated if it is to be structured into the personality of an individual woman or man. The *Tzimtzum*, therefore, represents the first notion of limitation or distinction within the human mind: the first mental act, a primordial repression that sets up a distinction between the infinite unconscious and the ego or self.

Tzimtzum acquired further ethical and psychological significance for the Chasidim, who understood it as an injunction to refrain from unduly interfering in the life and action of others. Just as God withdraws from and limits his power over the world in order that humanity may develop in its freedom, each of us must similarly limit ourselves in our relationships with others, so that they can develop according to their own nature and will.[45]

This theme is taken up by the neo-Jungian James Hillman, who relates the symbol of *Tzimtzum* to the need for each of us to "get out of the way so that our families can breathe (and) so our dreams can stay close in the morning...[and for] the simple admission of ignorance."[46] Hillman speaks of a strong influence of this Kabbalistic symbol on what he takes to be the alchemical view of "the application of power as an artful encouraging and releasing of the powers innate in others, maximizing through discretion, rather than direction."[47] This notion is beautifully expressed in the Chasidic Rabbi Dov Baer's description of the human act of *Tzimtzum*:

> As in the case of the father who sees his son playing with nuts, and then due to his love plays with him, although for the father this seems a childish act of "smallness," nonetheless out of love for his son and so that he should receive pleasure from his son, he contracts his mind and remains in "smallness" so that the little one will be able to bear him.[48]

(4) *Tehiru*, the Primordial Space: With the Godhead's contraction and withdrawal there remains a metaphysical void (*tehiru*) that serves as the "space" for all finite nature whatsoever.

The initial distinction wrought by *Tzimtzum* is without a definite form: it is simply a psychic space that is separate from the plenum of the infinite unconscious. The Kabbalists referred to this space as the metaphysical void (*tehiru*) within which creation develops. Psychologically, this void represents an unconscious that is at least potentially knowable but that is still formless and undifferentiated. It is, as Jung says, "what comes after the door to the unconscious" is *opened*. Jung tells us this unconscious is:

> a boundless expanse full of unprecedented uncertainty with apparently no inside and no outside, no above and no below, no here and no there, no mine and no thine, no good and no bad.[49]

However, as the *Tzimtzum* proceeds, as the process of psychic differentiation coalesces, an initial unity is rent into opposites that form the foundation of the human personality: being and nonbeing, self and other, inside and outside, good and bad, knowledge and ignorance, fullness and emptiness, love and hate, etc., all emerge as a result of this primal concealment/repression. In *Tzimtzum* the infinite Godhead creates a world, and a dialectic is set up between the basic oppositions that define "reality." It is from this dialectic that the psyche emerges. Psychologically speaking, this is the unknown of the primal, chaotic, and boundless unconscious, which the ego rushes to fill with its own contents.

The "primordial space" can be understood as the *place* of fantasies and dreams. Indeed, in fantasy and dreams we each perform an act of *Tzimtzum* and, in effect, play God to worlds of our own creation. In dreaming, we perform an act of contraction whereby we withdraw or remove our cathexis from the world, creating a "dream space" in which a new (dream) world or reality emerges in the dream. This dream or fantasy "space" is the psychological equivalent to the Kabbalist's *tehiru*, or "void," which emerges as the result of the initial withdrawal of *Ein-sof*. Yet just as the world is said to complete God, our dreams can be said to complete ourselves, for it is only through our dreams and fantasies that we can achieve the full measure of our human potential and gain interpretive insight into who we are. Jung viewed the dream as the "guiding words of the soul,"[50] and as a portal into both "heaven" and the self, for in the dream we gain access to the archetypes that, according to Jung, are the psychological elements of both the self and the gods.

We can see a dialectic at work on both the theological and psychological levels, for in both instances we find that reality gives rise to illusions that are in turn productive of the very realities that brought them into being. The "illusion" of a finite world is theologically the perfection and completion of God, and the "illusion" of a world of fantasies and dreams is the ground and the depths of the *reality* of man. This is another example of the Kabbalistic (and Jungian) principle of *coincidentia oppositorum*, the principle that profound opposites complement and complete each other. It also illustrates the Kabbalistic (and Jungian) principle that the unknown (or unconscious) is not simply a contingent by-product of repression, but lies at the very core of the human psyche.

(5) *Reshimu*, the Divine Residue: The withdrawal and contraction of *Ein-sof* cannot be complete without defeating its own purpose. A "residue" (*reshimu*) of divine light remains in the *tehiru* even after the *Tzimtzum*. Moreover, a thin line, or *kav*, of divine light (*Or Ein-sof*) penetrates the void without transversing it.

This *kav* represents the element of awareness that extends even into the unconscious but fails to circumscribe it or even penetrate it completely. There is some awareness of the unconscious, otherwise we could neither speak of it nor experience spontaneous archetypal and symbolic ideas. Jung makes reference to the alchemical idea of a small globe that exists happily in the midst of chaos, which he interprets as the germ of unity that exists even in the unconscious.[51] We might say that this globe, like the *kav* and *reshimu* of the Kabbalists, represents an element of consciousness and ego in the midst of unconscious chaos. It is perhaps this element that prompts the Kabbalists to "speak the unspeakable" and dare to enter into descriptions of the ultimate nature of *Ein-sof* itself, for example, articulating that *Ein-sof* is the supernal thought, as in the following passage in the Zohar:

> What is within the Thought no one can conceive, much less can one know *Ein-sof*, of which no trace can be found and to which thought cannot reach by any means. But from the midst of the impenetrable mystery, from the first descent of the *Ein-sof* there glimmers a faint indiscernible light like the point of a needle, the hidden recess of thought, which even yet is not knowable until there extends from it a light in which there is some imprint of letters, and from which they all issue. First of all is *Aleph*, the beginning and end of all grades, that in which all grades are imprinted and which yet is always called "one," to show that although the Godhead contains many forms it is still only one....The top point of the *Aleph* symbolizes the hidden supernal thought.[52]

This passage is notable not only for its daring to penetrate the unknowable "Thought" (psychologically, the unconscious) but for its equation of this mystery with the "imprint of letters," i.e., language. The "line" that penetrates the unconscious is the imprint of writing, and the unconscious itself is revealed via language. For Jung, it is only through myth, poetry, literature, art, and analytic psychotherapy—in short, through linguistic metaphor and symbolic representation—that the unconscious becomes at least partially accessible. As we will see, the Kabbalists suggest that the revealed world, which emerges out of the depths of *Ein-sof*, is structured by the letters in the "holy tongue."

(6) *Adam Kadmon* (Primordial Human): The modicum of divine light that remains in the void forms the "body" of *Adam Kadmon*, the Primordial Human, who according to Luria is the first figure to emerge as a result of the *Tzimtzum*, and who embodies in potentia the entirety of all created worlds.

Jung, who himself explored the Kabbalistic notion of *Adam Kadmon*, held that this Primordial Human is the *archetype of humanity*, the primal undifferentiated unity of the collective unconscious and the *goal of humankind*. *Adam Kadmon* is the "universal soul,"[53] the archetype of the self[54] and the process of transformation. He is humankind's invisible center, the core of the great religions, and, as the self-archetype, the psychological equivalent of the creator God.[55]

From a psychological point of view, the spontaneous emergence of *Adam Kadmon* from the unknowable void is symbolic of the birth of the self. However, at this stage the "self" is far from complete. The Primordial Man must first embark on a journey of creation (*Sefirot*), destruction (*Shevirah*), and restoration (*Tikkun*) before the archetype of the self can fully emerge.

The Kabbalists reinterpreted the symbol of *Adam Kadmon* from an almost kaleidoscopic variety of points of view. For example, they alternately understood *Adam Kadmon* to be comprised of (1) a system of physical orifices (the ears, nose, mouth, eyes) and the relative coarseness of the air entering through them; (2) the *Sefirot* or value archetypes of the world; (3) the various levels of the human soul; (4) the *Partzufim*, divine faces or personalities; (5) a variety of metaphysical "worlds"; (6) letters in the Hebrew language; and (7) the various "names of God." These diverse descriptions of *Adam Kadmon*, which are tantamount to the various perspectives within Lurianic theosophy, can also be understood as a *phenomenology of the self*. It is easy to see how these symbols and aspects of *Adam Kadmon* can each be taken to represent differing aspects of the self, and the foundation for distinct psychological points of view. For example, the metaphor of bodily orifices and organs defines the self in terms of its physical being and sensual relations; the *Sefirot* metaphor defines the self through its values and ideas; in the metaphor of *Partzufim*, the self is defined through its "personas" or the multivalent nature of its developing character; the metaphor of "worlds" defines the self through the physical and psychical environments that it inhabits; "letters" define it through narrative and language; and the "names of God" through its connection with a higher spirituality. Indeed, it is doubtful whether an adequate theory of the self cannot but include each of these aspects, perhaps nested hierarchically, or perhaps, as in the Kabbalah, in a condition of reciprocal and mutual determination. With the emergence of *Adam Kadmon*, we have left the realm of the primordial unconscious and entered the realm of the developing conscious psyche.

(7) *Kelim* (Vessels) and *Orot* (Lights): Lights flashing and then recoiling from the ears, nostrils, mouth, and eyes of *Adam Kadmon* create the structures that become the *Sefirot*. Each light beams down and then returns, leaving a residue from which a vessel is formed. A second light beams down and then returns, leaving behind another residue that fills the vessel and thus completes the *Sefirah*. The lights from the eyes play a dominant role in this process.

Neumann has pointed out that the idea of creation as a manifestation of light is ubiquitous in the history of religions. For Neumann, "the coming of consciousness, manifesting itself as light in contrast to the darkness of the unconscious, is the real 'object' of creation mythology."[56] In psychological terms, the Lurianic image of lights emanating from *Adam Kadmon* is a mythical account of the formation of both the ego and its representation of the external world. We can interpret the Lurianic image as a reaching out beyond the self and a confrontation with that "beyond." The psychic energy from a "primal man" radiates outward and returns, resulting in the formation of psychic structures. As Freud understood it, *thought itself* results from the libido's confrontation with a partially hostile environment and the consequent modification of that libido as it recoils back on itself in response to that confrontation.

The recoil of the lights in *Adam Kadmon* does not simply occur in a void prior to creation but is rather an archetype for the interaction between the individual's libidinal energy, broadly conceived, and the environment. Indeed there is, psychoanalytically speaking, no conception of an *external world* until the individual creates one out of the failures of his or her desire. When desire fails, an object is set up in consciousness that becomes the representation of a future need. The sum total of such representations is the "external world."

It is significant that the lights from *Adam Kadmon* extend from each of his facial orifices, representing four of the five senses, underscoring the view that it is through the human's projection of interest and desire (through his senses) that his experience of a world is formed. Here, as with the *Tzimtzum*, we must not think of this process as an original, onetime event, but rather as ongoing throughout life.

(8) The *Sefirot* are dimensions of mind and value that structure the light emanating from the Primordial Human and interact with one another dynamically. As their names suggest, they reflect specific psychological states, processes, and values: will, thought, wisdom, knowledge, loving-kindness, judgment, beauty, compassion, etc.

The *Sefirot* can readily be understood as representing the structures of the ego and its variety of psychological functions—desire, cognition, love, the aesthetic sense, conflict resolution, sexuality, etc. In psychological terms, we might contrast these ego functions with the unknown realm of the unconscious represented by *Ein-sof*. But as we shall see, with the Breaking of the Vessels much of what was destined for the "ego" becomes, in the Kabbalistic scheme, unconscious as well.

(9) The Order of the *Sefirot*: The Kabbalists' ordering of the *Sefirot* suggests a hierarchy of archetypal values and tendencies that can apply both to the differentiation of the Godhead and to the human psyche. The highest of the *Sefirot*, the one closest to the infinite Godhead (and, by extension, to the primal unconscious) is *Keter* (Crown), variously identified by the Kabbalists with *Ratzon* (will, desire) or *Tinug* (delight). In Hebrew, the word *ratzon* is used in the commonest expressions of desire, suggesting that desire (sexual and otherwise) is the basic manifestation of the human psyche. One step removed from this "desire" is intellect (*Chochmah*). This ordering suggests that cognition only emerges as a superstructure built upon desire. The next *Sefirah, Binah* (understanding), is, according to the Kabbalists, a blending of the first two. As the origin of creativity, it is equated with *Imma*, the Celestial Mother. It is through *Binah* that the will, directed by the intellect, can first make its creative mark on a world.

The next three *Sefirot* represent a second triad that in effect repeats on a more concrete level the dialectic of the first three. *Chesed* (love) is, according to the Kabbalists, fundamentally an *expression* of desire, whereas *Din* (judgment) is an *expression* of intellect, for in judgment, distinctions that have been held in theory are actually made and implemented in *reality*. This implementation of distinctions is perhaps the reason why *Din* is sometimes referred to as *Gevurah* (strength or power), and serves as the foundation for the harsh, punitive judgments that the Jewish tradition identifies with evil. Love and Judgment are reconciled in the *Sefirah Tiferet/Rachamim* (Beauty/Compassion), which according to the Kabbalists serves as a paradigm for all further reconciliations, both within the Godhead and in man. The next two *Sefirot, Netzach* (Glory) and *Hod* (Splendor), can be interpreted as the *further* instantiation of humanity's desire and intellect in the "glorious" and "splendorous" mani festations of human individual and collective creativity and culture. These two *Sefirot* are reconciled by *Yesod* (foundation), which the Kabbalists equated with the phallus, and which in turn engages in a coupling with the final *Sefirah* (*Malchut/Shekhinah*), representing the feminine aspect of the psyche. Indeed, it is the erotic coupling of male and female, and particularly the masculine and feminine aspects of the psyche, that serves as the most prominent Kabbalistic metaphor for the completion of both God and creation. As we have seen, Jung's "alchemical" works explore this *coniunctio* theme as a symbol of the unification of the self.

The bisexuality of the deity and the conjugal relationship between man and woman are represented in each of the *Sefirot*. Each *Sefirah* is conceived bisexually, as male to the *Sefirah* below it and female to the *Sefirah* above it. In effect, the entire sefirotic scheme announces the idea that the basic dynamics of the cosmos reflect the erotic and romantic union of man and woman. For example, *Chochmah* is frequently equated with the Celestial Father (*Abba*), while *Binah* is understood as the Celestial Mother (*Imma*), and the lower *Sefirot* are spoken of as children formed in *Binah's* womb. The union of *Tiferet* with *Malchut* (*Shekhinah*) is said to give rise to the lower worlds. Here the understanding of the *Sefirot* in *sexual* terms subtly passes over into a symbolism of birth and human development, and ultimately into a symbolism of the family. The two pairs of *Sefirot* we have just discussed, *Chochmah* and *Binah* (the Celestial Father and Mother) and *Tiferet* and *Malchut* (Son and Daughter), play an important role in what can only be described as a *family romance*.

The Zohar describes how the Father, *Chochmah*, has a particular fondness for his daughter (*Shekhinah/Malchut*), which stirs the jealousy of *Binah*, the Celestial Mother:

> The father's continual desire is solely for the daughter, because she is the only daughter among six sons, and he has shared out portions, gifts and presents to the six sons, but to her he has appointed nothing, and she has no inheritance at all. But despite this he watches over her

with more love and longing than over anyone else. In his love he calls her "daughter"; this is not enough for him and he calls her "sister"; this is not enough for him, and he calls her "mother"...therefore, the supernal world [mother] says to her [to the daughter]: "Is it a small matter that you have taken away my husband? (Genesis 30:15) for all his love is centered on you."[57]

Conversely, the "mother" is said to favor the son over her husband,[58] thus completing a sort of cosmic Oedipal triangle—a vision of the world that from a psychological point of view can be understood as a projection of archetypal family dynamics onto the cosmos as a whole.

(10) The Primordial Language: According to the Kabbalists, the *Sefirot* (and hence, the whole of creation) are comprised of the twenty-two letters of the Hebrew alphabet, each of which bears its own unique meaning and significance. For the Kabbalists, everything in the world, includeing inanimate objects such as stones, water, and earth, has a soul or spiritual life-force, which is to be found in the letters of divine speech from which they and their names are comprised.[59] The soul (and by this the Kabbalists refer not only to the human psyche but the world-soul as well) is a structure of significance and meaning, and the key to understanding both humanity and the world is to be found in those hermeneutic dis-ciplines that apply the methods of textual interpretation. Psychologically, this doctrine presents us with a hermeneutic/linguistic theory of mind and self, one in which psychological understanding is akin to the interpretation of texts.

(11) *Ha-Olamot* **(Worlds):** The *Sefirot* are organized into a number of worlds, of which the Kabbalists highlighted five, from *Adam Kadmon*, the highest, to *Assiyah*, the lowest. Psychologically, these worlds can be said to represent the various psychical "environments" that each individual constitutes for him or herself, some of which are extremely subjective and nearly identical to the personal psyche, while others are more objective and link the individual to other people, the world, and ultimately to God. Jung suggests such a distinction between subjective and objective worlds when he writes:

There arises a consciousness which is no longer imprisoned in the petty, oversensitive, personal world of the ego, but participates freely in the wider world of objective interests. This widened consciousness is no longer that touchy, egotistical bundle of personal wishes, fears, hopes, and ambitions which always has to be compensated or corrected by unconscious countertendencies; instead, it is a function of relationship to the world of objects, bringing the individual into absolute, binding, and indissoluble communion with the world at large.[60]

(12) The Instability of the *Sefirot*: There is an inherent weakness and disunity in the *Sefirot* that results in their displacement and shattering. The *Sefirot* "closest" to the Primordial Human—i.e., *Keter, Chochmah,* and *Binah*—are comprised of the most powerful vessels, and they alone can withstand the impact of the lights emanating from the eyes of *Adam Kadmon,* and as such they are merely displaced. All of the other *Sefirot,* save the last, *Malchut* (which is broken only partially), are shattered by the divine emanations.

Psychologically speaking, we might say that the values and psychic structures as they are constituted from birth through the first half of life do not serve the individual well as he matures. The strongest aspects of the ego, those most resistant to psychological disintegration in the face of a surge of libidinous energy, are the basic structures of will, cognition, and understanding, as represented in the highest *Sefirot* in the Kabbalistic system. However, it is those aspects of the ego that bind, contain, and structure *emotion* (the seven lower *Sefirot,* which are in fact spoken of by the Kabbalists as "emotional") that are subject to a psychic shattering as a result of a surge of libidinal energy from the unconscious. Jung held that the intellectual and moral values keep the archetypal images of the unconscious in check until the former are "weakened by age or criticism."[61] As we have seen, such weakened structures are subject to being overwhelmed by a flood of unconscious material.

(13) *Shevirat ha-Kelim,* the Breaking of the Vessels: The seven lower *Sefirot* shatter. Even the highest *Sefirot,* which do not shatter, fall from a higher to a lower place. This is the *Shevirat ha-Kelim,* the Breaking of the Vessels.

The structures of the ego are insufficient for the individual to contain the energy and imagery of the unconscious. These structures must shatter, creating a chaotic, disjointed, and dangerous (but necessary) state from which a new self can eventually emerge. Will and intellect have fallen in status. Reason can no longer resolve all difficulties in its path. The ego has been deflated.

The contemporary neo-Jungian psychologist James Hillman provides a key to a psychological interpretation of the Breaking of the Vessels. According to Hillman, psychology universally understands psychopathology, and the consequent experience of "falling apart," as ills to be cured, or at most as phases leading to the reorganization of the self or ego.[62] Hillman, however, argues that such "falling apart" lies at the core of our very being and has an intimate connection with our uniqueness and individuality. The psyche, according to Hillman, does not exist at all without its own inner sense of "deconstruction." He cites Freud to the effect that we can only "catch" the unconscious in pathological material and argues that it is precisely through our major and minor life crises, through our confrontation with death, and in our uncanny sense of "crazy" differentness, that we glimpse the unconscious chaos that is at the root of our psychic selves. As Jung observed in *The Red Book*:

...if you enter into the world of the soul, you are like a madman, and a doctor would consider you to be sick.[63]

...we do not love the condition of our being brought low, although or rather precisely because only there do we attain clear knowledge of ourselves.[64]

We need the coldness of death to see clearly...[65]

I experience the God in sickness. A living God afflicts our reason like a sickness.[66]

According to Hillman, the soul produces crazed patterns of sickness, perversion, and degeneration in dreams and behavior, and in art, thought, politics, religion, and war, because pathologizing is a basic archetype of the soul, a fundamental psychic activity *per se*. Indeed, from a certain perspective, the seemingly uncontrollable fragmentation embodied in the Lurianic notion of the Breaking of the Vessels, and expressed in what is to some a perverse proliferation of fragmentary images in the Kabbalistic sources, is an example of the soul's pathologizing. Hillman's dictum that such activity must be respected and understood echoes the Zohar's maxim that man must give his due to the "Other Side." According to Hillman, the multiplicity of mythical images (embodied in Greek mythology and such systems of thought as Gnosticism and the Kabbalah) "provides archetypal containers for differentiating our fragmentation."[67] Hillman points to the Greek myths of Bellerophon falling from his white crazed horse, Icarus falling into the sea after flying too close to the sun, and Phaeton's sun chariot hurtling into flames. These myths provide graphic analogs to the Kabbalists' Breaking of the Vessels, as each of them expresses the sense of humanity that is, paradoxically, to be gained through the shattering of the ego and the consequent fall from the "heavens." Kabbalistically, it is only when the "vessels break" that individuals can become truly human.[68]

(14) The Separation of Male and Female: With the Breaking of the Vessels, unities within the *Sefirotic* system—such as the union between *Chochmah* and *Binah* (wisdom and understanding, father and mother)—that had once been stable are now broken. The Celestial Father turns his back on the Mother and vice versa. The harmony of the *Sefirot* is destroyed.

With the shattering of the ego caused by an overwhelming upsurge of unconscious material, the individual experiences himself or herself as disjointed and conflicted. In particular, there is a separation and conflict between his masculine (ego-oriented) *animus* and his feminine (soul and unconscious oriented) *anima*, a rift that calls out to be healed. Further, there is a division between self and other.

In some instances, the shattering of the ego is so violent as to cause a "nervous breakdown"; in others, only a neurotic conflict or personal (e.g., "mid-life") crisis. However, such shattering provides an opportunity for both a deepening of the individual's humanity and his psychological restoration.

(15) *Netzotzim* (Sparks), *Kellipot* (Husks), and *Sitra Achra* (the "Other Side"): Shards from the shattered vessels tumble through the metaphysical void, entrapping some of the sparks (*netzotzim*) of light that the vessels were meant to contain. These shards, together with their entrapped light, form the *Kellipot* (husks), and fall into a netherworld known as the *Sitra Achra* (the Other Side), which in psychological terms can be described as the personal unconscious or the individual's "shadow."

A secondary repression occurs in which elements of the ego and energy from the primal unconscious that had originally been in the ego's service are shattered and repressed, forming neurotic complexes that inhibit the individual's ability to obtain pleasure, integrate his or her personality, and achieve life goals. As each individual contains within his or her soul unique sparks and is responsible for raising them, we witness the development of a personal (repressed) unconscious to complement the collective unconscious that one participates in simply by virtue of being human.

As we have seen, the image of the fallen sparks evolved into the Kabbalistic/Chasidic doctrine that the individual is responsible for redeeming sparks of spiritual energy in each of his or her encounters with self, others, and the world, thus providing the foundation for a Kabbalistic (and in contemporary terms, a psychoanalytic) ethic. It is not only the individual's task to bring to light those complexes that have become unconscious within his or her own psyche, but also those aspects within others and the environment that have, as a result of the Breaking of the Vessels, become repressed or obscured. Like James Hillman, the Kabbalists saw the entire world in psychological terms. All things, for the Kabbalah, are repressed, alienated, and unconscious, and must be liberated and brought to full consciousness through the emotional, intellectual, and spiritual activities of humankind. Not only the psychotherapist, but the physicist, the engineer, the artist, and the poet engage in making the unconscious conscious. They do this by liberating the wisdom, knowledge, beauty, etc. (indeed, each of the values represented by the *Sefirot*) that lay hidden in all things.

(16) Return of the Lights: Not all of the divine light (*Or Ein-sof*) is entrapped in the *Kellipot*. Some lights return spontaneously to their source.

These lights can be said to represent elements of the primal unconscious that are experienced as archetypal ideas and can be put to the service of healing the shattered psyche. These are the same archetypal ideas that—when they are overwhelming even to the intact *Sefirot*, from *Keter* to *Binah*—can be experienced as the disjointed imagery and ideas of psychosis. However, if they are reintegrated into aspects of a functioning "self" they become the foundation for creativity and profound personal change. The lights (archetypes) thus have the power both to heal and disrupt the psyche.

(17) *Tikkun ha-Olam,* **the Restoration of the World:** The whole *Sefirotic* realm must now be reconstituted and restored via *Tikkun haOlam* (the repair and restoration of the world). The restored cosmos, however, will differ considerably from the *Sefirot* as they were originally emanated.

The restored self is an achievement that transcends the biologically and environmentally determined development of the ego in childhood. When the structures and values that served the nascent ego are shattered by personal crisis—e.g., in adolescence or mid-life—the relations between the primal unconscious, the ego, and the personal unconscious must be restructured into a more unified, flexible (and hence more livable) arrangement. According to Jung, the archetype of the self emerges after mid-life to perform this formidable task. Unlike the ego, the self is not a bastion of consciousness, which, like a rider on a horse, limits and controls the forces of the unconscious psyche. Jung observes, "If one has done one's best to steer the chariot, and then notices that a greater other is actually steering it, then magical operation takes place."[69] Just as the Kabbalist's restored cosmos involves an integration rather than separation of its various levels, the Jungian self involves an integration between "conscious," "pre-conscious," and "unconscious"; between "superego," "ego," and "id," and even madness and reason.[70] The self manages its desire through wisdom rather than repression and control, for its desire is already integrated with the higher elements of the soul. In Kabbalistic terms, the psyche after *Tikkun* is one in which each of the *Sefirot* are fully integrated with each of the others. *Chesed,* for example, which originally represented unbridled beneficence or Love, is now comprised of and realizes within itself aspects of Wisdom, Understanding, Judgment, Beauty, etc.

(18) The Lights of *Tikkun:Tikkun* is brought about by means of lights streaming from the forehead of *Adam Kadmon.*

While the original development of the ego proceeded through the bodily senses (the ears, nose, mouth, and eyes), the restoration proceeds from the mind (aptly represented by the forehead), the storehouse of archetypal images and ideas.

(19) *Partzufim* **(Divine Personalities):** The lights are reordered and reconstituted as *Partzufim*—visages, configurations, personalities. Each *Partzuf* is a combination of all ten *Sefirot* and is thus stronger than the original *Sefirot* were in and of themselves. The lights from the forehead meet the broken vessels and the entrapped sparks that vivify them. Many of these sparks are freed, rising to join the reconstituted *Partzufim*. However, this spontaneous restoration is incomplete. The *Partzufim* require further assistance before there can be true harmony in the cosmic realm. This assistance must come from humanity.

As a first step in the restoration of the self, the energy of the psyche must be ordered into integrated self-images or personas that are better able to withstand and contain the upsurge of energy from the unconscious mind. A second step involves the freeing of libidinous energy from the neurotic complexes of the personal unconscious, which bind that energy and render it inoperative for the individual. Much of this occurs spontaneously, but it cannot be completed without an active effort on the part of the individual.

(20) Order of the *Partzufim*: The *Partzufim* are understood as partial personalities of the deity. As we have seen, the main *Partzufim* are:

Attika Kaddisha (The Holy Ancient One) or Arikh Anpin
1 (The Long-suffering One)
2 Abba (The Father)
3 Imma (The Mother)
4 Zeir Anpin (The Impatient One) or Ben (The Son)
5 Nukvah (The Female) or Bot (The Daughter)

The restored self is constellated around a series of archetypal images, each of which represents a different aspect of the individual's personality, and each of which can come to dominate the individual at any given time. Jung makes reference to a variety of alchemical and early Christian sources that suggest that man in his unredeemed state is multiple. For example, we read in Origen:

> "There was one man." We, who are still sinners cannot obtain this title of praise, for each of us is not one but many...see how he who thinks himself one is not one, but seems to have as many personalities as he has moods.[71]

The Kabbalists affirm that a form of multiplicity is a stage in the process of personal and psychological redemption. The archetypal images that constitute the self are many, and we cannot and should not strive for a premature integration. The entire Kabbalah affirms the unity of God (and hence the self) but only in the context of a "one in many" view of the divine persona. Jung himself held that our own era is dominated by a monolithic and therefore ultimately godless view of the self:

> ...our time has become so utterly godless and profane: we lack all knowledge of the unconscious psyche and pursue the cult of consciousness to the exclusion of all else. Our true religion is a monotheism of consciousness, a possession by it, coupled with a fanatical denial of the existence of fragmentary autonomous systems.[72]

As Thomas Moore has put it: "The psyche is not only multiple, it is a communion of many persons, each with specific needs, fears, longings, style and language. The many persons echo the many gods who define the worlds that underlie what appears to be a unified human being."[73]

The *Partzufim* correspond to basic archetypes within Jungian psychology, archetypes that, according to Jung, express essential organizing principles of the human personality. *Attika Kaddisha* (the Holy Ancient One) corresponds to the Jungian *Senex* (the old man: wise, conservative, reasonable, beneficent); *Abba*, to the archetypal father; *Imma*, to the mother; *Zeir Anpin* to the *Puer* (emotional, romantic, impulsive); and *Nukvah* to the *anima* (the feminine, seductive, soulful side of the individual). Each of these archetypes has its place in the unity that constitutes the overarching archetype of the Jungian self (*Adam Kadmon*, or God).

(21) Erotic Unifications: The *Partzufim* engage in certain regular relationships or unifications. *Abba* and *Imma* are unified in an enduring relationship of mutual friendship and support; *Zeir Anpin* and *Nukvah* are unified in a passionate romance, which brings them alternately together and apart. The lower *Partzufim* (and *Sefirot*) are "born" in the womb of *Imma*, the Mother.

Humanity's spiritual task is to help raise the sparks of divine light that had been entrapped by the husks of the Other Side, thereby liberating divine energy for the service of erotic unions among the various *Partzufim*; not only between the "Mother" and "Father," but between the Son and the Daughter and even between the "Old Holy Man" (*Attika Kaddisha*) and his mate. In raising these sparks, humankind is said to provide the "feminine waters" for renewed divine activity. As we saw in Chapter 7, Jung learned from the Kabbalah that humankind "is the *nymphagogos* of the heavenly marriage."[74]

The psyche itself must be unified through a coincidence of opposites, especially between its masculine and feminine elements. These inner unifications are reciprocally modeled from, and model, the significant relationships of human life in such a manner that the inner dynamics of the human psyche reflect the structure and vicissitudes of interpersonal existence. Eros plays a critical role in the psyche's personal and interpersonal development. Even in the depths of the individual psyche, man is essentially a social, interpersonal being. The deeper one probes into one's self, the surer one finds a representation of the "other." The formation of a self is hardly a solitary enterprise but is, as the Kabbalists imply, conditioned upon relationships of passion, friendship, and mutual support. The individual, like God himself, cannot hope to be complete outside of such relationships. It is for this reason that the Zohar can say "'Man' implies the union of male and female, without which the name 'man' is not applied."[75]

(22) The Raising of the Sparks: The Lurianic notion of "raising the sparks" is psychologically equivalent to the psychotherapeutic process of making the unconscious conscious, or perhaps better put, of bringing one's alienated and isolated complexes into conjunction and harmony with the self. Another related Lurianic metaphor, the "extraction" (*birur*) and liberation of entrapped divine light from the dark shells of the "Other Side," is also, as we have seen, an important precursor to the psychotherapeutic endeavor, but extends the psychotherapeutic ethic beyond the individual to the world as a whole.

(23) The Reunification of Male and Female: The raising of the sparks has the effect of not only reunifying masculine and feminine aspects of the divine (and human) psyche but of harmonizing all other contradictions within the psyche as well. As we have seen, for Jung such unification is the most important psychotherapeutic principle. The fully individuated self is one that, having seen the multiplicity, disharmony, and conflict of an actual lived existence, comes to experience a harmony behind all of its manifold expressions and appearances.

(24) Theurgy: In performing *Tikkun* on earth, humanity actually influences and restores the realms on high.

The Kabbalists provided a number of metaphors for the influence that humanity has upon the spiritual realms. According to the Kabbalist R. Meir ibn Gabbay, the deity is like a shadow of the human hand, which is forced to precisely reflect the changes in that hand's activity.[76] Ibn Gabbay introduces a second image, that of "acoustical resonance," in which the note of one violin (humanity) causes a second violin (God) to resonate in kind.[77] Theurgic influence can be for either good or ill. According to one anonymous Kabbalist, since "man is composed of all the spiritual entities...one who kills a man diminishes the form of the *Sefirot*."[78]

As we have seen, the Lurianists held that human activity can impact upon divine eros in a manner that is critical for the restoration of all the worlds. For example, according to Vital, the mystical secret of the biblical verse "three times each year all your males will be seen in Jerusalem" is that the presence of the males (and not the females) in Jerusalem on the festivals of Passover, Shavuot, and Sukkoth is designed to cause a supernal conjunction between masculine (represented by the male Israelites) and feminine aspects of the Godhead.

Psychologically speaking, we might interpret the Kabbalistic notion of theurgy as a recognition that behavior can impact greatly upon the personal and collective unconscious mind. A similar concept, I believe, is symbolized in the Hindu-Jaina concept of Karma, which expresses the belief that all the actions a person undertakes impact upon the future status and vicissitudes of his own (and the world's) soul. In Jungian terms, just as the personal and collective unconscious can impact on behavior, a change in behavior and our conscious attitude can impact upon the deeper layers of our personal psyche, even (for example, in great creative works) impacting upon the collective psyche as well.

Humanity's divinely appointed purpose is to reclaim the sparks that have fallen both into the world and his soul, and to release a portion of the divine light imprisoned in the Kellipot. In doing this, humanity performs its role in *Tikkun ha-Olam*, the restoration of the world. All levels of the cosmos are restored and set aright, including the Godhead itself.

The raising of the sparks and its consequence, *Tikkun ha-Olam*, involve bringing the ego into accord with the collective unconscious. But this does not simply amount to a reversion to unconsciousness. Just as the world after *Tikkun* is not by any means the same as the world prior to creation, the transformation of the psyche resulting in individuation is not a reversion to an original unconscious state. The world of *Tikkun* is one where God's unity is realized through creation. Similarly, the psychical condition that results from *Tikkun* involves a dialectical union of the unconscious with consciousness and ego, unified in a Jungian "self," which is then able to creatively act in the world. With the raising of the sparks, the ego is not escaped (as in Gnosticism and some other forms of mysticism) but is instead transformed in a manner that brings benefit to itself and humankind.

(25) The Limits of Humanity's Efforts: Humanity cannot, by its own efforts, reclaim all of the sparks that have fallen into the realm of the *Kellipot*. Only those that remain in the uppermost layer of the realm of evil, in what the Kabbalists referred to as *Kellipot nogah* (brightness or electrum), can be reclaimed by individual efforts. Only through a great love (*ahavah rabbah*) and grace can some of the lower sparks be redeemed. The unconscious is not completely accessible to man. Even the personal unconscious cannot be totally reclaimed. Certain repressions, as Freud held, form the bedrock of civilization and are not to be reclaimed by ordinary individuals. Perhaps they can be reclaimed only by those such as a Freud or Jung who, in so doing, would transform civilization itself.

Archetypal Forms of Consciousness

While the developmental account of the psyche that we have found to be implicit in the Lurianic system provides a very useful psychological template through which to understand the Lurianic theosophy, it is not the only approach to the archetypal riches that are implicit within the Kabbalistic symbols. This is because these symbols organize experience in a manner that differs from our customary psychological schemas and cannot be said to be exclusively equivalent to any conventional psychological terms. Further, on Kabbalistic hermeneutical principles there can never be anything like a simple one-to-one correspondence between symbols and their interpretations, which are potentially infinite in number. Such interpretations provide what is, in effect, a still photograph of what must be regarded as a kaleidoscopic connection between Kabbalistic symbols and our own language regarding the psyche.

In the following sections, rather than equate the Lurianic symbols with specific psychological structures and processes, I will develop the notion that each of the Lurianic symbols implies an archetypal *form of consciousness* and an *ethic* that carries the psyche forward in its development and connection with self, others, and world.

Coincidentia Oppositorum

Wolfgang Giegerich has suggested that with the transition to modernity, mythological symbols are not simply interpreted, rationalized, and translated into psychological ideas, but are rather transformed into, or "born," as (dialectical) consciousness.[79] Giegerich's view brings to mind the thought of the French anthropologist Claude Lévi-Strauss, who held that because all cultures organize thought and knowledge into binary oppositions, cultures require myth and symbols to reconcile the conflicts that are thereby engendered. Lévi-Strauss writes that myth "provides a logical model capable of overcoming contradictions."[80] For Lévi-Strauss, the dialectical thought that Giegerich sees as being *born out of* the mythical symbol in the modern era, is actually the intrinsic and original purpose of the symbol itself. Dennis McCort, in his book *Going beyond the Pairs*, holds that the dialectical thought and experience embodied in the coincidence of opposites is the most fundamental archetype (or in McCort's view, "*meta-archetype*"), as it reconciles distinctions and oppositions that are created by language and thereby reveals the universal principle or "nothing" that makes everything possible.[81] We should also recall that for Jung the "self" is a *coincidentia oppositorum*, and that a reconciliation of opposites is the *sine qua non* of psychotherapy.

Indeed, the Kabbalists themselves regarded the reconciliation and unification of opposites to be a critical function of their symbols; as we have seen, the thirteenth-century Kabbalist Azriel of Gerona went so far as to declare that *Ein-sof* is "the union of all contradictions" and thus "the common root of both faith and unbelief."[82] Further, in the eighteenth and early nineteenth centuries an important school of Chasidism, Chabad (Lubavitch), understood the coincidence of opposites to be one, if not the most fundamental, of the teachings of the Lurianic Kabbalah. For example, the first Lubavitcher rabbi, Schneur Zalman (1745–1813), held that truth involves a blending of two perspectives, an earthly one in which this world contains being and truth and the heavens are an illusion, and a Godly one in which the precise opposite is the case,[83] and one of Schneur Zalman's pupils, R. Aaron Ha-Levi Horowitz of Staroselye (1766–1828), held that "the revelation of anything is actually through its opposite."[84]

Generalizing from this example, there can be little doubt that the Kabbalists themselves understood their symbols as revealing an archetypal form of dialectical consciousness. Indeed, we might hypothesize that each of their mythical symbols has been and continues to be transformed into "forms of consciousness" and "modes of understanding," and that this transformation constitutes at least part of these symbols' archetypal character and significance for contemporary life and thought.[85] In the pages to follow, I will argue that this is indeed the case. While I believe that this transformation typically involves a reconciling of opposites, and that something like dialectical thinking or *coincidentia oppositorum* is a fundamental, if not the fundamental, archetype that emerges in and from the Kabbalah, dialectics is not the only form of consciousness to emerge from mythological and religious symbols in general and the Kabbalistic symbols in particular.

Leibniz, Van Helmont, Schelling, Hegel, and Derrida

Before discussing the other archetypal modes of understanding that emerge from several of the Kabbalist's symbols, I would like to briefly trace some of the early history of the transformation of these symbols into modern forms of consciousness and modes of understanding.

In two important books,[86] Allison Coudert has marshaled evidence suggesting that the transformation of certain Kabbalistic symbols into (contemporary) forms of consciousness began very early in the modern era, with the interest that such thinkers as Leibniz and Van Helmont took in the Lurianic Kabbalah. Coudert argues that the Kabbalistic symbols were not only understood by these thinkers as heralding new modes of understanding, but that they were in fact an impetus to modern modes of open, *scientific* thought. According to Coudert, Gottfried Wilhelm Leibniz (1646–1716), in part through the influence of Francis Mercury Van Helmont (1615–98), was deeply influenced by the Lurianic Kabbalah, especially by the idea of *Tikkun ha-Olam*, the notion that human beings have the power to perfect creation and impact upon and alter the course of the world. Coudert cites manuscripts that indicate Leibniz not only discussed Kabbalah with Van Helmont, but also took dictation from him and served as a ghostwriter for Van Helmont's Kabbalistic work, *Thoughts on Genesis*. Coudert argues that the concept of *Tikkun* was a very liberating idea, one that provided a rational/spiritual justification for science and the emerging free inquiry of the Enlightenment.

Today we tend to read intellectual history through categories that make a clear demarcation between science and what we have come to know as the "occult." However, the sharp distinction between rationalism and mysticism does not reflect the way in which thinkers like Leibniz and Van Helmont thought themselves, and it is thus important to examine the interactions between mystical and rational thought during the early years of the Enlightenment. If Coudert is correct in her views, Van Helmont and Leibniz had already "extracted" modern forms of consciousness from Kabbalistic symbols in the seventeenth century, or in Giegerich's terms, these symbols were at that time already on their way to being reborn as rational modes of understanding and ideas. According to Coudert, the Kabbalistic symbol of *Tikkun* provided the Enlightenment with a religious mandate for the reform and improvement of the world, and thus served as one important impetus to modernity.

A similar argument can be made with respect to the impact of Kabbalistic symbols and ideas on the dialectical philosophies of both Schelling and Hegel, who appear to have become familiar with Kabbalistic sources through their reading of the German philosopher Jacob Boehme (1575–1622).[87] Each of these thinkers extracted what they believed to be the philosophical core of mystical views on the unity of opposites, and traces of mysticism can be found in both Schelling's and Hegel's thought. While the impact of the Kabbalah upon Hegel is likely to have been less direct than on Schelling, Hegel does make reference to Kabbalistic symbols such as *Adam Kadmon* (which he speaks of as "the archetype of humanity"[88]), and it is not too much of a stretch to suggest that this and other mystical symbols were not only being (re)born as dialectical thought, as Giegerich argues, but were in fact an impetus to nineteenth-century dialectical philosophy.

Finally, the connection between Kabbalah and postmodernism and deconstruction has been noted by a number of scholars.[89] Moshe Idel has gone so far as to suggest that Derrida's famous dictum "There is nothing outside the text"[90] may well bear the mark of Kabbalistic influence.[91] At the very least, the postmodern notion that the world can be understood as an infinitely interpretable linguistic text was clearly anticipated in the Kabbalistic sources. Through the writings of Gershom Scholem and others, these Jewish mystical ideas have entered into a dialog with postmodern and deconstructive thought.[92]

With the continuing dialectic between Kabbalah and contemporary thought it becomes possible to understand each of the major symbols of the Lurianic Kabbalah as revealing archetypal forms of consciousness that are both relevant and vital to contemporary life and thought. We have already seen how the Kabbalistic symbol of *Ein-sof* (the Infinite) articulates a form of consciousness and experience that allows for the coincidence of and interdependence of opposites. I will now consider several other symbols that serve to expand consciousness by widening our horizon of possible being, thought, experience, and ethical action.

Otiyot Yesod: *Infinite Interpretation*

The Kabbalists' understanding of language and Torah gives rise to an archetypal form of consciousness that understands the world as a narrative *text* that is subject to an indefinite, if not infinite, number of interpretations.[93] The Kabbalists held that the cosmos, including the upper, divine worlds, is comprised of the "foundational letters" (*Otiyot Yesod*), which through an infinity of recombinations, produce everything that exists.[94]

Conversely, the interpretive, hermeneutic process is one that penetrates beyond the superficial appearance and significance of the letters, and is itself a mystical act that brings one into proximity with the divine essence.[95] However, for the Kabbalists, such "proximity" is hardly fixed and unchanging. For example, Moses Cordovero, who preceded Isaac Luria as the leading Kabbalist in Safed, held that there are 600,000 "aspects and meanings in the Torah,"[96] corresponding to the 600,000 souls of Israel who ventured forth from Egypt, and whose soul sparks are present in each subsequent generation.[97] The Lurianists held that scripture, text, and cosmos change their meaning and/or reveal ever new depths of significance in response to changing inquiries and circumstances, and some, including the followers of Israel Sarug, even went so far as to identify Torah with all of the potential letter combinations in the Hebrew language![98] Such interpretive latitude leads to an archetypal mode of understanding that opens up a myriad of hermeneutic and epistemological possibilities. In contemplating the interpretive possibilities inherent in the Zohar, the Lurianist Chayyim Vital exclaimed:

> At every hour of the day the worlds change, and each hour is not the same as the next....You have to come to some kind of intellectual middle ground because a human mind cannot understand it all. With this you'll understand how the worlds change (with) the garments of *Ein-sof*, and, according to these changes, the statements in *Sefer ha-Zohar* change.[99]

Ayin: "Unknowing"

Ein-sof (the Kabbalists' Absolute/Infinite) is paradoxically both everything and nothing (Ayin). As we have seen, according to Azriel of Gerona, Ein-sof is completely unknowable, ineffable, and unsayable, and also that about which everything is said.

Ein-sof, as Ayin, is precisely that which is impossible to know, as it lies behind and before the subject-object, word-thing distinctions that make knowledge and description possible. As such, the Kabbalists' Absolute lies completely outside the realm of "thinghood," conceptualization, and comprehension, and is thus clearly not the sort of thing that can or cannot be "cognized." All experience, according to the Kabbalah, from our perception of everyday objects to our intuition of "higher worlds," is a construction of the human mind, and, as such, "the world" exists and has its character and definition only "from the point of view" of humankind. The discrete things that make up the world are the necessary by-products of the Tzimtzum, the rupture between subject and object, words and things, mind and matter that sets into motion all distinction, finitude, and experience.

For these reasons, the appropriate mode of understanding Ein-sof involves a deconstruction or "forgetting" of conventional knowledge, and indeed an "unknowing." According to David ben Judah ha-Hasid, "The Cause of Causes...is a place to which forgetting and oblivion pertain...nothing can be known of It, for It is hidden and concealed in the mystery of absolute nothingness. Therefore forgetting pertains to the comprehension of this place."[100] According to the Maggid of Mesiritz, who succeeded the Baal Shem Tov as the leader of the nascent Chasidic movement, intuiting the divine involves a forgetting in which one returns to a preconceptual, pre-linguistic, preconscious state. For the Maggid, "Thought is contained in letters, which are vessels, while the preconscious is beyond the letters, beyond the capacity of the vessels. This is the meaning of: 'Wisdom comes into being out of nothingness.'"[101]

As a form of consciousness, "unknowing" complements infinite interpretation and helps free us from the view that there must be a specifiable truth, meaning, or answer to our theological, philosophical, and psychological questions.[102] While infinite interpretation opens us to multiple perspectives and an open economy of thought and experience, "unknowing" opens us to the possibility that there is an inscrutable "remainder" that cannot be encompassed by thinking at all. As Jung himself observed, "there will always exist an indeterminate and undeterminable amount of unconscious material which belongs to the totality of the self."[103]

Shevirah: *The Shattering of Dogma*

The symbol *Shevirat ha-Kelim*, the "Breaking of the Vessels," suggests an archetypal mode of understanding in which each of our ideas, experiences, systems, and structures are continually shattered in the face of that which they cannot adequately contain. The *Shevirah* implies a mode of consciousness that involves a continual unraveling and revision of our concepts and experience of God, self, and world. The symbols of *Shevirah* (rupture) and *Tikkun* (emendation, restoration) are said by the Lurianists to apply to all things, events, and times. The dynamic implicit in these symbols is one in which humanity, the world, and even God himself are in a continual state of *revision*. The Kabbalists held that the divine can only be realized in a ruptured world that is emended and restored through the ethical, aesthetic, spiritual, and intellectual acts of humankind. The dialectic of rupture/emendation further reinforces a conception of thought and experience that stands in stark contrast with religious dogma. There can, of course, be no dogma for a mode of thought and experience that by its own principles must continually be subject to revision and transcendence.

The transition from dogma to an open economy of thought and experience is also implicit in the Lurianic symbol of *birur*, the extraction of divine speaks (*netzotzim*) from the "husks" (*Kellipot*) that entrap the sparks and alienate them from their source. The *Kellipot*, which the Jewish mystics held to be the source of both cosmic evil and personal suffering, were understood by them to represent a malevolent *constriction* in being, intellect, experience, behavior, and—given that the Kabbalists understood divine energy in erotic terms—sexuality; in short, a "closed economy" of experience, thought, faith, emotion, etc. On the other hand, the process of *birur* (extraction) and the consequent "raising of the sparks," in which divine light is liberated from the *Kellipot*, produces a continual emendation of the world by allowing the "masculine and feminine divine energies" to flow freely through both the cosmos and man, thereby restoring an *open economy* of ideas, experience, action, and interpretation.

Tikkun: The Expansion of Ethical Consciousness

In addition to empowering humanity to repair and restore a broken world, the Kabbalistic symbol/archetype *Tikkun ha-Olam* provides for an expansion of ethical consciousness, one that complements the expansion of being, thought, and experience implied by the other symbols we have examined. We have already seen how, according to Coudert, the symbol provided thinkers like Leibniz and Van Helmont a justification for certain of the goals of the Enlightenment, and how Jung, in his 1954 letter to Reverend Evans, became fascinated with the *Tikkun* idea.[104] That the symbol of "*Tikkun*" continues its development in our time as an archetypal *form of consciousness* is testified to by the fact that it has come to represent, both within and even beyond Jewish circles, a spiritually informed progressive politics, in part prompted by the appearance of *Tikkun Magazine*, a major, politically progressive periodical bearing its name.

As we have seen, for Luria and his followers, every moment, act, and encounter that an individual has in life is an opportunity for *Tikkun*, the repair and restoration of the self and world. The Chasidim developed this theme in their view that there is a spark of divinity in all things, a spark that is at once the true reality of the things it informs and an exiled aspect of the light of *Ein-sof*. The purpose of human existence is for the individual to raise (highlight, understand, develop) these divine sparks, both within him or herself and the objects he or she encounters in the world. An individual, as he or she proceeds through life, encounters objects, people, and events that are uniquely suited to aid in raising the sparks within his or her own soul. Conversely, each encounter provides the individual with a unique opportunity to raise the sparks in those people, things, and events that are encountered on life's path. The events in an individual's life constitute the unique opportunities for *tikkun* for that individual, defining that individual's potential identity in the process.

The Kabbalists, and Chasidim after them, held that each individual contains within him or herself sparks of divine light that are entrapped in the negativity of the "husks" (*Kellipot*). These sparks must be released and put to divine service if individuals are to fulfill the purpose of their souls. The parallels to the *psychotherapeutic* process are clear. Jung himself suggested that the "sparks" represent aspects of the collective unconscious, and it is a small step to understand the *entrapped* sparks as fully akin to neurotic complexes that prevent the individual from actualizing his or her full potential, and which must be released as part of the therapeutic and individuation process. However, for the Kabbalists and Chasidim, the raising of the sparks is not just an individual affair. Psyche, as James Hillman has taught us, is also in the world, and the process of *therapy* (*tikkun*) is incomplete if it remains exclusively on the personal level.

For the Jewish mystics, the holy sparks inherent (and entrapped) in all things derive from the ten *Sefirot*, each of which is said to instantiate a divine value. In this way, the processes of *Tikkun ha-Olam* and the Raising of the Sparks amount to the realization of *intellectual, spiritual, and ethical values* in each of one's life encounters. The pursuit of these values constitutes an archetypal form of ethical consciousness and also the *raison d'être* of the individual self and the completion and perfection of God and creation.

Conclusion

The psychological interpretations of the Lurianic theosophy I have offered in this chapter are meant to be more suggestive than complete. It is my hope that this effort will encourage others to mine the "gold" that, according to Rabbi Chayyim Bloch, Freud thought to be present in its myths and symbols.[105] The reader may be surprised at the degree of concordance between the Lurianic symbols (e.g., the *Partzufim*) and various concepts in the psychology of C. G. Jung. As I have argued throughout this book, this is likely no accident, as the Kabbalists held that the heavens reflect basic human experiences and relationships, and the very alchemical texts upon which Jung anchored his archetypal psychology were themselves imbued with Kabbalistic ideas. Regardless, the Kabbalah can provide archetypal psychology with an extremely rich source of symbols and theory. On the other hand, Jungian thought can help unlock the meaning of the Kabbalah from a psychological point of view. While by no means exhausting the significance of the Lurianic Kabbalah, a psychological interpretation of its myths and symbols can provide both a contemporary approach to understanding Jewish mysticism and a Jewish dynamic perspective on the development and structure of the human mind.

Chapter 10

Carl Jung, Anti-Semitism, and National Socialism

At long last we arrive at the question that has haunted our investigation from the very beginning, a question that is as troubling—given the results of the rest of our investigation—as it is unavoidable. The questions of Jung's so-called anti-Semitism and sympathies with National Socialism loom over any inquiry into the theoretical relationship between Jungian and Kabbalistic ideas, and had we explored these issues deeply at the beginning of this study, the rest of our inquiry might well have been drowned in the intensity of the discussion. Now, however, having made significant theoretical headway, we can no longer avoid examining the biographical and historical issues in some detail, and considering the question of whether these issues might also be of theoretical moment.

The Questions

The question of Jung's personal attitude towards Jews and Judaism actually expands into a whole host of questions that go far beyond the issue of whether to apply to Jung the epithets "anti-Semitic" or "Nazi sympathizer." On the one hand, it is important to understand precisely what it is that Jung said, advocated, and did with respect to Judaism as a religion, the Jewish people in general, and individual Jewish psychotherapists, colleagues, and associates. However, we must also go beyond Jung the man, and as far as possible make a separate inquiry into how the answer to our initial queries should impact upon our views of Jungian thought and its connection to Jewish mysticism. In doing so, we must also question whether Jungian psychology, as distinct from Jung the man, tends towards irrationalism, racism, and/or anti-Semitism, and whether the Kabbalah might itself predispose to the first two of these tendencies. If, as I have argued, Kabbalism is very close to Jungianism, and if Jungianism tends towards irrationalism, racism, and even fascism, we are then forced to ask whether Kabbalism itself is a morally dangerous doctrine.

Another question, relevant from at least a traditional Jewish point of view, involves the ethics of utilizing ideas from morally tainted sources.

DOI: 10.4324/9781003027041-11

Assume for the moment, as I have argued, that Jung not only borrowed Jewish mystical categories but had something very important to say about them, and also assume that, at least during the 1930s, Jung flirted with anti-Semitism and welcomed National Socialism. Does this mean that we should ignore Jung's contributions to the study and interpretation of Jewish mysticism? This is, at least for some, a difficult question.

We must confront each of these questions if we are to properly conclude our investigation into Jung and the Kabbalah. However, the answers to each of them are likely to be more finely and subtly textured than any "labels" can convey. With respect to our evaluation of Jung's so-called anti-Semitism, we must recognize the possibility that Jung expressed and even held different views in different contexts and at different times, that his words were not consistent with his behavior (e.g., his assisting Jews in escaping from Nazi-occupied territory), that he was *ambivalent* regarding Jews and Judaism, and that such ambivalence sprang from various historical and personal sources and was expressed on a number of conscious and *unconscious* levels. Indeed, as depth psychologists, we have no reason to suspect that *any individual* is anything but highly ambivalent and conflicted, even about those values that, in his conscious awareness, he holds most sacrosanct. Finally, we should be open to the possibility that Jung, in the course of a long life and career, changed his views and behavior regarding Judaism. Indeed, the thesis that Jung experienced such a change will emerge as a major theme both in this chapter and Chapter 11.

Is the Issue Really Relevant?

Some Jungians hold that Jung's personal behavior and political beliefs are irrelevant to an evaluation of his theory. While I believe this view should be considered, I do not think it can be evaluated a priori, without a full examination of the historical and literary record. I do not, for example, believe, as Wolfgang Giegerich has suggested, that the question of the relevance of Jung's purported anti-Semitism to his theory can be compared to questions such as those pertaining to Newton's unpleasant character or Picasso's treatment of women.[1] Indeed, it is the tendency of certain Jungians to dismiss the problem of Jung's purported anti-Semitism as irrelevant that has at times fueled antipathy to Jung and his theories in the wider depth-psychological community.

I applaud the efforts of those who have contributed to the "Lingering Shadows" conference and the volumes edited by Maidenbaum and Martin, to treat this issue squarely and seriously,[2] and this and the following chapters are deeply indebted to their dialog. If the issue were one of Jung's extramarital affairs or even his alleged boundary violations with clients, I might agree that these were personal to Jung and not really relevant to Jungian theory and practice. However, as will become clear, Jung justified his optimism regarding Hitler and National Socialism on psychological grounds. For example, Jung initially believed that the Nazis could revitalize the German spirit by channeling archetypal energies that remained latent in the German psyche. Further, Jung's early fascination with Hitler and the Nazis stemmed from what he saw as their appeal to the irrational aspects of the collective unconscious,[3] and as late as 1938 he seemed to praise Hitler as a man who is not directed by his ego consciousness, but rather heeds a deeper voice, one that emanates from what Jung, in other places, calls the "self."[4] We are therefore entitled to *ask* if Jung's psychological theories led to his optimism, even enthusiasm, for Nazism. If, as has been argued by Jung's critics, aspects of Jungianism undermine consciousness and reason, if Jung could have encouraged his followers to express anti-Semitic sentiments as a means of their getting in touch with their Shadow,[5] if National Socialism evolved out of the same cauldron of ideas that also led to Jungian psychology,[6] and if Jung could praise Hitler in terms that suggested Hitler had achieved something valued by Jungian psychology, then Jungians need to examine not only Jung's anti-Semitism and Hitler-optimism but perhaps also those elements in his way of thinking that may have led to or justified it.

Richard Martin puts the question squarely when he writes:

> Insofar as Jung seemed fascinated by the unconscious power of the German psyche, could his psychology not be judged as one that is too susceptible to intoxication with the irrational at the terrible expense of the rational?[7]

Martin concludes that the "answer to this basic question, both for psychoanalysis and for Jungian psychology, must be an unequivocal 'No.'" He argues that "to hold a creation accountable for the flaws of its creator would leave us with little if any greatness or breadth in our culture." While I *generally* agree, more than this is necessary to answer the question in Jung's own case, for Jung's behavior and writings suggest that his psychology, or at least certain interpretations of it, may well be susceptible to the very "intoxication with the irrational" that Martin speaks of.

I believe that the question of Jung's accountability, repentance, and/or compensation for his pre-war views becomes significant (though not necessarily determinative) both for an evaluation of Jung's own personality and, more importantly, for a complete assessment of the transformative possibilities inherent in Jungian psychology. Minimally, those who are in the process of creating a dialog between Jungian psychology and Jewish mysticism need to examine this issue and come to their own conclusions regarding the relevance of this issue to such integrative work.

We should note that, with regard to the Nazi atrocities, Jung himself demanded no less than a full accounting on these matters from his own patients, stating that if individuals seeking treatment:

come from those "decent Germans" who want to foist the guilt onto a couple of men in the Gestapo, I regard the case as hopeless. I shall have no alternative but to answer the applications with a questionnaire asking certain crucial questions, like "What do you think about Buchenwald?" Only when a patient sees and admits his own responsibility can individual treatment be considered.[8]

Furthermore:

The only redemption lies, as I have already indicated, in a complete admission of guilt. *Mea culpa, mea maxima culpa!* Out of honest contrition for sin comes divine grace. That is not only a religious but also a psychological truth.

In this chapter, then, I will address the historical record, explore Jung's early, highly ambivalent attitude towards Judaism and "Jewish psychology," and consider the degree to which Jung later altered his attitudes and views. In general, I will argue that, without announcing or even acknowledging that he had done so, the Jung of after about 1950 reversed himself, and instead of using the term "Jewish psychology" in a pejorative manner as he had done in the 1930s, adopted the view that his own psychology was corroborated, and even anticipated, by the Jewish mystical tradition.

The Historical Record

A great deal has been written on Jung's alleged anti-Semitism, probably enough at this point to fill several volumes,[9] and here I cannot hope to provide anything more than a general survey of the biographical and literary data that are relevant to this question. A complete study of the issue would, of course, delve deep into Jung's personal background, his relationship with Freud, and the cultural and historical situation in Europe prior to World War II, all topics that must, unfortunately, be treated cursorily, if at all, in this brief presentation. (Those interested in a more in-depth examination of these matters are referred to Jay Sherry's important 2010 Palgrave Macmillan volume, *Carl Gustav Jung: Avant-Garde Conservative.*) My main interest is in presenting the major issues of the debate and providing some perspective on its impact upon Jungian studies of Jewish mysticism.

From the time of Carl Jung's break with Freud, charges of anti-Semitism followed him and placed something of a taint on Jungian psychology. In speaking of their parting, Freud wrote in 1914 that Jung "seemed ready to enter into a friendly relationship with me and for my sake give up certain racial prejudices which he had previously permitted himself."[10] Despite Jung's denials, accusations of anti-Semitism and even Nazism followed him throughout his career, and persisted even after his death. In 1989 a group of Jungian analysts organized a conference on these "Lingering Shadows" at the New School for Social Research in New York, and a similar symposium was held in Paris. The Jungian community, to its credit, has attempted to confront the issue directly, and some of its leaders have concluded that there is indeed a stain on Jung's personal record that contemporary Jungians need to acknowledge.[11] Jungians have also been forced to consider the question of whether Jung's questionable record on the issues of anti-Semitism and Nazism are of more than personal moment and cast a shadow upon Jungian theory.

Jung and Freud

As is well known, Jung was placed by Freud in the unenviable position of playing guarantor that psychoanalysis would not be looked upon as a "Jewish national affair."[12] In 1908, over two years after Jung had initiated a correspondence with Freud and more than a year after the two had first met, Freud wrote to Karl Abraham: "Our Aryan comrades are really completely indispensable to us; otherwise psychoanalysis would succumb to anti-Semitism."[13] The following year, Jung traveled with Freud to America as part of the contingent that delivered lectures on psycho-analysis at Clark University. In March 1910, at the Second International Psychoanalytic Congress in Nuremberg, Freud nominated Jung as pre-sident. In response to colleagues who were protesting Jung's nomination, Freud declared that by electing Jung, a Swiss and a non-Jew, they could be assured of winning friends for their teaching.[14]

With the publication of the first edition of *Symbols of Transformation* in 1912, Jung clearly marked his divergence from Freud, and, after this, Freud began to bemoan the fact that he had been unable to successfully unite Jews and Gentiles (Freud used the Yiddish word "goyim") under his banner.[15] By 1913 Freud and Jung had, in effect, ended their personal relationship. The following year, in his "On the History of the Psycho-analytic Movement," Freud implied that Jung ended their relationship because of "certain racial prejudices."[16] In a letter to James Putnam in 1915, Freud specifically accused Jung of anti-Semitism.[17]

According to Jung, these accusations stemmed not from anti-Semitism but rather from the fact that Jung could not abide Freud's "soulless materialism."[18] However, there is evidence that even in his youth Jung had associated Judaism with materialism and in the process had used anti-Semitic language. In a lecture Jung delivered to a Swiss student fraternity while in medical school at Basel University in 1897, Jung makes reference to Johann Zollner's scientific defense of spiritualism, and writes:

> But his was "a voice crying in the wilderness." Mortally wounded in his struggle against the Judaization of science and society, this high-minded man died in 1892, broken in body and spirit.[19]

Jung thus expressed anti-Jewish sentiments (that were in all likelihood almost taken for granted by his audience) long before meeting Freud. However, the bitter feud with the founder of psychoanalysis appears to have further confirmed and deepened Jung's negative view of Judaism. Jung's later identification of psychoanalysis as a "Jewish psychology" was at least in part fueled by his personal animosity towards Freud.[20] Indeed, Jung links Freud's materialism and reductionism with his Judaism,[21] relates the (Freudian) castration complex to the Jewish rite of circumcision,[22] and later contrasts the Jewish relationship with God, as a covenant or legal contract, with the Christian conception of a relationship based in love, a long-standing view of the church that had long been linked with anti-Jewish sentiment.[23]

However, according to John Kerr, Jung was hardly anti-Semitic at the time of his early encounters with Freud and was indeed experiencing a "Jewish romance."[24] Jung was attracted to the "Jewishness" of psychoanalysis, and personally very much attracted to Jewish women. Jung, according to Kerr, saw Judaism as he had seen the occult: as a means of expressing his dissatisfaction with his own Swiss Calvinist upbringing. Sabina Spielrein, Jung's Jewish patient, lover, and later colleague, spoke of Jung's interest in Judaism as stemming from "the drive to explore other possibilities through a new race, the drive to liberate himself from the paternal edicts."[25] According to Kerr, it was only after his break with Freud that Jung began to express anti-Jewish ideas. Soon, Jung was to identify more strongly with occultist, Gnostic, and German *Volkisch* trends, then the rage in middle Europe. These identifications afforded him not only a means to continue his rebellion against his father's Calvinism, but also a vehicle for his later identifying himself as an "Aryan psychologist," and to contrast his own views with Freud's "Jewish psychology."

Jewish and Aryan Psychology

Around the time of the final split with Freud (1914), Jung published a paper in which he contrasted Jewish and Aryan psychology. His words in "The Role of the Unconscious"[26] are somewhat prophetic, as he relates that as Christianity is losing authority the "repressed dark side" of the German psyche, the "blond beast," is "ready at any moment to burst out with devastating consequences" that can bring about a psychological or social revolution. According to Jung, the Jew, by virtue of his having taken on two cultures—his own ancient one as well as the culture of the nation within which he dwells—is far more "domesticated" than the Aryan. However, in Jung's view, the Jew lacks the "chthonic quality," the quality that draws strength from the earth and the dark, primitive side of the unconscious. By way of contrast, "this chthonic quality is found in dangerous concentration in the Germanic peoples."[27]

Jung argued that the Jews' tendency "to reduce everything to its material beginnings" is, in effect, a means of counterbalancing a dangerous over-ascendancy of his "two cultures." It is for this reason that Freud and Adler, respectively, can reduce the psyche to the sexual and power drives. While these reductions give a certain (compensatory) satisfaction to the Jew, "these specifically Jewish doctrines are totally unsatisfactory to the Germanic mentality," which is still largely conditioned by the "barbarian" within. This "anti-Christian" barbarous element of the German mind is both "danger-ous" and "congenial." For Jung, "it is a still untouched fortune, an uncor-rupted treasure, a sign of youthfulness, an earnest of rebirth."[28] However, Jung soberly concludes that "to value the unconscious exclusively for the sake of its positive qualities and to regard it as a source of revelation would be fundamentally wrong."[29]

Jung held that the very structure of the Jewish psychical apparatus was con-ditioned by the Jewish Diaspora. While the German psyche is split between a Christian upper half representing the forces of goodness and light and a pagan lower half representing the forces of darkness, the Jew's upper half is identified with their host country, while their lower, unconscious half is identified with biblical culture and religion.[30] This comparison, while not necessarily unflat-tering to the Jew, underscored for Jung the difference between German and Jewish psychology, and suggested to Jung that his project of reuniting the Christian trinity with its dark, Satanic "fourth," which Jung prescribed for the Germanic peoples, might not be applicable to the Jewish mind.

In *The Red Book* Jung describes entering into a dialog with "The Red One," that more than touches upon anti-Semitism. In this dialog with a figure that Jung identifies as the devil, it is indeed the devil who comes to the Jews defense! Jung says that he believes "it was the task of Western man to carry Christ in his heart and to grow with his suffering, death, and resurrection," to which the Red One responds, "Well there are also Jews who are good people and yet had no need for your solemn gospels." The dialog continues with Jung's response:

I: "You are, it seems to me, no good reader of people: have you never noticed that the Jew himself lacks something, one in his head, another in his heart, and he himself feels that he lacks something?"

T.R.: "Indeed Im no Jew, but I must come to the Jew's defense: you seem to be a Jew hater." I: "Well, now you speak like all those Jews who accuse anyone of Jew hating who does not have a completely favor-able judgment, while they themselves make the bloodiest jokes about their own kind. Since the Jews only too clearly feel that particular lack and yet do not want to admit it, they are extremely sensitive to criti-cism. Do you believe that Christianity left no mark on the souls of men? And do you believe that one who has not experienced this most intimately can still partake of its fruit?"

[Jung's draft for *Liber Secundus* continues: "No one can flout the spiritual development of many centuries and reap what they have not sowed."]

T.R.: "You argue your case well. But your solemnity?! You could make matters much easier for yourself. If you're no saint, I really don't see why you have to be so solemn. You wholly spoil the fun. What the devil is troubling you? Only Christianity with its mournful escape from the world can make people so ponderous and sullen."[31]

During the same period, in *Psychological Types*, Jung provided an analysis of the inquisition that is hardly unsympathetic to its victims. There it is anti-Semitism (and not the Jews' sensitivity to it) that is explained in psychological terms:

> The only defence available to the Christian consciousness was fanaticism. The frenzied horror of the Inquisition was the product of over-compensated doubt, which came surging up from the unconscious....[32]

It was not until 1928 that Jung again publicly discussed the differences between Jewish and Christian psychology. In "The Relations between the Ego and the Unconscious," he writes that it is "unpardonable to accept the conclusions of a Jewish psychology as generally valid," just as it would be unheard of to accept the universality of Indian or Chinese psychology.[33] Yet at this point Jung held that on the *deepest level* of the collective unconscious it is impossible to distinguish between the races.

The General Medical Society and the *Zentralblatt für Psychotherapie*

In 1933, after Hitler's rise to power in Germany, Ernest Kretschmer resigned as president of the General Medical Society for Psychotherapy, and Jung was prevailed upon by Matthias Göring (psychiatrist, and cousin of Hermann Göring) to take over the presidency, which Jung did on the condition that, while Jews were banned from the German section of the organization, the society be reorganized as an international organization that permitted Jewish psychotherapists to join as full members. While Jews remained banned from the German section of the organization, Jung made many efforts on behalf of his Jewish colleagues to enable them to continue their profession[34] and, when things became totally untenable, to leave Germany.[35]

Nevertheless, Jung's tenure as president of this society was filled with gaffes, misstatements, and gross insensitivities. For example, early in his tenure Jung wrote an editorial in the society's journal that underlined the differences between Germanic and Jewish psychology, insisting, however, "that this implies no deprecation of Semitic psychology."[36] That same year, in an interview on Radio Berlin with his former student and now German psychiatrist Adolf Weizsäcker, Jung spoke about psychology's role in the development of "consciously responsible spokesmen and leaders of the collective movement." He immediately followed this with an approving quotation from the new German leader: "As Hitler said recently, the leader must be able to be alone and must have the courage to go his own way."[37] Later in the interview, Jung declares: "It is perfectly natural that the leader [Der Führer] should stand at the head of an elite, which in earlier centuries was formed by the nobility. The nobility belies the law of nature in the blood and exclusiveness of the race."[38] In these remarks Jung appeared to give his approval to Hitler's leadership, and to place himself in league with the racial purity doctrines of National Socialism.

Of equal or greater significance was the appearance, late in 1933, of a "manifesto" written by Matthias Göring, likely without Jung's consent but nonetheless under his editorship, that called for psychotherapists to rally behind the racial theories of National Socialism. Göring's December 1933 *Zentralblatt* manifesto reads in part: "the society expects all members who work as writers or speakers to work through Adolf Hitler's Mein Kampf with all scientific effort and accept it as a basis."[39]

While Jung stated he had thought this manifesto would only appear in a special German issue of the *Zentralblatt für Psychotherapie*, which was only nominally under Jung's editorship, the article appeared in the full, international edition, edited by Jung.[40] Moreover, it was accompanied in the same issue by Jung's "The State of Psychotherapy Today," in which Jung highlighted differences between German and Jewish psychology and made a number of statements about the Jewish people that, at least in the context of the rise of Hitlerism, could well have been understood as comporting with the Nazi agenda. Jung made unflattering comparisons between the Jews and both women and nomads. For example, he wrote:

> The Jews have this peculiarity in common with women; being physically weaker, they have to aim at the chinks in the armour of their adversary, and thanks to this technique which has been forced upon them through the centuries, the Jews themselves are best protected where others are most vulnerable. Because, again, of their civilization, more than twice as ancient as ours, they are vastly more conscious of the shadowside of things, and hence in this respect much less vulnerable than we are.[41]

Jung further opined:

> "The Jew who is something of a nomad has never yet created a cultural form of his own and as far as we can see never will, since all his

instincts and talents require a more or less civilized nation to act as host for their development."

(Compare Hitler in *Mein Kampf*: "The Jewish people, despite all apparent intellectual qualities, is without a true culture, and especially without any culture of its own. For what sham culture the Jew today possesses is the property of other peoples, and for the most part ruined in his hands."[42]). Jung then goes on to state:

> The Jewish race as a whole—at least in my experience—possesses an unconscious which can be compared with the "Aryan" only with reserve. Creative individuals apart, the average Jew is far too conscious and differentiated to go about pregnant with the tensions of unborn futures. The "Aryan" unconscious has a greater potential than the Jewish: that is both the advantage and the disadvantage of a youthfulness not yet fully weaned from barbarism.[43]

Jung then made what some believed, given the circumstances of its writing, to be an opportunistic slur against Freud:

> In my opinion it has been a grave error in medical psychology up till now to apply Jewish categories—which are not even binding on all Jews—indiscriminately to Germanic and Slavic Christendom. Because of this the most precious secret of the Germanic peoples—their creative and intuitive depth of soul—has been explained as a morass of banal infantilism, while my own warning voice has for decades been suspected of anti-Semitism.[44]

Jung continues that Freud did not understand the German psyche, and that the phenomenon of National Socialism that has gripped the entire German nation reveals "tensions and potentialities" within the German mind that were not even considered by Freud and his followers.

Jung also opined more positively: "As a member of a race with a three-thousand-year-old civilization, the Jew, like the cultured Chinese, has a wider area of psychological consciousness than we." However, on Jung's view, such wider consciousness would only serve to constrain the free, barbarous, passionate (and dangerous) spirit that is present in the Aryan soul.[45]

Later in 1934, Jung published an article in which he responded to the accusations of anti-Semitism that had been leveled against him in print by a Dr. Bally.[46] In this article Jung defends his decision to take on the presidency of the General Medical Society for Psychotherapy on the grounds that he was pressed to do so by colleagues and that he did so in the interest of science and loyalty to his fellow psychotherapists. He reminds the reader that he took on the presidency of an "International" society, one that continued to grant Jews full membership. He further defended his right to distinguish various ethnic psychologies and, in particular, as a medical doctor to deal with "the Jewish problem," which he regarded as a "regular complex."[47]

In this rejoinder Jung points out that he had been speaking about differences between Jewish and Aryan psychology since 1913, and that his views have had nothing to do with the current "form of the German state." He speaks of his "total inability to understand why it should be a crime to speak of a 'Jewish' psychology." He relates that he is politically "neutral" and says, "If I am to be exploited for political ends, there's nothing I can do to stop it." Jung concludes that it is unfortunate that against his express wishes his scientific program should be linked to a political manifesto.

However, in that same year, 1934, Jung, along with the German psychiatrist Matthias Göring, published an article in tribute to the German psychiatrist Robert Sommer, in which they praised a chapter added by Sommer in 1927 to a book he had first published twenty years earlier. The chapter, entitled "Raceology and Racial History," speaks of "an intrusion of alien blood into the Germanic race," links "practical psychiatry...with raceology," and describes "the formation of the nose...as a racial criterion in human anthropology."[48] It is unclear why Jung would have given praise to such a work: certainly, unlike the eugenicists who justified Hitler's program for exterminating the Jewish race, Jung never advocated a racially based eugenics.

"JEWISH POINTS OF VIEW...HAVE AN ESSENTIALLY CORROSIVE CHARACTER"

On February 9, 1934, at roughly the same time that the "State of Psychotherapy Today" was published, Jung wrote what some regard to be his most clearly anti-Semitic[49] comments in a letter to his former assistant W. M. Kranefeldt:

> As is known, one cannot do anything against stupidity; but in this instance, the Arian [sic] people can point out that with Freud and Adler specifically Jewish points of view were publicly preached, and, as can be proven likewise, points of view that have an essentially corrosive (zersetzend) character. If the proclamation of this Jewish gospel is agreeable to the government, then so be it. Otherwise, there is also the possibility that this would not be agreeable to the government.[50]

This letter has been characterized by Jung's Jewish disciple James Kirsch as "really quite devastating."[51] Richard Stein points out that the Nazis at the time were using the word "corrosive" (*zersetzend*) to refer to the negative effects of Jews on Aryan culture.[52] On the other hand, we cannot read too much into this private correspondence, in which Jung is clearly venting his anger against Freud and Adler. This is perhaps clarified when several weeks later, in a letter to B. Cohen, dated March 26, 1934, Jung writes that while Cohen's criticism of his lack of knowledge of Judaism is justified: "I [Jung] am absolutely not an opponent of the Jews even though I am an opponent of Freud's."[53] This is a rather telling selfobservation, for it is indeed the case that in many if not most of the instances in which Jung appears to make specifically anti-Semitic remarks he does so in the context of his polemic against Freudianism. In the interim, Jung had written a letter to A. Pupato where he stated: "The question I broached regarding the peculiarities of Jewish psychology does not presuppose any intention on my part to depreciate Jews," because to point out differences between Jewish and other national psychologies "cannot possibly be in itself an insult to the Jews so long as one refrains from value judgments."[54]

Jung's Defense

Two days after his March 1934 letter to Cohen, Jung, in a letter to Max Guggenheim, writes: "People do not know, nor is it said in public, that I have intervened personally with the regime on behalf of certain Jewish psychotherapists." Jung says that the Jews should be thankful to him for assuring their membership in the Society for Psychotherapy, and indeed there is much evidence that Jung was committed to enabling Jewish psychotherapists to maintain their professional standing in Germany.

In a letter to James Kirsch, one of Jung's early Jewish disciples, dated May 26, 1934, Jung writes: "The Jew directly solicits anti-Semitism with his readiness to scent out anti-Semitism everywhere."[55] Jung goes on to state that "Freud previously accused me of anti-Semitism because I could not abide his soulless materialism." Jung tells Kirsch: "You ought to know me sufficiently well that an unindividual stupidity like anti-Semitism cannot be laid at my door." He continues that his goal as a psychotherapist is to facilitate the individuation of his patients and that this is only possible if they recognize their unique particularity. Jung adds, "No one who is a Jew can become a human being without knowing that he is a Jew, since this is the basis from which he can reach out towards a higher humanity."[56]

It is important to point out that the charge of anti-Semitism cannot automatically be leveled against Jung on the simple grounds that he distinguishes between Jewish and Gentile psychology, as this very distinction has been foundational for Judaism itself. To see that this is the case one need only look at the various Talmudic, midrashic, and halakhic (Jewish legal) and mystical sources that place the Jewish soul in a different and superior light. The Chasidim, for example, held that, in comparison to the

Gentile, the Jew has an extra "Godly soul" that brings him closer to God.[57] In his letter to Roback of September 29, 1936, Jung writes: "It is true I have insisted upon the *difference* between Jewish and Christian psychology since 1917, but Jewish authors have done the same long ago as well as recently. I am no anti-Semite."[58] In the same letter, Jung writes that Jews have an extension into their own subconscious which is rare among non-Jews. Jung's own descriptions are, at times, even flattering to the Jew, as Jung bases his distinction between Jewish and Aryan psychology on the grounds that "the Jews have a cultural history that is 2,000 years older than the so-called Aryan."[59]

Interestingly, Freud himself, in his 1926 address to the B'nai Brith, spoke of his irresistible attraction to Jews and Jewry as stemming from "many obscure emotional forces, which were the more powerful the less they could be expressed in words." The real issue, it seems to me, is why Jung chose to emphasize the distinction between Jews and Aryans and to make critical remarks regarding Jewish psychology at a time when anti-Semitism was beginning to run rampant in Europe. Jung's reply to Bally that he had been distinguishing between Jewish and Aryan psychology for twenty years hardly settles the issue, as Jung in the mid-1930s clearly took the opportunity to emphasize these distinctions and to escalate a controversy that had dire political implications.

One way of understanding Jung's decision to emphasize the distinction between Jewish and Germanic psychology at this time is to appeal to Jung's need to address the crisis into which he saw Germany heading, and his belief that the "Jewish" psychologies of Freud and Adler were not up to this task. Indeed, in 1936, in "Wotan" Jung presented an archetypal explanation of Nazism that rested on the idea that a "fundamental attribute of the German psyche" could be summed up via the god or archetype "Wotan." According to Jung:

> The emphasis on the Germanic race (vulgarly called "Aryan"), the Germanic heritage, blood and soil, the Wagalaweia songs, the ride of the Valkyries, Jesus as a blond and blue-eyed hero, the Greek mother of St. Paul, the devil as an international Alberich in Jewish or Masonic guise, the Nordic aurora borealis as the light of civilization, the inferior Mediterranean races— all this is the indispensable scenery for the drama that is taking place and at bottom they all mean the same thing: a god has taken possession of the Germans....[60]

For Jung, "rational" (i.e., economic, political, and non-archetypal psychological) factors are incapable of explaining the German people's acceptance of Hitler and the Nazis. Certainly, Jung thought, Adlerian and Freudian principles, based as they are on the "over-civilized" psychology of Judaism, will be useless in comprehending the barbarous and creative nature of the German psyche.

On the other hand, in a letter to Gerhard Adler (June 9, 1934), Jung suggests that the mechanization he so abhors in Freud is not so much due to Freud's *Jewishness*, but rather due to the fact that Freud has forgotten and become estranged from his Judaism, an act that Jung nevertheless believes to be "typically Jewish." He concludes, "So when I criticize Freud's Jewishness I am not criticizing the Jews but rather the damnable capacity of the Jew, exemplified by Freud, to deny his own nature."[61] Jung challenges "religious Jews" to summon the courage to distinguish themselves from Freud. While one can certainly accuse Jung here of making a "reinterpretive distortion" of anti-Semitic statements made earlier that year, his views *as stated here* are hardly anti-Semitic, but are actually consistent with a *religious* Jewish critique of Freudianism. Perhaps a wider point should also be made here—that for Jung the notions of "Jewish" and "Aryan" psychology served as shorthand for certain "ideal types," in Weber's sense of this term, that are, as Jung had put it, not binding on any particular Jews or members of any other ethnic group. However, even if we grant that Jung's use of these phrases was not intended to create rigid distinctions along ethnic or racial lines, their effect in Jung's time could only have been to contribute to the ethnic divisiveness propagated by the Nazi party.

In June of 1934, in two letters—one to Gerhard Adler, the other to C. E. Benda—Jung responded to questions about his previously published comments that the Jew has never created a "cultural form" of his own. He tells Benda that there is an "essential difference" between a "culture" and a "cultural form" (the difference escapes this writer) and that "No one is more deeply convinced than I that the Jews are a people with a culture."[62] He further argues that if he had said of the Jews what, in the same article, he had said of the Germans (regarding whom he used the word "barbarism"), such a statement "might have been some cause for excitement."

In a letter to another of his early Jewish disciples, Erich Neumann (December 22, 1935), Jung writes: "The 'cultivated Jew' is always on the way to becoming a 'non-Jew,'" and that for many of his patients "Jewishness" is a personal insult.[63] Jung implies that in his work with such patients he must bring them back to their Jewish roots. In the same letter he tells Neumann: "I find your very positive conviction that the soil of Palestine is essential for Jewish individuation most valuable." Jung wonders whether the Jew, who has grown accustomed to being a non-Jew, may need a concrete reminder of his Jewishness.

It is of note that Neumann, in his letters to Jung during the mid1930s, had expressed a hope that Jung would become a mentor for him in his quest for a deeper understanding of his own Judaism, even going so far as to refer to Jung as "one of the righteous of the nations" (a traditional Jewish designation later conferred by the State of Israel on those Gentiles who rescued Jews from the Holocaust). Neumann had hoped that Jung would become the spiritual teacher that, owing to the "present spiritual bankruptcy of Judaism," was not available to him within the Jewish world.[64] Still, Neumann foresaw a danger that analytical psychology would lead to a "betrayal to [his] own Jewish foundations, for something that is more beautiful, wider, and more modern."[65]

Jewish Refugees and the Effort to Convince Freud to Leave

On December 19, 1938, Jung wrote to Erich Neumann: "I have a lot to do with Jewish refugees and am permanently occupied with finding a place for all my Jewish acquaintances in England and America."[66] Bair has documented that Jung was indeed at this time making significant efforts on the part of individual Jews, treating many Jewish patients without charge, and assigning numerous attestations of financial support in order to arrange for their exit from Germany and entry into Switzerland.[67] In his letter to Neumann, Jung advises Neumann not to make too much of his specifically Jewish psychology in the context of the tragic events that were then unfolding in Europe. Jung wrote: "the specific Christian or Jewish traits have only a secondary significance," and "Especially small is the difference between a typical Protestant and a Jewish psychology as far as the historical problem of the time is concerned."

Earlier in 1938, in cooperation with other Swiss Jungians and several Jews, Jung reportedly made an effort to convince Freud and other Jews to leave Austria. There are at least two extant versions of the events surrounding these efforts (neither of which is clearly documented[68]), one recounted in a biography of Jung by Barbara Hannah, and a second recounted by Robert S. McCully.[69] The details vary, but in both accounts, a young man, Franz Riklin, Jr., the son of a former associate of Freud's who was now a Jungian, was sent to Austria to present Freud with a significant sum of money so that Freud might leave the country. In Hannah's account the money was sent by "some exceedingly rich Swiss Jews," whereas in McCully's account, the money was from Riklin's father and Jung. In both accounts, Freud is said to have rejected the offer, saying, "I refuse to be beholden to my enemies." Riklin returned, disappointed, to Switzerland and soon thereafter Freud found other means to leave Austria for England.

Jung and Hitler

While Jung saw Hitler speak on at least one occasion, he apparently never met or had any direct dealings with the German dictator.[70] Still, Hitler exercised a certain fascination for Jung, one that can be traced through a series of rather disturbing letters, reports, and interviews during the 1930s.

In a letter to Erich Neumann dated August 12, 1934, but which was withheld from publication, Jung writes:

> Jacob, in contrast to Esau, constitutes a symbolic attempt at collective individuation or, better, a stage in collective development, as, for instance, historically Hitler is an attempt at collective individuation for the German, or mythologically, Jesus, Mithras, Attis, Osiris, etc.[71]

While Jung here compares Hitler to both the biblical Jacob and Jesus of Nazareth, the comparison is descriptive and is meant to underline the undoubtedly powerful role that men like Jacob, Jesus, and Hitler play in the collective psyches of their respective peoples. Still, there is a positive tone to the comparison as Jung speaks of "collective individuation... [and] development."

In a series of lectures given at the Tavistock Clinic in London, in 1935, Jung described the hypnotic effect that Nazism had, not only upon the German people, but even, when he was in Germany, upon Jung himself:

> Would you have believed that a whole nation of highly intelligent and cultivated people could be seized by the fascinating power of an archetype? I saw it coming, and I can understand it because I know the power of the collective unconscious. But on the surface it looks simply incredible. Even my personal friends are under that fascination, and when I am in Germany, I believe it myself, I understand it all, I know it has to be as it is. One cannot resist it. It gets you below the belt and not in your mind, your brain just counts for nothing, your sympathetic system is gripped. It is a power that fascinates people from within, it is the collective unconscious which is activated....We cannot be children about it, having intellectual and reasonable ideas and saying: this should not be.[72]

Regarding Germans caught up in the Third Reich, Jung said: "An incomprehensible fate has seized them, and you cannot say it is right, or it is wrong. It has nothing to do with rational judgment, it is just history."[73] One cannot necessarily fault Jung for having become temporarily mesmerized with what he himself described as the archetypal aspect of Hitler's hold upon the German psyche. One wonders, however, how on further reflection he could possibly deny that the categories of "right" and "wrong" apply to those caught up in the tide of National Socialism.

In a letter to Aaron Roback (September 29, 1936), Jung writes: "I am no Nazi, as a matter of fact I am quite unpolitical."[74] That same year, Jung took up the psychology of National Socialism in the oft-cited article "Wotan." Wotan is the Teutonic God whom Jung equates with the irrational, barbarous, yet creative depths of the German psyche. As we have seen, on Jung's view, Wotan, as "god" or "archetype," "has taken posses-sion of the Germans."[75] For Jung, "All human control comes to an end when the individual is caught in a mass movement. Then the archetypes begin to function."[76] Jung then quite decisively repudiates both Hitler and the Nazis when he says, "The impressive thing about the German phe-nomenon is that one man, who is obviously 'possessed,' has infected a whole nation to such an extent that everything is set in motion and has started rolling on its course to perdition."[77]

The Knickerbocker Interview

In 1938, Jung was interviewed by H. R. Knickerbocker, an American for-eign correspondent. During this interview, Jung spoke rather freely about the German dictator. His remarks, which were apparently intended to be purely descriptive, nevertheless suggest that Jung was deeply impressed by Hitler's archetypal power over the masses. Jung then says: "There is no question but that Hitler belongs in the category of the truly mystic medi-cine man. As somebody commented about him at the last Nurnberg [Nuremberg] party congress, since the time of Mohammed nothing like it has been seen in this world." Jung goes on to describe the mystical sig-nificance of Hitler's dictatorship:

> This markedly mystic character of Hitler's is what makes him do things which seem to *us* illogical, inexplicable, curious and unreason-able. But consider—even the nomenclature of the Nazis is plainly mystic. Take the very name of the Nazi State….Only the Nazis call theirs the Third Reich. Because it has a profound *mystical* meaning: to every German the expression "Third Reich" brings echoes in his unconscious of the Biblical hierarchy. Thus Hitler, who more than once has indicated he is aware of his mystic calling, appears to the devotees of the Third Reich as something more than a mere man.[78]

Jung's remarks here are profound and must be understood as purely descriptive. He is not providing a (Jungian) psychological *justification* for Hitler's behavior, nor advocating the notion that Hitler is "more than a mere man," but only that the German leader functions within a certain archetype that prompts his devotees to experience him in this manner. The comparison to Mohammed and the biblical interpretation of the Third Reich suggests that, for the German people, Hitler's calling is a "third" revelation, superseding those given to Moses and Jesus! While this is a disturbing message, it was certainly one that contained more than a mea-sure of truth.

For Jung, Hitler is not a man who is directed by his ego consciousness, but rather one who heeds a deeper voice, one that emanates from what

Jung, in other places, calls the "self." Jung is deeply impressed by Hitler's intuitive powers, and he tells Knickerbocker:

> Hitler's secret is twofold: first, that his unconscious has exceptional access to his consciousness, and second, that he allows himself to be moved by it. He is like a man who listens intently to a stream of suggestions from a whispered source and then *acts upon them*. In our case, even if occasionally our unconscious does reach us through dreams, we have too much rationality, too much cerebrum to obey it. This is doubtless the case with Chamberlain, but Hitler listens and obeys. The true leader is always *led*.

Jung goes on to say that because of his "*unconscious perception....*[Hitler] makes political judgments which turn out to be right against the opinions of all his advisers and against the opinions of all foreign observers."[79]

In an article published after his father's death, Micha Neumann spoke candidly about Erich Neumann's distress during the mid-1930s over Jung's failure to adequately denounce the dangers of Nazism:

> My father told me that he tried to convince Jung of the terrible danger of the Nazi movement, of the brutality and inhumanity of the Nazis. He asked Jung to express himself openly and clearly against their ideologies and especially their anti-Semitic ideas and policies. He admitted that he failed to change Jung's attitude. My father warned him that if he kept quiet at such a bad time for the Jews, then it would always be remembered and he would never be forgiven. Jung, believing in the qualities of the German collective unconscious, insisted that something positive might still emerge from the situation.[80]

It is not difficult to see why Neumann was unable to persuade Jung, who even several years later continued to express a certain fascination with Hitler. Again and again, in his interview with Knickerbocker, Jung uses religious metaphors in speaking of Hitler. While Jung's words are intended as description as opposed to endorsement, a certain fascination, if not enthusiasm, is revealed in his choice of language and metaphors: "Hitler is a medicine man, a form of spiritual vessel, a demi-deity or even better, a myth," and "Yes, it seems that the German people are now convinced they have found their Messiah." Jung goes on to say: "In a way, the position of the Germans is remarkably like that of the Jews of old," for like the Jews the Germans have an inferiority complex and await a savior.[81] According to Jung:

> If he [Hitler] is not their true Messiah, he is like one of the Old Testament prophets: his mission is to unite his people and lead them to the promised land.[82]

Jung goes on to say that Hitler will pursue his campaign against the Catholic and Protestant churches because he wishes to substitute a new faith for these old creeds. In response to a question from Knickerbocker, Jung says that it is "highly possible" that Hitlerism could become the permanent German religion, just as Mohammedanism is for the Moslems. Jung suggests that one piece of evidence for this idea is that German communities in parts of the world such as Chile, that are far from Berlin, have adopted Hitlerism.

At the time of this 1938 interview, Jung was clearly aware of Hitler's anti-Semitism and even suggests that Mussolini adopted an anti-Jewish position because he became "convinced that world Jewry was probably an incorrigible and effective force against Fascism."

In fairness to Jung, it should again be emphasized that most of what he says in the Knickerbocker interview should be understood as a *description* as opposed to *endorsement*.[83] Further, it is clear in this interview that Jung saw Hitler as a great threat: "With Hitler you are scared. You know you would never be able to talk to that man; because there is nobody there. He is not a man, but a collective. He is not an individual; but a whole nation." Jung suggests that Hitler should somehow be encouraged to take a bite out of Russia. "Nobody," he says, "has ever bitten into Russia without regretting it. It's not very palatable food. It might take the Germans a hundred years to finish the meal. Meanwhile we should be safe, and by we, I mean all of Western civilization." Jung suggests that the democracy of America must be saved "else we all go under."[84] Jung is mistrustful of nationalism: "Everybody ought to fear a nation. It's a horrible thing. How can such a thing have honor or a word? That's why I am for *small* nations. Small nations mean small catastrophes. Big nations mean big catastrophes."[85]

A full reading of the Knickerbocker interview thus reveals Jung to be *fascinated* by Hitler's mysticism but *fearful* and *distrustful* of it. At least at the close of his interview with Knickerbocher, he aligns himself with the West. However, one can get the sense in reading the Knickerbocker interview that Jung was, as it were, talking out of both sides of his mouth and hedging his bets. Some of his language was such that it could be reinterpreted at a later date as either extremely flattering to Hitler or purely "descriptive" and even condemnatory. We should note parenthetically that Jung exhibited the same tendency with respect to his so-called "theology." While he said many things that could readily be interpreted as metaphysical or theological, he spoke in a manner that permitted him to deny that these statements were metaphysical at all, and claim that they were merely "descriptive."[86] Whether he was conscious of this or not, Jung seems to have had a way with words that enabled him to make certain rather dramatic statements and later claim that he was being misunderstood by those who took these statements in a literal or concrete manner.

Jung's Hitler Dream(s)

In 1939, around the time of the Hitler-Stalin non-aggression pact, Jung is said to have had a dream about Hitler that was not recorded until several years later, first by E. A. Bennett in 1946, and then by Esther Harding in 1948. In Bennet's version,[87] Jung is in a vast field filled with buffalos (i.e., Germans). He and Hitler were each on separate mounds, and Jung felt that "as long as he fixed his gaze on Hitler all would be well." In the end, Cossacks round up the buffalos and drive them from the field, and Jung awakens glad, knowing that Germany would be defeated by Russia. Jung told Bennett that this was a very important "collective dream." In the version recorded by Harding,[88] which may well have been a different dream altogether, Jung finds himself in a castle made of dynamite where Hitler enters and is "treated as divine." Hitler and Jung stand on adjoining mounds and the parade ground before them is filled with buffalos and yak steers. The herd is restless, and Hitler asks Jung about a lone cow that was apparently sick. Jung says, "It's obviously very sick," at which point Cossacks ride in and began to drive off the herd. Jung interprets for Harding that Hitler's being treated as divine shows that he, like Judas and the Antichrist, is yet an instrument of divine forces; the cow's sickness is the anima or feminine element, missing from the Third Reich, and "very sick" in Germany. The Cossacks represent the defeat of Germany by the Russians, who are more directly primitive and instinctual than the Germans themselves. Hannah, in her biography of Jung, tells us that Jung immediately afterward dreamed that Hitler was the "devil's Christ."[89] Hannah relates this to Jung's lifelong preoccupation with the dark side of God, a preoccupation that is finally articulated in his *Answer to Job*.

The War Years

By 1940, Jung's name was apparently on the Nazi's "blacklist," and at a point when it appeared that Switzerland would be invaded, Jung was asked to leave Zurich.[90] Certainly, by the time of the war, Jung lost any of the optimism he may have felt in connection with the Nazi regime, and participated in discussions regarding a plan to remove Hitler.[91] Jung also acted as an advisor to Allen Dulles, an American spy, who entered Switzerland in November 1942, and who based many of his communiqués to Washington upon Jung's observations of Nazi conduct and character.[92]

On the other hand, Paul Roazen reports on the existence of a 1946 British Foreign Office booklet entitled "The Case of Dr. Carl G. Jung— Pseudo-Scientist Nazi Auxiliary," by Maurice Leon. The file was classified, and was therefore not accessible to Roazen, but he reports that there were apparently Foreign Office minutes regarding a "proposed trial" of Jung as a "war criminal."[93]

In a document dated December 1944, there is a record of a secret agreement limiting the percentage of Jews in the Analytical Psychology Club of Zurich, a group that Jung was intimately involved with. While some apparently held that this was a means to safeguard Jung lest Switzerland were to be invaded by the Nazis, all agree that Jung was aware of the quota system, which did not come to an end until Siegmund Hurwitz (Jung's student and dentist) threatened to withdraw his application for membership unless the offending rule was eliminated. Maidenbaum and Martin were told that the club's records were a shambles when they attempted to pursue the question of whether or not there continued to be discrimination against Jews after the war and before the rule was rescinded in 1950.[94]

After the War

In "After the Catastrophe,"[95] which was published in 1946, Jung confesses that he did not realize how deeply he had been affected by the Nazi era. The "participation mystique with events in Germany has caused me to experience how painfully wide is the scope of the psychological concept of collective guilt."[96] He adds: "So when I approach this problem it is certainly not with any feelings of cold-blooded superiority, but rather with an aroused sense of inferiority." In this essay, Jung's understanding of Hitler is quite different and far less complimentary than the description he provided Knickerbocker in 1938. In this article he says, "The pseudoscientific race theories with which it was dolled up did not make the extermination of the Jews any more acceptable."[97] Jung diagnoses Hitler as having suffered from *pseudologia fantastica*, which Jung describes as a hysterical condition in which one believes one's own lies. Now Jung tells us: "Hitler's theatrical, obviously hysterical gestures struck all foreigners (with a few amazing exceptions) as purely ridiculous."[98] Whereas, in the 1938 Knickerbocker interview, Jung stated that he was struck by Hitler's "dreamy look,"[99] Jung now says, "When I saw him with my own eyes, he suggested a psychic scarecrow (with a broomstick for an outstretched arm) rather than a human being." Now, instead of appealing to analogies with Jacob, Jesus, and Mohammed as an explanation of Hitler's hold on the German people, Jung pins the label "psychopathic inferiority" on the whole of the German nation, and says that this is "the only explanation which could in any way account for the effect this scarecrow had on the masses."[100] Jung acknowledges that his judgment *would* have been different in 1933 and 1934 when, in Jung's view, the renewed economic situation in Germany gave one hope in the Hitler regime, but he makes no specific reference to his earlier archetypal analysis. Jung speaks in general terms regarding personal guilt vis-à-vis the "catastrophe":

> We must all open our eyes to the shadow who looms behind contemporary man....As to what should be done about this terrifying apparition, everyone must work this out for himself. It is indeed no small matter to know of

one's own guilt and one's own evil, and there is certainly nothing to be gained by losing sight of one's shadow. When we are conscious of our guilt we are in a more favourable position—we can at least hope to change and improve ourselves.[101]

As we have seen, in his Tavistock speech in 1935 Jung had described the phenomenon of Hitler's Germany as being totally beyond rational reflection, that it must be the way it is, that it cannot be resisted, cannot be said to be right or wrong, and "has nothing to do with rational judgment."[102] However, ten years later, in the "Epilogue to 'Essays on Contemporary Events,'" Jung put a different slant on his perceptions of what was occurring before the war: "When Hitler seized power it became quite evident to me that a mass psychosis was boiling up in Germany. But I could not help telling myself that this was after all Germany, a civilized European nation with a sense of morality and discipline."[103] In contrast to his earlier fascination with Hitler's acting in response to the call of his unconscious, Jung now says, "As a psychiatrist, accustomed to dealing with patients who are in danger of being overwhelmed by unconscious contents, I knew that it is of utmost importance, from the therapeutic point of view, to strengthen as far as possible their conscious position and powers of understanding so that there is something there to intercept and integrate the contents that are breaking through to consciousness."[104]

Jung gave a talk, broadcast on the BBC in 1946, "The Fight with the Shadow," which is printed in his *Collected Works* and in which he described Hitler as "the most prodigious personification of all human inferiorities."[105] In this talk, Jung describes Hitler as "an utterly incapable, unadapted, irresponsible, psychopathic personality, full of empty, infantile fantasies, but cursed with the keen intuition of a rat or a guttersnipe." People identified with him because in him they saw their own "shadow." This way of speaking contrasted markedly with his earlier comments to Knickerbocker, in which he appeared to laud Hitler's direct, unmediated access to his unconscious as the key to his leadership.

Also in 1946, in the "Epilogue to 'Essays on Contemporary Events,'" Jung wrote that as early as 1933 he had an "extremely unfavourable impression of the Nazi party, but indicates that he did not want to rush to judgment about it.[106]

In 1949, the *Saturday Review of Literature* published an article by Robert Hillyer that accused Jung of being anti-Semitic and pro-Nazi. Hillyer reported, "at the luncheon for the Harvard Tercentenary in 1936, Dr. Jung, who was seated beside me, deftly introduced the subject of Hitler, developed it with alert warmth, and concluded with the statement that from the high vantage point of Alpine Switzerland Hitler's new order in Germany seemed to offer the one hope for Europe."[107] Jung later told Philip Wylie that although he did not recall having told Hillyer this, he might have done so, as he had often expressed this belief in conversation prior to 1937.[108] In this context, it is worth noting that shortly after departing from Harvard, Jung was interviewed in London by *The Observer* (October 18, 1936), and while he called Roosevelt "perfectly ruthless... the stuff of a dictator absolutely," he said that Hitler was "a Sybil, the Delphic oracle," ruling Germany "by revelation."[109] However, the offense of Jung's optimism regarding the potential of Hitler's Germany is tempered somewhat by the fact that no less an opponent of Hitler's than Winston Churchill wondered in 1935 whether Hitler would "let loose upon the world another war in which civilization will irretrievably succumb, or whether he will go down in history as the man who restored honour and peace of mind to the great Germanic nation."[110]

Jung responded to Hillyer's attack in an interview in which he stated that anyone who has read his writings would understand that he was neither anti-Semitic nor pro-Nazi, and that the Nazis had "played double," by on the one hand blacklisting him and destroying his books and on the other hand publicizing that he supported them.[111] With regard to his article "The State of Psychotherapy Today," Jung stated that since the article was to be printed in Germany he "had to write in a somewhat veiled manner." He further said that he was simply pointing out "certain psychological differences" and that a full reading of the article would reveal that he was actually being "complimentary to the Jews" who "are in general more conscious and differentiated than the average Aryan."[112]

The Research of Richard Noll

Richard Noll has argued that the controversy over Jung's anti-Semitism and Nazi sympathies must be understood within the larger context of German *Volkisch* philosophy and spirituality, that informed both Jung's thought and National Socialism.[113] Noll's work created considerable controversy both within and beyond the Jungian community when it was published in the mid-1990s. I believe we can accept and learn from Noll's scholarship, without necessarily adopting each of Noll's assumptions or conclusions. In his review of Noll's two books, the British Jungian and evolutionary psychiatrist Anthony Stevens acknowledges that "Noll marshals extensive evidence designed to prove that Jungian psychology shares precisely the same Germanic, Aryan, 'volkisch,' Nietzschean sun-worshipping roots as National Socialism."[114] While Stevens (and many others) are justifiably critical of some of Noll's more extreme theses (e.g., that Jung established a religious cult with himself as God or the "Aryan Christ"; that because Jung experienced what many others have described as "the god within" that Jung must have "believed that he *was* a god"; and that Jungianism is a thinly disguised "institutionalized capitalist enterprise"!), he largely accepts Noll's contribution to our understanding of

Jung and his thought, holding that Noll was accurate in recording the development of Jung's researches on Mithraism, Gnosticism, and alchemy, and that had Noll refrained from some of his more outrageous conclusions he could well have provided us with "a scholarly examination of the cultural antecedents of Jung's thought, and a creative exposure of the shadow side of Jungian training and practice."

Here I will summarize some of Noll's less controversial claims, several of which cast considerable light on Jung's relationship to both Judaism and the occult. According to Noll, while the official history places Jung squarely within the psychiatric tradition of Bleuler and Freud, Jung was actually deeply involved with and influenced by a group of loosely related, largely Germanic movements and ideas.

Nietzscheism: Jung took an enormous interest in Nietzsche, devoting seminars to Nietzsche's *Zarathustra* at the psychology club throughout the late 1930s.[115] Early on, Jung had taken a keen interest in the revitalization of spiritual movements that were founded on the heels of Nietzsche's proclamation of the death of God and the deconstruction of traditional religious belief. According to Noll, Jung is part of, and indeed at the forefront of, a form of nontraditional spiritualism rooted in Nietzschean philosophy.

The Wagner Cult: Jung was fascinated with the composer Richard Wagner[116] (1813–83), whose devotees, particularly after Wagner's death, became nationalistic and openly anti-Semitic. Wagner selectively treated Germanic mythology in his operas, focusing especially on the heroic Siegfried, who became an important mythic figure for Jung. Sabina Spielrein, who was Jewish and deeply in love with Jung, wrote in her personal diaries that she and Jung both had fantasies about having a Germanic child named Siegfried. Hitler regarded Wagner as a progenitor of Nazism and made Bayreuth, where Wagner's operas were performed, a sacred national shrine.

Haeckelism: Ernst Haeckel (1834–1919), professor of zoology, anti-Christian, and the founder of "Monistic Religion," held that each adult is a "living museum" of the species history.[117] Jung took up Haeckel's recommendations regarding a "phylogeny of the soul" and a "phylogenetic psychology." Haeckel was anti-Semitic and helped formulate the notion that Jews were biologically inferior.

Sun worship: The sun as a prominent symbol of the inner God or self became an important theme in the *Volkisch* movement,[118] as expressed, for example, in the writings of such authors as Herman Alexander Keyserling (1880–1946). Richard Wilhelm (1873–1930) was a lecturer at Keyserling's school of wisdom and become a close personal friend of and collaborator of Jung's.[119]

Diederichs Verlag: Jung was familiar with many of the works published by Eugen Diederichs,[120] including those by such classic authors as Eckhart, Silesius, Boehme, Bruno, Paracelsus, Goethe, and Carus, many of whom were extremely important in Jung's own intellectual development. Diederichs believed in the nonrational character of religion and the spiritual reawakening of the German people, themes that were soon taken up by Jung himself. In the German reawakening, intuition would be placed above reason and, as Lukács argued, lead to an initiated, spiritual elite who would bring about society's redemption.[121] Diederichs also popularized Gnosticism in a series of popular works between 1903 and 1910 (Jung wrote his own Gnostic myth in 1916[122]), and promoted interest in Aryan mythology and symbolism, including the swastika and mandala symbolism,[123] the latter of which became of great interest to Jung.

The Occult: Noll points out that Jung took a great interest in spiritualism and the occult, working on the border between hysterical and spiritual phenomena. Jung was undoubtedly familiar with such occultists as Helena Petrovna Blavatsky (1831–91), a Russian spiritualist who claimed to be in contact with ascended masters, who imparted to her a "secret doctrine." Her work *Isis Unveiled* surveys the occult traditions of alchemy, astrology, ritual magic, witchcraft, and Eastern philosophies,[124] each of which became part of the spiritual climate that imbued many young Germans and Swiss, including Jung, during the late years of the nineteenth and early years of the twentieth century.

Land Mysticism: Jung took up another common *volkisch* theme in his doctrine that landscape or terrain has a decisive impact upon a people's psychology, and utilized this idea in his differentiation of the Jewish and Aryan minds.[125] Jung's distinction between the overcivilized Jew and the repressed barbarian German echoes a century-old German distinction between the natural, chthonic man and his overly constricted civilized counterpart.[126] As we have seen, Jung held that the Jew is not rooted in the land. (Here we should note that similar doctrines about the land and rootedness are major themes in Zionism and may have in fact later prompted Jung's sympathies with the Zionist movement.[127])

The "Life Tone": Jung was clearly attracted to the German ethnonaturalist or *volkisch* belief in a "life tone" linking all Germans together in a common emotional experience.[128] For Jung, this common feeling was the basis for a powerful transference, e.g., Hitler's impact upon the German masses.

Noll understands the impact of these *volkisch* ideas on Jung, as well as the popularity of Jung's ideas among astrologers and New Age and neopagan spiritualists, as signs that Jungian psychology is really nothing but an intellectualized version of occult ideas and practices. According to Noll, Jung presented his theories in terms of the metaphors of alchemy, which "were less nakedly volkisch."[129] Noll concludes that "the evidence is compelling that Jung's work arose from the same Central European cauldron of neopagan, Nietzschean, mystical, hereditarian, volkisch utopianism that gave rise to National Socialism."[130] However, Noll situates

Jung within these contexts without seriously considering the possibility that despite these indubitable associations, Jung and his followers developed an intellectually sophisticated and defensible psychology. This is because Noll works under the tacit (initially plausible, but questionable) assumptions that (a) there is virtually nothing of value in the occultist, theosophical, and "neo-pagan" movements of the late nineteenth and early twentieth century; (b) the association of elements of these movements with the *volkisch* philosophy that eventually contributed to Nazism is sufficient to damn these movements; (c) if Jungian psychology can be associated closely with religion or spirituality, this is sufficient to expose Jungianism as a fraud; and/or (d) the spirituality offered by Jung and his followers is a pseudo-spirituality unworthy of either theological or psychological attention.

"The Aryan Christ"

In a second work, *The Aryan Christ: the Secret Life of Carl Jung*, Noll discusses certain evidence regarding Jung's purported anti-Semitism. On Noll's reading, Jung had an abiding interest in the spiritual renewal of the Aryan race, and his love of pagan and *volkisch* myths and symbols initially attracted him to the Nazis, as they had constructed their own ideology on the basis of the same German myths and ideas that Jung had found so attractive. However, on Noll's view, Jung was uninterested in politics and he read National Socialism in purely psychological terms, as an expression of the mythic "archaic man" who would revitalize German culture.[131] Noll quotes one of Jung's longtime disciples, Jolande Jacobi:

> His idea [about the Nazi movement] was that chaos gives birth to good or something valuable. So in the German movement he saw a chaotic (we could say) pre-condition for the birth of a new world.[132]

Despite the evidence of the Nazi threat, Jung continued to view the goings-on in Germany through the lens of his own psychology, telling Jacobi, after she warned him of the dangers of Nazism, "Keep your eyes open. You can't reject evil because evil is the bringer of light."[133] According to Jacobi, Jung simply had no understanding of the outside world.

In all fairness to Jung, the mere fact that his psychology may in large part be rooted in many of the same philosophical and religious ideas that influenced National Socialism does not make Jung a Nazi, any more than the violent deeds of Christian zealots (e.g., during the Inquisition or Crusades) make all Christians a party to their acts. It has been lucidly pointed out by Noll and others that Zionism is in many ways a "volkisch" movement that was rooted in certain ideas that were also influential upon the Nazis.[134] The evidence linking Jung to anti-Semitism and Nazism must be more direct.

Noll points out that Jung could be openly anti-Semitic, particularly when in the company of non-Jews. In 1933, the prominent British Jungian Michael Fordham met with Jung in Zurich. Fordham reports that Jung spent three-quarters of an hour ranting about the Jews, saying, among other things, that when the Jews were in the desert for forty years they were "feeding off other people's crops," and that Jews "ought to be dressed up in different clothes because otherwise we might mistake them for people like ourselves."[135] Irene Champernowne, who had begun an analysis with Jung in 1936, later reported that Jung had made anti-Semitic remarks and actually encouraged his patients to do the same as a means of staying in touch with one's "shadow."[136] However, another of Jung's associates, Cornelia Brunner, recalled that Jung had been "terribly upset" when he learned that the German synagogues had been burned.[137]

"Guilt" and "Repentance"?

The extent of Jung's "guilt" with regard to his words and behavior prior to World War II remains open to considerable controversy.[138] A consensus has emerged, however, even among many Jungians, that while Jung was neither a rabid anti-Semite nor a Nazi, and personally did much to help individual Jews during the Nazi era and throughout his life, his words and attitudes during the 1930s were at times irresponsible, inflammatory, opportunistic, naïve, and perhaps even openly anti-Jewish. Jung never publicly acknowledged any specific personal wrongdoing after the war. I believe that the closest he came to doing so was in the comments he made in "After the Catastrophe," which we have already reviewed. There he implies that he himself was not immune from the "collective guilt" stemming from the Nazi era. Further, in an article entitled "Carl Gustav Jung and the Jews: The Real Story,"[139] James Kirsch, a longtime Jewish disciple of Jung, relates that the first thing Jung did when they met after the war was to express regret for his view that something good might come of the Third Reich and "to apologize for some of the things he had written at that time." Kirsch writes that he very much regrets that this apology was not made in a public forum.[140] It is noteworthy that Jung, who earlier in his life was scathing in his self-criticism,[141] never seems to have come to a full self-accounting with regard to his words and actions during the ascent of the Nazi state.

Gershom Scholem's letter to Aniela Jaffé, written on May 7, 1963, is worth quoting at length in this context, not only because it comes from the pen of the greatest modern scholar of Jewish mysticism, but also because it has been said to indicate that Jung, at least privately, accepted a certain responsibility and repented for wrongs he committed prior to World War II. Scholem writes:

> In the summer of 1947 Leo Baeck was in Jerusalem. I had then just received for the first time an invitation to the Eranos meeting in

Ascona, evidently at Jung's suggestion, and I asked Baeck whether I should accept it, as I had heard and read many protests about Jung's behavior in the Nazi period. Baeck said: "You must go, absolutely!" and in the course of our conversation told me the following story. He too had been put off by Jung's reputation resulting from those well known articles in the years 1933–4, precisely because he knew Jung very well from the Darmstadt meetings of the School of Wisdom and would never have credited him with any Nazi and anti-Semitic sentiments. When, after his release from Theresienstadt, he returned to Switzerland for the first time (I think it was 1946), he therefore did not call on Jung in Zurich. But it came to Jung's ears that he was in the city and Jung sent a message begging him to visit him, which he, Baeck, declined because of those happenings. Whereupon Jung came to his hotel and they had an extremely lively talk lasting two hours, during which Baeck reproached him with all the things he had heard. Jung defended himself by an appeal to the special conditions in Germany but at the same time confessed to him: "Well, I slipped up"— probably referring to the Nazis and his expectation that something great might after all emerge. This remark, "I slipped up," which Baeck repeated to me several times, remains vividly in my memory. Baeck said that in this talk they cleared up everything that had come between them and that they parted from one another reconciled again. Because of this explanation of Baeck's I accepted the invitation to Eranos when it came a second time.[142]

Scholem points out that, for the Swiss, the term Jung used, "slipped up," often refers to losing one's footing on a dangerous mountain path; however, the reader can judge for himself the degree to which this story reflects Jung's acceptance of responsibility for his words and actions.

Did Jung Ignore the Jewish Mystical Bases of His Own Thought?

The question of Jung's writings and attitudes during the early years of the Nazi regime is further complicated by the possibility that during that same period Jung suppressed the Jewish mystical basis for some of his own thought. We have already seen in Chapter 2 how Jung appealed to alchemy as a basis for his psychology without at first acknowledging the enormous impact of the Kabbalah on the very alchemical ideas that he found so appealing. Here, as promised, I will more thoroughly examine the evidence regarding Jung's possible suppression of the Jewish mystical basis of his thinking.

As we have seen, in a letter to the Reverend Erastus Evans written on the February 17, 1954, Jung describes what he says was his *first* encounter with the Kabbalistic symbols of *Shevirat ha-Kelim* (the Breaking of the Vessels) and *Tikkun ha-Olam* (the Restoration of the World). Jung's report that he first came across these Kabbalistic notions in 1954 is difficult to understand, because, as Jung's editors point out, he alludes to these Kabbalistic doctrines in Chapter 2 of *Answer to Job*, which was first published in 1952.[143] There Jung writes of a "new factor" that has never occurred before in the history of the world, the unheard-of fact that, without knowing it or wanting it, a mortal man is raised by his moral behavior above the stars in heaven, from which position of advantage he can behold the back of Yahweh, the abysmal world of "shards" (i.e., the broken vessels),[144] which he explains as "an allusion to an idea found in the later cabalistic philosophy."[145]

Jung himself notes that "shards" is a reference to later (i.e., Lurianic) Kabbalistic philosophy. He later adds that God had "banished Adam and Eve, whom he had created as images of his masculine essence and his feminine emanation, to the extra-paradisial world, the limbo of the 'shards.'"[146] In other places in *Answer to Job*, Jung expresses quintessential Lurianic ideas. For example, Jung suggests that God must have man for a partner in completing creation (an idea which, as Jung points out in his letter to Evans,[147] has a strong antecedent in the Lurianic notion of *Tikkun*), that "Whoever knows God has an effect on him"[148] (a parallel to the Kabbalistic doctrine of theurgy), and declares that the worlds are born as a result of the divine marriage (*hierosgamos*) of God and his feminine counterpart, a Kabbalistic theme that is prominent in the Zohar and that was passed on to alchemy via the Kabbalah.[149]

While it is certainly possible that some of Jung's ideas came to him independently of any knowledge of Kabbalistic sources, it is difficult to take Jung completely at his word that he found "confirmation" of his theodicy after first coming across the Lurianic concept of *Tikkun* in 1954, if only for the fact that he was reportedly quite familiar with *Kabbalah Denudata*[150] (a Latin compendium of Kabbalistic writings), cited the works of Gershom Scholem,[151] and, as we shall see, evidenced an apparently sophisticated awareness of Kabbalistic symbols in his 1944 visions. One possibility is that Jung's theodicy in *Answer to Job* and other writings is at least in part a result of "cryptomnesia," a reworking of old ideas that Jung experienced as his own because he had forgotten their source.[152] However, it is also possible that a more conscious cause than cryptomnesia may well have been at work in Jung's own case, as during the 1930s Jung saw an opportunity to distinguish his "Christian/Western" psychology from the "Jewish" psychology of Freud.

As we have seen, Erich Neumann, who had recently emigrated to Palestine, wrote Jung in 1935 expressing his fear that his absorption in Jungian psychology would place him in "danger of betrayal to [his] own Jewish foundations."[153] One of the things that Jung said in response was that "analytical psychology has its roots in the Christian middle ages and ultimately in Greek philosophy, with the connecting link being alchemy."[154] What Jung failed to mention is that the Kabbalah was an important spiritual foundation for alchemy.[155] It was only after World War II that Jung openly acknowledged this important connection. "Directly or indirectly," Jung writes in the *Mysterium*, "the Cabala [Jung's spelling] was assimilated into alchemy."[156] As we have seen, Jung was aware that by the end of the sixteenth century the alchemists began making direct quotations from the Zohar[157] and that a number of alchemists, including Khunrath and Dorn, had made extensive use of Kabbalistic symbols. In addition, Jung noted that works by Reuchlin (*De Arte Cabbalistica*, 1517) and Mirandola had made the Kabbalah accessible to non-Jewish alchemists,[158] and that Paracelsus had introduced the sapphire as an "arcanum" into alchemy from the Kabbalah. Finally, two of the alchemists (Knorr and Khunrath) Jung most frequently quoted wrote treatises on the Kabbalah, and others (e.g., Dorn and Lully) were heavily influenced by Kabbalistic ideas. Given Jung's claim to have extracted the psychological and spiritual gold from the dross of alchemical pseudoscience, it is hard to imagine that he was not aware that in doing so he was, at least in part, reconstituting aspects of the Kabbalah.

It is difficult to ascertain precisely how well-versed Jung was in Kabbalah prior to his 1954 letter to Evans. As we will see, his later report of his1944 Kabbalistic visions, if they can be taken at face value, suggests a quite sophisticated knowledge of Kabbalistic texts. Werner Engel relates that Siegmund Hurwitz, whom he describes as a "Jewish Jungian in Zurich deeply involved in Kabbalah studies," confirmed to him that Jung, with occasional assistance from Hurwitz, had "undergone intensive studies to deepen his knowledge of Judaism, including Isaac Luria's Kabbalistic writings."[159] Hurwitz himself told Maidenbaum that subsequent to Jung's 1934 *Zentralblatt* article, Jung changed his point of view. At that time, Jung "did not know much about Judaism but in the later years he was very much interested in Kabbalah and he bought books [on the topic]....I brought him together with [Gershom] Scholem and I helped him with Kabbalistic texts."[160]

James Kirsch, whose association with Jung dated back to the 1930s, wrote that Jung read the whole of Knorr von Rosenroth's *Kabbalah Denudata* (The Kabbalah Unveiled), a three-thousand-page Latin compendium of Kabbalistic texts.[161] While Kirsch does not indicate when such reading took place, it should be pointed out that Jung cites Knorr's text in *Psychology and Alchemy*, a work which was originally written during the 1930s and completed in 1943.[162]

Apart from his knowledge of Knorr's Latin translations of original Kabbalistic sources, Jung was likely early on familiar with German and/or French translations of the Zohar, the German text of Bischoff's *Die*

Elemente der Kabbalah (each of which are cited in his prewar works on alchemy), and the German writings of Gershom Scholem, who by the late 1930s had begun detailing the doctrines of the Kabbalah to a wide European audience. In addition, Jung was exposed to Kabbalistic symbols and ideas through his reading of sixteenth- and seventeenth-century alchemical texts, which borrowed heavily from Jewish Kabbalism.

The notion that Jung made intensive studies of Judaism and the Kabbalah prior to World War II is contradicted by Micha Neumann's claim that his father, Erich Neumann, encouraged, even pleaded with Jung to undertake such studies without any success. Micha Neumann writes: "Even though Jung promised my father that he would study Judaism, he never really kept his promise."[163] In 1935, Erich Neumann wrote to Jung that he lacked "knowledge and understanding of Judaism."[164] Jung's disciple, confidante, and secretary, Aniela Jaffé, held that Jung's early statements about the Jewish mind "spring from a lack of comprehension of Judaism and Jewish culture which is scarcely intelligible today."[165]

I do not know that Jung consciously ignored the Jewish mystical origins of some of his ideas. Given Jung's avowed efforts to distinguish his psychology from Freud's "Jewish psychology," and the opportunities such a distinction would have afforded him, he certainly would have had a motive for denying or suppressing any of his own Jewish sources. As we will see, if Jung had consciously or unconsciously ignored or suppressed the Jewish mystical sources of some of his ideas, his Kabbalistic visions during his mortal illness in 1944 might be understood (in Jungian terms) as a powerful compensation for that suppression, as well as for his anti-Jewish writings and sentiments.[166]

Jung, Ambivalence, and the Context-Dependence of Belief

The portrait of Jung that emerges from an examination of his purported anti-Semitism is confusing and often contradictory. On the question of his relation to National Socialism, Jung seems to have been capable of generating diametrically opposed reactions in two individuals who spoke with him at the identical time and place. As we have seen, Robert Hillyer, writing in 1949, reported that in 1936 at the luncheon for the Harvard Tercentenary, Jung raised "the subject of Hitler, developed it with alert warmth, and concluded...Hitler's new order in Germany seemed to offer the one hope for Europe."[167] However, Allen W. Dulles, who under President Kennedy was later to become Director of the CIA, wrote in 1950:

> I first met Dr. Jung in 1936 when he was here in connection with the Harvard Tercentenary. At that time I had a long talk with him about what was going on in Germany and Italy and I do not recall anything which Jung said which indicated other than a deep anti-Nazi and anti-Fascist sentiment.[168]

Jung's apparent duplicity with respect to such issues as anti-Semitism and Hitlerism, his "double-speak" on the question of whether his psychology has metaphysical as opposed to only empirical import, the belief among his disciples that there was a written and an "oral" Jungian teaching, and the fact that he was able to appear to Freud as a loyal psychoanalyst without revealing his roots in *volkisch* mysticism might simply be chalked up to the complexities of his great mind confronting the contradictions inherent in the human psyche. I will consider two other possibilities here, the first that Jung exhibited normal "context-dependent" contradictions in his personality and behavior, and the second that there was a potentially pathological rift in Jung's personality that could be described utilizing the terms "splitting" or "dissociation."

Walt Whitman, in his "Song of Myself," wrote: "Do I contradict myself? Very well, then I contradict myself, I am large, I contain multitudes." The idea that a special explanation is required in order to explain contradiction in human attitudes, beliefs, and assertions is itself contradicted both by human experience and by those such as Whitman (and Jung himself), who held that the self is indeed a unity of contradictory ideas, beliefs, and emotions. That Jung could be anti-Semitic in some contexts and appalled at the charge of anti-Semitism in others follows not only from Jung's theory of contradiction and ambivalence in the normal self but from recent research and theory on the context-dependence of ordinary beliefs and attitudes. According to "discourse theory," individuals' inconsistency in their talk and even their beliefs is the expected consequence of their engaging in discourse in varying contexts, with different audiences, on different occasions.[169] The theories of Festinger ("cognitive dissonance") and Bem ("self-perception theory") suggest that the context of one's behavior has an enormous impact upon one's beliefs (hence, Jung's comment: "When I am in Germany, I believe it myself, I understand it all, I know it has to be as it is").

The context-dependence of thought and (especially) prejudice was apparent to this author in the course of formulating the ideas and writing this very book. When I imagined myself addressing an audience of committed Jews I found myself writing and believing that Jung was clearly an anti-Semite. However, when I imagined myself addressing an audience of psychologists, and particularly Jungians, I found myself writing and believing that Jung was confused by the times and that the accusations that he was a Nazi sympathizer or anti-Semite were and are overblown, resting as they do upon a misunderstanding that Jung had advocated things that he clearly intended merely to describe. I don't think that such shifts in discourse and belief can be explained simply as "playing to an audience" (though they can at times be that as well), but rather reflect the fact that one's thoughts and beliefs are conditioned, at least in part, by one's real and imagined audience and context, a testimony to the power of the imagined "other" in shifting the sands of one's mental life. Jung, like many others who were caught between radically different "others" in the period before World War II, naturally responded by saying and believing a variety of patently contradictory notions and ideas.

Jung and Dissociation

The idea that there were dissociative tendencies in Jung's personality would be purely speculative but for the fact that Jung, in his auto-biography, describes a whole host of experiences that both in his time and today would be considered highly "dissociative,"[170] and the recent pub-lication of Jung's *Black Books* and *The Red Book* shows how readily he entered into apparently dissociative dialogues with internal, partial per-sonalities.[171] In *Memories, Dreams, Reflections*, Jung relates that in early adolescence he developed the notion that he was "actually two different persons."[172] The first, which he referred to as "Personality No. 1," was "the schoolboy who could not grasp algebra and was far from sure of himself." Personality No. 2 "was important, a high authority, a man not to be trifled with…, an old man who lived in the eighteenth century, wore buckled shoes and a white wig."[173] Jung reports that he experienced him-self as actually having lived in the seventeenth century and believing that certain objects from those times were his—even going so far, at the age of eleven, to habitually "write the date 1786 instead of 1886" and being "overcome by an inexplicable state of nostalgia" each time this occur-red.[174] While Jung himself said that "the play and counterplay between personalities No. 1 and No. 2, which has run through my whole life, has nothing to do with a 'split' or dissociation in the ordinary medical sense," we may be entitled to think otherwise. Indeed, one need only compare Jung's descriptions here with the descriptions, for example, made by Freud and Breuer and of the hysterics they treated to realize how close some of Jung's symptomatology was to those of hysterical-dissociative patients.

Years later, after Jung fell into a deep depression consequent to his split with Freud, Jung, as recorded in the *Black Books* and *The Red Book*, began to have vivid fantasies and waking visions, including visions of the Hebrew prophet Elijah and the Hellenistic pagan seer, Philemon. Of these figures Jung relates that they "produce themselves and have their own life." Jung held conversations with Philemon, and the vision seems to have responded with things that Jung "had not consciously thought." Jung relates: "For I observed clearly that it was he who spoke, not I."[175] "At times," Jung tells us, Philemon "seemed to me quite real…I went walking up and down the garden with him, and to me he was what the Indians call a guru."[176]

Jung composed his own Gnostic myth,[177] the "Seven Sermons to the Dead," in response to what he termed a "parapsychological" (and visionary) experience that occurred one evening in 1916, during which his "whole house was filled as if there were a crowd present, crammed full of spirits....[who] cried out in chorus 'We have come back from Jerusalem where we found not what we sought.'"[178] Jung's "Sermons," which are written in the style of an ancient prophecy, and are attributed to the ancient Gnostic Basilides and only "transcribed by Carl Gustav Jung," circulated for many years among his disciples but were not published until after Jung's death. These sermons, which gave expression to many themes that Jung would return to throughout his career, such as the "coincidence of opposites" and the impersonal nature of many psychic processes, were apparently written in a dissociative state.

To be sure, Jung advocated *techniques* (e.g., active imaginative conversation with alter selves) that involved dissociative processes, and it is clearly a one-sided oversimplification to hold that Jung's visions were a product of a dissociative disorder. However, unless we are willing to either normalize Jung's highly unusual and, at times, contradictory behavior or dismiss him as an opportunist who manipulated those around him by saying things that they wished to hear, the hypothesis of dissociation goes some distance in explaining certain aspects of Jung's behavior. It may indeed be because Jung dissociated that he was able to be both spiritually supportive of such Jewish disciples as Neumann and Kirsch, while at the same time commiserating with anti-Semites and making approving remarks regarding Hitler's reign over Germany.

Again, to say that Jung was "dissociative" is not to simply dismiss him as pathological. Recent interest in dissociation has focused upon its pathological manifestations (of which there are many) to the neglect of its creative and insightful potential. (By contrast, in the nineteenth century, a certain "hysteria" was considered to be almost a prerequisite for creativity and genius.[179]) By dissociating aspects of his own personality, Jung may have been able to obtain insights into elements of the human psyche that are obscured by virtue of being more or less commingled in the "normal" mind. Further, like the prophets and mystics of earlier time, Jung's dissociative visions may well have provided him and others with inspiration as well as insight into the spiritual aspects of human experience. Still, the fruits of his dissociation may well have been at a great cost—one that compromised his moral vision. That Jung achieved a certain integration, integrity, and wisdom in old age is quite clear, and the fact that this integration/integrity was achieved by an individual who was himself so conflicted and divided is rather remarkable, and speaks, I believe, to the depth of his achievement. Yet, one area that he failed fully to integrate into his "*senex*" or "wise old man" involved his ambivalence about the Jews and his grievous judgment and behavior prior to World War II. For many, even those who are sympathetic to Jungian psychology, this remains a significant obstacle to their fully embracing Jung and his work.

Jung's "Gnosticism" Revisited

Mention of Jung's "Seven Sermons" brings us back to our earlier discussion in Chapter 1 regarding the efforts of certain of Jung's critics (Buber, Friedman) and admirers (Altizer) to pin the epithet "Gnostic" on Jung's entire psychology. As noted earlier, Jung in the "Seven Sermons" had advocated an escape from the worldly realm of "creatura" in favor of an "inner star" that lies both within the human psyche and beyond the physical universe. We also saw how Jung had identified the physical world with consciousness and ego and the "inner star" with both the Gnostic Pleroma and the unconscious mind. Finally, following Robert Segal, we argued that insofar as Gnosticism advocates an escape from the physical world, it can in Jungian terms be understood as advocating an immersion of the self in the unconscious and an abandonment of the ego and conscious reason. In this sense, Gnosticism is completely antithetical to Jung's mature thought, where he insists upon an individuation process that is *consciously* realized.[180]

Here, however, we must consider the possibility, indeed the likelihood, that during the Nazi era Jung had become seduced by the Gnostic myth, just as he had been when he composed the "*Septem Sermones ad Mortuos*," and came to place his hopes in a leader, Hitler, whom he perceived to be immersed in the unconscious. As we have seen (for example in his interview with Knickerbocker), Jung was temporarily carried away by the archetypal power of the Nazi movement: "One cannot resist it...your brain just counts for nothing."[181] At the very least, it is clear that Jung was *fascinated* by the charismatic power of a leader who is led, not by the dictates of reason, but by the voice of the unconscious.[182]

Jungs early ambivalence towards reason is evident in *The Red Book*, where he states:

> The world accords not only with reason but with unreason.[183]
>
> We spread poison and paralysis around us in that we want to educate all the world around us into reason.[184]
>
> Whenever I want to learn and understand something I leave my so-called reason at home....[185]

We might say that throughout his career Jung's Gnostic tendencies remained in conflict with his more sober identification with the ego, science, and the rational mind. Indeed, for many of his admirers a significant part of Jung's appeal is derived from the access he appears to have had to the (collective) unconscious, as is evident in such works as the "Seven Sermons" and *Memories, Dreams, Reflections.* This direct access to the unconscious is, as Jung himself noted, the appeal of the prophet, the mystic, the shaman and medicine man, but it is also the appeal of Hitler and other demagogues. Even the attraction (and genius) of a figure like Isaac Luria rests on a similar access to the unconscious mind. Indeed, one might say that if not for its grounding in a very worldly, rational, and ethically conscious religious practice, the Kabbalah would be no more immune from such "Gnostic tendencies" than Gnosticism itself. How to harvest the mystical unconscious without being swallowed up by it was Jung's dilemma, a dilemma that caused him, as he put it, to "slip up" during the Nazi era. However, the dilemma does not end with Jung and the Nazis and continues today for anyone who is open to the spiritual value of the nonrational, unconscious mind.

Jung's Motivation for Writing *Answer to Job*

It will be useful to consider Jung's *Answer to Job* in the context of Jung's reflection upon his own behavior during the Nazi era. Tony Woolfson has argued that Jung's *Answer to Job* was written as a response to "the spectacle of suffering of so many innocent people during the Nazi time and in order to provide the answer to all unjustified suffering."[186] While this is certainly a reasonable motivation for Jung's having written this work, it may well be that Jung also had a personal motivation for writing *Answer to Job*, and we might therefore ask a more specific question. Why did Jung, at this point of his career, write a book that was focused upon the good and evil *in God*—in particular, Yahweh, the Jewish God of the Old Testament?

In order to address this question I will, for the moment, turn to one of Jung's earliest works, *Wandlungen und Symbole der Libido* (*Symbols of Transformation*), which was originally published in 1912, but which Jung was in the process of revising around the same time as he was writing *Answer to Job*. In that work, Jung makes reference to Anatole France's story *Le Jardin d'Epicure*, in which the pious Abbé Oegger is obsessed with trying to prove that the evil Judas, who betrayed the Son of God, was chosen by God as an instrument for the completion of redemption and will therefore be saved as opposed to eternally damned.

Jung asks, "Why should our pious Abbé worry about the old Judas legend?" and his answer is that the Abbé's "doubts and hopes are only apparently concerned with the historical purpose of Judas, but in reality revolve round his own personality, which was seeking a way to freedom through the solution of the Judas problem."[187] Indeed, we learn that the Abbé would soon himself *betray* the Catholic Church by leaving it and becoming a Swedenborgian.

In the same vein, we are entitled to ask: Why should Jung be so concerned about proving that even God, the Jewish God, contains radical evil, and further that this evil is necessary for the world's redemption? Following Jung's own thinking on such matters, we might answer that he was concerned with working through the shadow elements he had discovered within himself—in particular, shadow elements with regard to the people symbolized by Job, the people of the Old Testament, the Jews. On this view, *Answer to Job* is not only, as Tony Woolfson has argued, Jung's response to "the spectacle of suffering of so many innocent people," but also Jung's, perhaps unconscious, response to the evil he was wrestling with in his own soul.

Late in *Answer to Job*, Jung writes: "God wants to become man, the amoral wants to become exclusively good, the unconscious wants to become consciously responsible."[188] However, at least with respect to the question of his attitudes towards Judaism, Jung seems never to have achieved full consciousness and responsibility. One of Jung's faults, perhaps his greatest, was that his own personality was centered too far in the direction of his unconscious; and this quality—which he saw so well and at first admired in Hitler—may have prevented Jung from making a conscious accounting for his terrible insensitivity to the Jews prior to World War II. Jung's accounting was, in effect, mostly unconscious—in his "visions" of 1944, in his writing of *Answer to Job*, each of which work through Jung's own guilt without ever naming it. Consciously, all he could say was that he had "slipped up."[189] Unconsciously, I believe, Jung knew that he had done far more, that he had fallen into the abyss, an abyss to which a celebration of the unconscious over the conscious, of the intuitive over the rational, can ultimately lead.

If there is something to learn from Jung's own case, I believe it is that with all the danger of an over-rationalized, obsessional, neurotic self, centered in thought and ego (a danger that Jung refers to in *Answer to Job* as "loss of soul"[190]), there are equal dangers of the "wider" self, centered deeper in the personality, in the unconscious. Such "wider selves" have a creativity and a charisma that makes them appeal to those who, for one reason or another, have lost touch with the underworld of myth, dreams, visions, and magic. Such charismatic individuals, centered as they are in intuition, and who listen to and follow the stirrings of their unconscious, can lead themselves and others to an experience of great emotional and spiritual moment, but can also, to use one of Jung's own phrases, lead them "down the path to perdition." The Jewish mystical tradition is itself hardly immune from such dangers, as attested to, for example, in Gershom Scholem's study of Sabbatai Sevi, the "false messiah" who in the seventeenth century declared himself to be Messiah, produced a huge following, abrogated Jewish law, and ultimately abandoned his followers by converting to Islam.[191]

To be sure, in *Answer to Job* Jung provides an account of God and the self that places a premium on conscious reflection.[192] In what amounts to a Lurianic/Hegelian account of God's evolution, Jung says that God, existence, or the absolute "needs conscious reflection in order to exist in reality. Existence is only real when it is conscious to somebody. That is why the Creator needs conscious man even though, from sheer unconsciousness, he would like to prevent him from becoming conscious."[193] Jung further speaks of God, and *ipso facto* the self, as experiencing "a gradual reawakening of an unutterable longing for something which would make him conscious of himself."

I believe that we are entitled to read this struggle for consciousness in two ways: a general one in which the struggle is God's and humanity's, and a more specific one, in which the struggle is Jung's own. In this sense, Jung's struggle with his own efforts at conscious awakening with respect to the Jews becomes the human quest, and in Jung's theological terms, the divine quest, in *exemplum*. The problem is that although Jung pointed clearly in the direction of a solution, he himself appears to have, in the case of his own attitudes towards Judaism, not fully succeeded in his quest. To see that this is so, all we have to do is imagine how differently we might feel about Jung, had he, in his later years— the very years when he assumed the role of, and the world celebrated him as, the "wise old man"—publicly and in detail reflected upon his own words from the 1930s, taken responsibility for them, and deeply and publicly mourned both his own insensitivity as well as the great catastrophe that, despite all the warnings and his own early and accurate diagnosis of the forces that would bring it about, he could not bring himself either to acknowledge or to speak out against. As Jung himself said in "After the Catastrophe": "Anything that remains in the unconscious is incorrigible; psychological corrections can be made only in consciousness."[194]

Answer to Job is about two men who were presented by God with an ultimate test. Job passed his test. We might ask if Jung passed his own. In addressing this question, we might consider why it is that Jung, in his later years, adopted a position that is in many ways both sympathetic to, if not derived from, the Jewish mystical tradition. I believe that an answer to this question can again be gleaned from certain comments Jung makes about God in *Answer to Job*, Jung's most obviously "Jewish" work. There, Jung interprets God's incarnation as man in Christ as, in part, an atonement for God's own sins. "Yahweh must become man precisely because he has done man wrong."[195] We might ask whether in promulgating an increasingly Jewish/Kabbalistic psychology, by developing many close ties with Jewish disciples later in life, and finally and most significantly, by experiencing himself as Rabbi Simon ben Yochai as Jung clung to life after his heart attack in 1944, Jung might be said to have followed his own maxim: *Jung must become a Jew precisely because he had done Jews wrong*. In Christ, Jung says, Yahweh and Job become, as it were, combined in one personality. In a sense, late in his life, a similar "coincidence of opposites" might be said to have occurred between Jung and the Jews.

It is noteworthy that Jung ultimately concluded that not only Freud's, but his *own* psychological theories were anticipated by the Jewish mystics.

As we have seen, in response to a letter from a Ms. Edith Schroeder, Jung commented that in order to comprehend the origin of Freud's theories one would need to explore both Chasidism and the Kabbalah;[196] and in an interview in 1955, on the occasion of his eightieth birthday, Jung made a startling claim about his own thought, remarking that "the Hasidic Rabbi Baer from Mesiritz, whom they called the Great Maggid...anticipated [his] entire psychology in the eighteenth century."[197] The same Jung who used the epithet "Jewish psychology" as an ugly and opportunistic means of attacking Freud and currying favor with the Nazi regime during the 1930s, in the end embraces a "Jewish psychology" and declares that it anticipated the entirety of his own.

Chapter 11

Jung's Kabbalistic Visions

> I myself was, so it seemed, in the Pardes Rimmonim,[1] the garden of pomegranates, and the wedding of Tifereth with Malchuth was taking place. Or else I was Rabbi Simon ben Jochai, whose wedding in the afterlife was being celebrated. It was the mystic marriage as it appears in the Cabbalistic tradition.

In this chapter I return to Jung's 1944 Kabbalistic visions, examining them from the standpoint of Jung's earlier provocative remarks about Jewish psychology and National Socialism, Jung's attitude towards the Jewish sources of his own theories, and from the perspective of both Jungian and Kabbalistic dream theory. An important goal of this chapter is to show that Jung's visions signaled a change in his attitudes and personality that is critical to a full understanding of his complex relationship to Judaism. We will see that Jung's visions not only had deep personal, psychological, and even mystical significance, but also portended an enormously creative period in Jung's career, during which his psychological theories became closely aligned with the Jewish mystical tradition. A second goal of this chapter is to compare Jungian and Kabbalistic dream theory, both in order to shed light upon Jung's visions and to further explore significant points of contact between Jewish mysticism and analytic psychology. Finally, I will consider how Jung's own *mystical* interpretation of his Kabbalistic visions raises important questions regarding his use of religious symbols and vocabulary, and the boundaries between psychological science and religious experience.

The Visions

Jung described his Kabbalistic visions,[2] which he experienced on a nightly basis for about three weeks after his heart attack in 1944, in his autobiographical *Memories, Dreams, Reflections*. There he writes that these visions were "the most tremendous things I have ever experienced."[3] The visions, which occurred at a point when, according to Jung's own report,

DOI: 10.4324/9781003027041-12

he "hung on the edge of death,"[4] involve decidedly Jewish, Kabbalistic themes. Jung describes these visions as having occurred in a state of wakeful ecstasy. He relates that it was "as though I were floating in space, as though I were safe in the womb of the universe."[5] The visions involved the divine wedding between *Tiferet* and *Malchut*, which, in the Jewish mystical tradition, are the divine archetypes or *Sefirot*[6] that represent the masculine and feminine aspects of both God and the world. Jung describes his experience as one of indescribable "eternal bliss," relating:

> Everything around me seemed enchanted. At this hour of the night the nurse brought me some food she had warmed....For a time it seemed to me that she was an old Jewish woman, much older than she actually was, and that she was preparing ritual kosher dishes for me. When I looked at her, she seemed to have a blue halo around her head. I myself was, so it seemed, in the Pardes Rimmonim, the garden of pomegranates, and the wedding of Tifereth with Malchuth was taking place. Or else I was Rabbi Simon ben Jochai,[7] whose wedding in the afterlife was being celebrated. It was the mystic marriage as it appears in the Cabbalistic tradition. I cannot tell you how wonderful it was. I could only think continually, "Now this is the garden of pomegranates! Now this is the marriage of Malchuth with Tifereth!" I do not know exactly what part I played in it. At bottom it was I myself: I was the marriage. And my beatitude was that of a blissful wedding.[8]

The vision continues with what Jung describes as "the Marriage of the Lamb" in Jerusalem, complete with "angels and light." "I myself," he tells us, "was the Marriage of the Lamb." The vision concludes with Jung in a classical amphitheater situated in a verdant chain of hills: "Men and woman dancers came on-stage, and upon a flower-decked couch Allfather Zeus consummated the mystic marriage, as it is described in the Iliad."[9]

Jung relates that as a result of these experiences he developed the impression that this life is but a "segment of existence," and that time as it is ordinarily experienced is an illusion, since during the visions, past, present, and future merged into one. There can be little doubt that Jung took these impressions seriously, as according to him, "the visions and experiences were utterly real; there was nothing subjective about them."[10] We will have occasion to examine Jung's claim to "objectivity" later when we consider the Zohar's parallel claims about prophetic dreams.

It is certainly noteworthy that what Jung describes as the most tremendous and "individuating" experience of his life should involve a Kabbalistic vision. In this vision, he finds himself in the "garden of pomegranates," an allusion to a Kabbalistic work of that name (*Pardes Rimmonim* in Hebrew) by Moses Cordovero (1522–70). Further, Jung identifies himself with the union of the *Sefirot Tiferet* and *Malchut*, the masculine and feminine aspects of God, and whose union, according to the theosophical Kabbalah, restores harmony to both God and the world. Finally, and perhaps most significantly, in his Kabbalistic vision Jung identifies himself with Rabbi Simon ben Yochai, who, according to Jewish tradition, is the author of the classical Kabbalistic text, *Sefer ha-Zohar*. Not only is the content of Jung's visions Kabbalistic, but the impressions that were imparted to him as a result of his visions echo both general mystical and specifically Kabbalistic themes. Jung describes these visions as filling him "with the highest possible feeling of happiness," and "a sense of eternal bliss." He reports that he came away from these visions with the conviction that he had somehow been granted a glimpse into a higher reality or world. By comparison, Jung tells us, our own world is grey, box-like, overly material and ridiculous.[11]

In describing his vision, Jung expresses the idea that this world is but "a segment of existence,"[12] an idea that calls to mind the Kabbalistic doctrine that ours is but one of a myriad of levels or "worlds." His impression that life in this world "is enacted in a three-dimensional boxlike universe especially set up for it" is reminiscent of the Lurianic doctrine that the spatiotemporal universe is a function of God's contraction (*Tzimtzum*), a contraction that creates a metaphysical square within which space, time, and finite beings appear.[13] Further, Jung describes experiencing a non-temporal state in which present, past, and future are one, and "everything that happens in time [is] brought together in a concrete whole." Such atemporality is also characteristic of the Kabbalistic conception of "higher worlds" and God.[14]

It is important to note, however, that the vision Jung describes does not *remain* Kabbalistic. Indeed, Jung's vision moves from the Garden of Pomegranates to the Jerusalem described in the book of Revelation (the "marriage of the lamb," the "angels of light"), and then to ancient Athens. Such a movement through Jewish, Christian, and Greek images is reflective of Jung's intellectual odyssey, i.e., his movement away from what he later termed the "Jewish psychology" of Freud to a psychology rooted in Christian and Greek ideas. One way of understanding the transitions from the Kabbalah to Christianity and Hellenism in Jung's visions is that these transitions represent Jung's psychological need to establish both the basis of his thought and his personality in Christianity and Greece as opposed to Judaism. We should here again recall Jung's 1935 letter to Neumann in which he claimed that "analytical psychology has its roots in the Christian Middle Ages and ultimately in Greek philosophy, with the connecting link being alchemy."[15]

Jung's Kabbalistic vision can perhaps be understood as reflecting Jung's (not fully conscious) recognition of the significance of the Kabbalah for his own work. Indeed, these visions coincide with what appears to have been a profound alteration in both Jung's personality and his attitude towards

Judaism. Rosen describes Jung's 1944 heart attack and visions as a "'soul/ spirit attack' based on the realization that he'd been wrong about the German psyche (and his own)."[16] Jung himself recognized that his visions were instrumental in transforming and individuating his own psyche. As a result of these visions, he experienced both a sense of immortality as well as personal individuation. Jung relates that his experience involved an "objective cognition" that transcended the normal interpersonal economy of desire. It was an experience in which all emotional ties, "relationships of desire, tainted by coercion and constraint" were transcended in favor of a real *coniunctio*, a relationship with oneself, others, and the world that is beyond, yet also *behind*, desire.

A Redemptive Vision?

A specifically redemptive theme appears in Jung's description of his Kabbalistic vision. Jung tells us: "There is something else I quite distinctly remember. At the beginning, when I was having the vision of the garden of pomegranates, I asked the nurse to forgive me if she were harmed."[17] While Jung opines that it was the "odor of sanctity in the room" (a Christian notion[18]) that might have been harmful, it is important to note that it was this nurse who appeared in Jung's vision as an old Jewish woman and who prepared "ritual kosher dishes" for him. Further it was this "kosher" nurse whom Jung describes as seeming "to have a blue halo around her head."[19] It is not a great interpretive leap to propose that in his vision, Jung appears to be asking forgiveness of the Jews, from whom he has been spiritually fed, and with regard to whom he is concerned that he has caused significant harm. A possible confirmation for this, one that we have already alluded to in the previous chapter, can be inferred from something Jung tells us in his *Answer to Job*, where he writes: "Yahweh must become man precisely because he has done man wrong."[20] Following Jung's own reasoning, we might be entitled to surmise that in his vision Jung *must become a Jew* for the same *redemptive* reason. Again, by symbolically becoming a Jew on his "deathbed" in 1944, by promulgating an increasingly Jewish/mystical psychology, by developing many close ties with Jewish disciples towards the end of his life, and, finally, by acknowledging that a Chasidic rebbe had anticipated his entire work, Jung can be said to have effected something akin to his own maxim: *Jung must become a Jew precisely because he had done Jews wrong*.

Jung clearly believed that the visionary experiences of his 1944 illness provided the impetus to his forging a more fully differentiated self, enabling him both to articulate his own individual nature, thoughts, and destiny and to affirm the reality of the unified timeless world he had experienced.[21] Further, it was only after these visions that Jung felt that he was able to write *Mysterium Coniunctionis* and several other of his principal works, including *Answer to Job*, in which Jewish, moreover Kabbalistic, themes play a far greater role than in any of his previous writings. Jung states: "After the illness a fruitful period of work began for me. A good many of my principal works were written only then. The insight I had had, or the vision of the end of all things, gave me the courage to undertake new formulations."[22]

Jung's 1944 visions might be understood as a turning point, what in Hebrew is spoken of as *teshuvah* ("turning," i.e., transformation), with respect to Jung's earlier views regarding "Jewish psychology." However, just as, according to Maidenbaum, Jung may never have been fully conscious of what others saw as his anti-Semitism,[23] he may never have become fully conscious of (in the sense of being able to own and articulate) his transformation with respect to Judaism, Jewish psychology, and the Jewish people. If true, this was of no small moment, for as Jung himself said in "After the Catastrophe," "psychological corrections can be made only in consciousness."[24] Indeed, even after experiencing his Kabbalistic vision, Jung continued to express rather negative views about the Jews in his private correspondence. In a letter to a former patient, Mary Mellon (who would later endow the Bollingen foundation, publisher of Jung's *Collected Works*), Jung in 1945 angrily defends himself against accusations of having been a Nazi, and in the process suggests that the Jews might well have been complicit in their own destruction. Jung writes that it is "difficult to mention the anti-Christianism of the Jews after the horrible things that have happened in Germany. But Jews are not so damned innocent after all—the role played by the intellectual Jews in pre-war Germany would be an interesting object of investigation."[25]

One might be justified in the feeling that Jung's transformation (or in his own terms, "compensation") was partial, in some ways profound, but not complete. He was transformed to the point where he ultimately embraced a "Jewish psychology" as anticipating his own psychology, after having used this very epithet as an ugly and opportunistic means of attacking Freud and currying favor with the Nazi regime during the 1930s. However, as has become painfully apparent since the question has been explored openly and in depth,[26] Jung never fully acknowledged nor disowned his earlier, seemingly sympathetic view of Hitler and the Nazi regime, and his insensitive and inflammatory remarks on the Jewish people and Jewish psychology. However, in contrast to many who are transformed in word but not in deed, Jung seems to have, in a sense, been transformed in deed, if not fully in word, as he not only embraced aspects of Jewish mysticism in his later years, but, as James Kirsch and others have affirmed, became something of a "rebbe" for a number of his Jewish disciples.

"The Great Maggid…Anticipated My Entire Psychology"

Despite all the attention to Jung's attitude towards Judaism, it is curious that Jung's later positive comments about Jewish mysticism (as well as his

Jewish mystical visions) are neglected in nearly all discussions of Jung's alleged anti-Semitism. By the 1950s, Jung began to include numerous references to Jewish and especially Kabbalistic ideas and sources in his works. For example, in *Psychology and Religion* Jung approvingly quotes a Talmudic view on the interpretation of dreams.[27] In *Answer to Job*, Jung undertook a serious meditation and study of the God of the Old Testament, and made significant use of Jewish mystical categories to come to grips with the purpose of creation, the darkness inherent in a divinely created world, and the depths of the human soul.[28] Finally, Jung's last great work, *Mysterium Coniunctionis*, completed in his eightieth year in 1954, though ostensibly a treatise on alchemy, is filled with discussions of such Kabbalistic symbols as *Adam Kadmon* (Primordial Human), the *Sefirot* (the archetypes of creation), and "the union of the Holy One and his *Shekhinah* (his feminine aspect or spiritual bride)." These *Jewish* symbols (which in some but not all instances were mediated for Jung through alchemy and the Christian Kabbalah) became important pivots around which Jung constructed his final interpretations of such notions as the archetypes and the collective unconscious, as well as his theory of the ultimate psychological purpose of man. While the Jewish mysticism that became increasingly significant for Jung late in his life differed from both the normative Judaism and "Jewish" (i.e., Freudian) psychology that Jung had targeted in the 1930s, it was, I believe, the catalyst for a reappraisal of his own attitudes towards the Jewish tradition as a whole.[29]

During the 1950s, Jung began to take a sympathetic view of the distinctively Jewish origins of both psychoanalysis and his own analytical psychology. As we have seen, during that period Jung commented on the Jewish mystical origins of Freudian psychoanalysis, stating that in order to comprehend the origin of Freud's theories one would need to explore "the subterranean workings of Hasidism…and…the intricacies of the Kabbalah."[30] Jung ultimately concluded that not only Freud's but his *own* psychological theories were anticipated by the Jewish mystics, commenting in 1955 that the Chasidic Maggid of Mesiritz had anticipated his (Jung's) "entire psychology."[31] The Maggid had held that the Godhead has a hidden life within the mind of man and that while the Godhead himself is the foundation and source of thought, actual thinking can only occur within the framework of the human mind,[32] a notion that clearly anticipates Jung's own psychologization of the objects of religious discourse. (Further discussion of the parallels between the Maggid and Jungian psychology can be found in the Appendix.)

Jung's postwar writings and statements obviously reflect a profound turn in Jung's (at least acknowledged) understanding and appreciation of at least some aspects of the Jewish faith and, in particular, Judaism's potential contribution to his own analytical psychology. What happened between 1934, when Jung was railing against a Jewish psychology, and 1954, when he was hailing Jewish mysticism as a forerunner and confirmation of his own thought? My research has suggested that two factors played a role in Jung's transformation. The first is that while Jung had motives for ignoring the Jewish sources of his own psychology during the 1930s, after the war he felt free to acknowledge them, both to himself and others. The second is that Jung experienced a more profound psychological, spiritual, and potentially redemptive transformation in the mystical, specifically Kabbalistic, visions he experienced after his near-fatal heart attack in 1944.

The Zohar on (Jung's) Dreams and Visions

One of the more remarkable aspects of Jung's account of his Kabbalistic vision is that it reflects a view of spirituality and mysticism that is decidedly non-psychological and even nonscientific. J. W. Heisig has argued that Jung's views on God and the spiritual world traversed three distinct stages. In the first stage (roughly, 1900–21), Jung understood religious experience to be a projection of the individual's emotions; in the second stage (1921–45), such experience was understood as corresponding to the archetypes, and thus a projection of the deepest layers of the collective psyche; and in the third stage (beginning around 1945), Jung appears to have suspended judgment regarding the objective nature of that which the archetypal patterns of the psyche represent.[33] While a reading of the "Seven Sermons," and now *The Red Book*, renders Heisig's distinctions problematic, it is clear that Jung had a decidedly non-psychoanalytic view of his 1944 visions. We should recall that, regarding these visions, Jung stated emphatically: "It was not a product of imagination. The visions and experiences were utterly real; there was nothing subjective about them; they all had a quality of absolute objectivity."[34] Indeed, these mystical visions appear to mark the beginning of a stage in Jung's thought in which he seriously entertained the possibility that "this life is [but] a segment of existence"[35] and that the archetypes point not only to an inner transpersonal reality but to an outer, "objective" one as well.

It is in this context that I undertake an examination of Jung's Kabbalistic vision from the point of view of the Kabbalists' own theories of dreams and visions. Such an examination will inevitably raise a series of questions regarding Jung's claims regarding the "objectivity" of his visionary/mystical experiences, and similar claims that serve as the foundation for the Kabbalah and mysticism in general. We will be prompted, for example, to ask whether Jung's experiences of immortality, that this world is not the whole of existence, that past, present, and future are somehow illusory, and that all is "brought together in a concrete whole" reflect psychological regression, ego-inflation, and, as Wolfgang Giegerich has recently suggested, a spiritual drugging and retreat into the imagination,[36] or an advance to a higher state of consciousness in which the veil of finitude, temporality, materiality, and difference is lifted in a *unio mystica* or other *ecstatic* experience. These are important questions, which may not, of course, be subject to definitive answers and may very well be *essentially unanswerable*. However, the way in which we position ourselves with regard to such questions is potentially determinative of our attitude toward both psychology and religion in general, and Jungian psychology in particular. I will return to this theme after a discussion of the Kabbalistic understanding of visions and dreams.

Sefer ha-Zohar[37] does not always draw a sharp distinction between dreams and visions. According to the Zohar, dreams that provide mystical or predictive insights derive from the angel Gabriel, are referred to as "visions," and are to be distinguished, on the one hand, from dreams that contain mostly falsehoods and, on the other hand, from true (wakeful) prophecy. This yields a tripartite distinction,[38] one that the Zohar derived from the Jewish philosophers, especially Maimonides. It is an interesting but perhaps anachronistic and therefore idle question as to whether Jung's Kabbalistic vision was indeed a vision in the Zohar's sense of this term. Jung described these experiences as visions because, although they occurred at night, they were experienced in a state of at least semi-wakefulness.[39] However, in what follows I examine Jung's experiences within the context of the Zohar's discussion of dreams.

According to the Zohar, in sleep and dreams the soul leaves the body and ascends into the upper worlds, leaving only a fraction of its energy to sustain the life of the dreamer.[40] As the Talmud had affirmed, "sleep is a foretaste of death."[41] Because of its association with death and destructiveness, sleep, in the Zohar, is connected to both the *Shekhinah* (God's feminine "presence") and the *Sitra Achra* (the "Other Side"), the former because of its association with "stern judgment" (*din*),[42] the latter because the Other Side is the negative counter-world of evil and death. Sleep, the Zohar tells us, is ruled by the "Tree of Death,"[43] and when the individual awakens in the morning it is as if he or she were reborn. Further, upon awakening, the dreamer is, at least potentially, spiritually reborn and renewed.[44] This occurs after the soul has ascended on high and testified regarding the dreamer's wakeful deeds.[45]

While on the one hand sleep is a frightening sojourn into the realms of judgment, evil, destruction, and death, it is also an opportunity for the soul to journey from earth and return to its place of origin in the higher worlds.[46] In these worlds, the souls of the righteous learn the mysteries of the Torah, as they are clothed by the *Shekhinah* (God's feminine presence) and bathed in the light of the upper *Sefirot*. While the journey is a dangerous one, for in its ascent it must traverse realms dominated by destructive spirits, the highest soul (*neshamah*)[47] of one who is worthy is able to pass beyond the evil realm, and ascend to the place where it enjoys not only the splendor of the *Sefirot* but a vision of the King.[48] While the souls of the wicked are entrapped by the dark forces of the Other Side during sleep, the souls of the righteous escape its clutches and ascend on high.

Dreams, for the Zohar, thus bring the soul experiences of both lower and higher worlds. As such, dreams potentially provide the dreamer with mystical and even prophetic insights[49] that can, on awakening, be expressed in speech.[50] Further, according to the Zohar, the dreamer is provided with clues regarding future events, so that he or she can take whatever corrective actions are necessary to ward off or assure their occurrence: "Happy are the righteous, for the Holy One Blessed be He, reveals to them His mysteries in dreams, so they can preserve themselves from judgment."[51]

While, theoretically, dreams derive either from the higher worlds or from the evil realm of the Other Side, in practice all dreams contain a mixture of both good and evil, truth and falsehood,[52] and in interpreting dreams one must always be careful to separate the wheat from the straw.[53] The Zohar is in accord with the Talmudic dictums that "a dream that is not remembered and interpreted is like a letter that is not read"[54] and that dreams "follow the mouth,"[55] i.e., that both the meaning and effects of a dream are dependent not on the "dream itself" but upon the dream as it is interpreted.[56] The Zohar affirms that language has power over dreams, and for this reason "all dreams follow their interpretation."[57]

According to the Zohar, a dream must be interpreted by disclosing its content to one's friends, in order that the dream may move beyond desire and thought (*Keter* and *Chochmah*, the highest of the *Sefirot*), and enter into speech (*Malchut*, the lowest *Sefirah*, which completes the sefirotic system). "Desire," the Zohar tells us, "which is Thought, is the beginning of all things, and Utterance is the completion."[58]

We will see that the Kabbalistic view of sleep, dreams, and visions is of interest not only for the light it enables us to shed upon Jung's visions, but also because the Zohar's view is in many respects quite close to the perspective that Jung took upon these visions himself and, moreover, is compatible with Jung's overall perspective on dreaming. However, before returning once again to Jung's visions, it will be worthwhile to summarize some of the key features of the Zoharic theory of dreams. These features, along with their "psychological equivalents" (which correspond to what Heisig refers to as Jung's "second stage" understanding of religious experience—as a reflection of the deepest layers of the collective psyche[59]), are enumerated in Table 11.1.

Each of the Zohar's key ideas about dreams is clearly applicable to Jung's own Kabbalistic vision (most of them having been recognized and understood by Jung himself).

With regard to the first of the Zohar's premises, i.e., that dreams and visions are a kind of "death," we find that Jung's visions actually occurred when he was in a state of near-death, and that the images he experienced prompted him to conclude that he was indeed dying.[60] There is what, in psychological terms, might be called a profound "thanatic" aspect to dreams, and Jung's vision illustrates this very clearly; his initial experience was a sense of "annihilation,"[61] which soon yielded to an irresistible urge towards what seemed to be his "origin."[62]

Table 11.1 Key Features of the Zoharic Theory of Dreams and their Psychological Equivalents

Features of the Zohar's Theory	*Psychological (Archetypal) Equivalents*
(1) Sleep, dreams, and visions are associated with death. The dreamer's soul leaves his body to sojourn among higher and lower worlds, leaving behind only a small modicum of vitality to sustain corporeal life. Further, dreams are in large measure a frightening sojourn into the realms of deceit, destructiveness, and death.	(1) Dreams reflect vital existential concerns and reveal the individual's position and attitude towards his or her own death. Because of this, they enable one to access both creatively illuminating aspects of the psyche as well as aspects that are repressive, deceitful, and destructive.
(2) The soul, in its ascent during sleep, must account for the dreamer's wakeful activities, and the dreamer himself is judged on high during sleep.	(2) A dream provides a proposition or judgment by the unconscious self regarding some aspect of the dreamer's wakeful life.
(3) A dream, however, also enables the righteous soul to sojourn among higher worlds, return to its origins, receive the radiance of the Sefirot (divine archetypes), attain mystical insight, and commune with the one on high.	(3) A dream places one in touch with the fundamental collective ideals, tendencies, and values of humanity. The dream, by providing one with a certain access to the archetypes of the collective unconscious, grants insights that go beyond one's personal psychology.
(4) Dreams or visions can provide the dreamer with clues regarding future events in relation to which the dreamer may be advised to take action.	(4) Dreams process data that may not be readily available or comprehensible to the conscious mind, but that is recorded subliminally in the individual's psyche, and therefore are able to anticipate future events that are relevant to the dreamer.
(5) Sleep and dreams, by virtue of their partaking in a portion of both death and prophecy, provide the dreamer with an opportunity for spiritual rebirth.	(5) Dreams have a great capacity to facilitate creativity and selfactualizing transformation in the dreamer.
(6) All dreams contain a mixture of good and bad, truth and falsehood, and must be interpreted so as to separate out the "wheat from the straw."	(6) Dreams do not always carry their interpretation on their face, are often disguised in symbols and, as Freud suggested, "intend" to deceive the waking dreamer.

Features of the Zohar's Theory	Psychological (Archetypal) Equivalents
(7) It is the interpretation of the dream, as rendered in wakeful speech, that is significant, and not the purported (original) dream itself. Further, the greater significance of the dream is not to be found in its origins, but rather in the interpretation accepted by, and the effects the dream has upon, the dreamer.	(7) Dreams must be interpreted if they are to be understood and to have the greatest and most meaningful impact upon the dreamer. The dream's significance is dependent, not on the dream as it might be "in itself," but on how it is processed, reported, and understood by the dreamer, especially with regard to its impact upon him and his future.
(8) The interpretation of any dream is only complete when it has traversed "desire," "thought," and "speech," and, in effect, mirrors the entire sefirotic system.	(8) Each dream presents numerous aspects, and each dream is subject to a wide variety of interpretations from the perspective of the dreamer's desire, cognition, emotion, ethics, spiritual life, etc.

According to Solomon Alimoli (1485–1542), whose book *Pitron Chalomot, The Interpretation of Dreams*, provides a Jewish, Kabbalistic theory of dreaming, dreams occur during sleep and are associated with death because it is only at such times when the body is nullified that "the soul speaks out with full clarity." He adds that for visions to occur outside of dreams, "prophetic inspiration could not take place unless the soul were on the verge of departing the body, as when one is on the point of death."[63] At the time of Jung's visions, his own approach to death was so strong that he reported feeling "violent resistance" to his doctor for having restored him to life.

Jung's proximity to death seems to have conditioned the very profundity of his vision, and indeed Jung early on held that an encounter with death is a *sine qua non* for spiritual growth.[64] However, like the Zohar, Jung affirms that a sojourn into the realm of death is not without its dangers. As we have seen, the Zohar informs us that the dreamer must first descend into the realm of the *Sitra Achra*, the realm of "evil Husks" and destructive spirits, and it is only the righteous who can emerge from that realm and ascend to visions of the *Sefirot* and the "King." Similarly, Jung tells us that in following the path towards individuation (the very path of his own visions) "there is no guarantee—not for a single moment—that we will not fall into error or stumble into deadly peril. We may think there is a sure road. But that would be the road to death."[65]

The possibility for "error," the chance that one may "stumble into deadly peril," brings us to the second Zoharic dictum regarding dreams, viz., that the dreamer is judged while he sleeps. As I have indicated above, Jung does not focus much on what Freudians would refer to as the "superego" aspects of his vision, those referred to by the Kabbalists as stemming from the *Sefirah* of "Judgment," or *Din.* In this regard, Jung relates that he remembers distinctly that he had asked the nurse (who had fed him kosher food) to "forgive [him] if she were harmed."[66] While Jung does not dwell on the nature of this harm, I have interpreted it as an unconscious reference of the harm Jung felt he might have done to the Jewish people. This interpretation receives some confirmation two pages later, when Jung uses the same ideas ("falling into error," "stumbling into peril"[67]) in describing the dangers associated with his path that he had used in describing his actions in relation to the Nazis before the war, i.e., when he told Leo Baeck that he had "lost his footing" and "slipped up."[68]

We have already seen how Jung's visions fulfill the third of the Zohar's dicta about dreaming, viz., that dreams enable the dreamer to experience the radiance of the *Sefirot* and higher worlds. Indeed, Jung's visions began with images of his being high above the earth, over the subcontinent of India and Ceylon, looking down over the desert of Arabia and the Red Sea,[69] as if he were anticipating the views that the astronauts would later observe from space. Jung's earthly life seemed to be stripped away as if it were a phantasm, and just prior to his Kabbalistic vision Jung experienced what he described as "eternal bliss," a sense of being safe in the "womb of the universe," which was also a "tremendous void."[70] Jung's vision can be understood as a modern version of the "Chariot" or "Throne" mysticism of the early Jewish visionaries, whose mystical meditations created a *merkaveh*, chariot or vehicle of ascent to God's celestial throne. His vision can also be understood psychologically as an experience of individuation, wholeness, and completion in the face of what he perceived as impending death.

We have also seen how Jung believed that his dream or vision afforded him mystical *insights.* Jung relates that he came away from his experiences with a renewed "affirmation of things as they are,"[71] a sense of absolute wholeness regarding his own past, present, and future,[72] a sense of the confluence between the "void" and the safety of the universe,[73] and a sense that earthly life is but a mere segment of a greater existence.[74]

(4, 5) In accord with the Zohar's fourth teaching, regarding the prophetic aspects of dreams, Jung interpreted his vision as actually having forecast the death of his own physician, whose own mortal illness began on the very day—April 4, 1944—that Jung's had begun to subside. While Jung regarded his vision as a portent of his physician's death, he also regarded it as a herald of his own rebirth, the fifth of the Zohar's dicta on dreams. In commenting on the coincidence between his own cure and the doctor's illness, Jung tells us that he was terrified by the thought that his doctor would die in his stead.[75] Indeed, Jung himself describes what is tantamount to a rebirth after emerging from his illness and visions, particularly in his remarks regarding how these visions prompted his own individuation[76] and enabled him to author his later alchemical and theological writings.[77]

The Zohar's sixth dictum, that all dreams contain a mixture of good and bad, truth and falsehood (and therefore must be interpreted so as to separate out the "wheat from the straw"), is illustrated (on the interpretation offered here) in those parts of Jung's vision that remove Jung from the arena of Jewish mysticism and revert to the "Marriage of the Lamb" in Jerusalem and to "All-father Zeus consummating the mystic marriage."[78] Bearing in mind the Talmudic, Kabbalistic, *and Jungian* notion that each dream has many possible interpretations (see below), as I have understood Jung's vision, the transformation into a Christian and Greek context reflected Jung's earlier efforts to *avoid* any Jewish pedigree for his own psychology, and thus constitutes the "straw" mixed in with the true wheat of his Kabbalistic vision.

It is of note that Jung pays virtually no attention to the origins of his visions in the experiences and conflicts of his past, but, in accord with what I have described as the Zohar's seventh dictum, Jung's attitude towards his visions is future-directed and linked to the dream's message as opposed to its underlying cause. What counts, for Jung, are the insights this vision provided him regarding the unity of his personality and the world as a whole. There is no "Freudian" effort to trace the dream's significance back to its latent content or historical antecedents. Of course, Jung's own interpretation is hardly the only one that could fit the material of his visions.

Alimoli refers to a passage in the Babylonian Talmud,[79] where it is recorded that a certain sage once dreamed and consulted all twenty-four dream interpreters then residing in Jerusalem. Each gave the dream a different interpretation, and yet all were fulfilled. Alimoli tells us the reason for this is that while God's communications in dreams cannot be interpreted arbitrarily, each skilled and knowledgeable interpreter brings his unique standpoint and interpretive power in focusing upon one of the many aspects of a dream. "In other words," he tells us, "dreams have a multifarious character and do not arrive to bring only a single communication or to deal with only one of the dreamer's concerns."[80] So, while Jung himself does not focus on the origins of his visions in past concerns and conflicts, we would, on Alimoli's view, be entitled to (and will in due course) do so.

As we have seen, the Zohar holds that the greatest significance of a dream or vision is not to be found through tracing its origins, but rather by observing the impact and effects of the dream upon the dreamer. As Jung himself averred, his Kabbalistic vision seems to have transformed him in a variety of ways, not the least of which was to inaugurate a certain generativity that enabled him to be more open to the Jewish tradition and its impact upon his life and work.

Jung's visions may well have had an enormous impact upon him both spiritually and psychologically, but they cannot, from the point of view I have adopted here, be said to have fulfilled the eighth of the Zohar's dicta concerning dreams and visions—i.e., that the interpretation of any dream is only complete when it has traversed "desire," "thought," and "speech," and, in effect, mirrors the entire sefirotic system. Jung himself never *articulated* the significance that I am here attributing to his vision, nor did he endeavor to articulate *any personal psychological significance* for it. On the view I have proffered here, had Jung examined this vision from a personal psychological point of view, he might have been moved to make public amends for his views on Judaism and National Socialism prior to World War II. As such, to use a Lurianic metaphor, while Jung's "vessels" seem to have broken during his heart/soul attack of 1944, his *Tikkun* (restoration-redemption) was incomplete, as he failed to put his transformation/emendation into active "speech."

Jung on Dreams

We have seen how Jung's Kabbalistic vision accords with most of the criteria set forth in the Zohar regarding the nature of dreams and their interpretation. In this section, I will turn to Jung's own *theories* of dreams and consider them in light of both Jung's visions and the Kabbalistic view of dreams and visions. We will see that not only Jung's vision, but his theory of dreams is in several ways highly "Kabbalistic" in nature.

As we have seen, whereas Freud had focused upon the anterior causes of dreams, e.g., the wishes, conflicts, and traumas of the dreamer's life, Jung focused on what he termed the dream's "finality," the purpose that it serves in the life of the dreamer.[81] For Jung, as for the Zohar, dreams are, in effect, messages from an unknown source and frequently serve to warn the individual that something is amiss in his or her psychic life. Specifically, for Jung, most if not all dreams can be understood as providing a "compensation," in which thoughts, desires, and tendencies that are ignored or devalued in conscious life emerge spontaneously to help restore balance to the psyche.[82] The dream, in effect, warns us that something is being ignored and that we should take heed.

While for the Kabbalists dreams are symbolic messages from God, for Jung dreams have their origin in the unconscious or the "self." However, for Jung, the self is the whole individual, within which there is not only an integration of conscious and unconscious, but also an integration of the personal psyche with the collective psyche of humanity, the "universal human"[83]—what the Kabbalists referred to as *Adam Kadmon*, the Primordial Man. Jung tells us that in dreams the personal psyche "is continually being corrected and compensated by the universal human being in us."[84] While for the Zohar and Alimoli dreams are a communication from God, and for Jung they are an utterance of the unconscious or the self, in Jung's view these two perspectives are empirically identical. This is because, according to the Jung, "God" is virtually indistinguishable from the archetype of the self.[85]

Unlike Freud, who saw in the unconscious only the more primitive, darker aspects of the human psyche, Jung (like the Kabbalists) understood the psychical "unknown" as containing both the dark, negative, repressed, "shadow" aspects of the self (what the Kabbalists spoke of as the "Other Side") and its beautiful, civilized, and spiritual aspects as well. For Jung, the "objective psyche" or "collective unconscious" is a repository of archetypes that have the capacity not only to disturb the ego, but to heal and enlighten it. These archetypes, which come to the fore in certain dreams, correspond to the main symbols of the Kabbalah—the *Sefirot*, the *Partzufim* (faces or personas of God), and other symbols such as the *Sitra Achra* or Other Side. Jung says of the archetypes that they "correspond to the human situations which have existed since primeval times: youth and old age, birth and death, sons and daughters, fathers and mothers, mating and so on."[86] Anyone who examines the Kabbalists' *Sefirot* and *Partzufim* will see that this is a perfectly apt description of them as well, for among these Kabbalistic symbols are representations of mother and father, youth and old age, wisdom, knowledge, kingship, birth, death, marriage, and virtually all of the archetypal figures and situations that are of significance in Jungian thought.

To take just a few examples, as we have seen, the main *Partzufim: Attika Kaddisha* (the Holy Ancient One), *Abba* (the Father), *Imma*, (the Mother), *Zeir Anpin* (the "Impatient" youthful male), and *Nukvah* (the youthful female) correspond almost precisely to Jung's *Senex*, Father, Mother, *Puer*, and Young Maiden. The Kabbalists' *Sitra Achra* (the Other Side) corresponds to the Jungian Shadow, and the *Sefirot* adumbrate a number of archetypal values, including will, wisdom, understanding, kindness, judgment, compassion, beauty, splendor, femininity, etc. The masculine and feminine *Partzufim* and *Sefirot* continually engage in conjugal relations, which constitute a divine marriage—hence Jung's wedding symbolism in his Kabbalistic vision.

Like the Kabbalists, Jung distinguished between "little dreams," which are limited to the affairs of the dreamer's everyday life, and significant or "big" dreams (or in Kabbalistic terms, "visions"), which often prove to be the greatest treasures of psychic experience,[87] and which, according to Jung, link the individual with the collective unconscious. Such "big dreams" can yield mystical, philosophical, creative and psychological insights.[88] According to Jung, such dreams invariably contain symbols that "permit comparison with the motifs of mythology."[89] This is because, for Jung, dream symbols and myths are alternate expressions of the archetypes of the collective unconscious. According to Jung, the archetypes that appear in dreams and mythology serve to reconcile antinomies and conflicts that cannot be reconciled in any other manner. This is the very function that the Kabbalists attributed to the pairs of masculine and feminine *Sefirot*, resulting in the view that the *Sefirot* ultimately embody the union of "everything and its opposite."[90] As we have seen, the idea referred to in the Kabbalah as *ha-achdut ha-shawah*, the union or coincidence of opposites, is an extremely important principle in both Jewish mysticism and Jungian psychology.[91]

Dreams, for Jung, not only provide the individual with guidance, but can also (as Jung's vision regarding his physician's death illustrates) portend a future event. However, Jung generally held that dreams are prophetic in the purely natural sense that they anticipate events on the basis of data that may not be readily available or comprehensible to the conscious mind, but which is recorded subliminally by the individual's unconscious, or which accords with a collective archetype.

Like the Kabbalists, Jung acknowledges the possibility of destructive dreams, though he does not necessarily attribute them to a source or dynamic different from dreams that are "compensatory." Destructive dreams occur in individuals whose social or other achievements have exceeded their psychic capacities, and the dream becomes a vehicle to "reduce" the individual back to his actual self. If unheeded, such dreams can portend the destruction of the personality. The same is true of certain compensatory dreams occurring in fragile individuals—where, for example, a dream with a compensatory upsurge of sexual, aggressive, or even spiritual libido can have a destructive impact upon a fragile dreamer, leading to psychosis or suicide. These are, I believe, the Jungian equivalents of dreams that the Kabbalists attributed to the destructive forces of the Other Side. Jung held that the destructive power of dreams was often necessary in order to shake the individual from a fixed point of view or routinized existence. In this idea, Jung moves very close to the Kabbalistic symbol of *Shevirat ha-Kelim*, the "Breaking of the Vessels" (also referred to as the "*death* of the kings"), the necessary tearing asunder of the world's and man's values as the key to world as well as individual redemption.[92] We should note that, like the Kabbalists, Jung and his disciples (notably Marie-Louise von Franz) recognized that death was a very important symbol or horizon that facilitates the experience of archetypal/spiritual dreaming as well as the process of individuation. While Jung did not for the most part experience his Kabbalistic visions as a destructive occurrence, from the perspective I have adopted here the result of these visions was a breaking asunder of aspects of Jung's former personality and a restructuring of his self on a more generative and individuated basis.

For Jung, as for the Kabbalists (and the Talmud) there cannot be a single valid interpretation of a dream or of dreams in general: "Only a combination of points of view can give us a more complete conception of the nature of dreams."[93] Further, Jung, like the Talmud and Zohar, placed the greatest value on a dream's *interpretation*. Jung in fact offered a parallel to the Talmudic/Zoharic dictum that "a dream that is not interpreted is like a letter that is not read"[94] in his statement that "a dream that is not understood remains a mere occurrence; understood it becomes a living experience."[95] While Jung did not believe that the impact of a dream on the dreamer was necessarily nil if it went uninterpreted, he did hold that one can enhance a dream's effect considerably by making it understood;

this because, as Jung repeatedly points out, the voice of the unconscious so easily goes unheard.

The "Objectivity" of Jung's Visions

I would like to return for a moment to Jung's claim that there was "nothing subjective" about his Kabbalistic and other visions. Throughout his career Jung used language that hung tantalizingly on the border between psychology and theology. The archetypes were conceptualized by Jung as psychological entities, but at the same time, as has been clear to many of his readers, they carry some if not all of the "numinosity" associated with mythical and mystical symbols. We might say that a certain ambiguity between the psychological and the theological is, for many, a good part of Jung's appeal, as it seemingly permits the modern, educated individual to speak of religious, mystical, mythological, and dream symbols in a "scientific" or "naturalistic" manner while at the same time retaining the wonder and magic that prior generations had believed to be inherent in such symbolism. The inevitable question arises as to whether such talk involves Jung and his followers in acts of self-deception or is rather a path to a profound understanding of aspects of the human psyche that naturally lie on the border between the subjective/psychological and the objective/spiritual. On the latter view, Jung's genius rests in his intuitive recognition that only an ambiguous and paradoxical language can express certain truths that cannot be expressed in either/or, linear form. Jung himself said: "If I make use of certain expressions that are reminiscent of the language of theology, this is due solely to the poverty of language, and not because I am of the opinion that the subject-matter of theology is the same as that of psychology."[96] As I have pointed out in some detail elsewhere,[97] the Kabbalists and Chasidim (as do mystics of many traditions) refused to make sharp distinctions between the outer and inner, the macrocosm and microcosm, the transcendent and the immanent, and the theological and the psychological, holding that such distinctions sever a unity and plunge one hopelessly into a (practically necessary, but) illusory world of dichotomous thinking and experience. The power of the mythical symbol, as both the Kabbalists and Jung surmised, is that it reconciles the opposites, provides an opportunity to transcend the dichotomies of ordinary life and thought, and yields a glimpse into a unified whole. Whether such a "unity" can be shown to have an objective or rational basis are questions that I will return to in Chapter 12.

Jung's Transformation

Our examination of Jung's Kabbalistic visions provides support for the hypothesis that Jung's 1944 visions not only had a mystical, but also a *compensatory* purpose, one that prompted Jung to openly embrace Jewish themes, compensating for a past of gross insensitivity to Jews and Judaism (if not outright anti-Semitism) and hostility to what he termed "Jewish psychology." Our comparison of Jungian and Kabbalistic dream theory provides another important example of the affinity between Jungian and Kabbalistic thought, an affinity that Jung was himself aware of, but which, as I have argued, he failed to emphasize prior to his Kabbalistic visions. Regardless of whether we understand Jung's visions in theological or psychological terms, we can say that these visions heralded and even precipitated a transformation in his attitude towards Judaism and life in general.[98] Further, the Kabbalistic content of Jung's visions and his subsequent embrace of many Jewish themes suggest that Jung was called to, and actually went quite far in, compensating for his insensitivities to the Jews during the 1930s.

Jung's actions and statements during the 1930s were deeply troubling—Rosen, following Jolande Jacobi, has commented that he "seemed gripped by a power complex and caught in a trancelike state by his shadow."[99] However, I think it is a serious error to assume that the Jung of the 1950s possessed the same character and attitudes that he exhibited during the 1930s. To make such an assumption undermines the very possibility of the spiritual transformation and psychological change that are foundational assumptions for both mysticism and psychotherapy. Jung's transformation was evident not only to himself, but to those who knew him, and was particularly pronounced with respect to his attitudes towards Judaism and Jewish thought. Small wonder that this should be so, given the fact that Jung appears to have transformed himself by envisioning himself as Simon ben Yochai, the patriarch of the Jewish mystical tradition.

Chapter 12

Philosophical and Theological Issues

For the Lurianists, *Tikkun ha-Olam,* the repair and restoration of the world, was at once a spiritual, metaphysical, ethical, political, and psychological event. The separation of the psychological from the metaphysical is an idea that was completely foreign to the Kabbalists. Indeed, for the Kabbalists, to consider the "psychological" in isolation from these other elements would constitute an alienation and separation itself, which would only contribute to, rather than ameliorate, the disharmony in man's psyche and the world as a whole. To consider, for example, the growth and harmony of one's self without paying simultaneous and equal regard to the interpersonal, theological, and political aspects of one's environment would have been unthinkable. Indeed, critics of contemporary depth psychology have argued that this has been precisely the course pursued by certain followers of Freud and Jung who have eschewed the world for the intricacies of the human mind.[1]

The limits of a psychology confined to the human psyche have been explored by the neo-Jungian James Hillman, whose *Re-Visioning Psychology* and other works have urged psychologists to move from a preoccupation with the human psyche towards an attention to the *anima mundi,* the soul of the world.[2] Hillman is steadfast in his belief that the soul is not to be identified with humanity, or even with humanity's essence or inner spirit. Like the Chasidim, Hillman holds that the world itself is filled with fantasy and soul (the "divine sparks") that exist beyond our own "personifications." As Thomas Moore points out, "for Hillman it is abundantly clear how much soul we can find on an ocean beach, in a cabinetmaker's shop, or on a neighborhood street."[3] Even the soul that we discover within ourselves is neither our exclusive property nor of our own making. Our soul, like the soul of any other aspect of the world, is a visitation of the divine, dependent upon archetypes that exist beyond the individual person, and, on Hillman's view, even beyond the collective unconscious of humanity. These archetypes are the very essence of the universe itself. They are the eternal Platonic forms that make themselves manifest not only in man, but in his products and in the natural order. As

DOI: 10.4324/9781003027041-13

Jung put it in *The Red Book*, "...the depths in me was at the same time the ruler of the depths of world affairs."[4]

For Hillman, the modern condition, in which individuals reside in a world of "private experiencing subjects and public dead objects,"[5] is a lamentable one. The Cartesian worldview, to which we are all heirs, has killed the soul in things, or at least envisioned them as dead, and has imprisoned man by placing him "in that tight little cell of ego."[6] Hillman tells us that when soul is removed from the world a number of insoluble problems emerge in humankind. Man becomes dependent upon himself for the relationship to "soul" that he once found in an encounter with God and nature. He becomes obsessed with the mysteriousness of his own psyche and invents an "interior witness" or witnesses who reside at the center of his own subjectivity.

Hillman, like the Kabbalists, holds that there is a piece of psyche, a portion of divine light, in all things, and unlike Jung (at least in his earlier formulations) he is clear that it is neither true nor useful to regard these elements of the world soul as a mere projection of the human mind.[7] The Kabbalists, in elaborating the prerequisites of *Tikkun haOlam*, do so in the context of their non-projective theory of the worldsoul. Among these prerequisites are:

(1) The capacity to unite opposing and often contradictory elements of the human psyche: male and female, judgment and kindness, and, according to the Zohar, "good" and "evil."

(2) The capacity to redirect and, as it were, sublimate one's natural instincts, the so-called "taming of the evil impulse," in the service of higher, cultural and spiritual ends.

(3) The capacity to sanctify elements of the world in symbolic, mythical rituals that "highlight" and "release" the sparks inherent in the material world. This activity is illustrated in the Chasidic notion of *avodah be-gashmiyut*, "worship through corporeality," the process through which the individual is able, for example, to raise the holy sparks in food or sexual activity by engaging in his or her activities with *devekut*, a unique spiritual frame of mind that involves a "clinging" to the divine. More generally, it involves the recognition of the sacredness in all things, material or otherwise, and a capacity to experience the spiritual light that suffuses all of creation.

These capacities, along with a variety of other introspective, developmental, and integrative processes are, in their psychical dimensions, fully paralleled in Jungian psychology. The emphasis upon the union of opposing or contradictory aspects of the psyche, the direction of psychic energy in the service of cultural and spiritual work, and the sanctification of (or bestowing of meaning upon) the psyche and world through the richness of symbolic discourse are all familiar Jungian themes.

The limitations of any comparison between the Kabbalah and Jung are evident, however, in the fact that while Jung provides us with a theory that is generally limited to the human psyche, the Kabbalah provides us with a theory that is at once about the human psyche and the world. It is to this critically important metaphysical difference that we will now turn our gaze.

The Question of Metaphysics

As we have seen, throughout the greater part of his career Jung rejected the notion that his descriptions of the *coniunctio, Adam Kadmon,* the sparks, or man's relationship to God have any implications for the *objective existence* of these, or any other, presumably metaphysical entities. Jung regarded, or at least presented, himself as an empirical scientist describing the nature of Western psychological and spiritual experience, in much the same way as an anthropologist might describe the religious practice and experience of an unfamiliar ethnic tribe. Jung claimed that his use of historical symbols and traditional religious vocabulary was a matter of expediency and linguistic precision rather than belief. According to Jung, in order to gain an adequate scientific understanding of numinous experience, one must use parallel religious or metaphysical vocabulary and ideas.[8] As he puts it in the introduction to *Mysterium Coniunctionis*:

> I do not go in for either metaphysics or theology, but am concerned with psychological facts on the borderline of the knowable. So if I make use of certain expressions that are reminiscent of the language of theology, this is due solely to the poverty of language, and not because I am of the opinion that the subject-matter of theology is the same as that of psychology. Psychology is very definitely not a theology; it is a natural science that seeks to describe experienceable psychic phenomena....But as empirical science it has neither the capacity nor the competence to decide on questions of truth and value, this being the prerogative of theology.[9]

At the close of the same work, Jung takes a skeptical stance towards even the possibility of theological and metaphysical truths:

> It seems to me at least highly improbable that when a man says "God" there must in consequence exist a God such that he imagines, or that he necessarily speaks of a real being. At any rate he can never prove that there is something to correspond with his statement on the metaphysical side, just as it can never be proved to him that he is wrong....Our metaphysical concepts are simply anthropomorphic images and opinions which express transcendental facts either not at

all or only in a very hypothetical manner....The physical world and the perceptual world are two very different things. Knowing this we have no encouragement whatever to think that our metaphysical picture of the world corresponds to the transcendental reality.[10]

There are, of course, those who, despite Jung's disclaimers, have drawn theological inferences from his writings, inferences that seem justified when one takes into account those writings such as *The Black Books* and *The Red Book* that were not published as a part of Jung's *Collected Works*. As we have seen, Buber had criticized Jung for being a metaphysical Gnostic who reduced God to humanity. Gilles Quispel, who is well known for his view that the roots of Gnosticism are Jewish, has drawn on Jung to formulate a *synchronous* as opposed to *projective* view of Gnosticism and religion in general. For Quispel, there is, as it were, a synchronous, mystical conjunction between heaven and earth; instead of God being a projection of man, both man and the world are projections of the deity.[11] In this connection, it is noteworthy that Jung, near the end of his life, said regarding Buber's accusations: "I never dreamt that intelligent people could misunderstand (my ideas) as theological statements."[12]

Excursus: The Philosophies of Kant and Hegel

In order to deepen our understanding of what I have characterized as the Kabbalistic view, and to understand why Jung is so readily "misunderstood" (or properly understood) as a metaphysician requires a brief excursus into the history of philosophy with specific reference to the philosophies of Kant and Hegel, each of whom had considered the possibility of metaphysical knowledge in philosophy prior to Jung's discussion of metaphysics and psychology.

Kant had held that metaphysical knowledge, knowledge of the ultimate nature of things (what he called "noumenal" reality), was impossible, on the grounds that all knowledge is conditioned by the a priori modes of apprehension of the human mind, which include space and time. According to Kant, it is possible, for example, for the mind to eliminate objects and yet retain space, but not possible for the mind to eliminate space and retain the experience of objects. The same is true for time, causality, substance, quantity, quality, possibility/impossibility, and a variety of the other categories. We cannot experience anything whatsoever without these categories and modes of apprehension. However, for Kant, all of this is true only for our *experience* of objects and not for the *objects themselves*. For Kant, the object itself is *completely unknowable*. We cannot say that objects really exist in space or time, or have substance, because the very ideas of space, time, and substance are, as it were, forced upon the object by the human mind. All knowledge, according to Kant, is of "appearances," and applies solely to the so-called *phenomenal realm*. Reality itself is beyond knowledge. Metaphysics is, therefore, an impossible pursuit.

It should be noted straight away that this is precisely the attitude taken by Jung with respect to the archetypes of the collective unconscious. Indeed, Jung has, in effect, added to Kant's "modes of apprehension" and "categories," a number of universal concepts of the collective unconscious. Here I will briefly comment on Jung's attitude towards many of the archetypes, an attitude that is virtually identical to Kant's attitude towards his modes and categories.

According to Jung's more conservative position, those archetypes that refer to metaphysical objects (such as God, *Adam Kadmon*, the sparks, and perhaps even the *anima*, the shadow, and the self) have no application outside the realm of human experience. While Jung considers the possibility that theology may have something to say about the existence of the correlates to these archetypes in the actual world, psychology can say nothing. Further, Jung holds that there can be no possibility of proof one way or the other regarding such metaphysical objects which, according to Jung, are grounded in "anthropomorphic images and opinions."[13] Jung's considered view is that the gods and heavens lie in man's unconscious mind and, like the Kantian modes and categories, they are projected outwards onto the world and our experience of that world. The difference is that while, according to Kant, we could have no experience whatsoever without the modes and categories of space, time, substance, causality, etc., we can (or at least we believe we can) experience a world without the soul, the anima, or God. Primitive and ancient humans projected the contents of his unconscious onto the world and heavens, but moderns, who are devoted to reason, believe we can experience a world without such projections, and further, that we can live without paying any heed to the unconscious archetypes at all. However, for Jung, such a rational view is a psychological as opposed to metaphysical impossibility, for when the archetypes are ignored or repressed they will return in the form of mental illness, disturbing (and at times potentially enlightening) dreams, irrationality, and superstitious beliefs. In the end, Jung holds his archetypes to be almost as ubiquitous and necessary as Kant's modes and categories. The important point to note here, however, is that Jung, like Kant, limits the application of his observations to the human mind and holds that it may be an illusion to hold, as ancient man did, that they apply to "the things in themselves."

It is here that we must consider, however briefly, the philosophy of Hegel.[14] Hegel accepted the Kantian notion that there are *a priori* categories of the human mind, but he rejected, on principle, the Kantian distinction between the *noumenal* and *phenomenal* realms. For Hegel, an unknowable existent is a contradiction in terms. According to Hegel, the reason that Kant had even spoken about a thing-in-itself is that he felt a need to posit a cause or substrate for phenomenal experience. But to regard the thing-in-itself as a substrate or cause is itself, on Kant's own principles, an impermissible application of a phenomenal category to the so-called noumenal realm. Further, if we know that the "noumenon" exists and it is indeed a cause of our experience, then it is no longer unknowable, and it itself becomes *phenomenal*. The only conclusion that Hegel believed could be drawn from this is that *if anything exists it must, at least in principle, be knowable*. It follows that the categories of the mind determine not just experience but reality as well, for they apply not just to appearances but also to the world itself. The hypothesis of a "world" that exists beyond knowledge makes no sense. The notion of a noumenal realm is a contradictory, self-defeating hypothesis that in Hegel's philosophy drops out altogether. In Hegel we have an objective idealism in which reality is held to be equivalent to the categories, concepts, and ideas of the mind. Such an *idealist* point of view has a venerable history going back at least as far as Plato and is a metaphysical position that is in many ways compatible with the theosophical Kabbalah.

What happens, however, when we apply the Hegelian critique of Kant to the "Kantian" ideas that appear in Jung? If the "thing-in-itself" is also eliminated for Jung, then the archetypes of the collective unconscious, which Jung says are only applicable to the limited realm of human experience, become applicable to the world itself. The deep, universal experience of the God archetype becomes indistinguishable from God himself, and the notions of Primordial Human, or the sparks, become spiritual truths about *reality*, which is now understood to be nothing over and above the experience of humanity. Indeed, this is the view that Jung seems to have adopted in *The Red Book* and other places where he allowed himself to follow through on the full implications of his notion of the objective psyche.[15]

Such a view is held implicitly by the Kabbalists. Indeed, the very theory of the *Sefirot* defines reality in obviously ideal and experiential terms. Despite Jung's protests, an idealist or, at the very least, *phenomenological* (metaphysically neutral) interpretation of the Jungian archetypes is most consistent with Jungian psychology. Jung himself seems to imply an idealist or phenomenological interpretation of the archetypes when he declares that the archetype of the self is indistinguishable from the archetype of God,[16] or more pointedly that "the unconscious as a unit is indistinguishable from God."[17] Since the two are indistinguishable, we are better off ending our talk about two distinct things (our ideas of God and God himself) and beginning to talk about one experiential reality that is neither simply the mind nor God, but which is both. In a somewhat more metaphysical mood, Jung says that the realm of the unconscious mind:

> is a self-contained world, having its own reality, of which we can only say that it affects us as we affect it—precisely what we say about our experience of the outer world. And just as material objects are the

constituent elements of this world, so psychic factors constitute the objects of that other world.[18]

Earlier, in his "Commentary on 'The Secret of the Golden Flower,'" Jung had mused:

it seems to me...reasonable to accord the psyche the same validity as the empirical world, and to admit that the former has just as much "reality" as the latter.[19]

Hegelian, Jungian, and Kabbalistic Dialectics

There is another arena in which a comparison between Jung and Hegel can be instructive for our understanding of the Kabbalah. Here I refer to the role that a dialectical synthesis of opposites plays in each of these systems of thought. It is certainly of interest that both Hegel and Jung placed a "synthesis of opposites" at the heart of their theories, the very kind of synthesis that is so prominent in much of Kabbalistic and especially Chasidic thought.[20] While Hegel's synthesis of opposites is conceptual, conscious, rational, and philosophical, Jung's is symbolic, unconscious, largely irrational, and psychological. The Kabbalah's own dialectic includes features of both the Hegelian and Jungian points of view.

For Hegel the dialectic of opposites is a *logical* progression in which the Absolute, the origin and essence of all concepts and ideas, becomes estranged from itself, first through a series of conceptual distinctions (beginning with "being" and "nothing"), then in nature, and finally in humanity, only to return to itself as the *Idea* of the Absolute Spirit in humanity's highest institutions and disciplines: politics, art, religion, and ultimately, philosophy. In philosophy an impersonal or collective Absolute becomes self-conscious through the reflection and self-awareness of humanity. For Jung, on the other hand, the dialectic or coincidence of opposites is a *mythological* progression, one in which a collective, archetypal, mythological mind (the collective unconscious) becomes estranged from itself in a conscious, personal, and rational ego. However, like Hegel's Absolute, the Jungian unconscious ultimately returns to itself through a series of symbolic unifications that merge unconscious and conscious into a unified "self" within living, individual men and women. Both of these processes, the Hegelian and the Jungian, lead to a higher, more inclusive kind of consciousness, and both—the one metaphysical, and the other psychological—are present in the Kabbalah. Indeed, in the Kabbalah, the metaphysical and the psychological are said to reflect one another, on the principle that the microcosm, the mind of man, mirrors the macrocosm, the cosmos as a whole. In light of the unique affinities between Jung and Hegel, it is of interest to note that Jung confessed to having never read Hegel in the original and having only the scantiest knowledge of

Hegelian philosophy.[21] When queried directly about his opinion of Hegel, Jung responded that Hegel was misguided in having taken truths regarding his own psyche as logical and metaphysical principles about the world. In various places in his work, Jung jibes against what appear to be typical Hegelian formulations. For example, in *Mysterium Coniunctionis* he says that "nature, not logic knows a resolution of conflicts in thirds,"[22] and "in logical analysis there is no third, the 'solvent' must be irrational."[23] Further, according to Jung, "Moral, philosophical, and religious problems are, on account of their universal validity, the most likely to call for mythological compensation."[24] Myth, rather than reason, Jung tells us, will satisfy the urges that led us to philosophy to begin with. This is because "reason alone cannot do... adequate justice to the irrational facts of the unconscious."[25]

It is almost as if Jung were saying to Hegel that the outline of his system, in which an infinite, indeterminate Absolute comes to know itself through its incarnation in nature and man, is a potentially adequate representation of the God archetype (and *ipso facto,* the development of the self). However, instead of filling his scheme with a nearly endless series of (mostly dubious) logical deductions, Hegel ought to have filled it with archetypal symbols and mystical ideas. The "how" of God's descent into multiplicity and his ultimate reunification is spelled out and achieved through archetypal images (as in the Kabbalistic and alchemistic *coniunctios*), not through rational thought.

Despite their differences, Jung can be said to have held that the goal of the individual, as expressed in the psychological process of *individuation*, is very similar to the goal the Kabbalists had articulated as the restoration, emendation, and reunification of the world and God. This should come as no surprise, since Jung, as we have seen, equates the self and God archetypes. The idea that human development parallels a process in the world and God goes a long way towards clarifying our understanding of the Kabbalah. For both Jung and the Kabbalah, humanity's (and God's) goal is achieved through a process that involves the integration of a variety of conflicting forces in the realms of gender, ethics, intellect, spirit, and emotion.

The process Jung describes is one of "self-actualization" in which the goal is man's realization of his own unique individuality, and through that individuality, his connection with humanity as a whole. Jung calls this process "individuation" and he defines it as "the process by which a man becomes the definite unique being he in fact is."[26] This definition is indeed very close to Hegel's notion of the Absolute becoming itself through its dialectical expression in nature and man, and also to the Kabbalistic idea that God only becomes himself by virtue of his being contracted in (and through the efforts of) humanity. For Jung, psychological growth involves an initial independence from the unconscious, the consequent formation of an ego and *persona*, and then a reconnection and reconciliation with the unconscious, in the second half of life.[27] The truly individuated soul is trapped neither in the unconscious nor in the ego but becomes in his being a dialectical resolution of the two. This dialectic is for Jung the meaning of life itself.

Jung even goes so far as to suggest that (at least for some) a life that does not take up the challenge of individuation is not worth living: "If the demand for self-knowledge is willed by fate and is refused, this negative attitude can end in real death....The unconscious has a thousand ways of snuffing out a meaningless existence with surprising swiftness."[28]

For Jung, the cosmic drive (posited by the Kabbalists and later by Hegel) for self-knowledge and realization must be duplicated in man. The life well lived is one that estranges itself into a world of "a thousand things" and then returns to itself in a form of spiritual, emotional, and intellectual self-knowledge. This is no Gnosticism, for such knowledge does not lead to an escape from the world, but rather, according to Jung, to a deeper, more socially responsible engagement with it.[29] This, after all, is the meaning and purpose of the Kabbalist's *Tikkun* as well: to discover the roots of one's soul and to thereby assist in the repair and restoration of the world.

Postmodernism, Kabbalah, and the Psychology of C. G. Jung

Philosophy over the past 250 years has seen what might be called a gradual dissolution of a transcendent God and the despiritualization of the external world, and a gradual re-centering of metaphysics in the human mind or self. As I have argued in this chapter, Jung, and by extension a Jungian or psychologistic understanding of the Kabbalah, fits squarely within this trend. In the realm of theology, Jungian thought, which places God in the collective mind of humanity (echoing a similar idea found among the Chasidim), would seem to be the crowning culmination of the tendency, which began with Kant, to psychologize those objects (i.e., God and the world) that had traditionally been thought to exist independently from the human mind.

More recently, however, as a result of philosophical developments that began in Jung's own time and continued with great force after his death, there has been a "deconstruction" or dissolution not only of God and the world, but of the human subject as well. The same critique that was applied to the idea of a transcendent God and a knowable, objective world has now been applied to the human subject or self. The notion that there are fixed "authorial intents," "structures of meanings," "archetypes," and ideas that somehow constitute or populate the human mind has been challenged by the view—articulated by Wittgenstein, Derrida, Foucault, and others—that the infinite reinterpretability of any phenomenon, thing, or idea applies equally to the mind as it does to the so-called objects of the external world. For such a deconstructionist, poststructuralist point of view, there can be no invariant structures, archetypes, or ideas—just an infinite, errant play of language and its multiplicity of interpretations. Not only God and the world, but the self has been decentered.[30] The deconstructive view goes beyond moving the position of the philosophical and theological anchor (from the external world to conscious subject), to an elimination of the notion of an anchor altogether.

As a result, we have witnessed a "deconstruction" of all categories, archetypes, and intentions that might be said to *constitute* the world and the human psyche. The notion that one can, through a process of individuation, "find oneself" comes square up against the idea that whatever one "finds" would itself be subject to a multitude of interpretations. In Kabbalistic terms, the archetypes, which Jung and others believed to be a secure anchor or foundation for an objective psychology, have themselves *broken apart under the force of deconstruction*. The *Sefirot* have been torn asunder, and there is little, if any, prospect of attaining anything more than a relative *Tikkun* or restoration. In the moment when we seemed to be on the verge of discovering a Kabbalistic/ Jungian "root" to our soul, we are confronted with the very impossibility of any such root or foundation.

A question arises concerning the extent to which Jungian psychology, which I have argued has close affinities with the Kabbalah, represents the modern or humanistic ideal, as opposed to sharing in a postmodern, deconstructivist point of view. Despite Jung's apparent Platonism, I think it is fair to say that Jung's thought ranges over traditional, modern (humanistic), and postmodern points of view without being adequately encompassed or characterized by any. While it is true that Jung, in essence, transfers the attributes of God onto the "self," Jung's "self" is hardly assimilable to the self of humanistic modernism. On the one hand, Jung's self harkens back to more traditional thought by continuing to embody the numinous qualities (what Jung refers to as archetypes) that made God and self spiritual, as opposed to purely material and utilitarian ideas. On the other hand, Jung's self is hardly the coherent, conscious, rational subject of modernism, but, like the Kabbalist's *Ein-sof*, is understood as a *coincidentia oppositorum*—a coincidence, or overcoming, of the very oppositions that are needed to define both the traditional God and the humanistic ego. Finally, Jung's "self," unlike the traditional God and the rationalist/empiricist ego (and again like the Kabbalist's *Ein-sof*), is not a given, but is rather something to be achieved; Jung's subject, and the Kabbalist's deity, is not so much the source of human life and striving but is rather its product or end. Thus, Jung's conception of the self and the Kabbalist's conception of *Ein-sof* share much with a postmodern sensibility.[31] However, in holding out a *potential* for coherence and centering, Jung does not go the whole distance toward a deconstructive analysis of God, self, and meaning. For Jung, the archetypes provide the *possibility* of an anchor for meaning, and psychotherapy the *possibility* of achieving an integrated whole self.

Jung, Derrida, and the Theosophical Kabbalah

In previous studies[32] I have argued that there is an extremely close affinity between the Lurianic Kabbalah and deconstructive thought; that the Kabbalistic preoccupation with language and interpretation and, in particular, the Lurianic symbol of the Breaking of the Vessels leads to an open-ended, non-foundationalist form of thinking that implies that any of the constructions we place on any idea, including the Kabbalistic symbols themselves, are and must be continually subject to revision and reinterpretation. As I put in my book, *Kabbalah and Postmernism*:

> Understood philosophically, the Kabbalah actually performs a radical deconstruction upon the very language through which it (and all philosophy, for that matter) must be expressed and understood. Symbolized in the Breaking of the Vessels, this deconstruction provides us with a caution against being too satisfied with any of the interpretations or constructions we place upon the Kabbalah specifically, or upon the world in general. Indeed, it is only by constructing, deconstructing, and then reconstructing our perspectives upon God, the world, and ourselves that we can hope to achieve anything near the breadth of view necessary for a valuable interpretation.[33]

Further, I have also argued that the major figure in postmodern deconstructive thought, Jacques Derrida, can be profitably understood as articulating Kabbalistic ideas.[34] How is it possible to make the claim that two twentieth-century thinkers as different from each other as Derrida and Carl Jung can each be interpreted in Kabbalistic terms? This is a complex question, one that I can only touch upon briefly. In the first place, it is by no means clear that Jung and Derrida are completely alien to one another. Each, in their own way, are heirs to Freud, and define themselves in large measure through what they accept and reject from psychoanalysis. Second, despite what may now be regarded as Jung's cultural prejudices, both Jung and Derrida are champions of difference;[35] indeed, Jung can be said to have been the single most important factor in the appreciation of the religions, myths, and spiritual practices of non-Western cultures by contemporary psychologists and intellectuals. Finally, both Jung and Derrida were deeply concerned with those implications of speech and writing that transcend the intentions of the individual speaker/writer; Jung via his notion of the collective unconscious, and Derrida through his meditations on iteration and the trace.

Having said this, there are of course vast differences to be noted between these thinkers. We might begin by noting that while Jung's psychology is filled with meaning and form and is in many ways an heir to Plato's doctrine of eternal ideas, Derrida's "grammatology" is concerned with bare grammar and the dissolution of "form." While Jung's avowed goal is a totally individuated and integrated "self," Derrida's work involves the dissolution of all purported integrations. Still, I believe that Derrida and Jung can each be understood in Kabbalistic terms. The reason for this is the dialectal comprehensiveness of the Lurianic system, which encompasses both "negative" and "positive" moments. Whereas Derrida's ideas fall naturally on the negative (deconstructive) side, Jung's are far more compatible with the positive (emanative, restorative) side of Luria's dialectic. In Derrida we find analogies to Luria's *Ayin* (nothing), *Tzimtzum* (contraction), and *Shevirah* (breakage) in such notions as *différance, khora* (borrowed from Plato's *Timaeus), deconstruction*, and *the trace*; while in Jung, as we have seen, we find analogies to Luria's more positive characterizations of *Adam Kadmon* (Primordial Human), the *Sefirot* (Archetypes of Being), the *Partzufim* (Divine Visages), and *Tikkun* (Restoration) in such notions as the self, the archetypes of the collective unconscious, and the therapeutic process of individuation. Derrida and Jung can thus be understood as opposing terms of a dialectic that is (and on my view must be) integrated in the Kabbalah.[36]

These considerations, as interesting and vital as they may be, take us beyond the parameters of the present study. However, having closed, as it were, on a deconstructive note, and having suggested that the Kabbalah, at least in its negative moments of *Ayin* (nothingness), *Tzimtzum* (contraction), and *Shevirah* (rupture), assures us that there can be no final word, we cannot expect anything more than a continued dialog, an open economy of thought that searches for but never quite grasps or achieves the archetypes, the soul, the self, individuation, God, the Absolute, etc. Our study of Jung and the Kabbalah will not sum up or conclude, as there is no final conclusion regarding the issues raised in this book. The relationship between Jungian and Kabbalistic thought, the nature (and value) of a Kabbalistic psychology, the question of Jung's purported anti-Semitism and his relationship to National Socialism, the meaning of Jung's visions, each will and must remain open to further dialog and interpretation. If I have opened up dialog on some issues and contributed to dialog on others, that is all the concepts afforded me by my subject will allow, and all that I or the reader can genuinely hope for from a study of this kind.

Appendix

"The Maggid Anticipated My Entire Psychology" Erich Neumann's "Roots" as an Articulation of Jung's Relationship to Jewish Mysticism

The publication of Erich Neumann's *The Roots of Jewish Consciousness*, Vols. 1 and 2[1] in 2019 opens up new vistas into the relationship between Jungian thought and the Jewish tradition. Neumann (1905–60) was among Jung's pre-eminent disciples, and this work, especially "Volume Two: Hasidism," sheds considerable light on Jung's late life claim that "the Hasidic Rabbi Baer from Meseretz,[2] whom they called the Great Maggid… anticipated my entire psychology in the eighteenth century."[3] Indeed, at times Neumann's work is written as if it was aimed explicitly at drawing what appear to be uncannily close parallels between Hasidic and Jungian thought, and one wonders if Neumann, was somehow the source of Jung's striking proclamation. The Maggid of Meseritz, Rabbi Dov Baer Friedman (1704–72) succeeded his teacher the "Baal Shem Tov," Rabbi Israel ben Eliezer (c 1698–1760) as the leader of the nascent Hasidic movement, and was the first to formulate the philosophy underlying Hasidic practice. Neuman in his "Roots, Volume Two," considers a number of the Maggid's (and other Hasidic masters') ideas in relation to Jungian psychology.

While it is tempting to speculate that Neumann influenced Jung with regard to the psychological significance of Jewish mysticism, and in a 1934 letter Neumann actually scolded Jung over his ignorance of Hasidism,[4] the evidence for a direct influence is limited. Prior to World War II, while Neumann was in Palestine, he sent Jung a manuscript, "Applications and Questions,"[5] in which he outlined some of the ideas that would later appear in "Roots" and without mentioning the Maggid of Meseretz, described how Hasidic theory of the sparks involving "the taking back of the world into internal space."[6] Jung read this manuscript and responded, mentioning Buber's "renewal of Hasidism."[7] Neumann later informed Jung of his work on "Roots" and that he was writing a "comprehensive chapter on Hasidism,"[8] and even wrote that he hoped to send Jung a copy of Part One.[9] However, while Neumann forwarded several of his other manuscripts to Jung there is no indication that he ever sent Jung either Part One or Part Two of "Roots," or that he provided Jung with any of the details regarding his work on Hasidism and depth psychology. Further, when Neumann resumed his correspondence with Jung after a five-year hiatus during the war, Neumann's interests had completely shifted to more general and secular topics. As Martin Liebscher, who edited the Jung-Neumann correspondence notes, Jung and Neumann appear to have "crossed paths" intellectually, as Jung, after his "Kabbalistic vision" in 1944, began to take a keen interest in Jewish mysticism, and Neumann by that time had essentially put that interest behind him.[10] Thus, while a plunge into Neumann's *The Roots of Jewish Consciousness* can provide us an understanding of why Jung could later claim that a Hasidic rabbi anticipated his entire psychology, it will not fully answer the question of exactly how it was that Jung arrived at this conclusion.

Neumann's *Roots* ranges over a wide range of Hasidic ideas and principles that were premonitory of Jung. Among these are the centrality of symbols for the human psyche, the importance of accessing deeper, unconscious layers of the mind and soul, the integral connection between the psyche and the world, the discovery of divinity within the Self, the importance of engagement with evil and the "shadow" elements of personality, the emphasis upon creative individuality, the decentering yet critical importance of the ego, reason and consciousness, the significance of "nothingness," the complementarity and coincidence of opposites, the bisexuality of the human psyche, the value of joy, and the acceptance of the world. Many of these ideas are attributable to the Maggid of Meseritz and taken together they provide warrant for Jung's late life assertion about him.

However, "Roots" is by no means simply a work that articulates the interface between Hasidic and Jungian thought. Indeed, it is primarily an original work of "psycho-theology" which contains important insights into the ethical, psychological, and spiritual condition of Neumann's (and our own) time and, despite some of Neumann's more controversial assertions about the "Christianization" of Judaism in Hasidism, provides the basis for a psychologically meaningful reinterpretation of the Jewish tradition. As a result, I will also examine Neumann's *Roots*, with particular attention to Volume 2, with the thought of elucidating his understanding (and contribution) to Jewish thought and practice.

Neumann was ambivalent about publishing his work and failed to do so during his own lifetime. He expressed concerns that his work was not adequately grounded in the traditional sources and that as a result he might have distorted the true nature of the Jewish traditions he examined. This was (and remains) a legitimate concern to the extent that we regard Neumann's *Roots* as historical and exegetical, as was undoubtedly part of his intention in writing it. However, if we regard Neumann's *Roots* as the creative product of his encounter with the ideas and symbols of the Jewish, and moreover, the Kabbalistic/Hasidic tradition, as these were mediated through the authors he relied upon, the problem of his faithfulness to the "original sources" becomes less problematic. Understood in this way, his work should not be judged against some presumed criteria of "accuracy" but rather in terms of the value of the creative synthesis which he forged, a synthesis between his unique understanding of both Jewish mysticism and Jungian thought.

Neumann could not have known that several years after his death in 1960 the philosophical (e.g. Buber) and academic (e,g. Scholem) interest in Kabbalah and Hasidism would become the basis for a renewed interest in and resignification of Jewish mystical symbols and ideas that would lend impetus to a psychologically-minded and universalizing trend within Judaism—a trend that would give impetus to the "Jewish Renewal" movement. As we will see, one of the key figures in this movement, Zalman Schachter-Shalomi, a Hasidic trained rabbi, took a great interest in Neumann's writings, and had even hoped to enter into analysis with Neumann prior to the latter's untimely death. Indeed, "Jewish Renewal" essentially followed Neumann's prescription for a psychologically minded, creative, individuating, inclusive and universalizing Judaism.

Neumann's work was incomplete and not intended for publication in its present form—and his endnotes read as abbreviated reminders to himself that he may have intended to elaborate upon should his book have proceeded into print. As such, Neumann's text is problematic; he has the habit of quoting sources without identifying them; and his notes, which on a number of occasions required correction by his editors, often refer to his secondary sources without indicating the original authors of the quotations in question. At times his text in *Roots*, Volume 2 reads as if he is quoting various Hasidic authors as representatives of the "Hasidic tradition" in general. While in this essay I have identified the Hasidic thinkers Neumann refers to, my purpose is to understand Neumann's interpretation of his sources and not to defend this interpretation in light of these thinkers' views, or even in light of the secondary sources—e.g. those by Buber and Horodezky, which Neumann relied upon. My view is that Neumann has presented us with an original psychology and theology, one that is clearly rooted in the Hasidic tradition, but which interprets that tradition in the light of modern, and especially Jungian, psychology.

Neumann makes an extraordinary effort to provide a depth psychological interpretation of Hasidism and the Kabbalistic symbols upon which it is based—one that is in many ways successful, but which also suffers because of his failure to adequately consider the full range of the Kabbalistic, and particularly, the Lurianic symbols upon which Hasidic thought and practice is grounded. While he placed a strong emphasis on the Hasidic theory of the "sparks" (*netzotzim*) of divine energy that lay hidden in all things, the *Shekhinah*, the feminine aspect of the divine, and *Adam Kadmon*, the primordial human who serves as a "template" for both humanity and the world, he paid less attention to the Hasidic understanding of such Kabbalistic symbols as the *Sefirot* (the divine value archetypes), and the *Shevirah* (the cosmic catastrophe which brought about our current world). As I proceed, I will at times amplify Neumann's account of the Kabbalistic symbols which informed his exposition of Hasidism, with the thought of providing a fuller context for our reflections on Neumann's Neo-Hasidic psychology and philosophy.

In addition, we should note that, as Moshe Idel points out in his Introduction to *Roots* II, Neumann followed Buber in emphasizing the "this worldly" aspects of Hasidism to the relative neglect of Hasidic theosophy, which involved a focus upon "the lifting of the divine sparks from the demonic realm and their purification and elevation on high."[11] In this connection, Neumann, like Jung, insisted that he was writing only about psychology and not about metaphysics or theology. Neumann writes:

> We are investigating these texts for their psychological, not their metaphysical reality ...the real aim of our interpretation is to reveal the psychic structure of the Jewish person... [and it] says nothing about a deity's existence independent of the human structure.[12]

However, like Jung, and perhaps even more pointedly, Neumann used theological language in an ambiguous manner which had the effect of floating theological claims under the guise of psychological observations. For example, Neumann writes: "In terms of the process of creation, the human Self is brought forth by divine self-union; it is the product of the connection between God's active, masculine aspect and his feminine, worldly aspect, the *Shekhinah*."[13]

Language like this produced ambiguities which Neumann never adequately resolved. Both Jung and Neumann risked appearing disingenuous when they used God-talk in (hidden) "scare-quotes" as a vehicle for speaking about psyche and self while simultaneously denying that they had any theological or metaphysical intentions.

Jung, Neumann and Judaism

As I indicated earlier in this volume the Jung who claimed that a Hasidic rabbi anticipated his entire psychology was the same Jung who in the 1930s had used the epithet "Jewish psychology" in his attacks on Freud and Adler in a rather obvious effort to curry favor with the Nazis.[14] As we have seen, during this period Jung, both in his published papers and private correspondence had made a series of comments that could hardly be construed as anything but Anti-Semitic. To recall just one particularly pointed example: In 1933 Jung published an article in the *Zentralblatt fur Psychotherapie*, which at the time was under his own editorship, and in the very issue of that journal in which Herman Goring (!) had published a directive which read in part, "the [psychotherapy] society expects all members who work as writers or speakers to work through Adolf Hitler's *Mein Kampf* with all scientific effort and accept it as a basis."[15] In this article, entitled "The State of Psychotherapy Today," Jung wrote, "The Jew who is something of a nomad has never yet created a cultural form of his own and as far as we can see never will, since all his instincts and talents require a more or less civilized nation to act as host for their development."[16] Hitler had claimed in *Mein Kampf*:

> The Jewish people, despite all apparent intellectual qualities, is without a true culture, and especially without any culture of its own. For what sham culture the Jew today possess is the property of other peoples, and for the most part ruined in his hands.[17]

We need only compare these two passages, Jung's and Hitler's to understand the level of Anti-Semitism rhetoric Jung was willing to adopt as his own.

In 1934 Neumann castigated Jung, writing that he could not comprehend how Jung could ignore the obvious fact "that a mind-numbing cloud of filth, blood and rottenness is brewing: in the German psyche.[18] He upbraided Jung for being conditioned by a "general ignorance of things Jewish" and while "knowing everything about the India of 2,000 years ago" knows "nothing about Hasidism."[19]

Jung's late life pronouncement regarding the Maggid is all the more startling when viewed in the context of his Ant-Semitic rhetoric. I have described Jung's "turn" towards Judaism as a result of the visions he experienced after his 1944 heart attack.[20] The publication of Neumann's *Roots* provides us with additional insight into Jung's late life about face on the topic of "Jewish psychology."

Judaism in its "Christian Stage"

Neumann's radical reflections on the history of the Jewish religion and, in particular, on the "Christianization" of Judaism in Hasidism provide an important context for our understanding of the (anticipatory) relationship of Hasidism to Jungian psychology.

Neumann. held that in post-biblical times Judaism lost the tensions between YWH and earth, and this loss resulted in a hypertrophy of the spiritual within the Jewish religion. He believed that rabbinism became overly rational and Kabbalism overly ascetic and mystical, and argued that these opposing excesses provided the context for the development of Hasidism. While the rabbinic tradition had rejected inner "religious experience"[21] and the Kabbalah, became rigid, punitive, and overly theosophical, Hasidism, in Neumann's view, at least initially, developed a psychologically balanced spirituality that promoted individual creativity.

Neumann held that "Hasidism, after almost 2000 years, involve[d] a delayed ripening of essential aspects of early Christianity within Judaism."[22] Neumann did not fully develop this intriguing, if highly unorthodox thesis, but the gist of his idea was that in Hasidism Judaism had "arrived at its Christian stage" in which "religious revelation became individualized and internalized."[23]

Jung had held that Christ was or, at least, had become a symbol of the self, and particularly in his early formulation in *The Red Book*, he saw Christ in existential terms as providing a call for individuals to actualize their unique creative and spiritual paths. Neumann was of the view that with the advent of "Judaism in its Christian stage" the "heavenly kingdom" was brought into the individual human being, the cultic law was rejected, and there was an emphasis on "direct revelation."[24] However, this creative, individuating tendency was, inhibited in Judaism until the advent of the Kabbalah, and, moreover, Hasidism, which forged "a reconnection with ancient Judaism in its primal Christian form," a form "which saw religious individualism as the core of religious revelation."[25] Neumann held that through the public figure of the Tzaddik (the spiritual leader of the Hasidic community) and the inner figure of *Adam Kadmon* (the Primordial Human or divine aspect of the inner Self) "the Christianization of Jewish individuals took a new historical form." As it would later become for Jung, spiritual and psychic development, at least in the earlier phase of Hasidism, became "the central and personal task of each individual."[26]

I will return to Neumann's controversial ideas about the "Christianization of Judaism" in my concluding remarks.

The Value and Degeneration of Hasidism

Neumann's project in both volumes of *Roots* involved an effort to demonstrate that Judaism has always struggled to create a balance between earth and sky, between the uncompromising masculine spiritual demands of Yahweh, and an awareness of the feminine depths of the unconscious. He argues that this balance was destroyed with the Jewish people's exile from their land, the end of the temple sacrificial cult, and the resultant hyper-legalization of rabbinic Judaism. According to Neumann, Hasidism represented a revival of the feminine, prophesy, and access to the unconscious within the Jewish collective.

However, the opportunity to turn this revival into a revitalization of the Jewish people (and person) was lost when Hasidism degenerated into *Tzaddikism*, which produced a cult around the religious leader—who then became the only one with access to the psychic depths which Hasidism had originally vouchsafed for each individual.

Neumann provides an account of Hasidism's failure to live up to its initial promise of providing an alternative to the Enlightenment for

Judaism in modern times—one that would have avoided the pitfalls of illusory assimilation, the hyper-rationalism of modernism, and what in Neumann's view was the soulless constriction of Jewish orthodoxy. According to Neumann, the early Hasidim emphasized the individual's role in the redemption of both the world and God, and the original task of the *tzaddik* was to guide his followers in this process and "give each individual what he and he alone needs."[27] However, Hasidism developed into a *tzaddik-centered* movement in which the rebbe/tzaddik became the sole mediator of the divine, and in the process, Hasidism lost its opportunity to provide a psychology/theology of the individuated self. Neumann writes that Hasidism "gave rise to a form of tzadikkism in which a mass of followers, stripped of selfhood, gathered around the mana-personality of the tzaddik."[28] While early on the Maggid of Meseritz pronouncement of the "Godlikeness of the human being within himself"[29] was initially meant to apply to all human beings, it increasingly came to be attributed to the tzaddik alone.

Neumann was highly critical of what he regarded to be excesses of Tzaddikism, writing that "the *tzaddik's* self-identification with *Adam Kadmon* [the 'Archetypal Human'] leads to an obvious inflation."[30] He points out that at least one Hasidic rabbi, Rabbi Nachman, went so far as to order "that his grave be worshipped."[31] A similar "inflation" is evident in our own time where the last Lubavitcher rebbe, Rabbi Menachem Mendel Schneerson (1902–1994), failed to discourage his adherents from regarding him as the messiah, resulting in a messianic cult around him which continues today.[32]

Neumann refers to "Hasidism's self-betrayal" and argues that its loss of its own "principle of inwardness" resulted in a diminution of thought and intelligence, one that surrendered to the Enlightenment the claim of "legitimacy as the pioneer of Jewish intellectual development," and led to "the secularizing and atomizing of the Jewish person."[33] Within Hasidism there was a decline into "superstition, amulets, exorcisms, magical cures" related to the "mana-personalities" within the movement.[34] This led to a fanatical rejection of Hasdism by (both Enlightenment Jews) and the non-Hasidic, "Mitnagdid" orthodox.

Neumann held that the decline in 'Hasidic inwardness' led to the Jews' alienation from their unconscious, in particular the collective unconscious, an alienation which continued with Freud, who despite having touched upon the collective layer of the unconscious (in his understanding of the Oedipus complex and later in *Moses and Monotheism*) failed to confront the obvious problem of the "Jewish collective."[35]

In his historical analysis Neumann followed the general cultural critique laid out by Jung in holding that the 19th century witnessed a "loss of memory" and alienation of large numbers of Jews from both their religious traditions and their "inner communal connection."[36] Many Jews believed that a return to Eretz Yisroel would provide a renewal of the Jewish spirit, and Neumann himself made *aliyah* in 1934.

For Neumann, the Jews' alienation from their own history resulted in a turn towards general culture and values, a turn which in his view had the most terrible consequences,[37] the secularization and assimilation which prompted many Jews to see themselves primarily as Europeans, Germans, etc. and which contributed to their failure to adequately recognize the growing power of anti-Semitism which eventuated in the Holocaust. Neumann calls 19th century Jewish assimilation a "grand delusion,"[38] writing: "As if blinded, this ancient people abandoned itself with the naïve trust of a child to the enticing deception of the west, and no pogroms, no ritual murder trials, no antisemitic movements persuaded it otherwise."[39]

Yet even as the Hasidim were among the greatest victims of the Holocaust, Neumann believed that Hasidism, which became historically powerless in regard to modern Jewish consciousness, continues to hold "a hidden, crucial meaning for the psychology of the modern Jew"[40] and also to the problems of "modern people in general."[41]

According to Neumann, Hasidism failed not only because it abandoned the "sacredness" and creative potential of the individual but also because it "never seriously attempted to push the boundaries of legalistic Judaism" and this "hindered its influence."[42] Certain of the Hasidim, according to Neumann, regressed into to a form of "Kabbalistic rationalism," one that attempted, as in the Chabad movement, to find a compromise with rabbinism, and this resulted in an equally sterile result, with these Hasidim being devoured by what Neumann referred to as the "dragon" of Torah (*halakhic*) Judaism.[43] While such later Hasidic figures as Nathan of Brezlav, endeavored to revive early Hasidism's ethos, they were, on the whole, unsuccessful, and a figure like Mendel of Kotzk, who "declared drives and desires to be parts of God,"[44] lived his last years in a Nietzsche-like atheism and insanity.[45]

"Jewish Renewal"

It is here worth noting, at least in passing, that Erich Neumann's psychologically minded vision of Judaism was brought to fruition, after Neumann's death, by Rabbi Zalman Schachter-Salomi (1924–2014), an émigré from Vienna who fled the Nazis and came to the United States in 1941 and was ordained as a rabbi with Chabad-Lubavitch. Reb Zalman, as he came to be known, originally led Chabad congregations in Massachusetts and Connecticut, but eventually left Chabad and Jewish orthodoxy, and became one of the moving forces in the "Jewish Renewal" movement which advocated for a far more open, ecumenical, and psychologically minded form of Jewish prayer and practice—one that was rooted in Kabbalah and Hasidism but which was committed to social justice and eschewed a slavish adherence to *halakha*, Jewish law. Reb Zalman became a committed feminist and advocated for the inclusion of LGBT individuals within Judaism, and he encouraged all individuals to develop their visions and talents and to bring these into their Jewish practice.

It is of significance in the present context that Reb Zalman developed a keen interest in the work of Erich Neumann and had, just prior to Neumann's untimely death in 1960 hoped to enter analysis with Neumann in Israel.[46] In a recent book Shoshana Fershtman writes:

> Reb Zalman was greatly influenced by the work of Erich Neumann. In my meeting with Reb Zalman just a year before his death, I was able to share my work researching the impact of Jewish Renewal on individuals reconnecting with Judaism. When I mentioned my training as a Jungian analyst, his whole being lit up as he began talking about Erich Neumann. "Oh, Neumann!" he said. "How I wanted to study with him![47]

Neumann, in *Roots*, shows that he is indeed a prophet of a psychologically minded Jewish mysticism, yet he ultimately abandoned his project of reinterpreting Judaism in order to focus upon a new ethic based in depth psychology, in effect, discarding his ethnic and religious interests for a more general, secular interests, the very thing he had, in *Roots*, warned against.

Having set the stage by examining Neumann's general understanding of Hasidism, we are now in a position to explore his understanding of its relationship to Jungian psychology.

The Truth of Symbols

Jung regarded the symbol as a bearer of psychic reality and truth. In *The Red Book* Jung writes: "If the word is a sign, it means nothing. But if the word is a symbol, it means everything."[48] In that work he explains that a symbol is "born of man's highest spiritual aspirations," and that it arises "from the deepest roots of his being...from the lowest and most primitive levels of the psyche."[49]

According to Neumann the symbol plays a critical role in Hasidism, a role that is rooted in the symbolic Kabbalistic world-view upon which Hasidism is based. Neumann writes that for Hasidism the allegorical nature of the world is revealed "only to those who stand on the highest, the *symbolic* level."[50] For the Hasidim as for Jung, the symbol reveals a "truth" that is beyond the truths of empirical observation. Perhaps the most important of the Kabbalistic/Hasidic symbols are the *sefirot*, which play a role similar to the archetypes in Jung's psychology. Neumann writes:

The *sefirot* may be called non-pictorial archetypal constellations. They are therefore conceived of as levels, aspects, characteristics, hypostases, principles, emanations, names, lights and forces. Like every archetype, each *sefirah* owes its nothingness to its energy, which infinitely surpasses ego-consciousness and thus has a disintegrating effect on the ego.[51]

For the Hasidim the "human form" is also understood as a symbol. The *sefirot* are said to be embodied in the form of *Adam Kadmon*, the Primordial Human. Neumann quotes from a German translation of the Zohar which suggests that the human form contains all existent things.[52]

Neumann sees the Hasidic reliance on story and parable as serving a similar function as the symbol. He writes: "The *tzaddik* speaks in parables as God does, for the parable is *tzimtzum*, contraction, concealment of light. The whole world is also a parable, in which God's light is hidden."[53]

The Importance of "This World"

Neumann's' account of the (early) Hasidic philosophy, a philosophy first formulated by the Maggid of Meseritz, focuses upon a series of symbols and ideas that were either discussed directly by Jung or readily assimilable to Jung's psychology. Chief among these is the "Raising of the Sparks."

The notion of a "spark" of divinity imprisoned in the material world is an old Gnostic idea which reappeared in the Lurianic Kabbalah and later served as an essential symbol and idea in Hasidism. Whereas the Gnostics held that by attaching oneself to the divine spark one could escape this world and merge with the divine pleroma, Isaac Luria (1534–72), and later, the Hasidim who based their philosophy on Luria's system, believed that the "entrapment" of the sparks produces negativity and evil in both human souls and the world and by liberating the divine sparks a person can initiate *Tikkun ha-Olam*, the redemption and perfection of both the individual soul and *this* world. As Neumann put it, while the Gnostic redemption of the sparks involves "extracting bits of light from the evil world" and "leaving it below and behind as evil," the Hasidim take the further creative step of "radiating back into the world" and causing the world to be "reborn" and redeemed.[54] In the process evil within both the self and the world is revealed as "a veiled, hidden goodness."[55] Neumann avers: "For Judaism and Hasidism, the human being's specific salvific task is to make the world holy by redeeming the sparks."[56]

I have argued that while Jung's understanding of "the sparks" was initially derived from Gnosticism, his psychology is ultimately in far better accord with the this-worldly understanding of the sparks in Hasidism. As I put it in Chapter 1 of this volume: *In Gnosticism the world is escaped; in the Kabbalah it is elevated and restored.* For Hasidism, the charge of individuals is to raise those sparks they encounter in the life journeys.

Neumann notes that according to the Maggid of Meseritz, the sparks constitute wisdom "mixed with all the contents of this world."[57] and one's "whole intention should be to lift the sparks to their roots, to the place of supreme holiness."[58]

Neumann writes that because a spark is latent, like an "embryo" within all things, revelation "can break forth from anything and everything."[59] Such revelation involves a collision and, ultimately, a union between a human soul and the spark, yielding a "cross-fertilization" and "procreation" on the analogy of male uniting with female.[60] This procreation results in the spark, in effect, becoming a "talking being," one that can release and express its living, mental and spiritual inwardness.[61]

Neumann points out that for Hasidism, the raising of the sparks and the ultimate redemption of the world is intrinsically tied to the development of human life and mind. He quotes Buber's translation of the Baal Shem Tov:

> The human being should raise the holy sparks that fell when God built and destroyed worlds. He should purify them upward, from stone to plant, from plant to animal, from animal to the talking being. He should purify the holy spark, which is enclosed in a powerful shell. Everyone in Israel shares this basic purpose...And the one who is able to raise the holy spark from stone to plant, from plant to animal, from animal to the talking being with the good power of his spirit leads it to freedom. No other liberation of the imprisoned is greater than this. It is like one who rescues a king's son from captivity and brings him to his father."[62]

As I have described in Chapter Eight of this volume, Jung discussed the symbol of the sparks as it appeared in Gnosticism and Alchemy but was also familiar with is presence in the Kabbalah, and he understood them as unconscious complexes, the freeing of which would result in psychological redemption.[63] Indeed, the notion of a hidden, encapsulated psychic energy that must be freed and returned to consciousness is a basic, perhaps *the most basic*, psychoanalytic idea. Neumann focused on the raising the sparks as a means of reclaiming the unconscious and the shadow, as a symbol for the individual's transition from the individual ego to an identification with the wider "Self," and as a symbol of the Hasidic charge that each individual has a role in repairing and restoring *this world*.

The Shadow and Evil

Neumann observed that the Hasidim recognized what Jung would later describe as the "shadow" side of the personality. He points out that according to the Baal Shem Tov, the *Shekhinah*, the feminine aspect of God, which symbolizes the divine presence on earth, encompasses both good and evil, "for evil is the throne of goodness."[64] Further, the Maggid of Meseritz held that "goodness is hidden in darkness and "there is good in all evil."[65] Neumann writes that for the Hasidim, "the task of higher service is to free the sparks even from evil."[66] Indeed, Neumann says that it was the Maggid's view that if a person repents then God even enjoys an individual's sin.[67]

He points out that according to the Maggid of Meseritz there are "divine sparks" even idols and idolatry. Indeed, "The holiest sparks exist on the lowest of levels."[68] For Neumann, the notion that divine sparks exist "[e]ven in idolatry[69]...has the widest implications because...it completely revolutionized moral and traditional values."[70]

According to Neumann, when "rightly perceived" sin and evil are not only inevitable "but also a crucial part of this existence."[71] One reason for this is that, "Only the knowledge of good and evil leads to consciousness,"[72] and consciousness, according to Neumann conditions freedom and choice. Further, "Whenever any real experience of inwardness occurs, the reality of demons and of Satan becomes the problem of the holy struggle."[73] Neumann follows Jung in declaring: "Only evil, the other side, brings about the energic tension called life."[74] He points out that in the book of Genesis "evil becomes the consciousness-enhancing principle that leads to the affirmation of the world" as well as the affirmation of time. For Neumann "only the world 'equipped' with evil is the real world."[75]

Neumann contrasted what he termed the "old ethic" of obedience to set values and ethical norms with a "new ethic" grounded in depth psychology involving a recognition of the shadow side or (what from a traditional perspective would be regarded as) evil within the individual. For Neumann the "world of knowledge and fixed values constitutes the old, pre-Hasidic world of rabbinism..."[76]

Nature of the Self

Neumann saw in Hasidism the (Jungian) notion of a partly unconscious, non-rational creative "self" Neumann held that throughout the history of Judaism "the chief emphasis is to develop, support, and expand the system of consciousness."[77] However, Hasidism which, while "still emphasizing consciousness...dethrone[d] the ego and pure rationalism."[78] Hasidism's renewed interest in accessing the unconscious is manifest in a variety of ways; for example, Rabbi Nachman's interest in "the night world" and dreams. According to Rabbi Nachman it is in dreams that one "sees the spiritual naked, without a shell."[79] Neumann quotes a translation of a saying of the Maggid of Meseritz: "God makes something out of nothingness, the *tzaddikim* make nothingness out of something.[80] Neumann holds that the import of the Maggid's aphorism is that by returning the individual to the "nothingness" of the creative unconscious the Tzaddik is able to effect the coincidence of opposites which completes the individual (and God). The individual person is the "something" which provides actuality to divine creativity, whereas God is the (unconscious) and pre-formed "nothingness" which brings creativity, spirit and meaning to the individual. We have here yet another of the Maggid's anticipations of Jungian psychology.

For Neumann, "The Copernican revolution in the development of Judaism, which begins with Hasidism, displaces the ego from its position at the center of the world,"[81] a view that was fully in accord with Jung's understanding of the relationship between the *ego* and the *self*. Neumann suggests that by expanding the psyche to include its unconscious, non-rational underpinnings this actually "highlights the human being as the bearer of consciousness...against the cosmos of the unconscious."[82]

Self and God

Jung is well known for his often quoted and frequently misunderstood asser-tion that there is an equivalence between God and the self, a view which evolved in his writings over time. In *The Red Book* Jung wrote: "through uniting with the self we reach the God" (*Durch die Vereinigung mit dem Selbst erreichen wir den Gott*).[83] In *Psychological Types*, a work that Jung authored during his *Red Book* period he quotes with apparent approval the Christian mystic, Meister Eckhart (c. 1260–c. 1328): "For man is truly God, and God is truly man."[84] In par. 421 of Psychological Types Jung writes that for Eckhart, "God is dependent on the soul...and the soul is the birthplace of God."[85] In that work Jung claimed: "God and the soul are essentially the same when regarded as personifications of unconscious content." Jung later asserted that he is not making claims about the metaphysical God *per se*,[86] but in *Aion* and elsewhere he held that the God image or archetype is identical with the "whole man" or "Self."[87]

In *Roots II* Neumann suggests that a similar equation of God and self is present in Hasidic theology. He writes that Hasidism heralds "the inward migration of the divine."[88] This is because, "The world becomes increasingly free of God, increasingly an outer world and free of revelation, and the human being becomes increasingly filled with God and pregnant with reve-lation."[89] There is, on Neumann's interpretation of Hasidism, a reciprocal relationship between God and the Self. Neumann speaks of "human activity as a prior cause" (*die vorlaufende Aktivität des Menschen*)[90] He is here making reference to the concept of "theurgy" the impact of human activity on the divine.[91] Humanity not only has the capacity to be transformed by God and the *Sefirot*, but also has it within its power to transform the very nature of God. Neumann refers to a view attributed to the Baal Shem Tov that "God is a human shadow, and like his shadow, he does whatever the human being does."[92] Neumann further notes that the Maggid of Meseritz held that God thinks what the Tzaddikim think, and that when the Tzaddikim "think with love, they bring God into the world of love."[93] Indeed, the Maggid held that while God is the foundation and source of thought, *actual thinking* only occurs within the human mind.[94]

Neumann quotes a Hasidic saying: "The prayer a man says, the prayer, in itself, is God."[95] Further, in his description of a view attributed to the Maggid of Meseritz, Neumann writes:

> The human love of God is God's attribute of grace. One is constituted by the other. It may also be said that God's attribute of grace does not exist beyond the human love of God and, conversely, that no human love of God exists beyond God's attribute of grace.[96]

These views are certainly congenial to Jung's identification of the "God" and "Self" archetypes.

The Individual and the Collective

Neumann argues that Hasidism, while clearly embedded within the Jewish "collective" placed an emphasis on the side of the individual, holding that "each person is always contained in the unconditionality and newness of the present moment."[97] In this way the Hasidic ethos is not only individualistic but situational: Neumann writes that for Hasidism, at least in its initial phase, "The weight of destiny, both for God and the world, is thus placed on the individual and his life. He is anointed in his irreplaceability, as the mid-point of the world."[98] Further, in Hasidism "Individual life actualizes messianism, and the messianic stage of the individual actualizes the work to be fulfilled."[99] Neumann quotes the Maggid: "[I]nner grace belongs to the one who begins with himself [through developing humility], and not with the Creator."[100] Here again, we have a principle, attributable to the Maggid, which coincides with Jung's early emphasis (most pointedly in *The Red Book*) on the individual "finding his own way," and overcoming one's pride and (e.g. in "Scritunies") grandiosity. While Neumann observed that the "importance of the individual is a basic principle of Hasidism,"[101] he was, as we have seen, of the view that this principle waned with the advent of Tzaddikism in later Hasidism.

Neumann follows Buber in holding that Hasidism originally placed a crucial emphasis on individual free-will: "The world was created only for the sake of the one who chooses."[102] For Rabbi Nachman, the possibility of free-will entails that "Every human being in the world can become worthy of the highest level."[103] Individuals are responsible not only for their own ethical choices and acts but for the actualization of their unique nature. Neumann quotes the famous dictum of the Hasidic Rabbu Meshulam Zusha of Hanipol (Meshulum Zusil of Anipoli) (1718–1800), known as Rabbi Zusya: "I shall not be asked: "Why were you not Moses?" I shall be asked: 'Why were you not Zusya.'"[104]

Neumann turns to Buber's *Tales of the Hasidim*:

> Rabbi Zusya taught: God said to Abraham: "Go out of your country, out of your birthplace, out of your father's house, into the land that I will show you." God says to man:" First you get out of your country, that means the dimness you have inflicted on yourself. Then out of your birthplace, that means, out of the dimness your mother inflicted on you. After that, out of the house of your father, that means, out of the dimness your father inflicted on you. Only then will you be able to go to the land that I will show you."[105]

Neumann comments that what is "inauthentic" "is the foreignness imposed on us by time, race and people, family, constitution, and type."[106] Here is an eloquent expression of the need for the individual to discover his/her "true self" by stripping away he obscuring identifications with what Jacques Lacan later spoke of as "the desire of the Other." Neumann quotes a Hasidic dictum: "There is no man who is not incessantly taught by his soul."[107] and argues that this is "the new thing that Hasidism brought and still must bring to Judaism."[108] Indeed, this is a major, if not the major theme of Jung's *Red Book*.

The quest for unmitigated individuality, however, is not without cost. Such a quest can lead to an "atomistic," alienated existence, if it is not paired with a personal (though not slavish) connection to the collective. Neumann writes that a "personal realization of collective destiny dissociates a person from the constraint of the outer collective...(and) also leads to a rooted connection with the inner collective's creative forces,"[109] an idea which echoes Jung's views on individuation and the collective unconscious. For Neumann "an individuated connection with "the inner seedbed of Judaism... prevents the individual from dissolving in the void of individualistic atomization."[110] This, in brief, is Neumann's philosophy of Judaism for "the modern person," a philosophy he apparently intended to detail in an unwritten part of his "roots" project.[111]

Neumann held that individuation can lead to a sense of guilt for not conforming to the collectives dictates and values. Jung, in a passage in which he made a nod towards ethical and (creative) value objectivity, wrote:

> Individuation cuts one off from personal conformity and hence from collectivity. That is the guilt which the individual leaves behind him for the world, that is the guilt he must endeavour to redeem. He must offer a ransom in place of himself, that is, he must bring forth values which are an equivalent substitute for his absence in the collective personal sphere. Without this production of values, final individuation

is immoral and-more than that suicidal. The man who cannot create values should sacrifice himself consciously to the spirit of collective conformity. In so doing, he is free to choose the collectivity to which he will sacrifice himself. Only to the extent that a man creates objective values can he and may he individuate.[112]

Creativity

Neumann writes that Hasidism stressed creativity over the "formally and rationalistically uncreative" aspect of consciousness emphasized in the rabbinic tradition.[113] According to Neumann, the rabbis' rejection of creativity was a principled one, parallel to their "rejection of inner religious experience."[114] By way of contrast, the early Hassidim welcomed innovation. Neumann again quotes an account of the Maggid of Zlovoch (1726–84) from Buber's *Tales of the Hasidim*:

> Just as our fathers invented new ways of serving, each new service according to his character: one of the service of love, the other that of stern justice, the third that of beauty, so each one of us in his own way shall devise something new in the light of the teachings and of service, and do what has not yet been done.[115]

Neumann held that according to Hasidism, "humanity, by naming the unnamed, and forming and shaping the formless, continues God's act of creating the world"[116] a notion which comports with Jung's later pronouncement in *Answer to Job* that humanity forms a partnership with God in completing creation, an idea that Jung explicitly states he found in the Kabbalah.[117]

Neumann writes that for the Hasidim creative nothingness is the source of regeneration and is "beyond space and time, beyond oppositions, beyond individual differences."[118]

Neumann points out that for Hasidism "nothingness breaks into the world, interrupts its continuity" and thus gives lie to a conception of a "cage-like" deterministic universe.[119] Nothingness is the source of both wisdom and creativity. Indeed, according to the Maggid of Meseritz, "all change in the world is impossible without wisdom, that is to say nothingness."[120] and "every being must come to the level of nothingness, after which it can be another thing."[121] Here we should note that in *The Red Book* Jung wrote about the "little drop of something that falls into the sea of nothingness" prior to the world's creation, and which widens into "unrestricted freedom."[122]

Neumann explains "creative nothingness" by stating that one cannot create through will power—but must, in effect, *empty* oneself in order to become a "tool of the contents passing through him."[123] For the Hasidic masters "free-will," in its mode of creativity, paradoxically relies upon an *emptying* as opposed to an *act* of the will, an idea that clearly anticipates Jung's (and others') view that creativity and personal growth most often result from acts that are devoid of intention.[124]

Indeed, Neumann writes that "Hasidism considers the law of creative energy, its freedom and spontaneity, to be a basic fact, which conditions the inconstancy of what is given," and that this freedom originates in the fact that "the psyche continually experiences itself as originating in creation from nothingness."[125] In this connection, Neumann quotes Buber:

> The world was only created for the sake of choice and the one who chooses. The human being, the lord of choice, should say: The whole world was created for my sake alone. Every person should therefore always and everywhere ensure that he redeems the world and fills its deficiency.[126]

The Return to Nothingness

The role of "nothingness" in the creative process leads to a broader consideration of the role of "Nothing" in Kabbalistic and Hasidic thought. Neumann emphasizes that within both of these traditions there is the view that divinity is *Ayin*, Nothingness, inasmuch as God completely transcends human consciousness. Yet, as Neumann points out, such "nothingness" is provided a positive interpretation as "the primordial idea,"[127] and the Hasidim made returning to such nothingness a primary goal of their theology. This return, Neumann suggests, involves a movement from what is known to what is unknown, and thus, a movement towards the unconscious. Neumann equates the divine nothingness with the unconscious when he writes: "The human task in the world is fundamentally bound up with God's hiddenness."[128]

Neumann writes that for Hasidism, "nothingness, is the root and source of the world...[129]and an ecstatic *return* to "nothingness" assures that "all existence is reborn." Neumann writes: "It is almost as if the dissolution of consciousness into nothingness had to be seen essentially as the apex of a parabola, where the soul hurls itself into nothingness, in order to pass through the point and return to the world in the other direction."[130]

The Kabbalistic notion of *Tzimtzum*, the negation/contraction of the infinite divine plenitude which allows for finite existence, implies that the world itself is a species of "nothingness," a subtraction, contraction and concealment of the infinite divine being. Neumann describes the *Tzimtzum* (which is often associated with *Din* or stern judgment) as a quality of creative mercy which permits the world to exist. He states that this mercy is the world's "inwardness."[131] In a confusing passage Neumann seems to suggest that this inwardness is the divine "nothingness" breaking through into the human realm. The confusion results from the fact that for

Hasidism there are two perspectives on reality—one in which divinity is nothingness and human reality an existing thing, and a second in which human reality is nothingness and divinity is the entirety of existence. According to Schneur Zalman of Lyadi (1745–1813), the founder of Chabad Hasidism:

> (Looking) upwards from below, as it appears to eyes of flesh, the tangible world seems to be *Yesh* and a thing, while spirituality, which is above, is an aspect of *Ayin* (nothingness). (But looking) downwards from above the world is an aspect of *Ayin*, and everything which is linked downwards and descends lower and lower is more and more *Ayin* and is considered as nought truly as nothing and null.[132]

These perspectives imply and complement one another in the manner which Jung referred to as a *coincidentia oppositorum*.

Neumann describes how a "return to nothingness" can result in a regeneration of faith for those who fall into spiritual doubt. He references a passage in the Zohar which states that each night "the soul takes off its bodily garment and ascends, is consumed by fire, and then created anew…"[133] Neumann quotes Rabbi Nahum of Tchernobil (1730–87), who wrote that those "who truly desire to come close to God, must pass through the state of cessation of spiritual life, and 'the falling is for the sake of the rising'"[134] Rabbi Nahum derived the phrase 'falling is for the sake of the rising' from the Maggid of Meseritz,[135] a phrase that is again relevant to Jung's claim that the Maggid anticipated his entire psychology, but in this case it is also an anticipation of Jung's *personal* psychology. This is because Jung, during his *Red Book* period, went through a "falling," a "dark night of the soul," which resulted not only in a personal and spiritual awakening but also in the psychological insights that he would spend a lifetime developing.

Neumann comments that sleep, spiritual seclusion and "pseudo-death" all involve a passage through nothingness which heralds a renewal and birth of the whole person.[136] He writes: "The intention is to link consciousness back to the creative aspect of nothingness, which today we typically call, just as negatively the un-conscious."[137] According to Neumann, this (unconscious) "nothingness is the source of consciousness and its mental contents."[138] Nevertheless an "affirmation of the world is a precondition for realizing the 'whole person,' regenerated in the slumber of nothingness."[139] Neumann writes: "The ascent to nothingness, which occurs through prayer and meditation, and the simultaneous transformation of the world's sparks and of God's reality, corresponds to a *process of psychic transformation* within the individual parts of the human soul."[140]

Readers of Jung's *Red Book*, and in particular his "Seven Sermons to the Dead" will be familiar with Jung's deep engagement with "nothingness." These sermons (which Jung variously attributed to his inner guide

"Philemon, or the 2nd century Gnostic Basilides open with: "Now hear: I begin with nothingness. Nothingness is the same as fullness. In infinity full is as good as empty."[141] We soon learn that this "nothingness" is the "Pleroma," the Gnostics unfathomable infinite, which Jung would later equate with the unconscious.[142] In the Sermons" "Jung writes that "the Pleroma is also in us," and "We are also the whole Pleroma."[143] Years later, in his May 1933 "Visions Seminar" Jung spoke about "approaching the void, which seems to me to be the most desirable thing, the thing which contains the most meaning."[144]

The engagement with "nothingness" takes us to the limits of what can be known and pushes us into the realm of the unknown, non-sensical and incomprehensible. In *The Red Book* Jung describes the "Supreme Meaning" as the melting together of sense and non-sense.[145] In November 1915, he wrote to Hans Schmid, that "the core of the individual is a mystery of life, which is snuffed out when it is 'grasped'...[146] In this connection, Neumann quotes the Maggid of Meseritz: "And every incomprehensible thing is a real part of God."[147]

Paradox and the Coincidence of Opposites

Closely related to the emphasis upon the significance and value of "nothingness" is the Hasidic view that paradox is essential to a description of the psyche and the world. Neumann held that the world is a "diffusively distributed creative nothingness," that human beings are "concentrated points" within this nothingness and it is only through contact with this nothingness that individuals are able to transform the world. Neumann suggests that "every individual is a nodal point in the world, a place where nothingness becomes incarnate, changing from anonymous infinity into named finitude."[148] One might here ask "if the world is nothingness" how can it be transformed, how can it have points of concentrated nothingness within it that come into contact with nothingness. Either such proclamations are nonsensical, "nothingness" (i.e. the unconscious) is actually "something," or, as Schneur Zalman held, both God and the world are each *nothing and something*, depending upon one's perspective.

Jung, in *The Red Book* wrote that his recognition of the coincidence and compensation of the opposites was his greatest innovation.[149] In this, he was again anticipated by the Chabad Hasidim. Schneur Zalman's son, Dov Baer Schneuri, wrote that, "within everything is its opposite and also it is truly revealed as its opposite." He continued: "For the principal point of divine completeness is that...in every thing is its opposite, and...that all its power truly comes from the opposing power."[150] A century prior to Jung's *Red Book*, Aaron Ha-Levi Horowitz of Staroselye wrote that "the revelation of anything is actually through its opposite."[151] According to R. Aaron Ha-Levi: "He [God] is the perfection of all, for the essence of perfection is that even those opposites which are opposed to one another be made one."[152]

Jung, of course, was not the only 20th century thinker to speak in such paradoxes—for example, Jean-Paul Sartre, in his epic *Being and Nothingness*,[153] equated human subjectivity with "nothingness" precisely because it has no fixed nature, is creative and free through its capacity for negation, a notion that Sartre adopted from Hegel, who wrote in his *Logic*:

> every actual thing involves a coexistence of opposed elements. Consequently, to know, or, in other words, to comprehend an object is equivalent to being conscious of it as a concrete unity of opposed determinations.[154]

Neumann references a Hasidic tale about a condemned man who told another how he was able to traverse a rope that was strung across a chasm: "I don't know anything but this: whenever I felt myself toppling over to one side, I leaned to another."[155] According to Neumann, Hasidism "refuses to acknowledge any position once acquired as having a fixed value." Further, "Hasidism insists that the conscious and common attitude must be compensated by its opposite" and that one must develop "the other side."[156]

Male and Female

In his Foreword to Neumann's *Roots*, Moshe Idel points out that Jung's interest in the archetype of the feminine was anticipated by both certain Kabbalistic texts and in particular in the thought of the Maggid of Meseritz. Idel relates that the Maggid was reported to say that "there is nothing which is not constituted by male and female."[157] Idel also quotes from the Maggid's disciple, Rabbi Abraham Yehoshu's Heschel of Apta: "[E]verything in the world necessarily possesses aspects of male and female... emanator and recipient."[158] Idel remarks that both the Maggid and his disciple anticipated "the famous Jungian theory of anima/animus."[159] Idel writes that Neumann's (and Jung's) interest in the archetype of the feminine goes beyond anything present in either Scholem's or Buber's interpretation of Hasidism.[160]

Neumann himself writes that the raising of the sparks, the key act of redemption in Hasidic thought, involves a (human) male penetration of a passive female vessel which results in the female becoming fertile and the production of an embryonic offspring.[161] It is through this process that the human female "conceives" and redeems the spark—which now demonstrates that it is "male."[162]

Neumann relates that in Hasidic theology God's feminine aspect, the *Shekhinah*, is in exile and must be redeemed by humankind. This notion is based upon one of the Kabbalist's major metaphors for *Tikkun Haolam*: the redemption of the *Shekhinah* involves "the creative union of masculine and feminine on which the life of the world depends."[163] Neumann quotes the Zohar:

> Every form in which one does not find the male and female principle is imperfect. The Holy One, the Blessed, only makes his abode where both principles are completely united...the name 'human' applies only to both together, man and woman in their union'"[164]

Neumann points out that according to the Great Maggid, "the inwardness of the male is female, and the inwardness of the female is male,"[165] a comment that is startlingly "Jungian." Neumann writes that according to the Maggid the energy of the world is derived from the tension of male and female and its redemption involves the confluence of opposing genders to, in effect, realize "the prehistoric double sexuality of *Adam Kadmon*,"[166] the Primordial Human. According to the Maggid, the *tazddik* is able to unite male and female.[167] It is interesting to note that Jung, in *The Red Book*, endeavors to unite male and female within himself.

Neumann points out that the "marriage" in which God is male and humanity female results in *Rachamim* (Compassion) and *Tiferet* (Beauty)[168] and is essential for the harmony and redemption of the world. A marriage is also said to take place between *Adam Kadmon* and the world and on the heavenly level between the *sefirot Tiferet* and *Malkhut*, i.e. the Holy One Blessed Be He and his feminine counterpart, the *Shekhinah*. It is precisely this union which Jung so strongly identified with in his 1944 "Kabbalistic Vision," recorded in *Memories, Dreams, Reflections*, when he experienced himself as the marriage of Malchuth with Tifereth!"[169]

Neumann understands the marriage between humanity and God as an awakening of the "transpersonal self" (represented by God) by "the activity of the human ego."[170] It is not a far stretch to see this as an analogy to the analytic or psychotherapeutic process. However, Neumann further relates that a union of the masculine and the feminine, between God and humanity, leads to the human being achieving identity with the divine.[171] This involves an act which is initiated by the ego but which eventuates in the "dethroning of the ego" from its central position in the psyche and a consequent "emergence of the Self."[172] It is, according to Neumann, an experience of "It teaches," as opposed to "I learn." In subordinating a short-sighted, outward facing "ego-consciousness" to the Self the individual allows God to enter the psyche, with the result that suffering, sin and negativity is overcome.[173] The "inner meaning, that all things are related to the whole" is grasped when the divine symbol of the Self emerges.

One might here fault Neumann (as one can at times fault Jung) for an overly romanticized and naïve faith in the potential for human wholeness.

Neumann suggests that a whole self will not see the world as disintegrating—
and in retrospect this view seems naïve and optimistic in light of the great
tragedy that was to befall Europe soon after *Roots* was written.

Neumann recognizes that the Kabbalistic tradition associates *Hesed*
(kindness and grace) with the male principle and *Din* (judgment) with the
female,[174] a view that is reflected in the tradition's negative view of Eve,
and which is so counterintuitive as to be suggestive of a projection of male
aggressivity. Neumann makes what, at least in retrospect, the misogynistic
observation that:

> The castrating, infantilizing dominance of the mother archetype in
> every dogma, in every 'mother church,' paralyzes consciousness in its
> active, masculine, enlightening aspect."[175]

Neumann holds that it is this paralysis which "leads Judaism to the often
sterile, formal *pilpul* rationalism...in which consciousness...demonstrates
its own sterility."[176] His remark is at once quite misogynistic and overly
dogmatic in its denigration of the Talmudic rational tradition. Neumann
is of the view that such rationalism constrains consciousness and must be
"transformed...into a dynamic relationship with existence...(and
between) consciousness and the creative unconscious," a transformation
that Neumann sees occurring in the Hasidic notion that "the sparks
enliven the world.[177]"

Neumann writes that the development of the idea of the *Shekhinah*, the
feminine aspect of the divine, reaches its zenith in Hasidism.[178] He indicates that the *Shekhinah* is identified with creation itself and this might
suggest that she serves as a counterbalance to the notion that the divine is
centered only in humanity and the self. Neumann. quotes the Yiddish
scholar, Salomo Birnbaum (1891–1989): "The Shekhinah encompasses all
worlds—inanimate, plant, animal, and human—everything created, the
good and the evil. The *Shekhinah* is the true union."[179] While Neumann
recognizes that Hasidism (as does Judaism in general) interprets the world
from an anthropocentric perspective,[180] this understanding of the *Shekhinah* gives warrant to the idea that the entire world is ensouled and that all
of its animate and inanimate entities are loci of value. This appears to
conflict with the biblical charge that humanity has dominion over the
earth, and (as discussed above) the Hasidic emphasis upon the sparks
being raised through human sentient activity,[181] but it suggests a wider,
more inclusive understanding of value, one that complements and stands
in *coincidentia oppositorum* with ethical anthropocentrism. This understanding is particulary suited to our time when so many are raising legitimate questions about humanity's dominion over the earth and whether we
have violated a sacred trust.

Joy and Passion

Hasidism is well known for its encouragement and celebration of joy as a holy value. Neumann writes that the Hasidim affirmed joy both because of its affirmation of the created world and because it unites the "human personality into wholeness."[182] He quotes Rabbi Nachman to the effect that it is a divine law "to always be joyful" and to derive pleasure from everything "even from pranks and jokes."[183] Neumann says that while joy, derived, for example, from dance and music is a "physical experience,"[184] it involves "a heightening of the process of life, which is meant to increase consciousness..."[185] Indeed, the Hasidim, even today, engage in a joyous, almost frenzied song and dance during religious celebrations.

In the Kabbalah, joy is associated with the highest *Sefirah, Keter*, which is also referred to as *Tinug* (delight). However, the Kabbalists were often quite ascetic, and Neumann points out that while the Hasidim adapted their theology from the Lurianic Kabbalah, they departed from its punishing approach to compliance with Torah law and introduced an emphasis upon its joyful fulfillment.

Neumann further relates that certain of the Hasidim held that a passionate engagement with both life and Torah is spiritually superior to a quiet and respectful one. He writes (without providing his source):

> A tzaddik spoke about two opponents of Hasidism, one of whom angrily threw a newly published Hasidic book on the floor, whereas the other picked it up because after all, it contained words of the Torah. And he said: 'The angry one will become a Hasid, but the mild one will always remain an opponent.[186]

(101)

Neumann points out that the theory of the sparks creates a metaphor for the fire of passion and that, "Passionate feeling, raised to ecstasy, melts the diverse parts of the human soul together into a whole."[187] The individual's personality, he tells us, is "unified in joy."[188]

In this connection we should note that in *The Red Book*, Jung is confronted by "The Red One," an internal, imaginal figure who Jung recognizes to be the devil. The Red One upbraids Jung for his Christian seriousness and ponderous attitude, and tells Jung, in Dionysian/Nietzschean fashion, that it would be better if Jung would "dance through life."[189] Finally, the Red One "burst(s) into leaf" and reveals himself as an embodiment of "Joy." Jung then declares that the Red One is his "beloved" and says that perhaps there is "a joy before God" that he has yet to discover. (It is interesting to note that in the midst of this transformational encounter, the devil criticizes Jung for his defense of Christianity and its traditional vilification of the Jews.[190])

Accepting the World

Jung wrote about his struggles with "accepting all," both the horrors and wonders of life in *this world*. In *The Red Book* his soul presents him with a progressively horrid sequence of artifacts, acts, and events as a measure of Jung's willingness and capacity to accept the evil, destructiveness and tragedy which is repeatedly caused by humankind.[191]

Neumann's *Roots* again provides the Hasidic antecedents to Jung's struggle. He quotes a passage from Buber's Tales (II, p. 166):

> "In this day and age," said Rabbi Mosche, "the greatest devotion, greater than learning and prayer, consists in accepting the world exactly as it happens to be.'"[192]

And according to the Maggid of Meseritz:

> The law of things is: everything that a person sees and hears, and all events that happen to him, come to stir him."[193]

Neumann tells us that "This is the background for the principle of accepting the world, of redeeming through acceptance whatever one encounters, every place, every moment, every situation."[194] According to the Hasidim, everything a person encounters contains holy sparks that he or she is uniquely suited to release and bring to light for the purpose of personal and world redemption. The Hasidic "accepting all" is not a passive resignation but rather "enables the human being to extract meaning from everything he encounters."[195] Such acceptance, according to Neumann, not only "delivers" the meaning of objects and events, but also the meaning of the individual: "When the sparks are raised to the 'human level,' they deliver to the human being not only their meaning but his as well."[196]

Even the acceptance of "unfaith" and atheism has a place in the world and provides an opportunity to raise holy sparks, as the denial that there is a God to protect us, rightly places the onus on the individual to act in a helpful and charitable manner.[197]

Concluding Reflections

As we have seen, Neumann's *The Roots of Jewish Consciousness* was a work in progress, one that Neumann himself abandoned and never completed. As such we must not regard it as either *his* or *the* final word on the relationship between Hasidism and Jung, or psychology in general, but rather as a valuable starting point for our own inquiries and reflections on these connections. In some instances I have found Neumann's analysis to be either problematic or incomplete.

As we have seen, Neumann, like Jung, equivocated on the relationship between psychology and theology—at times making what appeared to be theological proclamations, and then "covering" himself by stating that he has no metaphysical intentions and is speaking only in psychological terms.

Neumann's understanding of the Kabbalistic symbol of the "sparks," was limited by his failure to fully consider the Lurianic notions of the "Breaking of the Vessels" (*Shevirat ha-Kelim*). More importantly, while Neumann inarguably made significant contributions to an ethic informed by depth psychology,[198] he failed to adequately consider the full ethical and axiological implications of the doctrine of the *Sefirot*, glossing over the fact that in both Kabbalah and Hasidism the *Sefirot* symbolize *objective values* that, in effect increases the depth of life and consciousness, e.g. *Chochmah* (wisdom), *Chesed* (love) *Tiferet* (Beauty).

Neumann (again, like Jung) tended to locate psychic development in inwardness and failed to adequately consider and account for the Hasidic emphasis on the relational aspect of psychic and spiritual life that was articulated in a philosophical idiom by Buber. We find in Neumann, as in Jung, a preference for the introverted stance. Neumann writes about "the path of turning [or repentance] from outside to inside, from extraversion, which stands in the sign of the ego and the world, to introversion, which stands in the sign of the Self and the soul."[199] It is interesting that Neumann, who relies so extensively on Buber, places such little emphasis upon Buber's view that it is primarily *an encounter between individuals*, or between humans and the world, the proverbial "I-thou" relationship, that is soul-making, and provides one with a window in the divine or "Eternal Thou." Indeed, Buber quite bitterly criticized Jung on this very point.[200]

Neumann, despite his ground-breaking work on the "mother archetype," and his awareness of the "the strange identification of the woman with evil"[201] in Judaism, also, in my view, failed to be sufficiently critical of the Kabbalistic and Hasidic degradation of the feminine. As we have seen, Neumann writes uncritically about the "The castrating...mother archetype (which) paralyzes consciousness in its active, masculine, enlightening aspect."[202]

From a Jewish perspective, Neumann's belief that Hasidism represents a "Christianisation" of Judaism, a delayed, and in Neumann's view, overdue ripening of essential aspects of early Christianity within Judaism"[203] comes dangerously close to justifying the Anti-Semitic Christian doctrine that the Jews are to be castigated (and persecuted) for their failure to accept Jesus Christ. One might even speculate that (despite Neumann's criticisms of Jung's views on National Socialism and ignorance regarding Judaism) that this served as a sort of concession to Jung who had, for example, in *The Red Book* claimed that the Jew has lacked or failed to "carry Christ in his heart" and as such "he himself feels that he lacks something?"[204]

Despite these controversies, and in this author's opinion, other limitations and defects, the publication of Neumann's "Roots" and in particular his analysis of the parallels between Hasidism and depth (especially Jungian) psychology has opened new vistas for our understanding of both Jung and the psycho-spiritual possibilities inherent in Judaism in particular and contemporary religious life in general. If the *Roots of Jewish Consciousness* does not completely unlock the mystery of Jung's 80th birthday pronouncement that "the Hasidic Rabbi Baer from Meseritz, whom they called the Great Maggid... anticipated my entire psychology..."[205] it certainly enhances our understanding and prompts us to make further inquiries into the relationship between depth psychology and Jewish mysticism.

Notes

Preface

1 See Sanford L. Drob, "Jung and the Kabbalah," *History of Psychology*, 2/2 (May 1999): 102–118; *Kabbalistic Metaphors: Jewish Mysticism, Ancient Religion and Modern Thought* (Northvale, NJ: Jason Aronson, 2000); "Jung's Kabbalistic Visions," *Journal of Jungian Theory and Practice*, 7/1 (2005): 33–54.

2 Sanford L. Drob, "Towards a Kabbalistic Psychology: C. G. Jung and the Jewish Foundations of Alchemy," *Journal of Jungian Theory and Practice*, 5/2 (2003): 77–100.

3 On the question of the relevance of Jung's purported anti-Semitism to his theories, see Wolfgang Giegerich's "Response to Sanford Drob," *The Journal of Jungian Theory and Practice*, 7/1 (2005): 55–68, and my "Response to Beebe and Giegerich," *ibid.*, pp. 61–64.

4 Zohar II: 184a; H. Sperling and M. Simon, *The Zohar*, 5 vols. (London: Soncino, 1931–1934), 4: 125.

Introduction

1 C. G. Jung, *Memories, Dreams, Reflections*, recorded and edited by Aniela Jaffé (New York: Random House, 1961), p. 289.

2 *Ibid.*

3 *Pardes Rimmonim*, the Garden of Pomegranates, refers to a sixteenth- century Kabbalistic work by R. Moses Cordovero (1522–1570).

4 Shimon ben Jochai: a second-century rabbi who is traditionally held to be the author of the Zohar, the most important and holiest of Kabbalistic works.

5 Jung, *Memories, Dreams, Reflections*, p. 294.

6 *Ibid.*

7 *Ibid.*, p. 295.

8 See A. Maidenbaum and S. A. Martin, eds, *Lingering Shadows: Jungians, Freudians, and Anti-Semitism* (Boston: Shambhala, 1992); F. McLynn, *Carl Gustav Jung* (New York: St. Martin's Press, 1996); and A. Jaffé, "C. G. Jung's National Socialism," in Aniela Jaffé, *From the Life and Work of C. G. Jung*, trans. R. F. C. Hull (New York: Harper, 1971).

9 See Maidenbaum and Martin, *Lingering Shadows*. See also A. Maidenbaum, ed., *Jung and the Shadow of Anti-Semitism* (Berwick, ME: Nicolas-Hays, 2002).

10 See Sanford L. Drob, "Jung and the Kabbalah," *History of Psychology*, 2/2 (May, 1999): 102–118; *Symbols of the Kabbalah* (Northvale, NJ: Jason Aronson, 2000); and *Kabbalistic Metaphors* (Northvale, NJ: Jason Aronson, 2000).

11   C. G. Jung, *The Red Book, Liber Novus*, ed. Sonu Shamdasani, trans. Mark Kyburz, John Peck, and Sonu Shamdasani (New York: W.W. Norton & Company, 2009), and C. G. Jung, *The Red Book, Liber Novus, A Reader's Edition*, ed. Sonu Shamdasani, trans. Mark Kyburz, John Peck, and Sonu Shamdasani (New York: W.W. Norton & Company, 2009).

12   The notion of a New Kabbalah is developed in the author's website, www. newkabbalah.com.

13   The publication of Jung's *Red Book* reveals that as early as 1914 he held a far more complex and nuanced view of the nature of the mystical symbol in relation to the purported objects of theological discourse. For example, he suggests that the then contemporary sickness of God can be cured by regarding God as a "fantasy," a fantasy that is as "real" as the so-called objects of the external world. We will see how this view, which regards certain "illusions" as the foundation for aspects of reality, is anticipated in the Jewish mystical tradition.

14   See note 10 above.

15   Interestingly, Jung's main accuser in this regard was the Jewish philosopher Martin Buber, who is well known for, among other things, his work on Chasidism. See Martin Buber, *Eclipse of God*, trans. M. Friedman et al. (New York: Harper & Row, 1952). Among Christian theologians who have hailed Jung's "Gnosticism" is the "death of God" theologian, Thomas J. J. Altizer. See his "Science and Gnosis in Jung's Psychology," *Centennial Review*, 3 (Summer 1959): 304. For a discussion of the whole question of Jung and Gnosticism, along with a collection of Jung's writings relevant to the subject, see Robert A. Segal, *The Gnostic Jung* (Princeton: Princeton University Press, 1992).

16   "An Eightieth Birthday Interview," in *C. G. Jung Speaking*, ed. W. McGuire and R. F. C. Hull (Princeton, NJ: Princeton University Press, 1977), pp. 271–272.

17   See Moshe Idel, Kabbalah: New Perspectives (New Haven: Yale University Press, 1988), pp. 146–153, and "Psychologization of Theosophy in Kabbalah and Hasidism," in his *Hasidism, Between Ecstasy and Magic* (Albany, NY: State University of New York Press, 1995), pp. 227–238.

18   See, for example, C. G. Jung, *Mysterium Coniunctionis*, CW 14, p. vii, where Jung writes: [I]f I make use of certain expressions that are reminiscent of the language of theology, this is due solely to the poverty of language, and not because I am of the opinion that the subject-matter of the- ology is the same as that of psychology. Psychology is very definitely not a theology; it is a natural science that seeks to describe experienceable psychic phenomena.... But as empirical science it has neither the capacity nor the competence to decide on questions of truth and value, this being the prerogative of theology.

19   Regarding his experience of God through uniting with the self, Jung wrote, "No insight or objection is so strong that it could surpass the strength of this experience....I could furnish [an explanatory] theory myself and be satisfied in intellectual terms, and yet this theory would be unable to remove even the smallest part of the knowledge that I have experienced the God" (Jung, *Red Book*, p. 338).

Chapter I

1   C. G. Jung, *Letters*, 2:358–359.

2   David Bakan, *Sigmund Freud and the Jewish Mystical Tradition* (Boston: Beacon, 1958; paperback edition first published, 1975), p. xvii.

3   "An Eightieth Birthday Interview," in *C. G. Jung Speaking*, ed. W. McGuire and R. F. C. Hull (Princeton, NJ: Princeton University Press, 1977), pp. 271–272.

4   See Gershom Scholem, *Jewish Gnosticism, Merkabah Mysticism and Talmu-dic Tradition* (New York: Schocken, 1960) and *Major Trends in Jewish Mysticism* (New York: Schocken, 1941), pp. 40–80.

5   On Sefer ha Bahir and the early Kabbalah in general, see Gershom Scholem, *Origins of the Kabbalah*, trans. R. J. Zwi Werblowsky (Princeton, NJ: Princeton University Press, 1987; originally published 1962). See also, Book Bahir, trans. Joachim Neugroschel, in David Meltzer, *The Secret Garden: An Anthology in the Kabbalah* (Barrytown, NY: Stanton Hill, 1998), pp. 49–98, and Aryeh Kaplan, *The Bahir: Illumination* (York Beach, ME: Samuel Weiser, 1989).

6   The main body of the Zohar, translated into English, appears in H. Sperling and M. Simon, *The Zohar*, 5 vols (London: Soncino, 1931–34) (hereafter, *The Zohar*). A more accessible treatment in which translated sections of the Zohar have been grouped topically and explained through extensive introductions and annotations is to be found in I. Tishby and F. Lachower, *The Wisdom of the Zohar: An Anthology of Texts*, trans. David Goldstein, 3 vols (Oxford: Oxford University Press, 1989). In the introduction to this work, Tishby provides a detailed discussion of the controversies surrounding the origin of the Zohar.

7   The classic scholarly sources on the Lurianic Kabbalah include Gershom Scholem, "Kabbalah," in *Encyclopedia Judaica* (Jerusalem: Keter Publishing, 1971), Vol. 10, pp. 489–654 (this and other articles on the Kabbalah by Scholem from the *Encyclopedia Judaica* have been collected in Gershom Scholem, *Kabbalah* [Jerusalem: Keter, 1974]). See also Gershom Scholem, *Major Trends in Jewish Mysticism*, rev. ed. (New York: Schocken, 1946), Lecture 7, "Isaac Luria and His School," and Gershom Scholem, *Sabbatai Sevi: The Mystical Messiah*, trans. R. J. Zwi Werblowsky (Princeton, NJ: Princeton University Press, 1973), chap. 1. In addition, a brief but comprehensive outline of the Lurianic system can be found in J. Schochet, "Mystical Concepts in Chassidism," which is appended to the Hebrew-English edition of S. Zalman, *Likutei Amarim-Tanya* (Brooklyn: Kehot, 1981); Louis Jacobs, "The Uplifting of the Sparks in Later Jewish Mysticism," in *Jewish Spirituality: From the Sixteenth-Century Revival to the Present*, ed. A. Green (New York: Crossroad, 1987), pp. 99–126. A fascinating discussion of Lurianic theosophy as interpreted by the Chabad Chasidim is to be found in R. Elior, *The Paradoxical Ascent to God: The Kabbalistic Theosophy of Habad Hasidism*, trans. J. M. Green (Albany, NY: State University of New York Press, 1993). Elior deals at length with the Lurianic/Chasidic conception of *coincidentia oppositorum*, a notion that plays a very significant role in Jung. Other important works on the Lurianic Kabbalah (e.g., by Tishby and Meroz) have yet to be translated from the Hebrew. Further, few of the relevant Kabbalistic texts have been translated into English. An exception is Donald Wilder Menzi's and Zwe Padeh's translation of the first "Gate" of Chayyim Vital's *Sefer Etz Chayyim: The Tree of Life: Chayim Vital's Introduction to the Kabbalah of Isaac Luria* (Northvale, NJ: Jason Aronson, 1999). More recently, James David Dunn's *Window of the Soul: The Kabbalah of Isaac Luria* (San Francisco: Weiser, 2008) provides a large selection, in English translation, of Lurianic passages from the writings of Chayyim Vital. Works attributed to Isaac Luria, the majority of which consist of notes by his pupils, can be found in a fourteen-volume Hebrew edition edited and annotated by Y. Brandwein (Tel Aviv, 1961–1964). Chayyim Vital is the author of several works purported to represent Luria's views, the most

important of which is Sefer Etz Chayyim, edited and annotated by Y. Brandwein (Tel Aviv, 1960). Readers interested in a fuller exposition of the theosophical Kabbalah, with particular reference to Isaac Luria, are also referred to Sanford Drob, *Symbols of the Kabbalah: Philosophical and Psychological Perspectives* (Northvale, NJ: Jason Aronson, 2000) and *Kabbalistic Metaphors: Jewish Mystical Themes in Ancient and Modern Thought* (Northvale, NJ: Jason Aronson, 2000).

8   On the Sabbatean heresy, see Scholem, Sabbatai Sevi

9   See Scholem, *Major Trends in Jewish Mysticism*.

10 As noted above, a portion of Sefer Etz Chayyim has been translated into English. See Menzi and Padeh, *The Tree of Life*.

11 M. C. Luzatto, *General Principles of the Kabbalah*, trans. P. Berg (Jerusalem: Research Centre of Kabbalah, 1970).

12 On Gnosticism, see Giovanni Filoramo, *A History of Gnosticism*, trans. Anthony Alcock (Cambridge: Basil Blackwell, 1990); Kurt Rudolph, *Gnosis: The Nature and History of Gnosticism*, trans. Robert M. Wilson (San Francisco: Harper & Row, 1987; first published in German, 1977; revised and expanded, 1980); James M. Robinson, ed., *The Nag Hammadi Library*, 3rd ed. (San Francisco: Harper & Row, 1988). The latter volume contains English translations of all the new Gnostic texts discovered in Egypt.

13 See Scholem, *Sabbatai Sevi*.

14 On Chasidism, see R. Schatz Uffenheimer, *Hasidism as Mysticism: Quietistic Elements in Eighteenth Century Hasidic Thought* (Jerusalem: Hebrew University, 1993); M. Idel, *Hasidism: Between Ecstasy and Magic* (Albany, NY: State University of New York Press, 1995). On Chabad Chasidism, see Elior, *The Paradoxical Ascent to God*, and S. Zalman, *Likutei AmarimTanya*, English-Hebrew edition (Brooklyn: Kehot, 1981). This is the spiritual bible of today's contemporary Lubavitch Chasidim. Daily lectures on this work can be heard in English by calling their "Tanya on Line" telephone number in Brooklyn (718-953-6100).

15 In the bibliography to *Mysterium Coniunctionis, CW*, 14, p. 630, Jung cites Christian Knorr von Rosenroth, *Kabbala Denudata* (Sulzbuch and Frankfurt a. M., 1677–84, 2 vols). Portions of Knorr von Rosenroth's Kabbala Denudata's Latin translations of *The Zohar* were translated into English by M. MacGregor Matthers as *The Kabbalah Unveiled* (London: Routledge & Kegan Paul, 1954).

16 As described in my book: Drob, *Kabbalistic Metaphors*.

17 This dialectical idea is present even among the earliest Kabbalists, for example, Azriel of Gerona (early thirteenth century); see Scholem, *Origins of the Kabbalah*, p. 423. Indeed, for the Kabbalists, *Ein-Sof* is so vast as to include both existence and nonexistence. A contemporary philosophical interpretation of this conception is provided in Robert Nozick, *Philosophical Explanations* (Cambridge, MA: Harvard University Press, 1981).

18 Again, this view is present in Azriel, see J. Dan, ed., *The Early Kabbalah*, texts trans. by R. C. Kieber (New York: Paulist, 1966), p. 94.

19 Tikkunei Zohar, Intr.: 17a-b, cited and translated in Immanuel Schochet, "Mystical Concepts in Hasidism," appendix to Schneur Zalman, *Likutei Amarim-Tanya* (Brooklyn, NY: Kehot, 1981), p. 827.

20 Vital, Sefer Etz Chayyim I:1, p. 21; Menzi and Padeh, *The Tree of Life*, p. 6.

21 Vital, Sefer Etz Chayyim, I:1, p. 22. (Translations of passages from Vital's *Sefer Etz Chayyim*, unless otherwise specified, are derived from working notes of my study of this work with Rabbi Joel Kenney. This passage in Vital

is discussed and translated somewhat differently by David Ariel, in his book *The Mystic Quest* [Northvale, NJ: Jason Aronson, 1988], p. 106ff. See also, Menzi and Padeh, *The Tree of Life*, op. cit., p. 1).

22 Vital, *Sefer Etz Chayyim* 1:2, p. 31; Menzi and Padeh, *The Tree of Life*, pp. 82–83.

23 Luzatto, *General Principles of the Kabbalah*, p. 64.

24 Scholem, *Kabbalah*, p. 142.

25 Zohar II:184a; *The Zohar*, 4:125.

26 Zalman, *Likutei Amarim-Tanya*, chap. 36, p. 165.

27 Jung, "An Eightieth Birthday Interview," pp. 271–272.

28 Dov Baer of Mesiritz, Maggid Devarev le-Ya'aqov, par. 73, pp. 126–127. Quoted in Uffenheimer, *Hasidism as Mysticism*, p. 121.

29 Zohar III:113a; *The Zohar*, 5:153. Idel translates this passage as follows: "Whoever performs the commandments of the Torah and walks in its ways is regarded as if he made the one above." Idel, *Kabbalah: New Perspectives*, p. 187.

30 See, for example, Emmanuel Rice, *Freud and Moses: The Long Journey Home* (Albany, NY: State University of New York Press, 1990); Dennis Klein, *Jewish Origins of the Psychoanalytic Movement* (Chicago: University of Chicago Press, 1985); and Moshe Gresser, *Dual Allegiance: Freud as a Modern Jew* (Albany, NY: State University of New York Press, 1994).

31 See Scholem, *Sabbatai Sevi: The Mystical Messiah*.

32 David Bakan, *Sigmund Freud and the Jewish Mystical Tradition*, p. xvii. The story may be apocryphal. Chayyim Bloch is known for having written a book about the legend of the Golem, the creation of an artificial anthropoid. Bloch's story may simply be another legend.

33 More recently, however, Peter Gay, in his book *Freud: A Godless Jew*, has argued that it was not Freud's Judaism but rather his godlessness, his atheism, that enabled him to make the discoveries leading to psychoanalysis (Peter Gay, *A Godless Jew: Freud, Atheism and the Making of Psychoanalysis* [New Haven: Yale University Press, 1987]). Gay comments that all of the comparisons between, for example, the methods of dream interpretation in the Talmud and psychoanalysis are superficial and coincidental, and that there is no real theoretical thread that can link psychoanalysis with any specific Jewish or other religious phenomenon. I am, unlike Bakan, not of the firm opinion that Freud consciously or unconsciously borrowed Kabbalistic or Jewish themes in creating psychoanalysis; this may or may not be the case. Gay, however, both in his work on Freud's Judaism and in his major biography of Freud, fails to take cognizance of any of the Kabbalistic ideas I have just outlined, nor does he consider the potential relevance of the Lurianic Kabbalah to psychoanalytic thought. The same is true for each of the other authors who have written about the impact of Judaism on psychoanalysis. However, if there is a specific convincing relationship between Judaism and psychoanalysis, it is to be found in the work of Luria and Vital, the very work that Freud himself presumably declared to be "gold." It is of further significance that Freud's father, who came from a Chasidic background, was himself more than likely conversant in the symbols of the Lurianic Kabbalah that lie at the foundation of Chasidism.

34 On Freud's Jewish background see, in addition to works already cited, *Sigmund Freud, An Autobiographical Study* (1925), in Standard Edition of the *Complete Psychological Works of Sigmund Freud* (hereafter cited as Standard Edition), ed. James Strachey (London: Hogarth Press, 1955–1967), vol. 20; A. A. Roback, *Freudiana* (Cambridge, MA: Sci-Art Publishers, 1957); Ernest

Jones, *The Life and Work of Sigmund Freud* (New York: Basic Books, 1953), vol. 1; W. Aaron, "Furzeichnugen Wegen Opshtam fun Sigmund Freud in wegan sien Yiddishkeit" [Notes concerning the genealogy of Sigmund Freud and concerning his Jewishness], Yivo Bleter, 40:166–174; Bakan, *Sigmund Freud and the Jewish Mystical Tradition*; H. W. Puner, *Freud: His Life and His Mind* (New York: Crown, 1949), p. 11; E. Rice, "The Jewish Fathers of Psychoanalysis," *Judaism*, 36/1 (1987): 109–115; E. Freud and L. Grinbrich Simitus, eds, *Sigmund Freud His Life in Picture and Words* (New York: Harcourt, Brace, Jovanovich, 1978); M. S. Bergmann, "Moses and the Evolution of Freud's Jewish Identity," *Israel Annal of Psychiatry Disciplines*, 14 (March 1976): 4; Sigmund Freud, *The Origins of Psychoanalysis: Letters to Wilhelm Fliess, Drafts and Notes: 1887–1902*, ed. M. Bonaparte, A. Freud, and E. Kris, trans. E. Mushacher and T. Strachey, intro. E. Kris (New York: Basic Books, 1954), p. 211.

35   C. G. Jung, *Mysterium Coniunctionis, CW*, 14, pp. 634, 647.

36   Knorr von Rosenroth's *Kabbala Denudata*, "The Kabbalah Uncovered, or, The Transcendental, Metaphysical, and Theological Teachings of the Jews," was the most important non-Hebrew work on the Kabbalah up until the close of the nineteenth century and was the major source on the Kabbalah for non-Jewish scholars at least up until that time. Knorr von Rosenroth, writing after the advent and dissemination of the Lurianic Kabbalah, includes (among many other things) Latin translations of portions of *The Zohar*, Cordovero's *Pardes Rimmonim*, a detailed explanation of the Kabbalistic tree after Luria, and even some of the writings of Luria himself. See Scholem, *Kabbalah*, Part III, Christian Knorr von Rosenroth, pp. 416–419.

37   James Kirsch, "Carl Gustav Jung and the Jews: The Real Story," in A. Maidenbaum and S. A. Martin, *Lingering Shadows: Jungians, Freudians and Anti-Semitism* (Boston: Shambhala, 1992), p. 68.

38   Jung, *Mysterium Coniunctionis, CW*, 14, p. 22. On Jung's visions inspired by *Pardes Rimmonim*, see C. G. Jung, *Memories, Dreams, Reflections*, recorded and edited by Aniela Jaffé (New York: Random House, 1961), pp. 293–295. See also Sanford Drob, "Jung's Kabbalistic Visions," *Journal of Jungian Theory and Practice*, 7/1 (2005).

39   Jung, Letters, 2:157. Jung relates that Knorr von Rosenroth's *Kabbalah Denudata* was influenced by Isaac Luria (*Mysterium Coniunctionis, CW*, 14, pp. 412, 198), but Jung's familiarity with Knorr von Rosenroth's work may not have made him aware of the fundamental Lurianic ideas of Tikkun or Shevirah prior to 1954.

40   Ibid., 2:122.

41   I am here again taking Jung at his word, i.e., that he was not familiar with basic Lurianic ideas prior to the early 1950s. There is, however, reason to believe that this may not have been the case—as such ideas were present in Kabbalah Denudata, which Jung is said to have read in its entirety, in all likelihood prior to the 1950s. Jung's first references to this work are from before World War II.

42   On Gnosticism, see Kurt Rudolph, *Gnosis; Giovanni Filoramo, A History of Gnosticism*; and Robinson, *The Nag Hammadi Library*. The Nag Hammadi texts, discovered in Jung's lifetime (but after his composition of the "Seven Sermons"—see below), greatly increased our knowledge of the Gnostics. For an account of their discovery see discussions in Filoramo, Rudolph, and Robinson. A number of scholars have posited a Jewish origin of Gnosticism, and hence a common Jewish origin for the ideas shared by Gnosticism and the Kabbalah.

On the subject of Jewish Gnosticism, see R. McL. Wilson, "Jewish 'Gnosis' and Gnostic Origins: A Survey," *Hebrew Union College Annual* 45 (1974): 179–189. Also, see Scholem, *Jewish Gnosticism, Merkabah Mysticism, and Talmudic Tradition*, and "Jewish Gnosticism" in *Major Trends in Jewish Mysticism*, pp. 40–79.

43 See Robert A. Segal, *The Gnostic Jung* (Princeton: Princeton University Press, 1992), for a collection of these writings.

44 Jung, "Gnostic Symbols of the self," in Aion: *Researches into the Phenomenology of the self, CW*, 9/2, pp. 184–221.

45 C. G. Jung, "Seven Sermons to the Dead," in Segal, *The Gnostic Jung*, p. 181.

46 *Ibid.*, p. 184.

47 *Ibid.*, p. 187.

48 Jung, *The Red Book*, p. 229

49 *Ibid.*, p. 273.

50 *Ibid.*, p. 317.

51 Segal, *The Gnostic Jung*, p. 184.

52 *Ibid.*, p. 185.

53 *Ibid.*, pp. 185, 193.

54 *Ibid.*, p. 193.

55 Jung, *The Red Book*, p. 232. Jung continues that one can only attain knowledge of the soul "by living your life to the full."

56 Segal, *The Gnostic Jung*, pp. 190–191.

57 *Ibid.*, p. 152.

58 As a result of discoveries at Nag Hammadi, we are in possession of many more original Gnostic texts than Jung had access to. See Robinson, *The Nag Hammadi Library*.

59 Segal, *The Gnostic Jung*, pp. 11–13.

60 Sigmund Freud, The Psychopathology of Everyday Life (1904), in the *Standard Edition*, Vol. 6, p. 256.

61 Jung, "Commentary on 'The Secret of the Golden Flower,'" in *Alchemical Studies, CW*, 13, pp. 1–56.

62 See Jung, "Flying Saucers; A Modern Myth" (1958), in *Civilization in Transition, CW*, 10.

63 Jung, "Commentary on 'The Secret of the Golden Flower,'" p. 37.

64 With the publication of *The Red Book*, we now have additional evidence that there was a strong current in Jung's thinking that understood such "psychological terms" as objective and real.

65 A similar view, interestingly enough, had been hinted at by Freud. See Sigmund Freud, "Shorter Works," vol. 23 of the *Standard Edition*, p. 300.

66 Jung, "Gnostic Symbols of the self," *CW*, 9/2, p. 190.

67 Jung, "Commentary on 'The Secret of the Golden Flower,'" p. 45.

68 Jung, *Psychology and Alchemy, CW*, 12, p. 228.

69 *Ibid.*, p. 132.

70 *Ibid.*, p. 242.

71 *Ibid.*, p. 232.

72 Jung, *Mysterium Coniunctionis, CW*, 14, p. xvii.

73 *Ibid.*, p. xiv.

74 *Ibid.*, p. 41.

75 *Ibid.*, p. xv.

76 Jung, *Psychology and Alchemy, CW*, 12, p. 34.

77 *Ibid.*, p. 24.

78 See Scholem, *Kabbalah*, Part III:14, "Chayyim Vital," p. 443.

79   Among these scholars are Gilles Quispel, George MacRae, B. Pearson, G. Stroumsa, and J. Fossum, as cited in M. Idel, *Kabbalah: New Perspectives*, p. 31.

80   See, for example, Scholem, *Major Trends In Jewish Mysticism*, p. 260. In this regard, it is interesting to note that Jung believed that such themes also arose *de novo* among certain sixteenth-century alchemists (Jung, *Mysterium Coniunctionis, CW*, 14, p. 563).

81   This positive characterization of the world is present in the earliest Kabbalistic source, *Sefer ha-Bahir*, which describes a "cosmic tree" that is the origin of both the "All" and all mundane things. Wolfson argues that this positive attitude toward the material world is evidence, contra the view of Scholem, that Sefer ha-Bahir is essentially non-Gnostic in character. See E. R. Wolfson, "The Tree That is All: Jewish Christian Roots of a Kabbalistic Symbol in Sefer Ha-Bahir," in his *Along the Path: Studies in Kabbalistic Myth, Symbolism and Hermeneutics* (Albany, NY: State University of New York Press, 1995).

82   We will see in Chapter 10 that, despite Jung's claim that the individuation process must result in full conscious awareness, he continued, especially during the beginning of the Nazi era in Germany, to be seduced by the "Gnostic" identification of the self with unconscious trends.

83   C. G. Jung, *Answer to Job* (New York: Meridian, 1960), p. 198.

84   Erich Neumann, as quoted in M. Idel, "Universalization and Integration: Two Conceptions of Mystical Union in Jewish Mysticism," in *Mystical Union in Judaism, Christianity and Islam*, ed. M. Idel and B. McGuinn (New York: Continuum, 1996), pp. 56–57.

85   J. L. Jarrett, ed., *Jung's Seminar on Nietzsche's Zarathustra*, abridged edition (Princeton, NJ: Princeton University Press, 1998), p. 117.

86   Segal, *The Gnostic Jung*, p. 32.

87   Jung, "The Relations between the Ego and the Unconscious," in *Two Essays on Analytical Psychology, CW*, 7, § 275.

88   Segal, *The Gnostic Jung*, p. 10.

89   See Gilles Quispel, "Jung and Gnosis," in Segal, *The Gnostic Jung*, pp. 219–238. Quispel writes that the "fundamentally Jungian interpretation, according to which the representation of God, and thus the godhead, encompasses both good and evil, has no analogy in the Gnostic sources. It is not Gnostic at all. One can call it magical, but only magic with a Jewish foundation."

90   See Gilles Quispel, "Jung and Gnosis," in Segal, *The Gnostic Jung*, pp. 228, 236.

91   Jung, *Letters*, 2:155.

92   Martin Buber, *Eclipse of God*, trans. M. Friedman et al. (New York: Harper & Row, 1952), p. 84. Buber had articulated a dialogical philosophy in I and Thou, trans. R. G. Smith (New York: Charles Scribner's & Sons, 1937).

93   Jung's attitude towards metaphysics will be discussed more fully in Chapter 10.

94   Jung, "Commentary on 'The Secret of the Golden Flower,'" *CW*, 13, p. 50.

95   As cited in Segal, *The Gnostic Jung*, p. 45.

96   T. J. J. Altizer, "Science and Gnosis in Jung's Psychology," *Centennial Review*, 3 (Summer 1959): 304. Altizer himself was inspired, in part, by Jung's pronouncement that for contemporary Protestants, "the person Jesus, now existing outside in the realm of history, might become the higher man within himself" (Jung, "Commentary on 'The Secret of the Golden Flower,'" *CW*, 13, p. 54).

97   Jung, *Memories, Dreams, Reflections*, p. 192.

98   Jung, *The Red Book*, p. 344: "human love...the holy source of life, the unification of everything separated and longed for." This would seem to be the answer to Jung's own question (p. 289) about the "bridge that could connect us."

99   *Ibid.*, p. 289.

Chapter 2

1   Micha Neumann, "On the Relationship between Erich Neumann and C. G. Jung and the Question of Anti-Semitism," in A. Maidenbaum and S. A. Martin, *Lingering Shadows: Jungians, Freudians, and anti-Semitism* (Boston: Shambhala, 1992), p. 280.

2   C. G. Jung, *Letters*, 2:206.

3   C. G. Jung and Erich Neumann, *Analytical Psychology in Exile: The Correspondence of. C. G. Jung and Erich Neumann*, Ed. Martin Liebscher. Trans. Heather McCartney. Princeton and Oxford: Princeton University Press, 2015, p. 13. Cf. M. Neumann, "On the Relationship between Erich Neumann and C. G. Jung," p. 279.

4   *C. G. Jung Speaking*, ed. W. McGuire and R. F. C. Hull (Princeton, NJ: Princeton University Press, 1977), pp. 271–272.

5   In this claim, Jung was indebted to the early Viennese psychoanalyst Herbert Silberer. See H. Silberer, *Hidden Symbolism of Alchemy and the Occult Arts*, trans. S. E. Jelliffe (New York: Dover, 1971; original English translation, 1917).

6   In the foreword to *Mysterium Coniunctionis*, written in October 1954, Jung writes: "This book—my last—was begun more than ten years ago"—which, interestingly, dates its origins to the period when Jung experienced his Kabbalistic visions. C. G. Jung, *Mysterium Coniunctionis, CW*, 14, p. xiii.

7   *Ibid.*, p. 24, cf. p. 384.

8   *Ibid.*, cf. p. 384–385.

9   *Ibid.*, p. 24.

10   *Ibid.*, pp. 486–487.

11   *Ibid.*, pp. 50, 383, 394, 411, 420, 424, 431; C. G. Jung, *Psychology and Alchemy, CW*, 12, p. 319.

12   Jung, *Mysterium Coniunctionis, CW*, 14, p. 383.

13   Ibid., p. 390.

14   Ibid., p. 390n

15   Ibid., p. 448.

16   References to these figures can be found in both *Psychology and Alchemy* (*CW*, 12) and *Mysterium Coniunctionis* (*CW*, 14).

17   Jung, *Mysterium Coniunctionis, CW*, 14, p. 54.

18   *Ibid.*, p. 55.

19   *Ibid.*, p. 55n.

20   Raphael Patai, *The Jewish Alchemists* (Princeton, NJ: Princeton University Press, 1994); B. Suler, "Alchemy," *Encyclopedia Judaica* (Jerusalem: Keter, 1972), vol. 2, p. 546.

21   Patai, *The Jewish Alchemists*. Patai holds that Jewish alchemy suffers from the same prejudice and consequent obscurity from which the Kabbalah suffered prior to the work of Gershom Scholem. On the relationship between Kabbalah and alchemy in general, an earlier important source is Gershom Scholem, "Alchemie und Kabbala: Ein Kapitel aus der Geschichte der Mystik," *Monatsschrift für Geschichte und Wissenschaft des Judentums*, 69 (1925): pp. 13–30, 95–110; also, an updated version of this article: Gershom Scholem, "Alchemie und Kabbala," *Eranos Jahrbuch*, 45 (1977). Scholem's views on Kabbalah and alchemy are discussed later in this chapter.

22   Patai, *The Jewish Alchemists*, p. 3; M. Idel, "The Origin of Alchemy according to Zosimos and a Hebrew Parallel," in A. Schwartz, *Kabbalah and Alchemy* (Northvale, NJ: Jason Aronson, 2000), pp. 97–111. Idel provides a more

complex argument for Zosimos's view that alchemy is fundamentally Jewish in origin.

23 Patai, *The Jewish Alchemists*, p. 66.
24 Patai, *The Jewish Alchemists*, p. 3.
25 *Ibid.*, p. 157.
26 *Ibid.*, p. 522.
27 Suler, "Alchemy," p. 546.
28 Patai, *The Jewish Alchemists*, p. 175ff. Suler, "Alchemy," p. 545, had earlier pointed out that Lully's work, *Ars Magna*, makes use of Kabbalistic methodology.
29 Patai, *The Jewish Alchemists*, p. 201.
30 *Ibid.*, p. 186.
31 *Ibid.*, p. 154.
32 Johann Reuchlin, *On the Art of the Kabbalah* (*De arte Cabalistica*), trans. M. and S. Goodman (Lincoln: University of Nebraska Press, 1993). Reuchlin's book was originally published in 1577.
33 Jung, *Mysterium Coniunctionis, CW*, 14, p. 410.
34 Phillip Beitchman, *Alchemy of the Word: Cabala of the Renaissance* (Albany, NY: State University of New York Press, 1988).
35 S. De Leon-Jones, *Giordano Bruno and the Kabbalah: Prophets, Magicians, and Rabbis* (New Haven: Yale University Press, 1997).
36 Jung, "Paracelsus as a Spiritual Phenomenon," in *Alchemical Studies, CW*, 13.
37 Suler, "Alchemy," p. 544.
38 Jung, *Psychology and Alchemy, CW*, 12, figs. 32, 95, 112, 134, 166, 219.
39 Suler, "Alchemy," p. 544; Patai, *The Jewish Alchemists*, p. 268.
40 Scholem, *Alchemy and Kabbalah*, trans. Klaus Ottmann (Putnam, CT: Spring Publications, 2006), p. 90.
41 *Ibid.*, p. 92.
42 *Ibid.*, pp. 94–96.
43 Patai, *The Jewish Alchemists*, p. 154. Gematria is a name given to several hermeneutic techniques that rely on the fact that each letter in the Hebrew alphabet has a determinate numerical value. The letters of a word, or each word in a phrase, are provided their numerical equivalents, and the words and phrases are interpreted to be equivalent in meaning or significance to other words or phrases of equal "numerical value." Gematria thus indefinitely multiplies interpretive possibilities and lends itself to the alchemist's "transformational" mentality.
44 Patai, *The Jewish Alchemists*, p. 156.
45 *Ibid.*, pp. 156–157.
46 *Ibid.*, p. 155.
47 *Ibid.*, p. 519.
48 *Ibid.*, p. 118.
49 Jung, *Mysterium Coniunctionis, CW*, 14, p. 383n.
50 Patai, *The Jewish Alchemists*, p. 118.
51 C. G. Jung, *Memories, Dreams, Reflections*, recorded and edited by Aniela Jaffé (New York: Random House, 1961), p. 289.
52 Patai, *The Jewish Alchemists*, p. 160.
53 *Ibid.*, p. 517.
54 *Ibid.*, p. 520.
55 Jung, *Mysterium Coniunctionis, CW*, 14, pp. 157, 251, 410ff., 446, 451.
56 Ibid. p. 415.

57 Patai, *The Jewish Alchemists*, p. 239.
58 *Ibid.*, p. 246.
59 *Ibid.*, p. 253.
60 *Jung, Mysterium Coniunctionis, CW*, 14, p. 50.
61 *Ibid.*, p. 410.
62 *Ibid.*, p. 251 and note.
63 *Ibid.*, p. 379.
64 Patai, *The Jewish Alchemists*, p. 154.
65 James Kirsch, one of Jung's Jewish disciples, whose association with Jung dated back to the 1930s, wrote that Jung read the whole of Knorr's 3,000page treatise. J. Kirsch, "Carl Gustav Jung and the Jews: The Real Story," in Maidenbaum and Martin, *Lingering Shadows*, p. 68.
66 Patai, *The Jewish Alchemists*, p. 323.
67 *Ibid.*, p. 324; cf. A. Schwartz, *Kabbalah and Alchemy*, pp. 86–87.
68 Scholem, however, regards *Esh M'saref* as a case of "kabbalist-alchemical syncretism." He sees it as a difficult and loose amalgamation, one that"speaks as much against the existence of a true kabbalist-alchemical tradition" (Scholem, *Alchemy and Kabbalah*, p. 78).
69 Suler, "Alchemy," p. 544.
70 Scholem, *Alchemy and Kabbalah*, p. 11.
71 *Ibid.*, p. 13.
72 Suler, "Alchemy," p. 545.
73 *Ibid.*, p. 546.
74 Jung, "The Spirit Mercurius," in *Alchemical Studies, CW*, 13, pp. 191–250.
75 Patai, *The Jewish Alchemists*, pp. 161–169.
76 H. Sperling and M. Simon, *The Zohar*, 5 vols. (London: Soncino, 1931–1934), 3:79–80.
77 Scholem, *Alchemy and Kabbalah*, pp. 33–34.
78 *Ibid.*, p. 41.
79 *Ibid.*, p. 42.
80 See M. Idel, *Golem: Jewish Magical and Mystical Traditions on the Artificial Anthropoid* (Albany, NY: State University of New York Press, 1990).
81 Suler, "Alchemy," p. 543.
82 Idel, *Golem*, p. 186.
83 *Ibid.*, p. 186.
84 Patai, *The Jewish Alchemists*, pp. 34–64.
85 *Ibid.*, p. 341.
86 Scholem, *Alchemy and Kabbalah*, pp. 50–51.
87 *Ibid.*, p. 46.
88 *Ibid.*, p. 52.
89 *Ibid.*, p. 53.
90 Schwartz argues that ancient alchemy, in its Indian, Chinese, and Hellenistic versions, was originally a spiritual discipline that degenerated into a material, pseudo-chemical practice during the Middle Ages (Schwartz, *Kabbalah and Alchemy*, p. xxxvi). Thus, in this view, in assimilating concepts from the Kabbalah, alchemy was in actuality rediscovering its own spiritual aspect.
91 Patai, *The Jewish Alchemists*, p. 7.
92 Scholem, *Alchemy and Kabbalah*, pp. 21–22.
93 *Ibid.*, p. 95.
94 Gershom Scholem, *Major Trends in Jewish Mysticism* (New York: Schocken, 1941), pp. 26–27.
95 *Ibid.*, p. 27.

96 Gershom Scholem, *On The Kabbalah and Its Symbolism*, trans. Ralph Manheim (New York: Schocken, 1965), p. 112.
97 Ibid., p. 113.
98 *Ibid.*, p. 117.
99 A fuller discussion of these antinomies is found in Chapter 7.

Chapter 3

1 C. G. Jung, *Memories, Dreams, Reflections*, recorded and edited by Aniela Jaffé (New York: Random House, 1961), p. 294.
2 Zohar I:53a; H. Sperling and M. Simon, *The Zohar*, 5 vols. (London: Soncino, 1931–1934), 1:167 (hereafter *The Zohar*).
3 J. Gikatila, *Sod Batt Sheva* (The Secret of Bethsabea), 1556, pp. 45–46; as quoted by A. Schwartz, *Kabbalah and Alchemy* (Northvale, NJ: Jason Aronson, 2000), p. 39.
4 I. Tishby and F. Lachower, *The Wisdom of the Zohar: An Anthology of Texts*, trans. David Goldstein, 3 vols. (Oxford: Oxford University Press, 1989), 1:298.
5 G. Dorn, "Congeries Paracelsicae chemicae..." in Theatrum Chemicum, 1581, p. 509; as quoted in Schwartz, *Kabbalah and Alchemy*, p. 41.
6 D. Gnosius, "Hermetis Trismegisti Tractatus Aureus de Lapidi Physici..." (1610), as quoted in Schwartz, *Kabbalah and Alchemy*, p. 41.
7 Schwartz, *Kabbalah and Alchemy*, p. 42.
8 Zohar I:49b-50a; see Sperling and Simon, *The Zohar*, 1:158.
9 R. Elimelekh of Lizhensk, "Noam Elimelekh, to Vayishalh, s.v. vayikah et shtei nashav," in Norman Lamm, *The Religious Thought of Hasidism, Text and Commentary* (New York: Yeshivah University Press, 1999), p. 65.
10 C. G. Jung, *Red Book*, p. 263.
11 C. G. Jung, "The Psychology of the Transference," in *The Practice of Psychotherapy, CW*, 16, p. 169.
12 Jung, *Memories, Dreams, Reflections*, p. 293.
13 The subject of Jung's possibly having suppressed his reliance on Jewish/Kabbalistic sources will be provided a more thorough treatment in chapter 10.
14 C. G. Jung, *Letters*, 1:356; 2:292.
15 Jung, *Mysterium Coniunctionis, CW*, 14, p. 22.
16 *Ibid.*, pp. 24, 396.
17 *Ibid.*, pp. 432–445.
18 *Ibid.*, p. 23. 19.
19 *Ibid.*, p. 442.
20 *Ibid.*
21 *Ibid.*, p. 23.
22 Ibid., p. 23 and note 123.
23 Ibid., p. 24, cf. p. 384.
24 Tishby and Lachower, *Wisdom of the Zohar*, 3:1369.
25 Jung, *Mysterium Coniunctionis, CW*, 14, p. 91. This "exaltation of transgression" is a theme that has remained implicit within the Kabbalah, but that has only occasionally been expressed in action. The followers of the messianic pretender Sabbatai Sevi, who created messianic fervor in Poland and the Holy Land in the century after Luria's death, used the Lurianic theosophy as a foundation for Sabbatai's "blessings over the forbidden" and his personal transgressions of Jewish law and faith. See Gershom Scholem, *Sabbatai Sevi: The Mystical Messiah*, trans. R. J. Zwi Werblowsky (Princeton, NJ: Princeton University Press, 1973).

26 Jung, *Mysterium Coniunctionis, CW*, 14, p. 41.

27 R. Elimelekh of Lizhensk, "Noam Elimelekh, to Vayishalh," p. 65.

28 Chayyim Vital, *Sefer Etz Chayyim*, 2:2 (*Sha'ar Shevirat HaKelim*, the Breaking of the Vessels).

29 According to Vital, with the original emanation of the worlds, the *Sefirot Chochmah* and *Binah*, which ultimately come to represent the *Partzufim* Father and Mother, were in a state of erotic union, presenting themselves to one another, as it were, "face to face" (*panim a panim*). Male and female were in a state of continuous, harmonious union, and the facets of the ideal or intellective realm represented by the *Sefirot Chochmah* and *Binah* were unified as well. Vital describes how the face-to-face (*panim a panim*) status of the Father and Mother visages was maintained by "feminine waters" (*mayim nukvim*) emanating from the interior of the Mother. However, with the Breaking of the Vessels, the cosmic Mother and Father turn their backs upon one another. It is only with the advent of *Tikkun*, in which man, through his ethical and creative acts, provides the "masculine waters" for a renewed *coniunctio* between the feminine and masculine aspects of the cosmos, that the Father and Mother are renewed in their face-to-face relationship and the spiritual harmony of the cosmos restored.

30 Jung, Mysterium *Coniunctionis, CW*, 14, p. 443n.

31 E. R. Wolfson, *Circle in the Square: Studies in the Use of Gender in Kabbalistic Symbolism* (Albany, NY: SUNY Press, 1995), p. 1.

32 *Ibid.*, p. xi.

33 M. Idel, "The Sexualizing Vector in Jewish Mysticism," foreword to Schwartz, *Kabbalah and Alchemy*, p. xv.

34 *Ibid.*, p. xiii.

35 Jung, *Mysterium Coniunctionis, CW*, 14, p. 91.

36 Wolfson, *Circle in the Square*, p. xiii.

37 *Ibid.*

38 Zohar I:85a; *The Zohar*, 1:285–286.

39 Zohar I:85a; *ibid.*, 1:286.

40 Zohar I:85a; *ibid.*, 1:285–286.

41 Zohar I:90b; *ibid.*, 1:298. The quotation continues: "and He fashions the forms of the offspring before they are born." It is unclear whether the world created by the *coniunctio* of male and female is the child itself and/or something more ethereal.

42 Zohar I:82a; *ibid.*, 1:274.

43 Zohar I:2b; *ibid.*, 1:10.

44 Zohar II:132b; *ibid.*, 2:28.

45 Zohar I:153a; *ibid.*, 2:89.

46 Zohar II:44b; *ibid.*, 3:135.

47 Zohar I:18b; *ibid.*, 1:79.

48 Zohar I:18b; *ibid.*, 1:80. Lest it not be obvious, the Zohar explains, "the dominion of the day belongs to the male and the dominion of the night to the female" (Zohar I:20a; *The Zohar*, 1:85).

49 Zohar I:55b; *ibid.*, 1:177.

50 Zohar I:19b; *ibid.*, 1:84.

51 Zohar I:20a; *ibid.*, 1:85.

52 Zohar I:49b; *ibid.*, 1:158.

53 Zohar I:50a; *ibid.*, 1:158–159.

54 Zohar I:49a; *The Zohar*, 1:155.

55 Jung, *Mysterium Coniunctionis, CW*, 14, p. 39.

56 Wolfson, *Circle in the Square*, p. xiii.
57 Zohar I:3b; trans. and cited in *ibid.*, p. 67.
58 Indeed, the Lurianists in their interpretation of the Zohar's account of creation held, "Before all the emanations the *Ein-Sof* was alone delighting in himself" (see Gershom Scholem, *The Kabbalah* [Jerusalem: Keter, 1974], p. 172). This delight, according to the disciple of Isaac Luria, Israel Sarug, produced a "shaking" movement within *Ein-Sof* that resulted in "the estimation of the engraving," and ultimately the engraving itself, which is the origin of both the Torah and all creation.
59 Zohar I:159a; *The Zohar*, 2:111.
60 ibid.
61 Wolfson, *Circle in the Square*, p. 70.
62 *Ibid.*, p. 74.
63 *Ibid.*
64 *Ibid.*, p. 83.
65 *Ibid.*, p. 84.
66 Zohar III:59b; *The Zohar*, 5:41.
67 Wolfson, *Circle in the Square*, p. 84.
68 Zohar III:81a-b; *The Zohar*, 5:93–94.
69 Wolfson, *Circle in the Square*, p. 85.
70 *Ibid.*, p. 98.
71 Cited in *ibid.*, p. 105.
72 *Ibid.*, p. 114.
73 *Ibid.*, p. 119.
74 Here I have in mind Jung's optimism regarding Hitler and National Socialism, and in the case of the Kabbalah the Sabbateian heresy with, among other things, its blessings over the "commandment to perform the forbidden." See Scholem, *Sabbatai Sevi*.

Chapter 4

1 See, for example, C. G. Jung, *The Red Book*, pp. 229, 243, 248, 254, 263, 273, 293, 315, 319, 350.
2 C. G. Jung, *Psychological Types, CW*, 6, chap. 5.
3 Cf. Jung, "The Transcendent Function" (1916), CW, 8; "The Structure of the Unconscious" and "On the Psychology of the Unconscious," *CW*, 7.
4 Jung, *Psychological Types, CW*, 6, p. 115, §184; pp. 126, 480.
5 Jung, *Psychology and Alchemy, CW*, 12, p. 186.
6 Jung, "Commentary on 'The Secret of the Golden Flower,'" in *Alchemical Studies, CW*, 13, p. 21.
7 *Ibid.*
8 A. Schwartz, *Kabbalah and Alchemy* (Northvale, NJ: Jason Aronson, 2000), p. 4.
9 *Ibid.*
10 *Ibid.*, p. 5.
11 Jung, *Mysterium Coniunctionis, CW*, 14, p. 65.
12 Jung, *Psychology and Alchemy, CW*, 12, p. 85.
13 *Ibid.*, p. 147.
14 *Ibid.*, p. 151.
15 *Ibid.*, p. 153, note.
16 *Ibid.*, p. 232.
17 *Ibid.*, p. 338.

18   Jung, *Mysterium Coniunctionis, CW*, 14, p. 43.
19   Jung, *Psychology and Alchemy, CW*, 12, p. 25.
20   Jung, *Mysterium Coniunctionis, CW*, 14, p. xvii.
21   Jung, "On the Relations between the Ego and the Unconscious," in *The Basic Writings of C. G. Jung*, ed. Violet S. de Laszlo, trans. R. F. C. Hull (Princeton, NJ: Princeton University Press, 1991), p. 151.
22   Jung, *Psychology and Alchemy, CW*, 12, p. 280
23   *Ibid.*, p. 330.
24   *Ibid.*, p. 25.
25   Jung, *Psychology and Alchemy, CW*, 12, p. 19.
26   Jung, *The Red Book*, pp. 253, 254, 274, 276.
27   *Ibid.*, pp. 243, 263, 274, 287 ("You are entirely unable to live without evil").
28   Jung, *Psychology and Alchemy, CW*, 12, pp. 294–295.
29   Jung makes reference to this in his correspondence. See C. G. Jung, *Letters*, 1:391.
30   Cited in Gershom Scholem, *The Kabbalah* (Jerusalem: Keter, 1974), p. 95.
31   Gershom Scholem, *Origins of the Kabbalah*, trans. R. J. Zwi Werblowsky (Princeton, NJ: Princeton University Press, 1987), p. 423.
32   I. Tishby and F. Lachower, *The Wisdom of the Zohar: An Anthology of Texts*, trans. David Goldstein, 3 vols. (Oxford: Oxford University Press, 1989), 1:230–255.
33   Scholem, *Origins of the Kabbalah*, p. 422.
34   *Ibid.*, pp. 441–442.
35   J. Dan, ed., *The Early Kabbalah*, texts trans. R. C. Kieber (New York: Paulist, 1966), p. 94.
36   See Tishby and Lachower, *Wisdom of the Zohar*, 1:245.
37   Rachel Elior, "Chabad: The Contemplative Ascent to God," in *Jewish Spirituality: From the Sixteenth Century Revival to the Present*, ed. Arthur Green (New York: Crossroads, 1987), pp. 157–205.
38   Zohar II:113a, quoted in Moshe Idel, *Kabbalah: New Perspectives* (New Haven: Yale University Press, 1988), p. 187.
39   Idel, *Kabbalah*, p. 188.
40   Ibid.
41   *The Gospel of Philip*, Nag Hammadi text II,3,72. See J. M. Robinson, ed., *The Nag Hammadi Library*, 3rd ed. (San Francisco: Harper & Row, 1988), p. 152. I have cited the verse as translated in Kurt Rudolph, *Gnosis: The Nature and History of Gnosticism*, trans. R. M. Wilson (San Francisco: Harper & Row, 1987), p. 93.
42   There, Jung quotes Meister Eckhart's saying, "For man is truly God, and God is truly man." *Psychological Types, CW*, 6, p. 245.
43   Chayyim Vital, *Sefer Etz Chayyim*, I:1,1a, ed. Y. Brandwein (Tel Aviv, 1960).
44   Quoted in Elior, "Chabad: The Contemplative Ascent to God," p. 162.
45   *Ibid.*, p. 166.
46   *Ibid.*, p. 167.
47   Jung, "The Hymn of Creation," in *Symbols of Transformation, CW*, 5, pp. 39–78.
48   Jung, *Letters*, 1:375.
49   *Ibid.*
50   Jung, *Psychology and Alchemy, CW*, 12, p. 186.
51   N. Mindel, *Philosophy of Chabad*, vol. 2 (Brooklyn: Kehot, 1973), p. 28.
52   Schneur Zalman, *Likutei Amarim-Tanya* (Brooklyn: Kehot, 1981), chap. 9.
53   *Ibid.*, chap. 13; cf. Mindel, *Philosophy of Chabad*, vol. 2, p. 54.

54 Zalman, *Likutei Amarim-Tanya*, chap. 26; cf. Adin Steinsaltz, *The Long Shorter Way* (Northvale, NJ: Jason Aronson, 1988), chap. 26.
55 Zalman. *Likutei Amarim-Tanya*, chap. 28; Steinsaltz, *The Long Shorter Way*, chap. 28.
56 Jung, "Psychological Aspects of the Mother Archetype," in *The Archetypes and the Collective Unconscious, CW*, 9/1, § 179.
57 Jung, "Some Crucial Points in Psychoanalysis: A Correspondence between Dr. Jung and Dr. Loÿ," in *Freud and Psychoanalysis, CW*, 4, p. 266, § 606.
58 Jung, "The Transcendent Function," in *The Structure and Dynamics of the Psyche, CW*, 8, pp. 67–91.
59 Robert J. Sternberg, "What Is the Common Thread of Creativity?: Its Dialectical Relation to Intelligence and Wisdom," *American Psychologist*, 56/4 (April 2001): 360–362.
60 Jung, "On Psychic Energy," in *The Structure and Dynamics of the Psyche, CW*, 8, § 61.
61 Jung, "Conscious, Unconscious, and Individuation," *CW*, 9/1, pp. 275–289.
62 Jung, "Some Aspects of Modern Psychotherapy," *CW*, 16, pp. 29–35.
63 *Ibid.* Interestingly, Jung's views here are quite similar to those of the structural anthropologist Claude Lévi-Strauss, who was to later hold that the very purpose of myth and symbols is to reconcile conflicts and contradictions that cannot be reconciled via other forms of thought or behavior. Lévi-Strauss writes that myth "provides a logical model capable of overcoming contradictions." Claude Lévi-Strauss, "The Structure of Myth, in Structural Anthropology" (1963). Originally published in the *Journal of American Folklore*, 67 (1955), pp. 428–444.
64 Jung, "The Conjunction: Stages of the Conjunction," in *Mysterium Coniunctionis, CW*, 14, pp. 469–477.
65 Jung, "Fundamental Questions of Psychotherapy," *CW*, 16, pp. 111–125.
66 Jung, "Medicine and Psychotherapy," *CW*, 16, pp. 84–93.
67 Jung, "Principles of Practical Psychotherapy," *CW*, 16, pp. 3–20.
68 Jung, "The Psychology of the Transference," *CW*, 16, pp. 163–201.
69 Jung, "Psychotherapy and a Philosophy of Life," *CW*, 16, pp. 76–83.
70 Jung, "The Psychology of the Transference," *CW*, 16.
71 Understanding (*Binah*) in the Kabbalah is associated with the Celestial Mother and has a creative, harmonizing role, one that brings it beyond pure reason, which is symbolized in the Kabbalah by the *Sefirah Chochmah*.
72 Jung, "The Psychology of the Transference: Purification," *CW*, 16, pp. 273–282.
73 An interesting discussion of Tzimtzum from a Neo-Jungian perspective can be found in James Hillman, *Kinds of Power* (New York: Doubleday, 1995), pp. 210–212.
74 See, for example, Jung, "The Psychology of the Transference: The Return of the Soul," *CW*, 16, pp. 283–305.

Chapter 5

1 C. G. Jung, "Answer to Job," *CW*, 11, § 755.
2 Jung, "The Shadow," in *Aion, CW*, 9/2, p. 8, § 14.
3 C. G. Jung, *Answer to Job* (New York: Meridian, 1960), pp. 198–199.
4 In *Answer to Job* (*ibid.*, p. 48), Jung makes a brief reference to the Lurianic *Sitra Achra* ("Other Side") when he says: "The new factor is something that has never occurred before in the history of the world, the unheard of fact that, without knowing it or wanting it, a mortal man is raised by his moral

behaviour above the stars in heaven, from which position of advantage he can behold the back of Yahweh, the abysmal world of 'shards.'" Jung himself notes that this is an allusion to later Kabbalistic philosophy.

5 C. G. Jung, *The Red Book*, p. 290.
6 *Sefer ha Bahir*, § 109, as cited in Gershom Scholem, *Origins of the Kabbalah*, trans. R. J. Zwi Werblowsky (Princeton, NJ: Princeton University Press, 1987), pp. 149–150.
7 Zohar III:63a-63b, *Raya Mehemna*; I. Tishby and F. Lachower, *The Wisdom of the Zohar: An Anthology of Texts*, trans. David Goldstein, 3 vols (Oxford: Oxford University Press, 1989), 2:523.
8 Zohar II:183b-184a; H. Sperling and M. Simon, *The Zohar*, 5 vols (London: Soncino, 1931–1934), 5:125; cf. Tishby and Lachower, *Wisdom of the Zohar*, 2:534.
9 Zohar II:108b; Tishby and Lachower, *Wisdom of the Zohar*, 2:496 (cf. p. 455); Zohar III:227a-227b, Raya Mehemna; Tishby and Lachower, *Wisdom of the Zohar*, 2:493ff.
10 Zohar II:173b; Tishby and Lachower, *Wisdom of the Zohar*, 2:468. For a discussion of snake symbolism in the Zohar, see Tishby and Lachower, *Wisdom of the Zohar*, 2:468ff.
11 Jung, *The Red Book*, p. 322.
12 Zohar III:70a; Sperling and Simon, *The Zohar*, 5:66.
13 Zohar III:63a-63b; Tishby and Lachower, *Wisdom of the Zohar*, 2:522–523.
14 Tishby and Lachower, *Wisdom of the Zohar*, 2:453.
15 Zohar II:34a; Sperling and Simon, *The Zohar*, 3:109.
16 Jung, "The Spirit Mercurius," in *Alchemical Studies, CW*, 13, pp. 191–250, p. 221.
17 Jung, *Answer to Job* (New York: Meridian, 1960).
18 Jung, "The Spirit Mercurius," *CW*, 13, p. 221.
19 *Ibid.*, p. 222.
20 Jung, *Answer to Job*, p. 28.
21 *Ibid.*
22 *Ibid.*, p. 174.
23 Tishby and Lachower, *Wisdom of the Zohar*, 2:453; Zohar II:184b-185a, *Wisdom of the Zohar*, 2:521–522; Zohar III:63a-63b, *Wisdom of the Zohar*, 2:522–523.
24 Zohar II:203b; Tishby and Lachower, *Wisdom of the Zohar*, 2:492, cf. p. 463.
25 Jung, "Commentary on 'The Secret of the Golden Flower,'" in *Alchemical Studies, CW*, 13, p. 48.
26 Zohar I:204a; Sperling and Simon, *The Zohar*, 2:275.
27 Zohar I:205a; Sperling and Simon, *The Zohar*, 2:278.
28 Zohar I:9b; Sperling and Simon, *The Zohar*, 1:39.

Chapter 6

1 C. G. Jung, *Psychology and Alchemy, CW*, 12, p. 319.
2 Jung, *Mysterium Coniunctionis, CW*, 14, p. 10.
3 Jung, "Christ, A Symbol of the self," in *Aion, CW*, 9/2, pp. 36–71.
4 *Mundaka Upanishad* II, 4, trans. R. C. Zaehner, in *Hindu Scriptures* (London: J. M. Dent and Sons, 1966), p. 208.
5 See Heinrich Zimmer, *Philosophies of India* (Princeton, NJ: Princeton University Press, 1971), pp. 366–367.
6 Gershom Scholem, "Adam Kadmon (Primordial Human)," in *Encyclopedia Judaica* (Jerusalem: Keter Publishing, 1971), 2:248.

7 Giovanni Filoramo, *A History of Gnosticism*, trans. Anthony Alcock (Cambridge: Basil Blackwell, 1990), p. 65.

8 Kurt Rudolph, *Gnosis: The Nature and History of Gnosticism*, trans. Robert M. Wilson (San Francisco: Harper & Row, 1987), p. 109.

9 As we have seen, Jung believed this text to have been written by a Christian posing as a Jew. However, Patai sees it is as the most Jewish of alchemical treatises.

10 Jung, *Mysterium Coniunctionis, CW*, 14, p. 50. On Eleazar's being Jewish, see p. 415.

11 *Ibid.*, p. 394; Jung, *Psychology and Alchemy, CW*, 12, p. 319.

12 Jung, *Mysterium Coniunctionis, CW*, 14, p. 386.

13 *Ibid.*, p. 390. The unity (*yechidah*) of one of the Kabbalist's highest worlds (*Atziluth* or "Emanation").

14 *Ibid.*, p. 407.

15 *Ibid.*, p. 390.

16 *Ibid.*, p. 409.

17 *Ibid.*, p. 16.

18 Gershom Scholem, *Kabbalah* (Jerusalem: Keter, 1974), Part II, "Samael," pp. 385–388.

19 Jung, *Mysterium Coniunctionis, CW*, 14, pp. 415–417.

20 *Ibid.*, p. 418.

21 *Ibid.*, p. 429.

22 *Ibid.*, p. 429.

23 On Hegel's notion of God (the Absolute), see *The Logic of Hegel*, trans. William Wallace, from the *Encyclopedia of the Philosophical Sciences*, 2nd ed. (Oxford: Oxford University Press, 1892); *Hegel's Science of Logic* (1812–1816), trans. A. V. Miller, foreword by J. N. Findlay (New York: Humanities Press, 1969); also, J. N. Findlay, *Hegel: A Re-examination* (New York: Oxford University Press, 1958); W. T. Stace, *The Philosophy of Hegel* (New York: Dover, 1955; originally published in 1924); F. G. Weiss, *Hegel: The Essential Writings* (New York: Harper & Row, 1974); and Cyril O'Regan, *The Heterodox Hegel* (Albany, NY: SUNY Press, 1994).

24 Jung, *Mysterium Coniunctionis, CW*, 14, p. 383.

25 *Ibid.*, p. 400.

26 *Ibid.*, p. 128.

27 See Jung, "Archaic Man," in *Civilization in Transition, CW*, 10, pp. 50–73, § 105.

28 Jung, *Mysterium Coniunctionis, CW*, 14, p. 420.

29 *Ibid.*, p. 7.

30 *Ibid.*, p. 407.

31 The distinction between "circles" and "lines" is discussed in Chayyim Vital, *Sefer Etz Chayyim* (Tel Aviv, 1960), I:1b, and VIII:1. See the discussion: "The Creation of the Sefirot: Circular and Linear Models," in Sanford Drob, *Symbols of the Kabbalah* (Northvale, NJ: Jason Aronson, 2000), pp. 167–171.

32 Jung, *Mysterium Coniunctionis, CW*, 14, p. 414.

33 Cf. *ibid.*, pp. 412–413, note.

34 Jung, "Commentary on 'The Secret of the Golden Flower,'" *CW*, 13, p. 29.

35 *Ibid.*, p. 25.

36 Jung, *Mysterium Coniunctionis, CW*, 14, p. 23 n. 118.

37 See Sanford Drob, "The Sefirot: Kabbalistic Archetypes of Mind and Creation," *Cross Currents*, 47/1 (Spring 1997): 5–29.

38 Jung, *Mysterium Coniunctionis, CW*, 14, p. 23.

39   See *ibid.*, pp. 43, 455.
40   Jung, "The Philosophical Tree," in *Alchemical Studies, CW*, 13, pp. 251–349, p. 340.
41   Jung, *Mysterium Coniunctionis, CW*, 14, p. 135. Jung's citations are through secondary sources.
42   Jung, *Alchemical Studies, CW*, 13, p. 312.
43   Estelle Frankel, *Sacred Therapy: Jewish Spiritual Teachings on Emotional Healing and Inner Wholeness* (Boston: Shambhala, 2003), pp. 257–258.
44   As I have discussed in Drob, "The Sefirot."

Chapter 7

1   See M. C. Luzatto, *General Principles of the Kabbalah*, trans. P. Berg (Jerusalem: Research Centre of Kabbalah, 1970), chaps. 3–8, and Part II, chap. 10.
2   C. G. Jung, *Letters*, 2:155, 157.
3   C. G. Jung, *The Red Book*, p. 264.
4   *Ibid.*, p. 295.
5   C. G. Jung, *Psychology and Alchemy, CW*, 12, pp. 202, 230, 254, 317, 340, 344; *Mysterium Coniunctionis, CW*, 14, pp. xiv, 156, 385.
6   Jung, *Mysterium Coniunctionis, CW*, 14, pp. 156, 197.
7   *Ibid.*, p. 197.
8   *Ibid.*, p. 156.
9   *Ibid.*, p. 9.
10   *Ibid.*, p. 80.
11   *Ibid.*, pp. 302, 359.
12   Gershom Scholem, *Major Trends in Jewish Mysticism*, rev. ed. (New York: Schocken, 1946), p. 217.
13   Jung, *Mysterium Coniunctionis, CW*, 14, p. 353.
14   *Ibid.*, p. 279.
15   *Ibid.*, p. 353, note 370.
16   *Ibid.*, p. 274.
17   *Ibid.*, p. 283. It is of interest that in the Lurianic account of the Breaking of the Vessels, the vessels are conceptualized as "Kings" in the womb of the Celestial Mother, the *Partzuf Imma*. (Chayyim Vital, *Sefer Etz Chayyim*. 2:8 [Tel Aviv, 1960]; see James David Dunn's *Window of the Soul: The Kabbalah of Isaac Luria* [San Francisco: Weiser, 2008], p. 74, § 40.) The Breaking of the Vessels or, what amounts to the same thing, the "Death of the Kings," results in a reduction in the flow of the "feminine waters" and, ultimately, a radical rupture in the relationship between the Celestial Mother and Father. The death of these "Kings" leads to their transformation and ultimate redemption in *Tikkun*. The origin of this idea is in the Zohar, which in the thirteenth century had already conceptualized the "Death of the Kings" as a world-cataclysmic event. See I. Tishby and F. Lachower, *The Wisdom of the Zohar: An Anthology of Texts*, trans. David Goldstein, 3 vols (Oxford: Oxford University Press, 1989), 1:276.
18   Jung, *Mysterium Coniunctionis, CW*, 14, p. 353; pp. 197, 253.
19   Jung, "Commentary on 'The Secret of the Golden Flower,'" *CW*, 13, p. 29.
20   Jung, *Psychology and Alchemy, CW*, 12, p. 74.
21   Jung, *The Red Book*, p. 211.
22   *Ibid.*, p. 298.
23   Jung, *Psychology and Alchemy, CW*, 12, pp. 194–195.

24 In *The Red Book*, Jung gave unusual expression to this egg symbol when he relates the fantasy that he had taken the sick God, Izdubar, squeezed him into the form of an egg and effectively became the God's mother. Interestingly, in describing this process Jung uses the metaphor of broken shells, a metaphor used in the Lurianic Kabbalah to represent the negativity and emptiness that remains after the breaking of the Vessels. Jung writes, "I was left with the broken shells and the miserable casing of his beginning: the emptiness of the depths opened beneath me" (Jung, *The Red Book*, p. 287).

25 Jung, *Psychology and Alchemy, CW*, 12, p. 202.

26 C. G. Jung, "Gnostic Symbols of the self," in Robert A. Segal, *The Gnostic Jung* (Princeton: Princeton University Press, 1992), p. 191.

27 *Ibid.*

28 Gershom Scholem, *Kabbalah* (Jerusalem: Keter, 1974), p. 140.

29 Jung himself says, "I planted my field and let the fruit decay," as part of his "incantation" to heal the sick God within his soul (*The Red Book*, p. 285).

30 Jung, *Letters*, 2:33–34.

31 *Ibid.*, 2:157.

32 For bibliographical references to Luria, see Chapter 1, fn 7.

33 As discussed in chapter 2, Chayyim Vital is the author of a number of works purported to be representative of Luria's views, the most important of which is *Sefer Etz Chayyim*, edited and annotated by Y. Brandwein (Tel Aviv, 1960). Chapters 12–40 of *Sefer Etz Chayyim* are devoted to the subject of *Tikkun ha-Olam*. In addition, see J. Dunn, *Windows of the Soul*, for relevant excerpts from Vital's works, and M. Luzatto, *General Principles of the Kabbalah*, an eighteenth-century work that summarizes much of the material in Vital's opus.

34 Chayyim Vital, *Sefer Etz Chayyim*, 50:3.

35 Moses Zacuto, commentary on Zohar 1:78a in Shalom b. Moses Busalgo, *Mikdash Melech* (Amsterdam, 1750), as quoted and translated by Gershom Scholem in *Sabbatai Sevi: The Mystical Messiah*, trans. R. J. Zwi Werblowsky (Princeton, NJ: Princeton University Press, 1973), pp. 41–42.

36 The concept of the "Godly self " or "Godly soul" is elaborated in Schneur Zalman, *Likutei Amaraim Tanya*, English-Hebrew edition (Brooklyn: Kehot, 1981), chap. 2 ff. For a discussion of *Tikkun ha-Olam* from the perspective of Tanya and Chabad Chasidism in general, see N. Mindel, *Philosophy of Chabad*, Vol. 2 (Brooklyn: Kehot, 1973).

37 While in some passages of *Sefer Etz Chayyim* the *Partzufim* appear to exist prior to the Breaking of the Vessels, this may simply be an artifact of the attempt by Vital to express a timeless notion in sequential language. Luzatto explains: "Each of [the] *Sefirot* is constructed of ten Lights, each of which in turn is composed of an equal number of Lights and so on *ad infinitum*. When, in one of these vessels only a single light is illuminated it is called a *Sefira*. When all ten Lights in a vessel are illumined then it is defined as a *Partzuf* (Person)" (M. Luzatto, *General Principles of the Kabbalah*, p. 45). However, the capacity for all ten lights to be illuminated together is a result of the process of *Tikkun ha-Olam*.

38 See Scholem, *Kabbalah*, p. 140; cf. M. Luzatto, *General Principles of the Kabbalah*, p. 244ff.

39 Scholem, *Major Trends In Jewish Mysticism*, p. 271.

40 *Ibid.*

41 *Ibid.*, p. 232.

42 Zohar II:184a; H. Sperling and M. Simon, *The Zohar*, 5 vols (London: Soncino, 1931–1934), 4:125.

43 *Ibid.*

44 Vital, *Sefer Etz Chayyim*, 1:1, p. 32; Menzi and Padeh, *The Tree of Life*, p. 102.

45 Elior, "Chabad: The Contemplative Ascent to God," p. 157.

46 Jung, *The Red Book*, p. 347.

47 Ibid., p. 310.

48 Jung, "A Review of the Complex Theory," in *The Structure and Dynamics of the Psyche, CW*, 8, § 201.

49 *Ibid.*, § 210.

50 An interesting question arises as to whether the Lurianic *Kellipot* develop or constellate around specific archetypes in the manner of Jungian complexes. It certainly make sense that they would—after all, the shattered *Sefirot*, which are the *Kellipot's* source, are each archetypes themselves that correspond to specific values, e.g., love, judgment, compassion, or specific archetypal figures (Mother, Father, Wise Old Man, Young Maiden, etc.). However, I have yet to find in the sources a description of the *Kellipot* sorted or classified according to their archetypal characteristics. One problem that arises in any effort to classify the *Kellipot* in this manner stems from the fact that, according to the Lurianists, not all of the *Sefirot* shattered (some were only displaced) and thus the Vessels that correspond to the Father and Mother archetypes—*Chochmah* and *Binah*—do not produce "shards" that become *Kellipot*. One way around this dilemma is to note that for the Kabbalists each of the *Sefirot* contain each of the others as parts of themselves, and to speculate that at the time of the *Shevirah*, the "Father," i.e., "Chochmah," elements of the seven *Sefirot* that did shatter, split off to produce the husks for *Kellipot* corresponding to the "father" complex, etc. Further, according to the Lurianists, everything that we encounter in the actual (i.e., material) world is comprised of *Kellipot*, and thus it would of course make sense to hold that there are *Kellipot* corresponding to each archetype and idea. Interestingly, the Kabbalists do hold that the "Other Side" does contain "counter-Sefirot" that are negative and evil counterparts to those in the upper worlds.

51 Jung, "Psychological Factors in Human Behavior," *CW*, 8, § 253.

52 Jung, "A Review of Complex Theory," *CW*, 8, § 204.

53 *Ibid.*, § 200.

54 Jung, "A Psychological Theory of Types," *CW*, 6, § 925.

55 See Adin Steinsaltz, "The Mystic as Philosopher," *Jewish Review*, 3/4 (March 1990): 14–17 (reprinted at www.newkabbalah.com "Jewish Review"); cf. Sanford Drob, Symbols of the Kabbalah (Northvale, NJ: Jason Aronson, 2000), p. 340.

56 Jung, *CW*, 6, § 925.

57 Jung, "Psychotherapy and a Philosophy of Life," CW, 16, § 179.

58 Jung, "Psychological Aspects of the Mother Archetype," *CW*, 9/1, § 184.

59 R. Schatz Uffenheimer, *Hasidism as Mysticism: Quietistic Elements in Eighteenth Century Hasidic Thought* (Jerusalem: Hebrew University, 1993), p. 1410.

60 R. Elimelekh of Lizhensk, "Noam Elimelekh, to Vayishalh, s.v. vayikah et shtei nashav," in Norman Lamm, *The Religious Thought of Hasidism, Text and Commentary* (New York: Yeshivah University Press, 1999), p. 66.

Chapter 8

1   On the Gnostic theory of the sparks see Kurt Rudolph, *Gnosis: The Nature and History of Gnosticism*, trans. Robert M. Wilson (San Francisco: Harper & Row, 1987), p. 90ff. Interestingly, a congress of scholars on the origins of Gnosticism (the Congress of Messina, organized in 1966) defined Gnosticism as follows: "The Gnosticism of the second-century sects involves a coherent series of characteristics that can be summarized in the idea of a *divine spark in man*, deriving from the divine realm, fallen into this world of fate, birth, and death, and needing to be awakened by the divine counterpart of the self in order to be finally reintegrated" (emphasis added). Quoted in Giovanni Filoramo, *A History of Gnosticism*, trans. Anthony Alcock (Cambridge: Basil Blackwell, 1990), p. 41.

2   C. G. Jung, *Psychology and Alchemy, CW*, 12, p. 301.

3   *Ibid.*, p. 301, note 26.

4   Jung, "Commentary on 'The Secret of the Golden Flower,'" *CW*, 13, p. 24.

5   Jung, *Mysterium Coniunctionis, CW*, 14, p. 8, note 26.

6   *Ibid.*

7   *Ibid.*, p. 48 and note 55.

8   *Ibid.*, pp. 48–49.

9   *Ibid.*, p. 50.

10 *Ibid.*, p. 51.

11 *Ibid.*, p. 54.

12 *Ibid.*, p. 55.

13 *Ibid.*, p. 54.

14 *Ibid.*, p. 55, note 113; Jung, *Psychology and Alchemy, CW*, 12, p. 509.

15 Jung, *Mysterium Coniunctionis, CW*, 14, p. 56.

16 Gershom Scholem, *Major Trends in Jewish Mysticism* (New York: Schocken, 1941), p. 260, and Scholem, *Kabbalah* (Jerusalem: Keter, 1974), p 143. Scholem holds that there was no direct Gnostic influence upon the Lurianists.

17 Ruach Elohim, the breath or spirit of God; Jung, *Mysterium Coniunctionis, CW*, 14, pp. 55–56.

18 *Ibid.*, p. 56.

19 *Ibid.*, p. 55, note 116; cf. Jung, "The Nature of the Psyche," in *The Basic Writings of C. G. Jung*, ed. Violet S. de Laszlo, trans. R. F. C. Hull (Princeton, NJ: Princeton University Press, 1991), § 388ff.

20 Jung, *Mysterium Coniunctionis, CW*, 14, p. 491.

21 *Ibid.*

22 Scholem, *Kabbalah*, p. 130ff.

23 Jung, *Mysterium Coniunctionis, CW*, 14, p. 487.

24 *Ibid.*, p. 453.

25 *Ibid.*, pp. 39–40.

26 *Ibid.*, p. 383.

27 *Ibid.*, p. 51.

28 *Ibid.*, p. 42.

29 *Ibid.*, p. 474.

30 Knorr von Rosenroth and other alchemists saw a justification for this view of the *lapis* in the Zohar, which relates:

    The world did not come into being until God took a certain stone, which is called the foundation-stone, and cast it into the abyss so it held fast there, and from it the world was planted. This is the central point of the universe, and on this point stands the Holy of Holies. This is the stone referred to in the verses "who laid the cornerstone thereof?" (Job 38:6), "a tried stone, a precious cornerstone" (Isaiah 28:16), and "The stone which the builders rejected has become the head of the corner" (Psalm 118:22). This stone is stone has on it seven eyes"...(Zech. 3:9). It is the rock Moriah, the place of Isaac's sacrifice. It is also the navel of the world. (Cited in Jung, *Mysterium Coniunctionis, CW,* 14, p. 447.)

That the alchemists related their concept of the *lapis* directly to those elements in the Zohar that were to evolve into the Lurianic notion of *Tikkun* (restoration/redemption) is evident from the fact that Vigenerus makes reference to a passage in the Zohar that comments on Genesis 28:22: "And this stone, which I have set for a pillar, shall be God's house" (*ibid.,* p. 396, quoting Zohar Chaye Sarah on Genesis 28:22). Vigenerus holds that Malchut is called the "statue" (i.e., for Vigenerus, the *lapis*) when it is united with *Tiferet.* In the Kabbalah, this union of *Tiferet* with *Malchut* (the masculine with the feminine aspects of God) is a prime metaphor for *Tikkun ha-Olam.* Jung, of course, sees this union of male and female as a bringing together of the *animus* and *anima* or of the masculine (conscious, ego) elements of the psyche with those that are feminine (unconscious and ego-alien).

31 R. Levi Yitzhak of Berdichev, "Kedushat Levi to Vayishev," in Norman Lamm, *The Religious Thought of Hasidism, Text and Commentary* (New York: Yeshivah University Press, 1999), p. 65.

32 Gershom Scholem, "Gilgul: The Transmigration of Souls," in *On the Mystical Shape of the Godhead* (New York: Schocken, 1991), p. 224.

33 *Ibid.,* p. 233.

34 *Ibid.*

35 Chayyim Vital, *Sefer Etz Chayyim* (Tel Aviv, 1960); I am indebted to Joel Kenney for this translation.

36 See Introduction, note 1.

37 Scholem, "Gilgul," pp. 246–250.

38 Louis Jacobs, "The Uplifting of the Sparks In Later Jewish Mysticism," in *Jewish Spirituality: From the Sixteenth-Century Revival to the Present,* ed. A. Green (New York: Crossroad, 1987), p. 117.

39 C. G. Jung, *Letters,* 2:157.

40 Jung, *Mysterium Coniunctionis, CW,* 14, p. 43.

41 Jung, "Archetypes of the Collective Unconscious," in *The Basic Writings of C. G. Jung,* p. 301.

42 *Ibid.,* p. 302.

43 *Ibid.,* p. 301.

44 *Ibid.,* p. 300.

45 Jung, *Mysterium Coniunctionis, CW,* 14, p. 87.

46 Ibid., p. 473.

47 *Ibid.*

48 *Ibid.,* p. xiv.

49 *Ibid.,* p. 438

50 Jung, "Archetypes of the Collective Unconscious," p. 335.

51 These parallels will be discussed in detail in Chapter 9.

52 Jung explores a number of other early Christian, Gnostic, and alchemical symbols that are parallel to important Kabbalistic ideas. Among other notions explored by Jung are the Gnostic concepts of alienation and exile (see Robert A. Segal, *The Gnostic Jung* [Princeton, NJ: Princeton University Press, 1992], p. 18) and the doctrine of "higher worlds," each of which have Kabbalistic parallels.

Chapter 9

1 See C. G. Jung, "Archaic Man," in *Civilization in Transition, CW,* 10, pp. 50–73; "Psychology and Religion," in *Psychology and Religion: West and East, CW,* 11, pp. 3–105; "The Undiscovered self," in *Civilization in Transition, CW,* 10, pp. 245–305. Also, Erich Neumann, *The Origins and History of Consciousness,* trans. R. F. C. Hull (Princeton, NJ: Princeton University Press, 1970), and Robert A. Segal, *The Gnostic Jung* (Princeton, NJ: Princeton University Press, 1992), esp. pp. 11–19.

2 The following discussion follows my treatment of the same issue in *Kabbalistic Metaphors* (Northvale, NJ: Jason Aronson, 2000), pp. 310–313.

3 See Moshe Idel, *Kabbalah: New Perspectives* (New Haven: Yale University Press, 1988), pp. 146–153, and "Psychologization of Theosophy in Kabballah and Hasidism," in his *Hasidism, Between Ecstasy and Magic* (Albany: State University of New York Press, 1995), pp. 227–238.

4 Gershom Scholem, *Origins of the Kabbalah,* trans. R. J. Zwi Werblowsky (1962; Princeton, NJ: Princeton University Press, 1987), p. 95.

5 Idel, *Kabbalah,* p. 146.

6 *Ibid.,* p. 147.

7 *Ibid.,* p. 176.

8 Chayyim Vital, *Sefer Etz Chayyim* (Tel Aviv: 1960), I.2.

9 Rabbi Jacob Joseph of Polonnoye, *Toldot Ya'akov Yoseph,* fol. 86a, quoted and translated in Idel, *Kabbalah,* p. 150.

10 Rabbi Levi Yitzhak of Berdichov, *Kedushat Levi,* Bo, p. 108, trans. A. Kaplan in *Chasidic Masters* (New York: Maznaim, 1984), p. 78.

11 Rabbi Yehoshua Heschel, *Ohev Yisrael,* Va Yetze 15b, trans. A. Kaplan in *Chasidic Masters,* p. 150.

12 *Ibid.*

13 Maggid, Dov Baer of Mesiritz, *Or ha-Emet* (Light of Truth), fol. 36c-d, quoted and translated in Idel, Kabbalah, p. 15.

14 "An Eightieth Birthday Interview," in *C. G. Jung Speaking,* ed. W. McGuire and R. F. C. Hull (Princeton, NJ: Princeton University Press, 1977), pp. 271–272.

15 Rifka Schatz Uffenheimer, *Hasidism as Mysticism* (Princeton, NJ: Princeton University Press, 1993), p. 207.

16 *Ibid.* Also see Rabbi Schneur Zalman's commentary in *Likutei AmarimTanya,* bi-lingual edition (Brooklyn: Kehot Publication Society, 1981), chap. 36, p. 163.

17 An attempt to provide a Jungian interpretation of Jewish mysticism was apparently undertaken by Erich Neumann. Unfortunately, his work in this area was never published. See M. Idel, *Hasidism: Between Ecstasy and Magic* (Albany, NY: State University of New York Press, 1995), p. 252, note 6.

18 Gershom Scholem, *Kabbalah* (Jerusalem: Keter, 1974), p. 89.

19 Gershom Scholem, *Major Trends in Jewish Mysticism* (New York: Schocken, 1941), p. 12.

20 Quoted by I. Tishby and F. Lachower, *The Wisdom of the Zohar: An Anthology of Texts,* trans. David Goldstein, 3 vols (Oxford: Oxford University Press, 1989), 1:234.

21 Zohar II:239a. The *Zohar* describes *Ein-sof* as "that which knows but does not know," and explains that the *Sefirot* are not themselves in a position to perceive *Ein-sof* (Tishby and Lachower, *Wisdom of the Zohar,* 1:257, see also 1:233).

22 Zohar II:239a; Tishby and Lachower, *Wisdom of the Zohar,* 1:257.

23   Zohar I:30a; H. Sperling and M. Simon, *The Zohar*, 5 vols. (London: Soncino, 1931–1934), 1:114.

24   Erich Neumann, *The Origins and History of Consciousness* (Princeton, NJ: Princeton University Press, 1954), p. 7.

25   C. G. Jung, *Answer to Job* (New York: Meridian, 1960), p. 199.

26   C. G. Jung, "The Relations between the Ego and the Unconscious," in *The Basic Writings of C. G. Jung* (Princeton, NJ: Princeton University Press, 1991), p. 151.

27   Quoted in C. G. Jung, *The Red Book*, p. 237, note 337.

28   Zohar I:1b; Sperling and Simon, *The Zohar*, 1:4–5.

29   See R. Elior, *The Paradoxical Ascent to God: The Kabbalistic Theosophy of Habad Hasidism* (Albany, NY: State University of New York Press, 1993), chap. 14ff.

30   Scholem, *Origins of the Kabbalah*, p. 416.

31   *Ibid.*, pp. 441–442.

32   Azriel, "The Explanation of the Ten Sefirot," in Joseph Dan, *The Early Kabbalah*, texts trans. Ronald C. Kieber (New York: Paulist, 1966), p. 94. Cf. Scholem, *Origins of the Kabbalah*, p. 423.

33   See R. Elior, "Chabad: The Contemplative Ascent to God," in *Jewish Spirituality: From the Sixteenth Century Revival to the Present*, ed. Arthur Green (New York: Crossroad, 1987), pp. 114, 163, 166, 167, for examples of *coincidentia oppositorum* in Chasidic literature.

34   In *Answer to Job*, Jung writes of the Jewish God that he is "an antinomy—a totality of inner opposites—and this is the indispensable condition for his tremendous dynamism, his omniscience and his omnipotence" (p. 28). Also: "The paradoxical nature of God has a like effect on man: it tears him asunder into opposites and delivers him over to seemingly insoluble conflict" (p. 174).

35   R. Aaron Ha-Levi, *Sha'arey ha-Yichud veha-Emunah*, IV:5, quoted in Elior, "Chabad," pp. 167–168.

36   M. de Leon, *Sheqel haQodesh*, quoted in Schwartz, *Kabbalah and Alchemy* (Northvale, NJ: Jason Aronson, 2000), p. 31.

37   Rabbi Aaron Ha-Levi, *Sha'arey ha-Yichud veha-Emunah*, LV:5; quoted in Elior, *The Paradoxical Ascent to God*, p. 70.

38   J. Dan, "The Name of God, the Name of the Rose, and the Concept of Language in Jewish Mysticism," in his *Jewish Mysticism*, Vol. III: *The Modern Period* (Northvale, NJ: Jason Aronson, 1999), pp. 131–162.

39   Jung, *The Red Book*, p. 229. Jung writes: "the melting together of sense and nonsense...produces the supreme meaning."

40   Jung, *Mysterium Coniunctionis, CW*, 14, p. 35.

41   For the Kabbalists, as for many other mystical traditions, individuality, however necessary to the world's plan, results from ignorance.

42   On the doctrine of "acosmism," see Elior, *The Paradoxical Ascent to God*, Chap. 11, and "Chabad: The Contemplative Ascent to God."

43   Jung, *The Red Book*, p. 283.

44   *Ibid.*

45   See Mordecai Rotenberg, *Dialogue with Deviance* (New York: University Press of America, 1993).

46   James Hillman, *Kinds of Power* (New York: Doubleday, 1995), p. 212.

47   Ibid., p. 210.

48   Maggid, Dov Baer of Mesiritz, *Maggid Devarav Yaacov*, p. 63; quoted by Rotenberg, *Dialogue with Deviance*, p. 82.

49 Jung, "Archetypes of the Collective Unconscious," in *The Basic Writings of C. G. Jung*, p. 317.
50 Jung, *The Red Book*, p. 233.
51 Jung, *Mysterium Coniunctionis, CW*, 14, § 511n.
52 Zohar I:21a; Sperling and Simon, *The Zohar*, 1:89.
53 Jung, *Mysterium Coniunctionis, CW*, 14, p. 409.
54 *Ibid.*, pp. 383–384.
55 This notion is confirmed by the fact that the *Sefirot* are said by the Kabbalists to emanate from *Adam Kadmon*, as explained in Chayyim Vital's *Sefer Etz Chayyim*.
56 Neumann, *The Origins and History of Consciousness*, p. 6.
57 Tishby and Lachower, *Wisdom of the Zohar*, 1:299.
58 Zohar II:145b; III:100b, 258a.
59 See S. Drob, *Symbols of the Kabbalah* (Northvale, NJ: Jason Aronson, 2000), chap. 5: "*Otiyot Yesod*: The Linguistic Mysticism of the Kabbalah," pp. 236–262.
60 Jung, "The Relations between the Ego and the Unconscious," *CW*, 7, § 275.
61 Jung, *Mysterium Coniunctionis, CW*, 14, p. 473.
62 On Hillman's views, see the anthology *A Blue Fire*, edited and introduced by Thomas Moore (New York: Harper & Row, 1989; paperback edition, 1991), and *Re-Visioning Psychology* (New York: Harper & Row, 1976; paperback edition, with a new preface by the author, 1992).
63 Jung, *The Red Book*, p. 238.
64 *Ibid.*, p. 364.
65 *Ibid.*, p. 274.
66 *Ibid.*, p. 338.
67 Hillman, *Re-Visioning Psychology*, p. 26.
68 Interestingly, Hillman argues that man is essentially fragmentary and multiple, and that the Jungian goal of a restoration to a unitary self is an illusion. I should here note the Kabbalistic notion that the Tikkun or restoration of the cosmos ends in the creation of multiple *Partzufim*, what amount to multiple "partial personalities" within an (ultimately) unified Godhead.
69 Jung, *The Red Book*, p. 317.
70 *Ibid.*
71 Jung, *Mysterium Coniunctionis, CW*, 14, p. 8, note 26.
72 Jung, "Commentary on 'The Secret of the Golden Flower,'" in *Alchemical Studies, CW*, 13, § 51, p. 36.
73 Thomas Moore cited from Hillman, *A Blue Fire*, p. 36.
74 C. G. Jung, *Letters*, 2:34.
75 Zohar I:18b; Sperling and Simon, *The Zohar*, 1:79.
76 See Idel, *Kabbalah: New Perspectives*, p. 175.
77 *Ibid.*, p. 179.
78 *Ibid.*, p. 180.
79 Wolfgang Giegerich, "The End of Meaning and the Birth of Man: An Essay about the State Reached in the History of Consciousness and an Analysis of C. G. Jung's Psychology Project," *Journal of Jungian Theory and Practice*, 6/1 (2004): 1–65; Wolfgang Giegerich, *The Soul's Logical Life* (3rd rev.ed.; Frankfurt am Main: Peter Lang, 2002).
80 Claude Lévi-Strauss, "The Structure of Myth," in *Structural Anthropology*, trans. Claire Jacobson and Brooke Grundfest (New York: Allen Lane, 1958).
81 Dennis McCort, *Going beyond the Pairs* (Albany, NY: State University of New York Press, 2001), p. 5.
82 Scholem, *Origins of the Kabbalah*, pp. 441–442.

83 Schneur Zalman, *Likutei Torah, Devarim*, fol. 83a (Brooklyn, NY: 1979).

84 Quoted in Elior, *The Paradoxical Ascent to God*, p. 64.

85 I should here caution that, on my view, these transformations do not exhaust the symbol qua symbol. On this question, see S. Drob, "Giegerich and the Traditions: Notes on Reason, Mythology, Psychology, and Religion," *Journal of Jungian Theory and Practice*, 7/2 (2005): 61–73.

86 Allison P. Coudert, *Leibniz and the Kabbalah* (New York: Springer-Verlag, 1995), and *The Impact of the Kabbalah in the Seventeenth Century: The Life and Thought of Francis Mercury Van Helmont (1614–1698)* (Boston: Brill Academic Publishers, 1998).

87 On Schelling and the Kabbalah, see: S. Drob, *Kabbalistic Metaphors*, pp. 83–85; Elliot R. Wolfson, *Language, Eros, Being: Kabbalistic Hermeneutics and Poetic Imagination* (New York: Fordham University Press, 2005), pp. 100–105. On Hegel and the Kabbalah, see S. Drob, *Kabbalistic Metaphors*, 185–240.

88 G. W. F. Hegel, *Lectures on the Philosophy of Religion*, ed. Peter C. Hodgson (Berkeley: University of California Press, 1985), pp. 99, 288.

89 See, for example, Elliot R. Wolfson, "Assaulting the Border: Kabbalistic Traces in the Margins of Derrida," *Journal of the American Academy of Religion*, 70 (September 2002): 475–514; Susan Handelman, *The Slayers of Moses: The Emergence of Rabbinic Interpretation in Modern Literary Theory* (Albany, NY: State University of New York Press, 1982); Moshe Idel, *Absorbing Perfections* (New Haven, CT: Yale University Press, 2002).

90 Jacques Derrida, *Of Grammatology*, trans. G. C. Spivak (Baltimore, MD: Johns Hopkins Press, 1974), p. 158. Derrida writes, "*There is nothing outside of the text*," or "*there is no outside-text*" (*il n'y a pas des hors-texte*). Idel points to the Italian Kabbalist R. Menahem Recanti, who in the early fourteenth century wrote: "All the sciences altogether are hinted at in the Torah, because there is nothing that is outside of Her....Therefore the Holy One, blessed be He, is nothing that is outside the Torah, and the Torah is nothing that is outside Him, and this is the reason why the sages of the Kabbalah said that the Holy One, blessed be He, is the Torah." Idel states that this passage had never been translated and was unknown outside of Kabbalistic circles prior to its discussion by Gershom Scholem at the 1954 Eranos Conference in Ascona. At that time, Scholem's comments and the passage itself were printed in English and French translations in the journal *Diogenes* (*Diogene*). The French translation (1955–1956), which was made by the distinguished Judaica scholar Georges Vajda, reads: "there is nothing outside her (i.e., the Torah)." Idel writes: "The fact that this statement about the identity between the Torah and God was available in French in 1957 may account for the emergence of one of the most postmodern statements in literary criticism: 'There is nothing outside the text.'" Idel suggests that in the *Grammatologie*, which was first published in 1967, Derrida, who maintained a certain interest in the Kabbalah, "substituted the term and concept of Torah with that of text" (Moshe Idel, *Absorbing Perfections*, p. 123).

91 Jacques Derrida, *Writing and Difference*, trans. Alan Bass (Chicago: University of Chicago Press, 1978), pp. 76–77.

92 See, for example, J. Derrida, "Edmond Jabes and the Question of the Book," in *Writing and Difference*, pp. 64–78; on Derrida on the Kabbalah, see Wolfson, *Assaulting the Border*, and S. Drob, "Derrida and the Kabbalah," online at www.newkabbalah.com.

93 On indefinite and infinite interpretability in Kabbalistic hermeneutics, see: G. Scholem, "The Meaning of the Torah in Jewish Mysticism," in his *On the*

Kabbalah and Its Symbolism (New York: Schocken, 1969), pp. 32–86; Idel, *Absorbing Perfections*, pp. 83–99; and Joseph Dan, "The Name of God, the Name of the Rose, and the Concept of Language in Jewish Mysticism," in his *Jewish Mysticism*, Vol. II: *The Modern Period* (Northvale, NJ: Jason Aronson, 1998), pp. 131–162.

94 See, for example, Zohar I:29b-30a: "Letters were imprinted on the fabric of the Whole, on the upper and the lower fabric....'The heavens' are the totality of twenty-two letters. The letter *hé* produced the heavens....The letter *vav* produced the earth." Sperling and Simon, *The Zohar*, 1:114.

95 For a discussion of the Kabbalah's linguistic mysticism, ontology, and metaphysics, see S. Drob, *Symbols of the Kabbalah*, pp. 236–262.

96 Scholem, "The Meaning of the Torah," p. 76.

97 *Ibid.*, p. 65.

98 Scholem, "The Meaning of the Torah," p. 73.

99 Chayyim Vital, *Sefer Etz Chayyim*, p. 29a, trans. Joel Kenney (personal correspondence).

100 Daniel Matt, "Ayin: The Concept of Nothingness in Jewish Mysticism," in *Essential Papers on Kabbalah*, ed. Lawrence Fine (New York: New York University Press, 1995), p. 81.

101 *Ibid.*, p. 87.

102 In *The Red Book*, one of Jung's interlocutors, the Anchorite, says, "I've spent many years alone with the process of unlearning. Have you ever unlearned anything?" (Jung, Red Book, p. 269).

103 Jung, "The Relations between the Ego and the Unconscious," in *Two Essays on Analytical Psychology, CW*, 7, § 274.

104 Jung, *Letters*, 2:157.

105 See above, Chapter 2; David Bakan, *Sigmund Freud and the Jewish Mystical Tradition* (Boston: Beacon, 1958; paperback edition, 1975), p. xvii.

Chapter 10

1 See Wolfgang Giegerich's "Response to Sanford Drob," *The Journal of Jungian Theory and Practice*, 7/1 (2005): 55–68, and my "Response to Beebe and Giegerich," *ibid.*, pp. 61–64.

2 A. Maidenbaum and S. A. Martin, eds, *Lingering Shadows: Jungians, Freudians, and Anti-Semitism* (Boston: Shambhala, 1992); A. Maidenbaum, ed., *Jung and the Shadow of Anti-Semitism* (Berwick, ME: Nicolas-Hays, 2002).

3 C. G. Jung. "The Tavistock Lectures." in *The Symbolic Life, CW*, 18, p. 164.

4 *C. G. Jung Speaking*, ed. W. McGuire and R. F. C. Hull (Princeton, NJ: Princeton University Press, 1977), p. 118.

5 C. G. Jung Biographical Archives, Irene Champernowne Interview, December 19, 1969, as cited by Richard Noll, *The Aryan Christ: The Secret Life of Carl Jung* (New York: Random House, 1997), p. 274.

6 See discussion of the work of Richard Noll below.

7 Stephen A. Martin, "Introduction," in Maidenbaum, *Jung and the Shadow of Anti-Semitism*, p. xxv.

8 *C. G. Jung Speaking*, p. 150.

9 I believe that the most comprehensive account is contained in Jay Sherry, *Carl Gustav Jung: Avant-Garde Conservative* (New York: Palgrave Macmillan, 2010).

10 Sigmund Freud, *The Standard Edition of the Complete Psychological Works of Sigmund Freud*, ed. and trans. James Strachey (London: Hogarth, 1957), 14:43.

11 See, for example, Maidenbaum and Martin, *Lingering Shadows; and Maidenbaum, Jung and the Shadow of Anti-Semitism.*

12 Freud to Abraham, May 3, 1908, in *A Psycho-Analytic Dialogue: The Letters of Sigmund Freud and Karl Abraham, 1907–1926* (New York: Basic Books, 1965).

13 Freud to Abraham, December 6, 1908, in *ibid.*

14 See Fritz Wittels, *Sigmund Freud: His Personality, His Teaching, and His School* (New York: Dodd, Mead, 1924), p. 140. According to Wittels, Freud had told his Jewish colleagues that because they are Jews they are "incompetent to win friends for the new teaching." However, the Swiss, as non-Jews, "will save me, and all of you as well."

15 Freud to Ferenczi, July 28, 1912. Cited in Peter Gay, *A Godless Jew: Freud, Atheism and the Making of Psychoanalysis* (New Haven: Yale University Press, 1987), p. 120.

16 Freud, *Standard Edition*, 14:43.

17 Cited in Martin, "Introduction," in Maidenbaum and Martin, *Lingering Shadows*, p. v.

18 C. G. Jung, *Letters*, 1:162.

19 C. G. Jung, "Some Thoughts on Psychology," *The Zofingia Lectures*, Supplementary Vol. A to *The Collected Works of C. G. Jung*, trans. Jan Van Heurck (Princeton, NJ: Princeton University Press, 1983), p. 35.

20 McLynn, *Carl Gustav Jung* (New York: St. Martin's Press, 1996), p. 362. McLynn argues that "Jung was not really an anti-Semite but he allowed his hatred for Freud to poison his mind and invade his thoughts; it is almost always the case that when Jung says 'Jew' he means Freud and when he says 'Jewish' he means Freudian." On the other hand, McLynn points out that Jung's choice of the 1930s as his time to focus on the "Jewish Question" "looks like the worst kind of opportunism, to say the least" (p. 363).

21 Jung, *Letters*, 1:172.

22 *Ibid.*, 2:16.

23 *Ibid.*, 2:43.

24 John Kerr, *A Most Dangerous Method* (New York: Knopf, 1993), p. 133.

25 *Ibid.*, p. 134. Interestingly, Spielrein, who had been in analysis with Jung, ended up as a Freudian analyst. Spielrein had dreams of producing a child, Siegfried, an Aryan-Semitic hero, with Jung (M. V. Adams, "My Siegfried Problem—and Ours: Jungians, Freudians, Anti-Semitism, and the Psychology of Knowledge," in Maidenbaum and Martin, *Lingering Shadows*, pp. 240–259, p. 245), and she conceived of the child as symbolic of a union between Jung's and Freud's theories (p. 246). See also Kerr, *A Most Dangerous Method*, pp. 161–165ff., re: Sabina Spielrein's "Siegfried Complex."

26 Jung, "The Role of the Unconscious," in *Civilization In Transition, CW*, 10, pp. 3–28, pp. 12–15.

27 *Ibid.*, p. 14.

28 *Ibid.*

29 *Ibid.*

30 *Ibid.*

31 Jung, *The Red Book*, p. 260.

32 Jung, *Psychological Types, CW*, 6, p. 236.

33 Jung, "The Relations between the Ego and the Unconscious," in *Two Essays on Analytical Psychology, CW*, 7, p. 152, note.

34 Deirdre Bair, *Jung: A Biography* (Boston: Little, Brown and Company, 2003), pp. 448–449. Bair obtained access to correspondence from Jung to

Vladimir Rosenbaum, as well as Rosenbaum's recorded memoirs of his encounters with Jung. Rosenbaum was an attorney and the husband of one of Jung's patients. Jung had known Rosenbaum, and had taken a liking to him, through their mutual attendance at the Eranos conferences during the 1930s. Jung consulted Rosenbaum in 1934 and asked him to revise Göring's proposed membership statutes for the General Medical Society, of which Jung had recently assumed the presidency. Jung implored Rosenbaum to rewrite the proposal in such a way that it would contain ambiguous language and subtle loopholes that would permit Jewish psychotherapists to remain individual members of a newly organized international society, and thereby maintain their professional standing. Rosenbaum was skeptical of the whole undertaking, but to his surprise Jung was able to get the "Nazi gathering to swallow statutes prepared by a Jew." Jung was clearly grateful to Rosenbaum, but in 1937, when Rosenbaum was jailed and then released by

Swiss authorities for illegally channeling money to the resistance in Franco's Spain, Jung bowed to pressure from other members of the Psychology Club who wanted Rosenbaum to resign and never attend another meeting. Divorced, disbarred, and penniless, Rosenbaum relates that in this moment of need Jung callously told him, "Even a mortally injured animal knows when to go off alone and die" (account provided to Bair by Christa Robinson, personal friend of Rosenbaum, keeper of his archive, and President of the Eranos Foundation).

35   See Bair, *Jung*, pp. 459–460.
36   Jung, *CW*, 10, pp. 533–534.
37   "An interview on Radio Berlin," *C. G. Jung Speaking*, p. 64.
38   *Ibid.*, p. 65.
39   Jay Sherry, "The Case of Jung's Alleged Anti-Semitism," in Maidenbaum and Martin, *Lingering Shadows*, p. 121.
40   See Bair, *Jung*, pp. 447ff.
41   Jung, "The State of Psychotherapy Today," *CW*, 10, p. 165.
42   Adolf Hitler, *Mein Kampf*, trans. Ralph Mannheim (1927; Boston: Houghton Mifflin, 1999).
43   Jung, "The State of Psychotherapy Today," *CW*, 10, p. 166.
44   *Ibid.*
45   Jung, it seems, took Judaism to exemplify what Nietzsche had described as the "Apollonian" consciousness, and as such as a culture that had lost its spirit and vitality, especially in comparison to the "Dionysian" German consciousness. Later, after his discovery of Jewish mysticism, it became clear to him that one could not simply equate "Jewish" with "Apollonian" psychology.
46   Jung, "A Rejoinder to Dr. Bally," *CW*, 10, pp. 535–544. Bally's article had been published in the *Neue Zürcher Zeitung*. It should be noted that not only Bally, but others—including Wilhelm Eich, Alfred Adler, and Thomas Mann—took great offense at Jung's writings during this period. Mann, for example, wrote in his diary that Jung would not declare his "affiliation" openly and later that the "revolting behavior of Jung" had caused him "to reflect on the ambiguousness of human and intellectual phenomena." (H. Kesten, *The Thomas Mann Diaries 1918–1939* [New York: Harry N. Abrams, 1982], pp. 201, 235).
47   Jung's full words are: "My esteemed critic appears to have forgotten that the first rule of psychotherapy is to talk in the greatest detail about all the things that are the most ticklish and dangerous, and the most misunderstood. The

Jewish problem is a regular complex, a festering wound, and no responsible doctor could bring himself to apply methods of medical hush-hush in this matter" (*CW*, 10, § 1024). As to why Jung raised the issue at this point in time, Jung says he has been speaking about it since 1913 and concludes by stating: "If I am to be exploited for political ends, there's nothing I can do to stop it" (§ 1034).

48 Quoted in Andrew Samuels, Sonu Shamdasani, Gottfried Heuer, and Matthias Von Der Tann, "New Material Concerning Jung, Anti-Semitism, and the Nazis," *Journal of Analytical Psychology*, 38 (1993): 464.

49 Hans Dieckmann has said that this is the only place in his writings where Jung is openly anti-Semitic. H. Dieckmann, "C. G. Jung's Analytical Psychology and the Zeitgeist of the First Half of the Twentieth Century," in Maidenbaum and Martin, *Lingering Shadows*, pp. 167–175, p. 168. My own view is that it is one of a number of anti-Semitic statements.

50 Jung to W. M. Kranefeldt, February 9, 1934; cited by M. Vannoy Adams and J. Sherry, "Significant Words and Events," in Maidenbaum and Martin, *Lingering Shadows*, pp. 349–396. (Portion of a letter originally published by I. A. Stargard Auction House, Marburg, Germany, Catalog No. 608; reprinted in *International Review of Psycho-Analysis*, 4 [1977]: 377.)

51 James Kirsch, "Jung's Transference on Freud: The Jewish Element," *American Imago*, 41/1 (Spring 1984): 72.

52 Richard Stein, "Jung's 'Mana Personality' and the Nazi Era," in Maidenbaum and Martin, *Lingering Shadows*, pp. 89–116, p. 109.

53 Jung to B. Cohen, March 26, 1935, Adams and Sherry, "Significant Words and Events," pp. 372–373.

54 Jung to A. Pupato, March 2, 1934, *ibid.*, pp. 371–372.

55 Jung to James Kirsch, May 26, 1934, *ibid.*, pp. 374–375.

56 *Ibid.*, p. 375.

57 See, for example, Schneur Zalman, *Likutei-Amarim-Tanya*, bi-lingual edition (Brooklyn: Kehot, 1981).

58 Jung to Abraham Aaron Roback, September 29, 1936, Adams and Sherry, "Significant Words and Events," p. 379; Jung, *Letters*, 1:224.

59 Letter to E. Beit von Speyer, April 13, 1934, Adams and Sherry, "Significant Words and Events," p. 373.

60 Jung, "Wotan," *CW*, 10, pp. 179–193, p. 186.

61 Jung to Gerhard Adler, June 9, 1934, Adams and Sherry, "Significant Words and Events," p. 376.

62 Jung to C. E. Benda, June 18, 1934, *ibid.*, p. 376.

63 Quoted by M. Adams and J. Sherry, *ibid.*, p. 378.

64 Erich Neumann to Jung, May 19, 1935; quoted and discussed in Micha Neumann, "On the Relationship between Erich Neumann and C. G. Jung and the Question of Anti-Semitism," in Maidenbaum and Martin, *Lingering Shadows*, pp. 273–289, p. 279.

65 Erich Neumann to Jung, October 19, 1935, *ibid.*, p. 280.

66 Jung to Erich Neumann, December 19, 1938, *ibid.*, p. 283.

67 Bair, *Jung*, pp. 459–460.

68 Jung's biographer Deirdre Bair writes that although Jung was quietly raising money to help Jews leave Germany, "to date, no documentary evidence has been found to verify that this [i.e., the story related by Hannah and McCully of the effort to assist Freud] actually happened, and if it did, no evidence connects Jung with it" (p. 458; note, p. 798).

69   Robert McCully, "Remarks on the Last Contact between Freud and Jung," *Quadrant*, 20/2 (1987), as quoted in Adams and Sherry, "Significant Words and Events," in Maidenbaum and Martin, *Lingering Shadows*, pp. 381–382.

70   A number of stories, most of them probably apocryphal, have circulated regarding Jung's supposed encounters with Hitler and other members of the Nazi hierarchy. For example, Philip Wylie, who hosted the Jungs for a weekend in Madison, Connecticut, in October 1937, related that Jung had told him that Joseph Goebbels, Nazi minister of propaganda, had summoned Jung to Berlin in order to observe Goebbels together with Hitler, Göring, and Himmler, in order to form an opinion of their mental status. Wylie relates that Jung "sat through enough of their show to know they were madmen." Wylie told Jung's biographer William McGuire that Jung had told him this story in the strictest of confidence and that he, Wylie, had never before repeated it to anyone. McGuire was unable to corroborate this story in any way. See Bair, *Jung*, p. 424; Philip Wylie to William McGuire, December 24, 1966, Wylie archives, Princeton University.

71   M. Neumann, "On the Relationship between Erich Neumann and C. G. Jung," in Maidenbaum and Martin, *Lingering Shadows*, p. 278.

72   Jung, "The Tavistock Lectures," Lecture V, *CW*, 18, pp. 135–182, p. 164.

73   *Ibid.*, p. 164.

74   Jung, *Letters*, 1:219.

75   Jung, "Wotan," *CW*, 10, pp. 185–186.

76   *Ibid.*, pp. 189–190.

77   *Ibid.*, p. 185, § 388.

78   *C. G. Jung Speaking*, ed. McGuire and Hull, p.118.

79   *Ibid.*, pp. 119–120.

80   M. Neumann, "On the Relationship Between Erich Neumann and C. G. Jung," p. 274.

81   *C. G. Jung Speaking*, p. 120.

82   *Ibid.*

83   *Ibid.*

84   *Ibid.*, p. 133.

85   *Ibid.*, p. 135.

86   See, for example, Jung, *Mysterium Coniunctionis, CW*, 14, p. vii.

87   E. A. Bennett, *Meetings with Jung, 1946–61* (Zurich: Daimon Verlag, 1955), p. 14.

88   *C. G. Jung Speaking*, pp. 181–182.

89   Barbara Hannah, *Jung, His Life and Work: A Biographical Memoir* (New York: G. P. Putnam's sons, 1976), p. 265.

90   *Ibid.*, p. 269.

91   Bair, *Jung*, p. 484.

92   This episode is recounted in detail in Bair, Jung, pp. 486–493. See also, Joan Dulles Buresch-Talley, "The C. G. Jung and Allen Dulles Correspondence," in Maidenbaum, *Jung and the Shadow of Anti-Semitism*.

93   Paul Roazen, "Jung and Anti-Semitism," in Maidenbaum and Martin, *Lingering Shadows*, pp. 211–221, pp. 218–219.

94   Aryeh Maidenbaum, "Lingering Shadows: A Personal Perspective," in Maidenbaum and Martin, *Lingering Shadows*, pp. 291–300, p. 297.

95   Jung, "After the Catastrophe," CW, 10, pp. 194–217. According to Richard Stein ("Jung's 'Mana Personality' and the Nazi Era," in Maidenbaum and Martin, *Lingering Shadows*, pp. 90–116), if one reads the entire essay, it is

evident that "the catastrophe" in "After the Catastrophe" refers to the spiritual downfall of Germany and not to the grim fate of European Jewry (p. 105). Stein continues: "I am aware of no place in his writings where he takes up the question of the Holocaust in depth."

96   Jung, "After the Catastrophe," *CW*, 10, pp. 194–195

97   *Ibid.*, p. 202.

98   *Ibid.*

99   *C. G. Jung Speaking*, ed. McGuire and Hull, p. 117.

100 Jung, "After the Catastrophe," *CW*, 10, pp. 203–204.

101 *Ibid.*, pp. 215–216.

102 Jung, "The Tavistock Lectures," *CW*, 18, p. 164.

103 Jung, "Epilogue to 'Essays on Contemporary Events,'" *CW*, 10, p. 236.

104 *Ibid.*

105 Jung, "The Fight with the Shadow," radio talk on a British Broadcasting Program, 1946, in *CW*, 10, pp. 218–226, p. 223.

106 Jung, "Epilogue to 'Essays on Contemporary Events,'" *CW*, 10, p. 236.

107 Quoted in Jay Sherry, "Bibliographic Survey," in Maidenbaum and Martin, *Lingering Shadows*, p. 399.

108 *Ibid.*

109 Quoted in Bair, *Jung*, p. 423; see also C. G. *Jung Speaking*, "The Psychology of Dictatorship," pp. 91–93.

110 Winston Churchill, *Great Contemporaries* (New York: W. W. Norton, 1991); quoted in Bair, *Jung*, p. 453.

111 C. G. Jung, Interview with Carol Baumann, 1949, reprinted in *C. G. Jung Speaking*, pp. 192–200.

112 *Ibid.*, pp. 193–194.

113 Richard Noll, *The Jung Cult: Origins of a Charismatic Movement* (Princeton, NJ: Princeton University Press, 1994), p. 103.

114 Anthony Stevens, "Critical Notice: A Review of Richard Noll's *Jung Cult* and *Aryan Christ*," *Journal of Analytical Psychology*, 42 (1997): 671–689.

115 See C. G. Jung, *Nietzsche's Zarathustra*, ed. James L. Jarrett (Princeton, NJ: Princeton University Press, 1991).

116 Noll, *The Jung Cult*, p. 73.

117 *Ibid.*, p. 48.

118 *Ibid.*, p. 94.

119 *Ibid.*, p. 95.

120 *Ibid.*, p. 86.

121 *Ibid.*, p. 87.

122 C. G. Jung, "Seven Sermons to the Dead," in Robert Segal, ed., *The Gnostic Jung* (Princeton, NJ: Princeton University Press, 1992), pp. 181–193.

123 Noll, *The Jung Cult*, p. 90.

124 *Ibid.*, p. 65.

125 *Ibid.*, p. 95.

126 *Ibid.*, p. 97.

127 Zeev Sternhell, *The Founding Myths of Israel* (Princeton, NJ: Princeton University Press, 1997).

128 Noll, *The Jung Cult*, p. 21.

129 Ibid., p. 274; Noll, *The Aryan Christ*, p. 277.

130 Noll, *The Jung Cult*, p. 135.

131 Noll, *The Aryan Christ*, p. 273.

132 C. G. Jung Biographical Archives, Jolande Jacobi Interview, December 26, 1969; Noll, *The Aryan Christ*, p. 274.

133   *Ibid.*
134   See, esp., Zeev Sternhell, *The Founding Myths of Israel.*
135   C. G. Jung Biographical Archives, Michael Fordham Interview, February 1969; Noll, *The Aryan Christ*, p. 275.
136   C. G. Jung Biographical Archives, Irene Champernowne Interview, December 19, 1969; Noll, *The Aryan Christ*, p. 274.
137   C. G. Jung Biographical Archives, Cornelia Brunner Interview, January 8, 1970; Noll, *The Aryan Christ*, p. 275.
138   Varied opinions are put forth in Maidenbuam and Martin, *Lingering Shadows*, and Maidenbaum, *Jung and the Shadow of Anti-Semitism.*
139   James Kirsch, "Carl Gustav Jung and the Jews: The Real Story," in Maidenbaum and Martin, *Lingering Shadows*, pp. 52–87.
140   *Ibid.*, p. 64. Kirsch, however, held that Jung overcame his anti-Semitism, working it through in his *Answer to Job*. According to Kirsch, "Jung was the only non-Jew I have ever known who, in my opinion, truly overcame the last trace of anti-Semitism" (James Kirsch, "Jung's Transference on Freud: The Jewish Element," *American Imago*, 41/1 [Spring 1984]: 77).
141   Jung, *The Red Book*, p. 334, where Jung writes: "Your inordinate ambition is boundless. Your grounds are not focused on the good of the matter but on your vanity. You do not work for humanity but for your own self-interest. You don't strive for the completion of the thing but for the general recognition and safeguarding of your own advantage. I want to honor you with a prickly crown of iron; it has teeth inside that bore themselves into your flesh. You play at modesty and do not mention your merit, in the certain hope that someone else will do it for you; you are disappointed and hurt if this doesn't happen." On one interpretation it was Jung's vanity and desire for recognition that prompted him to proclaim that his psychology, unlike the "Jewish psychologies" of Freud and Adler, was suited to the Aryan temperament.
142   Gershom Scholem to Aniela Jaffé, May 7, 1963; Aniela Jaffé, *From the Life and Work of C. G. Jung*, trans. R. F. C. Hull and Murray Stein (Einsiedeln, Switzerland: Daimon Verlag, 1989), pp. 97–98. Also quoted in Adams and Sherry, "Significant Words and Events," pp. 395–396.
143   C. G. Jung, *Answer to Job* (New York: Meridian, 1960), pp. 48, 73; note 7, p. 206.
144   *Ibid.*, p. 48.
145   *Ibid.*, p. 206, note 7. An editor's note in the English edition explains that the "shards" refer to Luria's doctrine of the "breaking of the vessels" through which "the powers of evil assumed a separate and real existence."
146   Jung, *Answer to Job*, p. 53.
147   Jung, *Letters*, 2:157.
148   Jung, *Answer to Job*, p. 64.
149   *Ibid.*, p. 74.
150   James Kirsch, "Carl Gustav Jung and the Jews: The Real Story," p. 68.
151   In *Mysterium Coniunctionis* (*CW*, 14), a work that Jung began in 1941 and completed in 1954, there are at least nine separate references to the works of Gershom Scholem.
152   Interestingly, nearly fifty years earlier, in a 1905 essay entitled "Cryptomnesia," Jung himself had argued that much creative work is produced in precisely this manner (Jung, "Cryptomnesia," CW, 1), and in his own doctoral dissertation had gone as far as to demonstrate that Nietzsche had unconsciously plagiarized sections of his Zarathustra from an essay he had read in his youth by Justinius Kerner. See Richard Noll, The Aryan Christ, p. 51.

153 Neumann to Jung, October 19, 1935, quoted in M. Neumann, "On the Relationship between Erich Neumann and C. G. Jung," p. 280.
154 Jung, *Letters*, 1:206.
155 See Sanford Drob, "Towards a Kabbalistic Psychology: C. G. Jung and the Jewish Foundations of Alchemy," *Journal of Jungian Thought and Practice*, 5/2 (2003): 77–100.
156 Jung, *Mysterium Coniunctionis, CW*, 14, p. 24, cf. p. 384.
157 *Ibid.*, p. 24.
158 *Ibid.*, p. 410. See also Johann Reuchlin, *On the Art of the Kabbalah* (*De Arte Cabalistica*), trans. M. and S. Goodman (Lincoln, NE: University of Nebraska Press, 1983).
159 Werner H. Engel, "Thoughts and Memories of C. G. Jung," in Maidenbaum and Martin, *Lingering Shadows*, pp. 261–272, p. 267.
160 A. Maidenbaum, "The Shadows Still Linger," in Maidenbaum, *Jung and the Shadow of Anti-Semitism*, p. 211. While Hurwitz's remarks suggest that Jung only became familiar with Jewish mysticism in his "later years," we should note that in November 1937 Jung wrote a letter to Professor M. H. Goering, who was the editor of the *Zentralblatt für Psychotherapie* in Berlin (which was under Jung's general supervision), which suggests at least some familiarity with this subject. In this letter, Jung was highly critical of a book that had stated that the Jews are contemptuous of mysticism (as cited by Engel, "Thoughts and Memories of C. G. Jung," p. 267).
161 Kirsch, "Carl Gustav Jung and the Jews," p. 68, states that Jung read the whole of Knorr von Rosenroth's *Kabbalah Denudata*, but he does not indicate when such reading took place.
162 However, Jung does not reference the Kabbalah with any abundance until after the end of World War II.
163 M. Neumann, "On the Relationship between Erich Neumann and C. G. Jung," p. 274.
164 *Ibid.*, p. 280.
165 Jaffé, *From the Life and Work of C. G. Jung*, p. 87.
166 This idea is suggested by Steven Martin in his introduction to Maidenbaum and Martin, *Lingering Shadows*, p. 10.
167 Quoted in Jay Sherry, "Bibliographic Survey," p. 399.
168 Allen W. Dulles, Letter to Paul Mellon of the Bollingen Foundation, February 17, 1950; quoted in Joan Dulles Buresch-Talley, "The C.G. Jung and Allen Dulles Correspondence," p. 45.
169 See, for example, Wood and Kroger, *Doing Discourse Analysis* (Thousand Oaks, CA: Sage, 2000); Potter and Weatherall, *Discourse and Social Psychology* (Thousand Oaks, CA: Sage, 1987); and Weiss and Wodak, *Critical Discourse Analysis* (New York: Palgrave MacMillan, 2002), which treats anti-Semitic discourse in varying historical contexts.
170 For many, pathological dissociation is typically a response to an early childhood trauma. Though trauma is not an absolutely necessary condition for pathological dissociation, there are indeed events that can be considered traumatic in Jung's life story. For discussion of Jung's own dissociative tendencies, as well as his views on dissociation, see Brian R. Skea, "Trauma, Transference and Transformation: A Study of Jung's Treatment of His Cousin, Helene (A Jungian Perspective on the Dissociability of the self and on the Psychotherapy of the Dissociative Disorders)," paper presented in a public lecture at the C. G. Jung Education Center, Pittsburgh, PA, on February 3, 1995.

Downloaded from ⟨http://www.cgjungpage.org/index.php? option=com_content&task=view&id=802&Itemid=40⟩, "The Jung Page," May 24, 2009.

171   C. G. Jung, *The Black Books 1913–32. Notebooks of Transformation.* Ed. Sonu Shamdasani. Trans. Martin Liebscher, John Peck and Sonu Shamdasani (New York: W.W. Norton & Company, 2020). Jung himself denied that these dialogs were poetry or a literary device (see Sonu Shamdasani, "Introduction," *The Red Book*, p. 213) and suggests in *The Red Book* that from a psychiatric perspective these dialogs were madness or incipient psychosis (*The Red Book*, p. 360).

172   C. G. Jung, *Memories, Dreams, Reflections*, recorded and edited by Aniela Jaffé (New York: Random House, 1961), p. 33.

173   *Ibid.*, p. 34.

174   *Ibid.* The Jung family had a tradition that Jung's grandfather, also named Carl Gustav Jung, was an illegitimate son of Goethe, and Noll marshals evidence suggesting that Jung may have considered himself a reincarnation of the great German poet (see Noll, *Jung Cult*, p. 20, and *The Aryan Christ*, p. 18).

175   Jung, *Memories, Dreams, Reflections*, p. 183.

176   *Ibid.*

177   Or, as he suggests in *The Red Book*, he received this myth from a spiritual guide, Philemon.

178   Jung, *Memories, Dreams, Reflections*, pp. 190–191.

179   See Mark S. Micale, *Approaching Hysteria: Disease and Its Interpretations* (Princeton, N.J.: Princeton University Press, 1995).

180   Jung, *Answer to Job*, p. 198.

181   Jung. "The Tavistock Lectures," *CW*, 18, p. 164.

182   *C. G. Jung Speaking*, p. 120.

183   Jung, *The Red Book*, p. 314.

184   *Ibid.*, p. 280.

185   *Ibid.*, p. 313.

186   Tony Woolfson, "The Meaning of Suffering in the Book of Job and in Jung's *Answer to Job*," *Harvest: Journal for Jungian Studies*, 44/2 (1998): 39–57.

187   Jung, *Symbols of Transformation, CW*, 5, § 44, p. 31.

188   Jung, *Answer to Job*, p. 124.

189   In fairness to Jung, Werner Engel points out that *"Ausgerucht,"* which is translated as "slipped up," is better understood as "lost my footing," which to Jung, a Swiss mountain climber, is a potentially fatal event. Engel, "Thoughts and Memories of C. G. Jung," p. 269.

190   Jung, *Answer to Job*, p. 132.

191   Gershom Scholem, *Sabbatai Sevi: The Mystical Messiah*, trans. R. J. Zwi Werblowsky (Princeton, NJ: Princeton University Press, 1973).

192   Jung, *Answer to Job*, p. 34.

193   *Ibid.*, p. 35.

194   Jung, "After the Catastrophe," *CW*, 10, § 440.

195   Jung, *Answer to Job*, p. 88.

196   Jung, *Letters*, 2:358–359.

197   "An Eightieth Birthday Interview," *C. G. Jung Speaking*, pp. 271–272.

Chapter 11

1   *Pardes Rimmonim*, the Garden of Pomegranates, refers to a sixteenth-century Kabbalistic work by R. Moses Cordovero (1522–70).

2   As we have seen, this was not the first time Jung had visionary experiences; three decades prior to his Kabbalistic vision, he recorded a series of visions in

his *The Red Book*, which he did not publish in his lifetime, and which did not fully see the light of day until 2009. As he did with regard to his Kabbalistic visions, Jung regarded these earlier visionary experience as extremely significant, and stated that they laid the groundwork for much of his later psychology and prepared him for his encounter with alchemy.

3　Jung's description is, of course, retrospective, and may not accurately reflect either the nature of his visions/dreams or his state of knowledge about the Kabbalah in 1944.

4　§ 728, p. 315.

5　*Ibid.*, p. 293.

6　The *Sefirot* are value archetypes as well as divine visages or personae, as discussed earlier in this volume. I have discussed the *Sefirot* in philosophical and psychological terms in "The Sefirot: Kabbalistic Archetypes of Mind and Creation," *Crosscurrents*, 47 (1997): 5–29, and in Chapter 4 of *Symbols of the Kabbalah: Philosophical and Psychological Perspectives* (Northvale, NJ: Jason Aronson, 2000).

7　Simon ben Yochai (or Shimon bar Yohai), a second-century rabbi who is traditionally held to be the author of the Zohar, the most important and holiest of Kabbalistic works.

8　Jung, *Memories, Dreams, Reflections*, p. 293.

9　*Ibid.*, p. 294.

10　*Ibid.*, p. 295.

11　*Ibid.*

12　*Ibid.*

13　As I have described in chap. 3 of my *Symbols of the Kabbalah*, the Kabbalists held that the earliest reference to the *tzimtzum* is in an early midrash, where it is said that when God descended to inhabit the holy *mishkan* or tabernacle, he "restricted his *shekhinah* [the divine 'presence'] to the square of an ell" (*Midrash Shemoth Rabbah*, 34:1). The description of this world as a square is also evident in Israel Sarug's conception of the *tzimtzum* as a square folding of the divine garment that provides a place for the emanation of the *Sefirot*.

14　The Kabbalist Moses Cordovero, for example, spoke of the deity as progressing through "non-temporal time" (G. Scholem, *Kabbalah* [Jerusalem: Keter, 1974], p. 103). Further, we read in Chayyim Vital's *Sefer Etz Chayyim* that "in Him there was no time or beginning to start, for He always existed and is everlasting and in Him there is no beginning (*rosh*) or end at all" (Vital, *Sefer Etz Chayyim*, 1:1 [Tel Aviv, 1960], p. 21; D. W. Menzi and Z. Padeh, trans., The Tree of Life, Chayim Vital's Introduction to the Kabbalah of Isaac Luria [Northvale, NJ: Jason Aronson, 1999], p. 6).

15　Jung, *Letters*, 1:206. However, as we have seen, Jung himself later acknowledged that many of the alchemists he studied regarded the Kabbalah to be the spiritual foundation of their work, and, as I have argued (in Chapter 2), in extracting the psychological "gold" that lay buried within the alchemists' pseudo-chemical operations, Jung was in effect reconstituting aspects of the Kabbalah, which had initially been absorbed by the alchemists themselves. See also S. Drob, *Kabbalistic Metaphors: Mystical Themes in Ancient and Modern Thought* (Northvale, NJ: Jason Aronson, 1999), chap. 8, pp. 289–343; S. Drob, "Jung and the Kabbalah," *History of Psychology*, 2/2 (May 1999): 102–118 (reprinted as "Jung, Kabbalah, and Judaism," in A. Maidenbaum, ed., *Jung and the Shadow of Anti-Semitism* [Berwick, ME: Nicolas-Hays, 2002], pp. 175–192); and S. Drob, "Towards a Kabbalistic Psychology: C. G. Jung and the Jewish Foundations of Alchemy," *Journal of*

Jungian Thought and Practice, 5/2 (2003): 77–100. We should note that this was not the first time that Jung had a visionary experience that moved from Jewish to Greek themes. In *The Red Book*, he relates how he is in a hall with glittering walls, and says, "As I look into its reflection, the images of Eve, the tree, and the serpent appear to me. After this I catch sight of Odysseus and his journey on the high seas" (Jung, *The Red Book*, p. 245).

16 David Rosen, *The Tao of Jung: The Way of Integrity* (New York: Penguin, 1996), p. 118.
17 Jung, *Memories, Dreams, Reflections*, p. 295.
18 The sweet smell or odor of sanctity would suggest both Jung's impending death and his increasing spirituality.
19 Jung, *Memories, Dreams, Reflections*, p. 294.
20 C. G. Jung, *Answer to Job* (New York: Meridian, 1960), p. 88.
21 Jung, *Memories, Dreams, Reflections*, p. 297.
22 *Ibid.*
23 See Aryeh Maidenbaum, "The Shadows Still Linger," in Maidenbaum, *Jung and the Shadow of Anti-Semitism*, pp. 193–217. Maidenbaum holds that "any anti-Semitism that can be attributed to Jung (and in his early career there clearly exists enough of his writings to make such a case) should be attributed to cultural, unconscious prejudice and not what one would define as consciously anti-Semitic" (p. 217).
24 C. G. Jung, "After the Catastrophe," *CW*, 10, pp. 203–204.
25 Quoted in A. Samuels, "New Material Concerning Jung, Anti-Semitism, and the Nazis," *Journal of Analytical Psychology*, 38 (1993): 469.
26 See A. Maidenbaum and S. A. Martin, eds, *Lingering Shadows: Jungians, Freudians, and Anti-Semitism* (Boston: Shambhala, 1992); F. McLynn, *Carl Gustav Jung* (New York: St. Martin's Press, 1996); and A. Jaffé, "C. G. Jung's National Socialism," in A. Jaffé, *From the Life and Work of C. G. Jung*, trans. R. F. C. Hull (New York: Harper, 1971).
27 Jung, "Psychology and Religion (The Terry Lectures, 1938/1940)," *CW*, 11.
28 Jung, "Answer to Job," *CW*, 11, pp. 355–370. Pagination of quotations are from C. G. Jung, *Answer to Job*, trans. R. F. C. Hull (New York: Meridian, 1960). Jung makes specific reference to the "shards," which in the Kabbalah are the remnants of the divine Sefirot subsequent to the "Breaking of the Vessels," on pages 48 and 73 of *Answer to Job*. In various other places in this work, Jung makes use of theological notions that echo fundamental Kabbalistic ideas. Among these are the idea of God as a "totality of inner opposites" or *coincidentia oppositorum* (pp. 33, 116, 134), that such opposites facilitate or express the union of opposites (p. 198), that humanity was initially created through a Primal Anthropos (p. 36), that there is a necessity for God himself to be completed through humanity's efforts (pp. 34, 124), that the paradoxical nature of the divine tears humankind asunder (p. 174), that God desires to regenerate himself in the mystery of the heavenly nuptials (p. 74), that humanity has a theurgic impact on God (p. 64), and that God limits himself, forgets himself, or becomes unaware of himself in the creation of the world and humankind (pp. 69, 84–85). It is not possible to determine which, if any, of these notions (other than the "shards," which Jung attributes directly to "the later cabalistic philosophy," note 7, p. 206) Jung borrowed or derived from Kabbalistic sources.
29 Moshe Idel holds that even in his later writings Jung remained somewhat negative in his attitude toward the Jewish religion. According to Idel, Jung wavered in his view as to whether the more primitive, archaic forms of

religion, as expressed in myth and symbolism, or the later monotheistic and mystical expressions of religion, as exemplified by Christianity, were the more authentic forms of religion. Idel suggests that for Jung, Judaism is either not mythological enough (too legal and Apollonian) or not mystical enough. Jung's view during the 1930s was that Judaism was too old, Apollonian, and conventional to participate in the mythic, if barbaric, consciousness that was about to creatively renew the German spirit. Later, Jung saw Judaism as not having reached "the more advanced and psychologically more correct view that not fidelity to the law but love and kindness are the antithesis of evil" (Jung, *Mysterium Coniunctionis*, *CW*, 14, p. 170). Jung refers to this view, introduced by "the reformer and rabbi Jesus" as "a *unio mystica*...the fundamental experience of all religions that have not yet degenerated into confessionalism" (*ibid.*, p. 171). Jung's critique, it seems to me, is focused upon his (rather narrow) understanding of rabbinic Judaism and did not at all prevent him from appreciating those aspects of Judaism that participated in the mythological and mystical aspects of the human psyche. Scholars of Jewish mysticism, including Gershom Scholem, have observed that the Kabbalah and Chasidism each reintroduced a mythical, emotional, and mystical element into a Judaism that, in their respective times and places, had been largely absent in Jewish orthodoxy. See M. Idel, "'Unio Mystica' as a Criterion: Some Observations on Hegelian Phenomenologies of Mysticism," *Journal for the Study of Religious Ideologies*, 1 (Spring 2002): 19; http://hiphi.ubbcluj.ro/JSRI.

30   Jung, *Letters*, 2:358–359.
31   "An Eightieth Birthday Interview," in *C. G. Jung Speaking*, ed. W. McGuire and R. F. C. Hull (Princeton, NJ: Princeton University Press, 1977), pp. 271–272.
32   Rifka Schatz Uffenheimer, *Hasidism as Mysticism: Quietistic Elements in Eighteenth Century Hasidic Thought* (Jerusalem: Hebrew University, 1993), p. 207.
33   J. W. Heisig, *Imago Dei: Jung's Psychology of Religion* (Lewisburg, PA: Bucknell University Press, 1979).
34   Jung, *Memories, Dreams, Reflections*, p. 295.
35   *Ibid.*
36   Wolfgang Giegerich, "The End of Meaning and the Birth of Man: An Essay about the State Reached in the History of Consciousness and an Analysis of C. G. Jung's Psychology Project," *Journal of Jungian Theory and Practice*, 6/1 (2004).
37   In what follows I will be making reference to the traditional Zohar pagination as well as to two English translations of the Zohar: H. Sperling and M. Simon, *The Zohar*, 5 vols. (London: Soncino Press, 1931–1934), which will be referred to as Sperling and Simon, *The Zohar*; and I. Tishby and F. Lachower, *Wisdom of the Zohar*, trans. D. Goldstein, 3 vols. (Oxford: Oxford University Press, 1989), which will be referred to as Tishby and Lachower, *Wisdom of the Zohar*. The Tishby volumes are an anthology of Zohar texts organized by themes.
38   Zohar I:183b; Sperling and Simon, *The Zohar*, 2:200; Tishby and Lachower, *Wisdom of the Zohar*, 2:826.
39   In *Memories, Dreams, Reflections*, Jung initially states: "in a state of unconsciousness I experienced deliriums and visions which must have begun when I hung on the edge of death and was being given oxygen and camphor injections" (p. 289). However, just prior to relating his Kabbalistic vision, he states

that "toward evening I would fall asleep, and my sleep would last until about midnight. Then I would come to myself and lie awake for about an hour, but in an utterly transformed state" (p. 293).

40 My discussion here follows closely upon that of the Zoharic text and commentary in Tishby and Lachower, *Wisdom of the Zohar*, 2:810–830.

41 Talmud, *Tractate Berakhot*, 57b. See Zohar I:206b, where we learn that King David never slept consecutively for more than 59 breaths in order to avoid being entrapped by the "taste of death" and an "evil power" (Sperling and Simon, *The Zohar*, 2:283).

42 In the Kabbalah, God's feminine aspect is frequently associated with the "left side" of the sefirotic tree and thus with stern judgment.

43 Zohar III:119a; Sperling and Simon, *The Zohar*, 5:170–171.

44 Zohar II:213b-214a; Sperling and Simon, *The Zohar*, 6:225–226. "The souls of the righteous, in ascending in the night into their own celestial spheres, are woven into a crown as it were, with which the Holy One, blessed be He, adorns himself....There all the souls are absorbed in the Supreme Point; as a woman conceives a child, so does the Supreme Point conceive them....The souls then re-emerge, that is to say, they are born anew, each soul being fresh and new as at its former birth."

45 Zohar III:121b; Sperling and Simon, *The Zohar*, 5:178–179.

46 Zohar I:83a; see Zohar II:213b; Sperling and Simon, *The Zohar*, 4:225: "at night all things return to their original root and source." See also Tishby and Lachower, *Wisdom of the Zohar*, 2:810–811, 828.

47 The Kabbalists held that each individual possesses four souls, of which the *neshamah* is the highest and closest to God.

48 Zohar III:25a; Sperling and Simon, *The Zohar*, 4:377; See also Tishby and Lachower, *Wisdom of the Zohar*, 2:811.

49 Zohar III:222b, *Raya Mehemna* (The *Raya Mehemna* is an "addition" to the basic Zohar text that is included in all traditional editions of the Zohar but which is not translated by Sperling and Simon). See also, Zohar I:183b; Sperling and Simon, *The Zohar*, 2:200: "For nothing happens in the world but what is made known in advance by means of a dream or by means of a proclamation." See Tishby and Lachower, *Wisdom of the Zohar*, 2:827.

50 Zohar I:200a; Sperling and Simon, *The Zohar*, 2:259–260.

51 Zohar I:83a, as translated in Tishby and Lachower, *Wisdom of the Zohar*, 2:818. See also Sperling and Simon, *The Zohar*, 1:277.

52 Zohar I:183a; Sperling and Simon, *The Zohar*, 2:199.

53 Zohar I:130a-130b; Sperling and Simon, *The Zohar*, 2:19.

54 See Zohar I:199b; Sperling and Simon, *The Zohar*, 2:258; Tishby and Lachower, *Wisdom of the Zohar*, 2:822.

55 Talmud, *Berakhot* 55b.

56 Zohar I:183a; "Since the dream contains both falsehood and truth, the word has power over it, and therefore it is advisable that every dream should be interpreted in a good sense" (Sperling and Simon, *The Zohar*, 2:199).

57 Zohar I:183a; Sperling and Simon, *The Zohar*, 2:199.

58 Zohar I:200a; Sperling and Simon, *The Zohar*, 2:259; Tishby and Lachower, *Wisdom of the Zohar*, 2:823. This notion—i.e., that a proper interpretation of a dream must traverse and parallel the development of the entire Kabbalistic system—is a critical element in the development of a Kabbalistic theory of dream interpretation. We will see that when this notion is applied to the Kabbalistic system as interpreted by Luria and his disciples, we have the foundation

for a powerful dream hermeneutic that is highly compatible with Jungian psychology.

59 In *Symbols of Transformation*, Jung writes: "For modern man it is hardly conceivable that a God existing outside ourselves should cause us to dream, or that the dream foretells the future prophetically. But if we translate this language into the language of psychology, the ancient idea becomes much more comprehensible. The dream, we would say, originates in an unknown part of the psyche and prepares the dreamer for the events of the following day" (Jung, *CW*, 8, p. 7). By the time he wrote *Answer to Job*, Jung stated: "We cannot tell whether God and the unconscious are two different entities" (p. 199).

60 Jung, *Memories, Dreams, Reflections*, p. 297.

61 *Ibid.*, p. 291.

62 *Ibid.*, p. 292.

63 Joel Covitz, *Visions of the Night: A Study of Jewish Dream Interpretation* (Boston: Shambhala, 1990), pp. 24–25.

64 See Jung, *The Red Book*, p. 267, 274, 275, 323.

65 Jung, *Memories, Dreams, Reflections*, p. 297.

66 *Ibid.*, p. 295.

67 *Ibid.*, p. 297.

68 See Aniela Jaffé, "C. G. Jung's National Socialism," *From the Life and Work of C. G. Jung*, trans. R. F. C. Hull and Murray Stein (Einsiedeln, Switzerland: Daimon Verlag, 1989).

69 Jung, *Memories, Dreams, Reflections*, p. 290. It is interesting that Jung should focus upon the Red Sea, a small landmark that was of inestimable importance in the liberation of the Jewish people.

70 *Ibid.*, p. 294.

71 *Ibid.*, p. 297.

72 *Ibid.*, p. 296.

73 *Ibid.*, p. 293.

74 *Ibid.*, p. 294.

75 *Ibid.*, p. 293.

76 *Ibid.*, p. 296.

77 *Ibid.*, p. 297.

78 *Ibid.*, p. 294.

79 Talmud, *Berakhot*, 55b.

80 Covitz, *Visions of the Night*, p. 46.

81 Jung, "General Aspects of Dream Psychology," *CW*, 8, § 456; reprinted in C. G. Jung, *Dreams*, trans. R. F. C. Hull (Princeton, NJ: Bollingen, 1974), pp. 23–66, p. 27.

82 Jung, "General Aspects of Dream Psychology," *CW*, 8, § 469; Jung, *Dreams*, p. 31.

83 Jung, "On the Nature of Dreams," *CW*, 8, § 557; reprinted in Jung, *Dreams*, p. 78.

84 Jung, *Dreams*, p. 78.

85 Jung, *Answer to Job*, p. 200.

86 Jung, "The Significance of the Father in the Destiny of the Individual," *CW*, 4, § 728, p. 315.

87 Jung, "On the Nature of Dreams," *CW*, 8, § 474; Jung, *Dreams*, p. 77.

88 For Jung, dreams are extremely variable in their significance. He writes: "Dreams may contain ineluctable truths, philosophical pronouncements, illusions, wild fantasies, memories, plans, anticipations, irrational experiences,

even telepathic visions, and heaven knows what besides" (Jung, "The Practical Use of Dream-Analysis," *CW*, 16, § 317; reprinted in Jung, *Dreams*, p. 95).

89 Jung, "General Aspects of Dream Psychology," *CW*, 8, § 555; Jung, *Dreams*, p. 33.

90 Azriel, "Explanation of the Ten Sefirot," in Joseph Dan, ed., *The Early Kabbalah*, trans. R. C. Kiener (New York: Paulist, 1986), p. 94.

91 On the coincidence of opposites in Jewish mysticism, see S. Drob, "The Doctrine of *Coincidentia Oppositorum* in Jewish Mysticism," www.newkabba lah.com, and S. Drob, Kabbalah and Postmodernism: A Dialogue (New York: Peter Lang, 2009), Ch. 6. On this doctrine in Jung, see, for example, chap. 3 of *Mysterium Coniunctionis*, "The Personification of the Opposites," and *Answer to Job*, chaps 17 and 19. In *Psychology and Alchemy*, Jung states: "The self is made manifest in the opposites and the conflicts between them; it is a *coincidentia oppositorum*" (Jung, *Psychology and Alchemy, CW*, 12, p. 186).

92 See Drob, *Symbols of the Kabbalah*, chap. 9, "*Tikkun ha-Olam*: The Restoration of the World," pp. 363–412.

93 Jung, "General Aspects of Dream Psychology," *CW*, 8, § 473; Jung, *Dreams*, p. 33; cf. § 491, p. 40. Jung further says that in interpreting dreams one "should give up all his theoretical assumptions and should in every single case be ready to construct a totally new theory of dreams" (Jung, "The Practical Use of Dream-Analysis," *CW*, 16, § 317; Jung, *Dreams*, p. 95).

94 Zohar I:199b; Tishby and Lachower, *Wisdom of the Zohar*, 2:822.

95 Quoted in Anthony Shafton, *Dream Reader* (Albany, NY: State University of New York Press, 1995), p. 115.

96 Jung, *Mysterium Coniunctionis, CW*, 14, p. vii.

97 See Drob, *Kabbalistic Metaphors*, chap. 8, pp. 289–343.

98 Several writers, including A. Altmann ("The Meaning and Soul of 'Hear, O Israel,'" in L. Meier, *Jewish Values in Jungian Psychology* [Lanham, MD: University Press of America, 1991], pp. 51–70), David Rosen (*The Tao of Jung*, chap. 5), and Aryeh Maidenba um ("The Shadows Still Linger") have commented on the change in Jung's attitude towards Judaism in his later years. Rosen attributes this change to the "soul attack" Jung experienced in connection with his 1944 heart attack. Rosen writes: "Until he had his heart attack in 1944, Jung remained unable to take in the meaning (and soul) of Judaism" (*The Tao of Jung*, p. 104).

99 Rosen, *The Tao of Jung*, p. 105.

Chapter 12

1 Here I have in mind Martin Buber, James Hillman, and Phillip Rieff, each of whom has criticized depth psychology for its exclusive, narcissistic focus upon the individual self.

2 See James Hillman, *Re-Visioning Psychology* (New York: Harper Perennial, 1977); *The Myth of Analysis: Three Essays In Archetypal Psychology* (New York: Harper & Row, 1978); *The Dream and the Underworld* (New York: Harper & Row, 1979); "Anima Mundi: The Return of the Soul to the World," *Spring* (1982): 71–93; *Anima: An Anatomy of a Personified Notion* (Dallas: Spring Publications, 1985); and J. Hillman and M. Ventura, *We've Had One Hundred Years of Psychotherapy and the World's Getting Worse* (San Francisco: Harper, 1992).

3   Thomas Moore, preface to chapter 5, in *A Blue Fire: Selected Writings by James Hillman*, introduced and edited by Thomas Moore (New York: Harper Perennial, 1991), p. 96.
4   C. G. Jung, *The Red Book*, p. 231.
5   Hillman, *Re-Visioning Psychology*, p. 99.
6   *Ibid.*, p. 100.
7   *Ibid.*, chap. 1, pp. 1–51.
8   C. G. Jung, *Mysterium Coniunctionis, CW*, 14, p. 547.
9   *Ibid.*, p. vii.
10 *Ibid.*, p. 548.
11 Robert A. Segal, *The Gnostic Jung* (Princeton, NJ: Princeton University Press, 1992), pp. 10ff.
12 C. G. Jung, *Letters*, 2:570, to Robert C. Smith, 29 June 1960, original in English.
13 Jung, *Mysterium Coniunctionis, CW*, 14, p. 548. Jung held a somewhat different view outside of his official, professional writings, especially in *Memories, Dreams, Reflections*, recorded and edited by Aniela Jaffé (New York: Random House, 1961).
14 On Hegel, see W. T. Stace, *The Philosophy of Hegel* (1924; New York: Dover, 1955), p. 39ff.
15 In *The Red Book*, Jung says, "your thoughts are just as much outside yourself as trees and animals are outside your body" (Jung, *The Red Book*, p. 249).
16 C. G. Jung, *Answer to Job* (New York: Meridian, 1960), p. 200.
17 Jung to R. J. Zwi Werblowsky, 2 September 1953, *Letters*, 2:122.
18 Jung, *Two Essays on Analytic Psychology, CW*, 7, p. 185.
19 Jung, "Commentary on 'The Secret of the Golden Flower,'" *CW*, 13, p. 133.
20 On the synthesis of opposites in Kabbalah and Chasidism, see R. Elior, "Chabad: The Contemplative Ascent to God," in *Jewish Spirituality: From the Sixteenth Century Revival to the Present*, ed. Arthur Green (New York: Crossroads, 1987), pp. 157–205; Sanford Drob, "The Doctrine of *Coincidentia Oppositorum* in Jewish Mysticism," www.newkabbalah.com/CoincJewMyst.htm; Gustav Derifuss, "The Union of Opposites in the Kabbalah," *Journal of Jungian Theory and Practice*, 7/1 (2005): 65–72.
21 C. G. Jung to Joseph F. Rychlak, April 27, 1959, *Letters*, 2:500–501.
22 Jung, *Mysterium Coniunctionis, CW*, 14, p. 473.
23 *Ibid.*, p. 495.
24 Jung, *CW*, 7, p. 180.
25 Jung, *Mysterium Coniunctionis, CW*, 14, p. 472.
26 Jung, *CW*, 7, § 267.
27 Segal, *The Gnostic Jung*, p. 40.
28 Jung, *Mysterium Coniunctionis, CW*, 14, p. 474.
29 29. Jung, *CW*, 7, § 267, 275.
30 This decentering may actually be akin to the mystic's "dissolution" of the ego in favor of a wider, transpersonal self (*Adam Kadmon, Atman*) and ultimately in favor of an "oceanic non-self" (*Ein-sof, Brahman*) upon which the individual ego is a transitory wave. On the archetypal and structuralist interpretation, even this transpersonal self involves certain invariant structures of meaning, consciousness, and language. A deconstructionist reading would see this non-self in completely negative, open, and/or errant terms.
31 See Sanford Drob, *Kabbalah and Postmodernism: A Dialogue* (New York: Peter Lang, 2009); Sanford Drob, *Symbols of the Kabbalah* (Northvale, NJ:

Jason Aronson, 2000), p. 37; Sanford Drob, "Derrida and the Lurianic Kabbalah" (www.newkabbalah.com).

32 Drob, *Kabbalah and Postmodernism.*
33 Drob, *Symbols of the Kabbalah*, p. 37.
34 Drob, "Derrida and the Lurianic Kabbalah."
35 We have seen how in *The Red Book* (p. 347), Jung writes, "Differentiation is creation. It is differentiated. Differentiation is its essence, and therefore it differentiates. Therefore man differentiates since his essence is differentiation." In this striking statement, Jung is undoubtedly influenced by Nietzsche and is premonitory of Derrida.
36 Of course, this is a task that deconstructionists will regard with a skeptical eye. I can only respond that deconstruction can hardly place a priori limits on thought or the manner in which language is used, and the only way to assess whether such an "integration" is possible is to attempt to perform it.

Appendix

1 Neumann, Erich. *The Roots of Jewish Consciousness, Volume Two: Hasidism.* Ann Conrad Lammers, ed., Mark Kyburz and Ann Conrad Lammers, trans, London and New York: Routledge, 2019. (Hereafter referenced as "Neumann, *Roots* II."). Hereafter, all citations to the second volume of this work.
2 Jung's spelling. There are many alternate English spellings. "Meseritz," is utilized in Neumann's "Roots." "Mezeritch" and "Mezhirichi" are also common spellings. It is a town in the Ukraine where the "Maggid" (itinerant Jewish preacher) spent the latter portion of his life.
3 "An Eightieth Birthday Interview." *C.G. Jung Speaking*, pp. 271–2.
4 C. G. Jung and Erich Neumann, *Analytical Psychology in Exile: The Correspondence of. C. G. Jung and Erich Neumann*, Ed. Martin Liebscher. Trans. Heather McCartney. Princeton and Oxford: Princeton University Press, 2015, p. 13.
5 Jung and Neuman, *Analytical Psychology in Exile*, pp. 37–50. Sent to Jung on July 19, 1934.
6 Jung and Neuman, *Analytical Psychology in Exile*, p. 42.
7 Jung and Neuman, *Analytical Psychology in Exile*, p. 52. Letter 7 J, August 12, 1934.
8 Jung and Neuman, *Analytical Psychology in Exile*, p. 141. Letter 27 N December 5, 1938.
9 Jung and Neuman, *Analytical Psychology in Exile*, p. 156, Letter 31 N, May 11, 1940.
10 Jung and Neuman, *Analytical Psychology in Exile*, p. xxxvi.
11 Idel, Moshe, *Foreword: On Erich Neumann and Hasidism.* Neumann, *Roots* II, p. xiv.
12 Neumann, *Roots* II, p. 3.
13 Neumann, *Roots* II, p. 83.
14 See Chapter 10 in this volume.
15 Jay Sherry, "The Case of Jung's Alleged Anti-Semitism," in Maidenbaum and Martin, *Lingering Shadows*, pp. 117–132, p. 121.
16 C.G. Jung, The State of Psychotherapy, in *Collected Works*, Vol. 10, pp. 157–173, p. 165.
17 Hitler, A. *Mein Kampf.* Translated by Ralph Mannheim. Boston: Houghton Mifflin, 1999 (Originally published in 1927).
18 Jung and Neumann, *Analytical Psychology in Exile*, p. 12.

19 Jung and Neumann, *Analytical Psychology in Exile*, p. 13.
20 See Chapter 11 of this volume and Drob, S., *Jung's Kabbalistic Visions. Journal of Jungian Theory and Practice*, 7(1), 2005, 33–54.
21 Neumann, *Roots* II, p. 32.
22 Neumann, *Roots* II, p. 18.
23 Neumann, *Roots* II, p. 164.
24 Neumann, *Roots* II, p. 164.
25 Neumann, *Roots* II, p. 164.
26 Neumann, *Roots* II, p. 165.
27 Neumann, *Roots* II, p. 8.
28 Neumann, *Roots* II, p. 171.
29 Neumann, *Roots* II, p. 123, 157n.24 referencing Samuel A. Horodezky, *Torat ha-maggid mi-Mezeritz ve-sihotav* (The Teachings of the Maggid of Meseritz and his Conversations, 1923, p. 108. [Referred to by Neumann (and hereafter in this essay) as Horodezky, *Great Maggid*]. Samuel Horodezky (1871–1957) was a respected Ukrainian scholar of Jewish mysticism who in 1935 founded the Hasidic archives for Schocken Press.)
30 Neumann, *Roots* II, p. 132.
31 Neumann, *Roots* II, p. 133.
32 See Elliot R. Wolfson, *Open Secret: Postmessianic Messianism and the Mystical Revision of Menahem Mendel Schneerson*. NY: Columbia University Press, 2009.
33 Neumann, *Roots* II, p. 173.
34 Neumann, *Roots* II, p. 173.
35 Neumann, *Roots* II, p. 177.
36 Neumann, *Roots* II, p. 174.
37 Neumann, *Roots* II, p. 177.
38 Neumann, *Roots* II, p. 178,
39 Neumann, *Roots* II, p. 178.
40 Neumann, *Roots* II, p. 178.
41 Neumann, *Roots* II, p. 179.
42 Neumann, *Roots* II, p. 171.
43 Neumann, *Roots* II, p. 172, cf. *Roots* I, p. 132.
44 Neumann, *Roots* II, p. 172. Neumann (p. 180, n, 29) references Martin Buber, *Die chassidischen Bucher* (1928), p. 403.
45 Neumann, *Roots* II, p. 172. On Menachem Mendel of Kotzk, see Joseph Fox, *Rabbi Menachem Mendel of Kotzk: A Biographical Study of the Chasidic Master*. New York: Bash Publications Inc., 1988, Available on line at: https://itethics.tripod.com/kotzk.pdf (Downloaded June 25, 2021).
46 Zalman M. Schachter-Shalomi with Edward Hoffman, *My Life in Jewish Renewal*, Plymouth, UK: Rowman & Littlefield Publishers, Inc., 2012, pp. 116–117.
47 Shoshana Fershtman, *The Mystical Exodus in Jungian Perspective: Transforming Trauma and the Wellsprings of Renewal*. London: Routledge, 2021, p. viii.
48 C. G. Jung, *The Red Book: Liber Novus*, ed. Sonu Shamdasani, trans. Mark Kyburz, John Peck, and Sonu Shamdasani (New York: W. W. Norton, 2009), p. 310b.
49 *Psychological Types*, Vol. 6 of *The Collected Works of C. G. Jung*, trans. R. F. C. Hull, ed. H. Read, M. Fordham, G. Adler, Wm. McGuire, 20 vols. (Princeton, NJ: Princeton University Press, 1953–1979). (Hereafter referenced as "CW") par. 823 (*CW*, 6:823).

50   Neumann, *Roots* II, p. 120.
51   Neumann, *Roots* II, p. 68.
52   Neumann, *Roots* II, p.72, citing Zohar III 144a (*Roots* II, p. 87, n.45).
53   Neumann, *Roots* II, p. 120.
54   Neumann, *Roots* II, p. 141.
55   Neumann, *Roots* II, p. 142.
56   Neumann, *Roots* II, p. 142.
57   Neumann, *Roots* II, p. 47, citing to Horodezky, *Great Maggid*, p. 35 (Neumann's editors note that the correct citation is p. 39), *Roots* II p. 54, n. 189.
58   Neumann, *Roots* II, p. 47, citing to Horodezky, *Great Maggid*, p. 36, correct citation should be p. 40, *Roots* II, p, 54, n.190.
59   Neumann, *Roots* II, p. 60.
60   Neumann, *Roots* II, p. 60.
61   Neumann, *Roots* II, p. 61.
62   Neumann, *Roots* II, p. 55. Neumann is quoting from Buber's *Unterweisung*, p. 28, *Roots* II, p. 85, n.1. cf *Roots* II, pp. 61, 65.
63   Jung writes that "sparks of light" (*scintillae*) are archetypes, hidden in the unconscious and "from which a higher meaning can be 'extracted.'"20 Jung, *Mysterium Coniunctionis, CW*, 14, p. 491.
64   Neumann, *Roots* II, p.106, citing Buber, *Unterweisung*, p. 86, *Roots* II, p. 118, n. 76.
65   Neumann, *Roots* II, p.105, citing Horodezky, *Great Maggid*, p. 15, cited as p. 40, *Roots* II p. 118, n. 67.
66   Neumann, *Roots* II, p. 107.
67   Neumann, *Roots* II, p. 107, citing Horodezky, *Great Maggid*, p. 193, *Roots* II, p. 118 n. 79.
68   Neumann, *Roots* II, p. 47, citing Great Maggid 135 (Neumann's editors point out that the correct citation is from p. 135), *Roots* II, p. 54, n. 184.
69   Neumann, *Roots* II, p.143, citing *Great Maggid*, p. 39, *Roots* II, p. 160, n. 116.
70   Neumann, *Roots* II, p.143.
71   Neumann, *Roots* II, p. 107.
72   Neumann, *Roots* II, p. 107.
73   Neumann, *Roots* II, p. 28.
74   Neumann, *Roots* II, p. 31.
75   Neumann, *Roots* II, p. 31.
76   Neumann, *Roots* II, p. 138.
77   Neumann, *Roots* II, p. 136.
78   Neumann, *Roots* II, p. 136.
79   Neumann, *Roots* II, p. 27, citing Horodezky, *Great Maggid*, p. 78, *Roots* II, p. 51, n. 92.
80   Neumann, *Roots* II, 29, citing Horodezky, *Great Maggid*, p. 200, *Roots* II, p. 52. N.103.
81   Neumann, *Roots* II, p. 136.
82   Neumann, *Roots* II, p. 137. One might even go so far as to argue that on Neumann's understanding of Hasidism it is not only the Jungian "self" but also the Hegelian "Absolute Spirit" that is completed by the incorporation of the unconscious and shadow!
83   C. G. Jing, *The Red Book*, p. 338b.
84   C. G. Jung, *Psychological Types, CW*, 6: p, 245, par. 416.
85   C. G. Jung, *Psychological Types, CW*, 6: p, 251, par. 426.
86   C. G. Jung, *Psychology and Alchemy, CW*, 12, p. 14, par 125; *Mysterium Coniunctionis, CW*, 14: p. 548, par. 781.

87   C. G. Jung, *Aion, CW*, 9, II: p. 40, par. 73, p. 63, par. 116, p. 109, par.170.
88   Neumann, *Roots* II, pp. 145, cf. 148.
89   Neumann, *Roots* II, p.145.
90   Neumann, *Roots* II, pp. 135, 147.
91   See Neumann, *Roots* II, p. 159, n 89).
92   Neumann, *Roots* II, p. 148, citing Horodezky, "Baal-Shem-Tom," *Jüdische Enzyklopädie*. (1928–34) col. 838, *Roots* II, p. 160, n.135.
93   See Neumann, *Roots* II, p. 148, citing Horodezky, *Great Maggid*, p. 201, *Roots* II, p. 160, n. 134.
94   See R. Schatz *Uffenheimer. Hasidism as Mysticism: Quietistic Elements in Eighteenth Century Hasidic Thought*. Jerusalem: Hebrew University, 1993, p. 207.
95   Neumann, *Roots* II, p.152, citing Buber, *Chassid Buch*, p. 574, *Tales of the Hasidim* I, p. 125, *Roots* II, p. 161, n. 153.
96   Neumann, *Roots* II, p.153,
97   Neumann, *Roots* II, p.103.
98   Neumann, *Roots* II, p.105.
99   Neumann, *Roots* II, p.103.
100 Neumann, *Roots* II, p.15, citing Buber, *Chassid Buch*, p. 437, *Roots* II, p. 50, n. 49.
101 Neumann, *Roots* II, p. 7.
102 Neumann, *Roots* II, p. 19, citing Buber, *Chassid Buch*, p. 33, *Roots* II, p. 50, n. 64.
103 Neumann, *Roots* II, p. 19, citing Samuel A. Horodezky, *Torat Rabbi Nachman mi-Bratslav ve-sihotav* (The teaching of Rabbi Nachman of Brezlav and his conversations, 1923 (Hereafter referred to as Horodezky, *R. Nachman*), p. 17. *Roots* II, p. 50, n. 65.
104 Neumann, Roots II, p. 20. Neumann's editors indicate that this passage is found in a 1948 pamphlet by Buber, *Der Weg des Menschen nach der schassidischen Lehre* (The Way of Man, According to the Teachings of Hasidism), p. 17. *Roots* II, p. 50, n. 40.
105 Neumann, *Roots* II, p. 124, citing Buber, *Chassid Buch*, p. 592, *Tales of the Hasidim* I, p. 244, *Roots* II, 157, n. 28.
106 Neumann, *Roots* II, p. 124.
107 Neumann, *Roots* II, p. 100, citing Buber, *Chassid Buch*, p. 591, Buber *Tales* I, p.121, *Roots* II, p. 117, n. 45.
108 Neumann, *Roots* II, p. 100.
109 Neumann, *Roots* II, p. 170.
110 Neumann, *Roots* II, p. 170.
111 See Neumann, *Roots* II, p. 180, n. 20.
112 C. G. Jung, "Adaptation, Individuation, Collectivity," *The Symbolic Life, CW*, 18, p. 451, par 1,095.
113 Neumann, *Roots* II, p. 32.
114 Neumann, *Roots* II, p. 32.
115 Neumann, *Roots* II, p. 32, citing Buber, *Chassid Buch* 581f, *Tales* I, p. 147, *Roots* II, p. 52, n. 115.
116 Neumann, *Roots* II, p. 33.
117 *C. G. Jung Letters*, ed. Gerhard Adler and Aniela Jaffé, trans. R. F. C. Hull, 2 vols. (Princeton, NJ: Princeton University Press, 1973) Vol. 2: p. 157.
118 Neumann, *Roots* II, p. 66, citing *R. Nachman*, p. 60 (Neumann's editors indicate that the actual cite is to p. 69) and Buber, *Chassid Buch*, p. 148. *Roots* II, p 86, n. 27, 28. Cf., *Roots* II, p, 139.
119 Neumann, *Roots* II, p. 39.

120 Neumann, *Roots* II, p. 40, citing Horodezky, *Great Maggid*, p. 46, *Roots* II, p. 53, n.158.
121 Neumann, *Roots* II, p. 39, citing Horodezky, *Great Maggid*, p. 215, (Neumann's editors indicate that the actual cite is to p. 296) *Roots* II, p. 53, n. 156.
122 Jung, *Red Book*, p. 320a, *Reader's Edition*, p. 424.
123 Neumann, *Roots* II, p. 40.
124 In *The Red Book*, Jung writes: "Do you still not know that the way to truth stands open only to those without intentions?... We tie ourselves up with intentions, not mindful of the fact that intention is the limitation, yes, the exclusion of life. We believe that we can illuminate the darkness with an intention, and in that way aim past the light. How can we presume to want to know in advance, from where the light will come to us?" Jung, *Red Book*, 236a–237b.
125 Neumann, *Roots* II, p. 142.
126 Neumann, *Roots* II, p. 102, citing Buber, *Chassid Buch*, p. 33f. *Roots* II, p. 117, n.55.
127 Neumann, *Roots* II, p. 21.
128 Neumann, *Roots* II, p. 22.
129 Neumann, *Roots* II, p. 22.
130 Neumann, *Roots* II, p. 32.
131 Neumann, *Roots* II, p. 25.
132 Schneur Zalman, *Likutei Torah, Devarim*, fol. 83a, as quoted in Elior, *Paradoxical Ascent*, p. 137–8.
133 Neumann, *Roots* II, p. 36. Zohar I, 19 a, b. Neumann quotes from a translation by Gershom Scholem, *Die Geheimnisse der Schöpfung: Ein Kapitel aus dem kabbalistischen Buche Sohar. Roots* II, p. 52, n. 134. Matt, in the Pritzker edition of the Zohar translates the passage as follows, "Every single night, the spirit strips itself of that garment and ascends, and the consuming fire consumes it. Later they are restored as before, figured in clothes" (Daniel Matt, *The Zohar: Pritzker Edition*, Vol. I, Stanford, CA: Stanford University Press, 2004, p. 147. See *Roots* II, Appendix A: Passages from the Zohar, p. 182). Matt comments that "that garment" refers to the body.
134 Neumann, *Roots* II, p. 37. Neumann references Buber, *Chassid Buch*, p. 632, *Tales* I, p. 173, *Roots* II, p. 52, n. 138.
135 Neumann's editors point out that the saying is found in Dove Baer of Meseritz, *Maggid Devarav le-Yaakov* (1780, Critical Hebrew Edition edited by Rivka Schatz Uffenheimer, Jerusalem: Hebrew University, 1976). Neumann, *Roots* II, p. 52, n. 138.
136 Neumann, *Roots* II, p. 37.
137 Neumann, *Roots* II, p. 38.
138 Neumann, *Roots* II, p. 39.
139 Neumann, *Roots* II, p. 38.
140 Neumann, *Roots* II, p. 69.
141 C. G. Jung, *The Red Book*, p. 346b, *Reader's Edition*, p. 509.
142 C. G. Jung, *Aion, CW*, 9ii, pp. 190–1, par. 298.
143 C. Jung, *The Red Book*, p. 347a, *Reader's Edition*, p. 510.
144 C. G. Jung, *Visions: Notes of a Seminar Given in 1930–1934*, Vol. II (31 May 1933), Claire Douglas, Ed. Princeton: Princeton University Press, 1997, p. 1026.
145 Jung, *The Red Book*, p. 229a.
146 Jung to Hans Schmid, 6 November 1915, C.G. Jung, *Letters*, Volumes I and II, eds., Gerhard Adler, Aniela Jaffe, and R.F.C. Hull (Princeton, NJ: Princeton University Press, 1973), Vol. I, p. 31.

147   Neumann, *Roots* II, p. 144, citing Horodezky, *Great Maggid*, p. 107, Roots
      II, p. 16, n. 117.
148   Neumann, *Roots* II, p. 46.
149   C. G. Jung, *The Red Book*, p. 319, *Reader's Edition*, p. 554.
150   Rabbi Dov Baer, *Ner Mitzvah ve-Torah Or*, II, fol. 6a. Quoted in Rachel
      Elior, *The Paradoxical Ascent to God*, trans. J. M. Green (Albany, NY: State
      University of New York Press, 1993). p. 64.
151   Elior, *The Paradoxical Ascent to God*, p. 64.
152   Quoted in Elior, Rachel Elior, "Chabad: The Contemplative Ascent to God,"
      in *Jewish Spirituality: From the Sixteenth Century Revival to the Present*,
      Arthur Green, Ed. (New York, NY: Crossroads, 1987), p. 166.
153   Jean-Paul Sartre, *Being and Nothingness*. Trans. Hazel Barnes. New York:
      Washington Square Press, 1966 (1943).
154   *Hegel's Logic*, William Wallace, trans., (Oxford, England: Clarendon Press,
      1975), par. 48, Zusatz 1, 78.
155   Neumann, *Roots* II, p. 111, citing Buber, *Chassid Buch*, p. 543, Tales II, p.
      60), *Roots* II, n.118, n. 83.
156   Neumann, *Roots* II, p. 144.
157   Neumann, *Roots* II, p. xvii. Idel cites *Or ha-'Emmet*, (Light of Truth) Bnei
      Beraq, 1967, fol. 37c.
158   Neumann, *Roots* II, p. xvii-xviii, citing *Ohev Israel* (Love of Israel), Zhiomir,
      12863, fol. 81cd.
159   Neumann, *Roots* II, p. xviii.
160   Neumann, *Roots* II, p. xvii.
161   Neumann, *Roots* II, pp. 60–1.
162   Neumann, *Roots* II, p. 61.
163   Neumann, *Roots* II, p. 81.
164   Neumann, *Roots* II, p. 82, citing Zohar I:55b, Bischoff Zohar p. 100f. Matt, in
      the Pritzker edition of the Zohar translates the passage as follows: "Any image
      not embracing male and female is not fittingly supernal...Anywhere male and
      female are not found as one, the blessed Holy One does not place his abode. One
      is not even called human, unless male and female are as one." Matt, *The Zohar:
      Pritzker Edition*, Vol. I, p. 314. See Appendix A, *Roots* II, p. 184).
165   Neumann, *Roots* II, p. 130, citing Horodezky, *Great Maggid*, p. 115, *Roots*
      II, p. 158, n. 153.
166   Neumann, *Roots* II, p. 130.
167   Neumann, *Roots* II, p. 130.
168   Neumann, *Roots* II, p. 150.
169   C. G. Jung, *Memories, Dreams, Reflections*, recorded and edited by Aniela
      Jaffé (New York: Random House, 1961), p. 293.
170   Neumann, *Roots* II, p. 150.
171   Neumann, *Roots* II, p. 151.
172   Neumann, *Roots* II, p. 151.
173   Neumann, *Roots* II, p. 151.
174   Neumann, *Roots* II, p. 130.
175   Neumann, *Roots* II, p. 166.
176   Neumann, *Roots* II, p. 166.
177   Neumann, *Roots* II, p. 166.
178   Neumann, *Roots* II, p. 145.
179   Neumann, *Roots* II, p. 146, citing Salomo Birnbaum, *Leben und Worte des
      Blaschemm nach chassidischen Schriften, Auswahl und Übertragung von
      Salomo Birnbaum*, Berlin: Welt, 1920, p. 86, *Roots* II, p. 160, n.126.

180 Neumann, *Roots* II, p. 62.
181 Neumann holds that foe the Hasidim, meaning is discerned when one sees the entire world as a "cipher" and this is achieved by viewing the external world through the prism of the psyche, thus making the world an "inner world." Neumann writes: "Every event that appears to come to a person from outside, if we look into its reality, reveals that it is related to something inside the person" (Neumann, *Roots* II, p. 115).
182 Neumann, *Roots* II, p. 93.
183 Neumann, *Roots* II, p. 93, Horodezky, *R Nachman*, p. 161, *Roots* II, p.116, n. 22.
184 Neumann, *Roots* II, p. 94.
185 Neumann, *Roots* II, p. 94
186 Neumann, *Roots* II, p. 101.
187 Neumann, *Roots* II, p. 102.
188 Neumann, *Roots* II, p. 102.
189 Jung, *The Red Book*, p. 260b.
190 Jung, *The Red Book*, p. 261a.
191 Jung, *The Red Book*, p. 305b.
192 Neumann, *Roots* II, p. 111, citing Buber, *Chassid Buch*, p. 638, *Tales* II, p. 166, *Roots* II, p. 118, n. 88.
193 Neumann, *Roots* II, p. 112, citing Horodezky, *Great Maggid*, p. 175, *Roots* II, p. 118, n. 94.
194 Neumann, *Roots* II, p. 122.
195 Neumann, *Roots* II, p. 112.
196 Neumann, *Roots* II, p. 112.
197 Neumann, *Roots* II, p. 112, citing Buber, *Chassid Buch*, p. 515. Neumann's editors point out that the correct citation is from p. 609 (and Buber, *Tales* II, p. 89), *Roots* II, p. 118, n. 98.
198 Especially in his *Depth Psychology and A New Ethic*. Eugene Rolfe, trans. Boston: Shambhala (Reprint Edition), 1990.
199 Neumann, Roots II, p. 125.
200 Martin Buber, "Religion and Modern Thinking," in his *Eclipse of God: Studies in the Relation Between Religion and Philosophy* (Amherst, New York: Humanity Books, 1988), pp. 63–92. Buber's dialog with Jung receives a thorough and sympathetic analysis by Barbara. D. Stephens in her "The Martin Buber-Carl Jung disputations: protecting the sacred in the battle for the boundaries of analytical psychology," *Journal of Analytical Psychology*, 46(2001): 455–91.
201 Neumann, *Roots* II, p. 31.
202 Neumann, *Roots* II, p. 166.
203 Neumann, *Roots* II, p. 18.
204 Jung, *The Red Book*, p. 260a, *Reader's Edition*, p. 215.
205 Jung, "An Eightieth Birthday Interview." *C.G. Jung Speaking*, pp. 268–72, 271–2.

Index